# DYNAMICS OF SOUTHWEST PREHISTORY

# DYNAMICS OF SOUTHWEST PREHISTORY

Edited by Linda S. Cordell

and George J. Gumerman

Smithsonian Institution Press

Washington, D.C.   London

A School of American Research Advanced Seminar Book

*Edited by Robin Gould*
*Designed by Lisa Buck Vann*

Library of Congress Cataloging-in-
Publication Data
Dynamics of Southwest Prehistory /
edited by Linda S. Cordell and
George J. Gumerman.
p.   cm.—(Smithsonian series in
archaeological inquiry)
"An advanced seminar entitled: "dynamics
of Southwestern prehistory", was held at
the School of American Research, in Santa
Fe, New Mexico, from 26th to the 30th
September, 1983."
Bibliography: p.
Includes index.
ISBN 0-87474-334-6 (cloth); 1-56098-307-8 (paper)
1. Indians of North America—Southwest,
New—Antiquities—Congresses.
2. Excavations (Archaeology)—Southwest,
New—Congresses.
3. Southwest, New—Antiquities—
Congresses.
I. Cordell, Linda S.
II. Gumerman, George J.
III. School of American Research (Santa Fe,
N.M.)
IV. Series.
E78.S7D96 1989
979'.01—dc19        89-5954

British Library Cataloguing-in-Publication
Data available

*Cover drawings taken from a*
*photograph by John Richardson*

⊗The paper used in this publication meets
the minimum requirements of the
American National Standard for
Permanence of paper for Printed Library
Materials Z39.48—1984.

Printed in the United States of America
10  9  8  7  6  5  4  3
98  97  96

# Contents

# List of Illustrations

# List of Tables

# Contributors

Linda S. Cordell, Irvine Curator, California Academy of Sciences, San Francisco, California.

Jeffrey S. Dean, Professor, Laboratory of Tree-ring Research, University of Arizona, Tucson, Arizona.

Paul R. Fish, Curator of Archaeology, Arizona State Museum, University of Arizona, Tucson, Arizona.

George J. Gumerman, Professor, Department of Anthropology, and Director, Center for Archaeological Investigations, Southern Illinois University, Carbondale, Illinois.

Gregory A. Johnson, Professor, Department of Anthropology, Hunter College, City University of New York, New York.

W. James Judge, Director, Fort Burgwin Research Center, Southern Methodist University, Taos, New Mexico.

Steven A. LeBlanc, Director, Mimbres Foundation, Albuquerque, New Mexico, and Curator of Archaeology, Southwest Museum, Los Angeles, California.

Fred Plog, Professor, Department of Sociology and Anthropology, New Mexico State University, Las Cruces, New Mexico.

J. Jefferson Reid, Professor, Department of Anthropology, University of Arizona, Tucson, Arizona.

Arthur H. Rohn, Professor, Department of Anthropology, Wichita State University, Wichita, Kansas.

Douglas W. Schwartz, President, School of American Research, Santa Fe, New Mexico.

# Foreword

The American Southwest has been the subject of a vast amount of archaeological research in the past century. Through a combination of excellent preservation, exceptional chronological control, and the presence of a variety of vigorous, contemporary native cultures, which have resided in the area since the prehistoric period, the Southwest has offered an unparalleled laboratory for the study of prehistoric culture. To review the results of this archaeological work and draw from it an overall conception of the prehistoric Southwest, an Advanced Seminar entitled "Dynamics of Southwestern Prehistory," was held at the School of American Research, in Santa Fe, New Mexico, from the 26th to the 30th of September, 1983.

Specifically, this seminar sought to review the general status of archaeological knowledge in 11 key regions of the Southwest, to examine broader questions of cultural development, which cross-cut these subregions, and to consider an overall conceptual model of the prehistoric Southwest after the advent of sedentism.

Ten archaeologists who had worked in separate, key areas of the Southwest participated in the seminar. While each participant had conducted extensive research in at least one southwestern area, they also controlled a significant amount of data that could be used to address the major questions on which the seminar focused. Each of these individuals also had shown an interest in questions relating to the larger pattern of southwestern prehistory and the direction of its development.

Each participant was asked to prepare a paper on the cultural sequence of his or her area and to consider several additional topics relating to that specific region: (1) the nature of population dynamics and sedentism; (2) the function and organizational significance of the large sites; (3) the main causes of culture change not related to environmental factors; (4) the social and political implications of major alterations in settlement patterns; (5) the balance between resource utilization and carrying capacity and its effects on demographic change; and (6) the special features of organization, adaptation, and change emerging from work in the region, which would illuminate our understanding of southwestern prehistory as a whole.

Each paper was circulated prior to the seminar and read by all other participants so that no further presentation was necessary when the seminar began. The first half of the week's discussion was spent in systematically and critically examining each paper. This process led to questions requiring additional data, clarification of interpretations, and inevitably to the introduction of broader problems that were pursued in a preliminary way and then set aside for later consideration. When the critique of the individual areal sequences had been completed, topics relevant to the whole Southwest, which had arisen in the course of the earlier discussions, were then methodically reviewed.

Linda S. Cordell, then of the University of New Mexico, presented the major paper on the Northern Rio Grande, and in the general discussion considered the role of migration as opposed to in situ cultural change. Jeffrey S. Dean of the Laboratory of Tree-Ring Research at the University of Arizona dealt with the Kayenta and the effects of climate on changes in population and culture. Paul R. Fish of Arizona State Museum at the University of Arizona handled the Hohokam and discussed Mesoamerican influences in the Southwest. George J. Gumerman from Southern Illinois University was assigned the topic of the Black Mesa-Hopi region. James W. Judge, then head of the National Park Service, Chaco Center, at the University of New Mexico, wrote a paper on the Chaco Canyon area. Steven LeBlanc of the Southwest Museum wrote two papers for the seminar, one on the Cibola area and another on the Mimbres Valley, and Fred Plog from New Mexico State University considered the Sinagua of north-central Arizona. J. Jefferson Reid from the University of Arizona was the key participant on the Mountain Mogollon, and Arthur H. Rohn from Wichita State University, covered the Mesa Verde and the general time period from A.D. 1050 to 1150.

Douglas W. Schwartz of the School of American Research served as organizer and chairman of the seminar.

At the end of the critique of papers and the considerations of selected topics, Gregory A. Johnson from Hunter College, City University of New York, served as general discussant with special responsibility for commenting on the Southwest as a region and the factors relating to the trajectory of its organizational change in comparison to other areas, such as the Near East.

During the last day of the seminar, an overall conceptual model of southwestern prehistory was developed. In this endeavor, the participants set aside the uniqueness of the individual sequences and focused on the commonalities of development. The goal was to determine whether a pattern of cultural development could be identified that characterized the entire Southwest from the beginnings of agriculture to the time of the Spanish entrada. The result of this exercise was both provocative and productive for understanding the totality of southwestern prehistory. It also raised additional questions regarding the interpretation of some of the areal sequences and boldly laid open the lack of critical data in other.

The National Endowment for the Humanities made the seminar possible through a grant to the School for a series of meetings on southwestern anthropology (R*1054−79). I gratefully acknowledge this support and hope the results justify the trust they showed in this endeavor. Jeton Brown, the School's executive secretary, ensured that all details were in order before the seminar participants arrived; she has our greatest thanks for her efficiency. Joe Sweeney, the School's physical plant supervisor, and his crew completed a new bedroom addition on the Seminar House just prior to the meeting, making our stay doubly enjoyable. All the seminar participants are grateful to Jane Baberousse, the manager of the School's seminar house. She has our thanks for supervising our welfare while the seminar was in progress. Jane and her crew, Sarah Wimett, Jill Hutson, and Steven Soule, made our life pleasant, kept us free from outside distractions, and amazed us with the meals they produced from their always wonderfully fragrant kitchen.

This seminar was devoted to understanding the complexity and the pattern of the prehistoric Southwest. Building on cultural and environmental change and the dynamics of its development, a model of southwestern culture history was constructed.

All the participants worked hard to fathom the evolving nature of the prehistoric southwestern culture, to understand its uniqueness, and to achieve an appreciation for the part the Southwest can play in considering the changes that operate in regions characterized by sustained cultural pluralism in the early centuries of settled, agricultural existence.

Douglas W. Schwartz
School of American Research
Santa Fe

# Preface to the Paperback Edition

A decade ago, the School of American Research in Santa Fe, New Mexico, hosted an advanced seminar that resulted in the original edition of *Dynamics of Southwest Prehistory*, published by Smithsonian Institution Press in 1989. Since its appearance, the volume has enjoyed considerable success as a source book and reference for comprehensive, clearly written presentations on the prehistory of major portions of the United States Southwest. This book is an unmodified edition of its parent volume. The intention of the publishers is to make the work available to a broader audience of interested students and public. We are gratified that they have chosen to do so.

The principal concerns of the seminar and of the book were to describe the themes that cross-cut the major traditions of the southwestern region and attempt to explain common processes that underlie them. Such region-wide syntheses, though rare, have been attempted in single or co-authored works beginning with A. V. Kidder's 1924 classic *An Introduction to the Study of Southwestern Archaeology*. In the latter half of the twentieth century, there is far more detailed knowledge about past events and the contexts in which they occurred than has been available up until now.

It is the tension between the detail of the specific mesas, valleys, and basins and the need to generalize about universal processes characterizing the evolutionary path of prehistoric peoples of the Southwest that is the challenge for contemporary archaeologists. Clearly, the dynamics of southwestern prehistory transcend the small areas that are the intellectual domain of individual archaeologists. Nevertheless, the detail is needed to construct realistic models of the evolution of prehistoric southwestern society. The seminar participants attempted to balance description of specifics of particular regions and generalization of broad scope by providing as much detail as possible in their contributions and by constructing an overarching scheme that underscores what were perceived to be similar processes operating in many subregions. A felicitous outcome is that chapters serve readers who are interested in either the particulars or the connective themes. As we discuss in the introductory chapter, the seminar produced a framework and attendant vocabulary for describing changes that occurred across the Southwest. This framework entails a particular perception of how prehistoric southwestern culture change took place. It is obvious in the chapters that follow that some authors feel more comfortable with this framework than do others. Nevertheless, since publication of the original edition, there has been no substantive refutation of the applicability of the proposed scheme.

This volume is a product of its time. Therefore, there is undue emphasis on the Anasazi with the result that the Mogollon and Hohokam are represented by too few chapters. The book also reflects the perspective of the 1970s and early 1980s in examining the Southwest as a relatively closed, highly articulated system. One result of relying on a systems model is that it becomes difficult to include multidimensional processes of interaction with other cultures, such as those with the more complex societies of Mexico. Another limitation is that it underestimates the now growing evidence for internal violence and social dysfunction that appeared at some times and places. Despite these admitted deficiencies, we believe that the book continues to provide a fine starting point for further consideration of Southwest prehistory, and we are very pleased that it does.

June 1993

# Preface

An effective conference uses the data and concepts that have been collected and generated in order to assess the current state of the discipline, and then uses that platform to address current concerns in new ways. The conference that was the genesis of this volume was proposed because Southwest archaeology is in a period of rapid change, both in terms of the amount and kinds of data that have been collected and in the development of various models that might be tested through the new data. It seemed a propitious time to assess the current state of Southwest archaeology and to attempt new insights about the nature of prehistoric southwestern society.

The conference participants were concerned with synthesizing the culture history of key regions of the Southwest and attempting to delineate underlying patterns and infer causes of stability and change. There was no narrowly defined goal as is so often the case in seminars of this type.

The participants were selected for their expertise in a specific geographic and cultural subarea of the Southwest. These scholars have all had a minimum of 10 years invested in the professional investigation of southwestern archaeology; most have been practicing for 20 or even 25 years. The long-term, collective experience of the participants does not mean, however, that there is a standard orthodoxy expressed in these papers. While individual authors do espouse a particular interpretation of the past for each area, attempts were made to discuss alternative explanations wherever possible. During the seminar, considerable time was spent trying to reconcile differences, note similarities, and explain differences among the areas. Toward the end of the seminar, the participants produced a framework that describes broad patterns of generally synchronous cultural events for all of the subareas represented. This scheme is discussed in Chapter 1. Some authors were more comfortable in using this scheme for their areas than were others. Finally, no one scheme was imposed on all the contributors. Authors used whatever cultural-historical or chronological framework they felt was most appropriate for their area. The overall conference scheme does highlight some pan-southwestern phenomena, and points of concordance and dissonance. These general patterns are noted and possible explanations for them are discussed by Cordell and Gumerman in Chapter 1 and by Johnson in Chapter 10.

The major charge to the participants was to examine the character of the archaeological manifestations in their area, and to explore the nature of change and the reasons for it. Most of the authors were particularly interested in patterns of interaction and isolation. They attempt to describe and explain the existence of periods when there were widespread social and economic networks, encompassing broad geographic regions, and other times during which these networks collapsed and were replaced by more localized and seemingly parochial traditions.

All of the authors use the detail of their area of study to address some of the larger questions of Southwest archaeology. In the best tradition of the archaeological study of a large region, the individual chapters in this volume demonstrate how data from smaller locales provide insight into the larger scheme. Being restricted to a relatively small area, however, the separate chapters cannot address all of the larger issues, and those which are addressed are examined within a necessarily limited context. An attempt to document the large areal patterns and synthesize regional data is reserved for the introductory chapter. Johnson's concluding chapter offers valuable commentary on the Southwest as a whole from the perspective of the Old World (especially Near Eastern) Neolithic and later developments.

Any volume about the Southwest must wrestle with the problem of its spatial definition. The seminar focus was on the core area of the Southwest and the major prehistoric cultures therein: the Hohokam, Mogollon, and Anasazi. The geographically, and perhaps culturally, more peripheral groups, such as the Patayan and Fremont, are not included here. The reasons for this are twofold. Most importantly, the seminar was to focus on documenting, and explaining culture change, especially patterns of interaction and isolation. Historically, most of these patterns had been formulated in the core area traditions. It was necessary to maintain the focus on the core areas in order to have enough cultural and environmental data so that potential explanations for, rather than simply descriptions of, these changing situations could be offered. The seminar also wished to bring the results of the most recent, high-quality data to the evaluation of older interpretations. The major, large-scale projects of the past five years have been in the core area where most land-modifying activities have taken place. The peripheral areas have not been subjected to the same recent intensity of archaeological scrutiny.

The relationship of the more elaborate cultures of Mexico to prehistoric southwestern societies is a perpetual line of inquiry that has involved scholars since the inception of organized investigations in the Southwest. Yet, this subject is not addressed in detail by any of the papers in this volume. This neglect of the Southwest-Mexico connection is not a denial of its existence or of its importance. None of the authors doubt that the connection existed and that its strength and character changed over time. The subject of Southwest-Mexico connections has been dealt with in numerous, very recent, symposia at professional meetings and in a newly published volume (*Ripples in the Chichimec Sea: New Considerations of Southwestern-Mesoamerican Interactions*, F. Joan Mathien and R. McGuire, eds., 1986, Southern Illinois University Press). Aside from these, there is a paucity of new cultural and environmental data, and a similar lack of new explanations or materials with which to evaluate old ones. For these reasons, the focus of this volume remains on what may be somewhat naively called the southwestern heartland.

As with any attempts at synthesizing and interpreting the prehistory of a large region, and one which has been perhaps more intensively scrutinized than any other comparable area in the world, the authors have relied on the many hundreds of projects conducted over many decades. In a very true sense, these papers are a culmination of efforts of those archaeologists who have reported on their work for a number of decades. In short, the seminar participants have had to consider not only the remains of native southwest-erners that are of primary concern, but they have also depended heavily on the published efforts of past archaeologists. Our thanks go to them.

The need for this conference was first recognized by Douglas W. Schwartz, President of the School of American Research. He selected the participants, made the many necessary arrangements, and most impor-tantly, chaired the seminar, leading the discussions in a thoughtful and orderly way. For his leadership, the volume contributors are deeply grateful.

Linda S. Cordell
and George J. Gumerman
September 1986

LINDA S. CORDELL AND
GEORGE J. GUMERMAN

1

# Cultural Interaction in the Prehistoric Southwest

## INTRODUCTION

The North American Southwest extends from southeastern Utah and south-western Colorado into Chihuahua and Sonora, and from central New Mexico to the Grand Canyon and the lower Colorado River (Fig. 1). As delineated, this geographically heterogeneous area is united by an arid to semiarid climate, a condition that has had major impact on cultural manifestations. The archaeological record extends some 11,000 years and encompasses ways of life characterized by highly mobile hunting and gathering, semisedentary and sedentary horticulture, and following the introduction of domestic livestock by Europeans, economies of mixed herding and horticulture.

The diversity of lifeways pursued over time, and at any one time, has led anthropologists to debate whether the Southwest is best described as a single culture area, as more than one culture area, or as a regional zone of cultural interaction (see Daifuku 1952; Kirchoff 1954; Kroeber 1939; Martin and Rinaldo 1951). Some scholars have employed a variety of trait lists in support of the general cultural unity of the Southwest (see Jennings and Reed 1956; Rouse 1962). We also favor emphasizing the essential unity of the Southwest, although our view focuses on the dynamics of cultural interactions over time in the area. The unity is reflected in the consistent sychroneity of changes

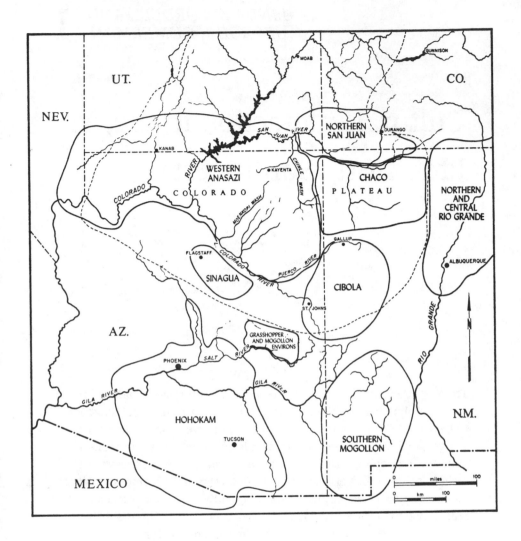

Fig. 1. General regions and groups discussed in this volume. Dashed line indicates extent of the Colorado Plateaus.

described in the framework of southwestern culture history that emerged from the conference and is described below. This framework also indicates that the greatest similarities in the material remains of the archaeological record of the area occur at the start of the time period under consideration, a time when both horticulture and sedentism began to set the Southwest apart from two adjacent regions—the Great Plains and the Great Basin—where hunting and gathering continued to be the primary mode of subsistence.

Despite increased regional variation over time in the Southwest, the complex and changing web of cultural interactions within the area becomes a hallmark of its unity and overshadows interactions with neighboring regions.

The Southwest enjoys a unique position in American archaeology. Due to the exceptional preservation of archaeological remains, the unmatched precision of temporal control and palaeoenvironmental data for the prehistoric periods, and the continued existence in the area of vital American Indian cultures, the Southwest is often seen as a natural laboratory appropriate for evaluating archaeological method and theories of cultural development and change. With the recent phenomenal growth of public archaeology in the western United States, the pace and scale of southwestern archaeological research has greatly accelerated. The vast quantity of literature of the 1970s and 1980s is difficult for even area specialists to control. Both the general interest in the prehistory of the Southwest and the avalanche of recent information suggested to the conference participants that this volume would be of interest to a broad community of scholars.

The Southwest has long been known for its archaeological conferences. The first, and still most famous, was the Pecos Conference of 1927. A. V. Kidder invited scholars to Pecos Pueblo in order to devise a scheme that would reflect the broad outlines of all southwestern prehistoric development, and to resolve issues of nomenclature and terminology (Kidder 1927). The Pecos Conference is now an annual event held at the end of the summer field season, and therefore serves primarily as a forum for discussion of current fieldwork with some topically oriented sessions. In addition to the Pecos Conference with its pan-southwestern focus, the recent volume of data recovery has been so great that there are now biannual conferences devoted to the Mogollon (e.g., Benson and Upham 1986), Hohokam (e.g., Dittert and Dove 1985a, 1985b) and the Anasazi (e.g., Smith 1983). In January of 1988, the first, in what may become a regularly scheduled pan-southwestern conference devoted to topical syntheses, was held in Tempe, Arizona.

Over the past decade, there have also been topically oriented conferences that have brought together specialists from diverse disciplines in order to address a particular problem area. These have included conferences aimed at developing detailed palaeoenvironmental reconstructions and relating these to prehistoric settlement and technological changes (e.g., Dean et al. 1985; Gumerman 1988) and conferences on specific topics in cultural resource management (e.g., Cordell and Green 1983; Green and Plog 1983; Plog and Wait 1982). Of a slightly different nature are conferences that bring southwestern archaeologists together to address broader thematic issues. The 1955 Seminars in Archaeology (Jennings and Reed 1956) focused on determining the extra-southwestern origins of various southwestern culture traits. The School of American Research seminar on prehistoric Pueblo social organization (Longacre 1970) was more restricted geographically, examining only those southwestern societies that could be construed as Pueblo. The seminar grew out of early processual archaeology in the attempt to reconstruct nonmaterial aspects of prehistoric culture and had an impact far beyond the scholarship of the Southwest.

The aims of the current seminar were, in some respects, broader than either the 1955 seminar or the seminar on prehistoric social organization. The conference was concerned, first, with synthesizing the culture history of key regions of the Southwest and, second, with describing and explaining underlying patterns of stability and change among the prehistoric cultures represented. In papers prepared for the seminar, participants were asked to provide background on the environment and paleoenvironment of their areas, review the culture history of their areas, and discuss the dynamics behind that culture history. As might be expected, considerable seminar time was spent learning the details of the sequences presented. Nevertheless, the seminar produced two worthwhile results: first, a framework with descriptive nomenclature relating to synchronous periods of stability and change, and second, discussions of cultural dynamics pertinent to periods of apparent isolation and interaction among local areas within the Southwest.

The patterns of interaction and isolation described during the conference were diverse. For example, a pattern such as the synchronous appearance of a distinctive ceramic style might suggest interaction that could have been the result of trade, migration, or the political ascendancy of a group whose pottery other cultures replicated. On the other hand, a pattern such as a synchronous shift in settlement distribution might be the result of purely local responses to a regional climatic event. There are also examples of times when distinctive stylistic features were restricted to local areas. These were generally interpreted as reflecting cultural isolation. After reviewing the local culture histories, much conference time was spent discussing the processes underlying similarities among the areas that seemed to indicate cultural interaction. It was in conceptualizing, describing, and discussing possible forms of political, social, and religious interactions that there was the most diversity in the vocabulary of the participants. Some used the term "alliances," some "interaction spheres," and some just the term "system." In part, the diversity reflects controversy over the nature of the interactions, and in part just the novelty in approaching these questions. Over the past ten years, southwesternists have moved far from developing the culture histories of single river valleys into discussions of a broadly regional nature.

Yet, there is still uncertainty about the way in which regional phenomena should be described.

One area of conference discussion involved attributing some of the evidence for interaction to the effects socially complex systems had on broad areas of the Southwest. Traditionally, the prehistoric Southwest has been considered an area that supported only egalitarian societies. Recently, there has been a great deal of discussion about systems that were socially hierarchical. While many investigators continue to be leery of ascribing hierarchical organization to any prehistoric southwestern group, most of the seminar participants acknowledged that at least a few of the prehistoric systems, notably those centered at Chaco Canyon, Casas Grandes, and the Hohokam region, influenced areas well beyond their own borders. Their degree of influence suggests organizational complexity beyond that of egalitarian groups as generally defined. There is continued disagreement among those participating in the conference (and probably among southwestern archae-ologists in general) about the degree of social complexity involved. Here we find Gregory Johnson's (this volume) observations and discussion most useful. Johnson's background in studying social hierarchies theoretically and in the early civilizations of the Near East allows us to see that in comparison to the early complex societies of the Old World, the southwest-ern examples are simple and modular.

A key element in this simplicity is the lack of obvious economic stratifi-cation in the Southwest that, in turn, is a reflection of the relatively low level of environmental productivity. From our perspective, the limitations of the southwestern environment and fluctuations in climate are crucial compo-nents in understanding prehistoric change. This is an issue we address in some detail below. We also believe that we need to develop broader and more innovative approaches to finding appropriate ethnographic analogs for the prehistoric societies of interest. Not only do we need to look regularly beyond the bounds of the geographic Southwest, but we need to isolate aspects of interest in a broad range of ethnographically and historically recorded societies, and develop ways of measuring these components in the archaeological record. Particularly distressing is our inability to understand regional population dynamics. Too often the seminar participants were un-able to offer convincing explanations for events or processes because demo-graphic data were unavailable or unreliable. Finally, we believe that agree-ment on the nature of social complexity reached in the prehistoric South-west is a long way in the future, but the issues that must be addressed are discussed in the papers included in this volume.

The framework developed during the conference provides a general temporal scheme with behavioral referents for the Southwest as a whole. The dates and period names are as follows:

| Date A.D. | Descriptive Title |
|---|---|
| 1275/1300 to 1540 | Aggregation |
| 1130/1150 to 1275/1300 | Reorganization |
| 1000/1050 to 1130/1150 | Differentiation |
| 770/800 to 1000/1050 | Expansion |
| 200/500 to 750/800 | Initiation |

There are several aspects of this framework that set it apart from others that are used in the Southwest (i.e., the Pecos Classification). It should first be noted that the dates which bracket each period are given as intervals (i.e., A.D. 1000/1050). In some cases, the dates unfortunately suggest a precision that may not exist. Also, we would not maintain that all changes took place simultaneously throughout the region. Rather, the intervals reflect the view that these times represent approximate *hinge points* when change from one set of characteristic modes of behavior to the next took place.

Importantly, the conference did not view change occurring gradually throughout a designated period. Rather, the scheme reflects the view that most often change was abrupt, occurring over a much shorter period of time. When it was first proposed, the Pecos Classification (Kidder 1927) was not tied into calendar dates. With the development of dendrochronology, tree-ring dates for the sequence were obtained, but often it was assumed that change was gradual and continuous. The two-hundred-year long stages of the Pecos chronology are artifacts of a gradualist intellectual stance that was rejected by the current conference on the basics of more recent information. Although the Pecos Classification was originally meant to refer to the entire Southwest, most of the data available in 1927 pertained only to the Anasazi. Thus, the terminology of the Pecos Classification (Basketmaker II, III, Pueblo I–IV) is culturally specific to the Anasazi. The current framework attempts to identify patterns of truly regional scope. Clearly, not all participants felt that the conference framework was entirely adequate for events in their particular area, although all agreed that for the Southwest as a whole, the scheme is relevant.

The various periods defined, as well as the hinge point dates, were derived from the discussions of culture history presented at the conference and in each paper. No attempts were made during the conference to link southwestern environmental change to pan-regional culture change. Long after the conference proposed the scheme, we noted some striking correspondence with the dates of various environmental episodes. Because we do address the environmental factors in our discussion of the cultural framework, their basis is addressed here. Dean and others (1985) synthesized several sources of paleoenvironmental data from the Colorado Plateaus and linked this with information on prehistoric population and a model of cultural behavior. We referred to that synthesis in developing our discussion of the framework presented here. We were impressed by the correlation between hinge point dates in the cultural scheme and the climatic changes reported (Dean et al. 1985). An obvious conclusion is that rather abrupt changes in climate triggered the cultural developments reported at the conference. We caution the reader against accepting the obvious on two points. First, we have no basis for generalizing paleoclimatic (or demographic) data from the Colorado Plateaus to the Southwest as a whole. Second, the correlations may not be as marked to others as they are to us. For this reason, we reproduce the chart from the 1985 publication with the conference framework added (Fig. 2).

## THE INITIATION PERIOD

The Initiation period is characterized as the time when the basic southwestern pattern is established. In essence, the change was away from the mobile, largely hunting and gathering strategies of the Archaic, to a way of life that included more dependence on crops and reduced residential mobility. With the reduction in mobility, the archaeological record contains tools and facilities that archaeologists recognize as distinctively southwestern, especially compared to the Great Basin and the Plains, where high mobility strategies persisted. The artifactual hallmarks of the period are residential architecture of a distinctive form and ceramics. Throughout the Southwest, the ceramics at this period are nondescript brown or gray wares. There is great similarity between Hohokam and Mogollon ceramics and general homogeneity in Anasazi ceramics throughout the Colorado Plateaus. The characteristic form of domestic architecture of this period is the pithouse.

The change from rather limited dependence on agriculture during much of the Archaic to somewhat more dependence on agriculture and probably to stored foods for part of the year during the Initiation period, seems to us to indicate a response to an imbalance between population and wild food resources. Looking at the environmental records of the Colorado Plateaus (Fig. 2), we note that the transition begins during a period of decreased ground water levels and decreased moisture. We would suggest that the move toward agricultural dependence may be related to a decrease in resources, whether or not population increased or remained stable. In

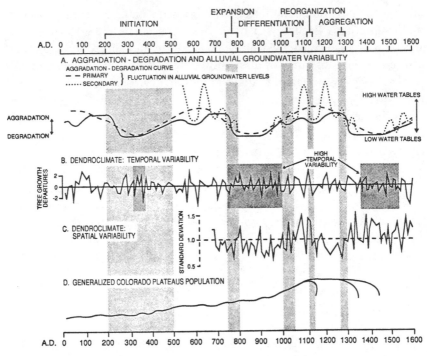

Fig. 2. *Periods of culture change in relation to environmental and demographic variables on the southern Colorado Plateaus,* A.D. *1–1600 (after Dean et al. 1985). Shaded vertical bars represent periods of cultural change for the prehistoric Southwest, as developed during the conference. These periods relate to the Southwest as a whole, not simply the Colorado Plateaus. (A) hydrologic fluctuations and floodplain aggradation-degradation; (B) decadal tree-ring growth departures in standard deviation units. The stippled section of the plot indicates periods of rapid oscillations between high and low precipitation values; (C) spatial variability in dendroclimate; (D) relative, generalized population trends. The curved downward lines indicate movement and reorganization.*

fact, we think there is little good evidence for increased population between about A.D. 1 and A.D. 200, just prior to the Initiation period. We follow Wobst (1977) and others (i.e., McLaughlin 1987) in suggesting that visually distinctive styles relate to social boundary mechanisms, which can become important in situations of increased regional population densities (Cordell 1987). The lack of stylistic differentiation in ceramics throughout the Southwest during the Initiation period may therefore imply little more than generally low population densities. On the other hand, it is possible that the stylistic homogeneity reflects the necessity for maintaining open social systems as people adjusted to environmental deterioration. Our position, not necessarily shared by others at the conference, is that increased dependence on agriculture by peoples in the Southwest, reflected by the use of stored foods and a decrease in residential mobility, may have been an attempt to reduce subsistence risk during a period of poor environmental conditions. We admit that by taking this position, we have not adequately addressed the question of why risk was not offset by further increases in mobility.

Finally, we would note that the appearance of pithouse architecture in the Southwest is but one example of a worldwide Neolithic phenomenon. This observation does not explain why pithouses were used in the Southwest or elsewhere. Discussions purporting to explain the use of pithouses have been advanced by others (i.e., Gilman 1987; McGuire and Schiffer 1983), and we offer no new ones here. We simply note that continued work on the subject is important and that no explanation for pithouse use that is particular to the Southwest is apt to be satisfactory.

## THE EXPANSION PERIOD

During the Expansion period, the broad, regionally differentiated patterns of the Southwest develop. Thus, with respect to ceramics, Hohokam, Mogollon, and Anasazi styles become recognizable. There is also a transition from homogeneity in architectural forms to differentiation among the subcultural areas. In the Anasazi region, surface rooms are built for storage or living. In the Hohokam area, platform mounds, which began late in the preceding period, become more formalized, and ballcourts appear and become more numerous throughout the period. The Hohokam area also evidences a change from small, highly localized communities to settlement over a much broader area. In the Mogollon area, the pithouse continues in use. Throughout the Southwest, there are more settlements and these occur in varied environmental situations. As our name for the period indicates, there is a definite geographic expansion of settlement and in some areas increased settlement density.

We note that the Expansion period in the northern portion of the Southwest is initiated by an interval of depressed water tables, erosion, and low effective moisture. These conditions, in fact, persist throughout the period and were accompanied by unpredictable precipitation from year-to-year, with little spatial variation in climate on the Colorado Plateaus (Fig. 2). The increased diversity of environmental settings that were settled in the Lower Sonoran zone and at higher elevations, suggests this may have been a time of experimentation for agriculturalists trying to find reliably productive locations for fields despite poor and variable climate. If the increase in settlements that we see is largely the result of rather short periods of occupation at particular locations, then population growth during the period may be overestimated. It is also possible that such experimentation in subsistence techniques might have been accompanied by an increase in exchange as groups compensated for local short-falls. Again, assuming that style is one mechanism of boundary marking, the distinctive stylistically defined regions we see may represent areas where exchange was intensive. The more elaborate Hohokam structures may indicate locations of ritual activity accompanied by resource sharing. The surface structures of the Anasazi suggest an increase in space allocated for storage. The Anasazi may have been attempting to store food (from years of good harvests) for longer periods of time in the face of deteriorating climatic conditions.

## THE DIFFERENTIATION PERIOD

The period from about A.D. 1000 to 1130 or 1150, which we term Differentiation, is characterized by two somewhat opposing trends. First, it was a time when much of the Southwest was characterized by extremely parochial stylistic behavior. For example, in the Hohokam area this takes the form of different ceramic styles for virtually every drainage. In parts of the Anasazi area, there are localized traditions in all aspects of the archaeological record. Second, and at the same time, this period witnessed the development of larger and apparently more complex systems, especially at Chaco Canyon and the Hohokam heartland. Casas Grandes was central to a regional system that flourished more than a century later.

Perhaps nothing in southwestern archaeology has changed so much in the past fifteen years as our characterizations of the large, complex systems (see Judge, this volume; LeBlanc, this volume; Fish, this volume). It is also clear that we have a very long way to go toward adequate descriptions of the development and functioning of these systems. What is clear in the conference papers is that the manifestations in Chaco Canyon, Casas Grandes, and the Hohokam heartland are not simply larger variants of parochial local traditions. It is apparent in the papers in this volume that the major regional systems had proportionately great and diverse impact on enormous areas. This impact included increased exchange of some items (primarily ceramics), procurement and differential distribution of other items (such as shell and turquoise), changes in settlement patterns in some adjacent regions (see LeBlanc's discussions of Chacoan influence on the Cibola area and Casas Grandes's influence on the Mimbres area, both in this volume), and the differential spread of stylistic elements throughout much of the Southwest. Throughout the conference, a commonly heard remark was that it would not be possible to understand what was occurring in "area x" without knowing the situation at Chaco, Casas Grandes, or the Hohokam heartland. If much of the Southwest was undergoing a period of extreme parochialism, then the large systems encouraged a great deal of interaction elsewhere.

Having acknowledged the impact of the large regional systems, we readily point out that there is no consensus regarding the degree they were internally hierarchically organized or precisely how they functioned within their cultural settings. It is likely that there were differences in organization among the three systems and that the ways they articulated with other areas also varied. We deliberately refrain from using descriptors such as ranked societies, chiefdoms, Big Man systems or the like. We do not believe that such terms are useful here, at least in part because they imply specific kinds of economic and social relationships that may not be appropriate for the societies of present concern. We are impressed by Johnson's observations (this volume) which suggest that these systems were not economically or socially stratified, nor were they on their way toward becoming small-scale states. We also suggest that whatever economic interactions characterized the big systems, the altruistic pooling and sharing of food resources between have and have-nots (as is sometimes described under the rubric of redistribution) does not appear to offer a reasonable or likely scenario of their function.

We note that the environment during virtually the entire period of Differentiation was characterized by favorable hydrologic conditions with relatively good rainfall maintained after A.D. 1000 (Fig. 2). It would appear that during this quite benign interval, a variety of farming strategies, modes of social integration, and economic systems were attempted and succeeded, at least for the short-term. As one of us commented: Virtually any economic strategy would work. We leave to others (e.g., Mathien and McGuire 1986) discussion of Southwest-Mesoamerican interactions at this time. We would comment that in the Southwest we find somewhat less artifactual and symbolic indications of direct ties to Mesoamerica than during the period after A.D. 1150. Nevertheless, with abundant and secure food resources, the Southwest may have interacted with Mesoamerican states in a variety of more complex and subtle ways.

## THE REORGANIZATION PERIOD

We have used the term Reorganization to refer to the period from A.D. 1130/1150 to 1275/1300. In general, it was a time of apparent instability, with changes in the nature of the previously strong large systems, some local abandonments, and the development of new centers. The environmental record indicates that the transition point, between A.D. 1130 and 1150, was one when there was a very marked decline in hydrological conditions. The effect of lower water tables and erosion was clearly major for Chaco and for outlying Western Anasazi areas. Within Chaco Canyon, there is a cessation in building, although neither the canyon nor the San Juan Basin were abandoned. There were abandonments in some Anasazi areas and reorganizations in others. For example, in this period the Yellow Jacket and Mesa Verde areas (see Rohn, this volume) underwent a major episode of building and an expansion of their influence. Mesa Verde styles of ceramics and architecture were widely copied. Elsewhere, over much of the Western Anasazi area, there was extreme heterogeneity in the form that the reorganization took (see Gumerman and Dean this volume).

The Hohokam area, which cannot be assumed to have undergone the same environmental problems, also shows major changes. There was contraction of its northern extent and less elaboration of ritual items. Carved stone bowls, censors, and palettes were no longer made. Hohokam platform mounds at this time assumed residential functions, again indicating major reorganization but not a real abandonment. The notion of reorganization is strengthened by evidence of an increase in trade and of possible development of local craft specialization in the Phoenix Basin (see Fish, this volume). In what may be a similar case of local craft production and trade at this time, we see the beginnings of the Salado manifestation in the Tonto Basin and Globe-Miami areas of central Arizona. The Salado sites themselves are large and produced polychrome ceramics that were widely traded and widely copied.

In general, it is difficult to escape the proposition that with the environmental stress beginning in A.D. 1130, a number of previously successful options were seriously curtailed or failed completely. As the systems themselves differed, their responses were neither uniform or simple. Some regimes saw population decline, others became more densely inhabited. Old exchange networks broke down, but some new ones developed. The older centers of major systems were not abandoned but they do seem to have ceased being centers of innovation and control.

## THE AGGREGATION PERIOD

We term the period beginning in A.D. 1275/1300 and lasting until A.D. 1540 Aggregation. This was, of course, the time initiated by the "Great Drought" and major abandonments occurred on the Colorado Plateaus. The use of the term Aggregation as a descriptor, however, reflects the degree to which southwestern prehistory is no longer written from the perspective of the San

Juan Basin and Mesa Verde areas, as well as the pattern of settlement change at this time. In virtually all the areas that continued to be inhabited during this period, very large sites with rooms numbering in the many tens and hundreds are common.

The beginning of the period is again initiated by environmental deterioration. This is in the form of lowered ground water levels, the major drought of A.D. 1275 to 1300, and a decrease in spatial variation in rainfall (Fig. 2). Mesa Verde and Chaco Canyon, as well as much of the San Juan Basin and large portions of the Western Anasazi homeland and other areas, were finally abandoned. At the same time, large settlements were established or maintained in the northern Rio Grande drainage, Grasshopper, Cibola, Tsegi Canyon, Hopi Mesas, Jeddito Valley, Little Colorado River Valley, and the southern Hohokam regions. The existence of large sites, however, should not imply similarity in occupation histories or organization. Dean's (1969) still classic study of the divergent occupation patterns of Betatakin and Kiet Siel remind us that we cannot assume that all large sites were organized in the same way or had similar histories of development.

In some regions, such as the Grasshopper (see Reid, this volume) and the Western Anasazi areas (see Gumerman and Dean, this volume), there seem to have been focal or central pueblos that were economic and social centers for surrounding settlements. This is particularly true in the early portion of the Aggregation period. Focal pueblos are larger than the sites that surround them, and in general, they yield higher quantities of ceramics made in the prevailing regional style than do their smaller neighbors. The ceramic distributions indicate that the focal pueblos interacted among themselves differently than they did with their neighboring settlements. Focal or central pueblos also contain larger quantities of trade goods, deriving from the region or from greater distances, than their neighbors. Again, however, we would caution that such similarities among the focal pueblos themselves may mask internal organizational differences.

There is a continuing debate whether the interaction implied by the homogeneity of styles and relative abundance of trade goods required coordination by an elite group or class of individuals (see discussions in Reid, this volume). The conference did not resolve this issue, and in our view, no compelling case has been made in support of either position. We could argue that the data analyzed by those with opposing views are in fact significantly different so that major organizational differences are at the center of the controversy; the ambiguity also probably reflects the weakness with which social hierarchies were developed anywhere in the Southwest. Essentially, while we do not claim that the focal or central communities were analogous in organization to modern Western or Eastern Pueblos, we also do not have evidence that would suggest social and economic stratification in the more usual sense (again, see Johnson, this volume). Rather than seeing our stand as one that begs the question altogether, we suggest that southwesternists need to be more open to a wide range of ethnographic cases and situations and expect to find parallels in a diverse range of ethnohistoric and ethnographic records. Furthermore, this approach might help to discover and explain many different types of variation in the archaeological record.

The issue of organization during this period emerges as one of major and continuing importance on more than one level of inquiry. We do not know why settlement size increased to such an extent at this time. In some areas there seems to have been settlement with a defensive posture, but there are also cases where warfare or raiding does not seem to have conditioned settlement placement (see Cordell, this volume; Fish, this volume). There is also heterogeneity in site layout, with some sites consisting of masses of roomblocks oriented toward central plazas and others without central plazas. Some sites are surrounded by low walls; others are not. At this point, we do not know precisely how these reflect differences in community organization (Reed 1956).

Significantly, many of the areas inhabited during this period ceased to be occupied into the Historic period. The paleoenvironmental data indicate a period of low water tables, expanding arroyo systems, and deficient and temporally highly variable precipitation from about A.D. 1475 to 1500. How many communities failed because of environmentally related factors and how many because of problems attendant upon social coordination of large numbers of people in the same village is unknown. The seminar considered the possibility that sites appearing to have been abandoned in the late prehistoric period, as determined from tree-ring dates, may actually have been inhabited into historic times when they may have been deserted due to the impact of Europeans, specifically European diseases. It is not uncommon to discover beams that have been cut hundreds of years ago in villages that are occupied today. For the period from A.D. 1400 to 1600, which brackets the first contact with Europeans, the issue of dating the *abandonment* of individual villages is crucial.

The seminar considered A.D. 1540 the beginning of the transition into the Historic period. Until this time, all the cultural systems under consideration were entirely native. From A.D. 1540 onward, these were variously disrupted and altered by external factors, among them European diseases, the introduction of new crops, and livestock, in addition to new forms of political and social interaction. Our discussion addressed the problem of our current inability to adequately identify various nomadic groups that should have been in the area at about the time of contact, if not slightly before. The primary difficulty is that we do not have methods to appropriately and unambiguously identify such groups.

As is often the case, the seminar raised as many questions and issues as it resolved. Many of the unanswered questions, however, have been brought into sharper focus with the result that they are more likely to be answered in the future. Those areas that we felt needed immediate attention were developing a less provincial ethnographic perspective, developing techniques and refining means of estimating prehistoric population size and structure, and working toward finer chronological control. In many ways, the Southwest is far ahead of other regions of the world in the precision and resolution of its data, but the nature of the problems we attempt to resolve requires even greater efforts. We are pleased that the seminar did reach major agreement on the broad outlines of southwestern prehistory. The novelty of the view incorporated by the papers in this volume is that each paper is regionally specific and detailed, however, each also acknowledges the impact of pan-southwestern factors. Those of environment have been part of the southwest-ernist's intellectual baggage for many years, but have only recently attained the remarkable level of detail reflected here. The influence of large, regionally based systems on local developments, we see as new in its current form. The influence was universally recognized but the manifestations across the areas represented, and interpretations of that influence, were diverse and intellectually interesting. We look forward to having the opportunity to explore them further in the future.

# REFERENCES

Benson, Charlotte, and Steadman Upham (editors)
  1986    *Mogollon Variability*. University Museum Occasional Papers No. 15. New Mexico State University, Las Cruces.

Cordell, Linda S.
  1984    *Prehistory of the Southwest*. Academic Press, Orlando.
  1987    Approaches to Ethnicity in Southwestern Archaeology. Paper presented at the 86th Annual Meeting of the American Anthropological Association, Chicago.

Cordell, Linda S., and Dee F. Green (editors)
  1983    *Theory and Model Building: Refining Survey Strategies for Locating Prehistoric Heritage Resources*. Cultural Resources Document No. 3. USDA Forest Service, Southwest Region, Albuquerque.

Daifuku, Hiroshi
    1952    A New Conceptual Scheme for Prehistoric Cultures in the Southwestern United States. *American Anthropologist* 54 (2):191–200.

Dean, Jeffrey S., Robert C. Euler, George J. Gumerman, Fred Plog, Richard H. Hevly, and Thor N. V. Karlstrom
    1985    Human Behavior, Demography, and Paleoenvironment on the Colorado Plateaus. *American Antiquity* 50(3):537–554.

Dittert, Alfred E., Jr., and Donald Dove (eds.)
    1985a    *Proceedings of the 1983 Hohokam Symposium*, Part 1. Phoenix Chapter. Arizona Archaeological Society, Occasional Paper No. 2.
    1985b    *Proceedings of the 1983 Hohokam Symposium*, Part 2. Phoenix Chapter. Arizona Archaeological Society, Occasional Paper No. 2.

Gilman, Patricia A.
    1987    Architecture as Artifact: Pit Structures and Pueblos in the American Southwest. *American Antiquity* 52(3):538–564.

Green, Dee F., and Fred Plog (editors)
    1983    *Problem Orientation and Allocation Strategies for Prehistoric Cultural Resources on the New Mexico National Forests.* Cultural Resources Document No. 1. USDA Forest Service Southwest Region, Albuquerque.

Gumerman, George J. (editor)
    1988    *The Anasazi in a Changing Environment.* The School of American Research and Cambridge University Press, Cambridge.

Jennings, Jesse D., and Erik K. Reed
    1956    The American Southwest: A Problem in Cultural Isolation, Seminars in Archaeology 1955. *Memoirs of the Society for American Archaeology* 11:59–129.

Kidder, A. V.
    1927    Southwestern Archaeological Conference. *Science* 68:489–491.

Kirchoff, Paul
    1954    Gatherers and Farmers in the Greater Southwest: A Problem in Classification. *American Anthropologist* 56(4):529–550.

Kroeber, Alfred L.
    1939    *Cultural and Natural Areas of Native North America.* University of California Publications in American Archaeology and Ethnology 38. Berkeley.

Longacre, William A. (editor)
    1970    *Reconstructing Prehistoric Pueblo Societies.* School of American Research and University of New Mexico Press, Albuquerque.

Martin, Paul S., and John B. Rinaldo
    1951    The Southwestern Co-tradition. *Southwestern Journal of Anthropology* 7(3):215–229.

Mathien, Frances J., and Randall H. McGuire (editors)
    1986    *Ripples in the Chichimec Sea, New Considerations of Southwestern-Mesoamerican Interactions.* Southern Illinois University Press, Carbondale.

McGuire, Randall H., and Michael B. Schiffer
    1983    A Theory of Architectural Design. *Journal of Anthropological Archaeology* 3:277–303.

McLaughlin, Castle
    1987    Style as a Social Boundary Marker: A Plains Indian Example. In *Ethnicity and Culture*, edited by Reginald Auger, Margaret F. Glass, Scott MacEachern, and Peter H. McCartney. Proceedings of the 18th Annual Conference of the Archaeological Association of the University of Calgary, Calgary.

Plog, Fred, and Walter Wait (editors)
    1982    *The San Juan Tomorrow*. National Park Service, Southwest Region, Santa Fe.

Reed, Erik K.
    1956    Types of Village Plan Layouts in the Southwest. In *Prehistoric Settlement Patterns in the New World*, edited by Gordon Willey, pp. 11–17. Viking Fund Publications in Anthropology 23. New York.

Rouse, Irving
    1962    Southwestern Archaeology Today. In *An Introduction to the Study of Southwestern Archaeology*, by A. V. Kidder, pp. 1–55. Revised edition, Yale University Press, New Haven and London.

Smith, Jack E. (editor)
    1983    *Proceedings of the Anasazi Symposium 1981*. Mesa Verde Museum Association, Mesa Verde National Park.

Wobst, Martin
    1977    Stylistic Behavior and Information Exchange. In *Papers for the Director: Research in Honor of James B. Griffin*, edited by Charles E. Clelland, pp. 317–342. Anthropological Papers of the University of Michigan 61. Ann Arbor.

# The Hohokam

## 1,000 Years of Prehistory in the Sonoran Desert

### INTRODUCTION

The Hohokam are the prehistoric desert farmers in central and southern Arizona below the Mogollon Rim, from the Dragoon Mountains on the east to the Growler Mountains on the west (Fig. 3). Discounting any portion of adjacent Mexico that might exhibit cultural similarities, these boundaries involve a territory of nearly 45,000 square miles or an area almost the size of the state of South Carolina. Expression of this cultural tradition is encompassed by the Lower Sonoran Desert, but considerable internal variation exists among local environments. Several models have been used to characterize the homogeneity perceived in Hohokam archaeological material across this broad swath in space and over more than 1,000 years in time. With greater or lesser explicitness, students of regional prehistory have treated this archaeological culture as one ethnic group, a collection of related ethnic groups, an underlying economic adaptation or peasant tradition, an interaction sphere, and a horizon style. Each of these models derives from a basic set of shared culture traits.

Artifactual traits that have come to be identified as hallmarks of the Hohokam were recognized for some time in the major ruins of the Salt and Gila River valleys when the Gila Pueblo Archaeological Foundation began

19

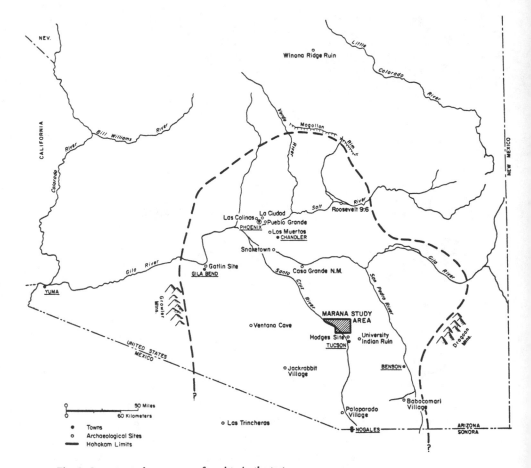

*Fig. 3. Important place names referred to in the text.*

studying the prehistoric cultures of southern Arizona in the 1920s. The geographic extent of red-on-buff ceramics found at these sites provided boundaries for the tradition by the early 1930s (Gladwin and Gladwin 1929a, 1929b, 1930, 1935). Additional organizational characteristics have come to parallel the distribution of Hohokam pottery and other artifact types. Villages consist of dispersed houses and house clusters. Larger settlements are often organized around formal arrangements of plazas, ballcourts, and platform mounds. Cremation is the primary method for disposal of the dead. Canal networks tap desert rivers and major tributaries, the largest carrying water more than 20 miles. Ak chin farming on alluvial fans and a variety of techniques utilizing floodwater and runoff complete a versatile agricultural repertoire. Widespread trade networks involve large amounts of shell and other exotic goods.

Disjunctions have been noted between the Hohokam and Puebloan peoples of the Southwest. A. V. Kidder (1924:298) was so impressed with these that he described Hohokam remains as "so unlike those of any of our other districts. . . . we should be forced to consider that we had overstepped the limits of the Southwest culture area." Though often used, the border with Mexico is an unconvincing boundary. Linguistic comprehensibility existed among Piman speakers from the Gila to Jalisco (Kroeber 1939:125; Sauer 1934:82–83; Hayden 1970:89; Wilcox 1986). On both stylistic grounds and settlement patterns, the Hohokam appear to have resembled the historic river-oriented rancheria cultures, extending into Sonora and Sinaloa, more than the ethnographic Puebloans of the southwestern United States.

Traits with a Mexican flavor are often used in differentiating Hohokam ceramics. Incising and grooving in the early part of the sequence, and later repetitious use of small elements are found to the south but not to the north. Forms such as molcajetes, comals, tripods, and censors occur in the same distribution. A suite of items with socioreligious implications finds northern limits among the Hohokam; three dimensional figurines, censors, and palettes occur very sporadically in the remainder of the Southwest, and are usually considered the result of trade or direct interaction with the Hohokam. In contrast with the Puebloan kiva complex, Hohokam public architecture in the form of platform mounds or ballcourts has Mesoamerican antecedents.

## SONORAN DESERT ENVIRONMENT

With rainfall seldom exceeding 12 inches, the Sonoran Desert has high summer temperatures and mild winters. The single outstanding characteristic that distinguishes the Sonoran Desert from other major deserts is the size, diversity, and wide distribution of trees and treelike cacti (Dunbier 1968:45). Giant cacti and small xerophytic trees dominate the landscape and have earned the designation "arborescent" for the Sonoran Desert.

The Sonoran Desert has a rich and varied set of vegetational resources. Desert plants tend to store starchy reserves, fruiting quickly and profusely in response to sporadic moisture. Apparent barrenness of the desert is contradicted by the abundance of gatherable plants. Ethnobotanists Richard Felger and Gary Nabhan (1976:74) compiled a list of 375 species and 40 staples for the Pimans. Many of these, such as mesquite beans and cholla buds, are seasonally predictable, easy to harvest, found in large quantities, and are readily processed into storable states.

The Lower Sonoran Desert is also characterized by widely spaced rivers draining distant upland areas. The major drainages flow through numerous basins with considerable elevational diversity. Elevational ranges result in diverse resources over short lineal transects. This pattern is repeated to an extent that individual groups have comparable access to similar, varied resources within less than one day's walk.

The region can truly be described as one of the major food-rich areas for a gathering economy in North America. Food is not only predictable, storable, and abundant, but harvest times for staples are spread over much of the year. Although food for large populations can be supplied from desert sources, important restrictions to settlement are present. The limited availability of potable water is most significant. Aside from day-to-day domestic use, processing of desert plants into storable forms frequently requires quantities of water. As a result, some areas containing much potential food were never exploited or were used only during periods of highest population density.

## FACTORS INFLUENCING HOHOKAM STUDIES

Hohokam archaeology follows a significantly different historical trajectory from that of the neighboring Mogollon and Anasazi areas. Basic research has been comparatively limited until recently. Investigations have focused on the study of a few sites and major publications have been widely separated in time. Further, only a few individuals have sustained an interest in the region spanning their professional careers.

More than for other major archaeological cultures in the Southwest, areas of greatest prehistoric population density and cultural elaboration have coincided with modern cities and agriculture. While many imaginative attempts are being made to salvage remnants of the settlement pattern in the central Hohokam area (Gregory and Nials 1985; Nicholas and Neitzel 1984; Wilcox and Sternberg 1983; Wilcox, in press; Howard 1987), the opportunity to study the Hohokam in a manner still possible at Chaco Canyon, Mesa Verde, or Casas Grandes is gone. Records of canal systems and locations of large sites are known to some extent, but overall patterns of the Salt and Gila settlements are essentially lost under urban sprawl and cotton fields. In fact, many larger sites had already been obliterated when Gila Pueblo investigations began shaping the concepts of a Red-on-buff Culture.

Unlike other southwestern traditions, the basic sequence and evolutionary scheme for the Hohokam were constructed by intensive excavation at a single, long-term site rather than by integrating studies at multiple sites. Emil Haury's (1976) detailed work at the large and elaborate site of Snaketown was completed by restudy in the 1960s and has not been repeated in other parts of the region. This emphasis has promoted a model of Hohokam culture as emanating from a strong central source, surrounded by less well developed, imitative, and colonial spheres. The core-periphery contrast is undoubtedly strengthened by lack of thoroughly excavated and reported large sites outside the Salt and Gila heartland. Comparison of poorly known materials from broad peripheral areas with the master sequence has shaped perceptions of Hohokam prehistory and the processes guiding it. In spite of the strong central focus, an overriding concept of cultural unity within a vast territory follows from the widespread distribution of Hohokam ceramic styles.

Quantitative treatment is often missing in presentation of Hohokam data, hindering distributional and other specific comparative studies. The quantities and proveniences of particular items may be buried or neglected in the literature in favor of more detailed discussion of typical examples. Contrasts between features, sites, and subareas have been based most frequently on undifferentiated presence and absence of traits. In the few instances where data on context and frequency have been assembled, results have suggested conclusions quite divergent from traditional trait comparisons (Fish et al. 1980; Nelson 1981; Howard 1983; McGuire and Downum 1982).

Difficulty in deriving quantitative data also stems from the physical nature of Hohokam remains. In much of the Southwest, prehistoric groups conveniently lived in above-ground, compact masonry sites with conifer beams. The Hohokam were much less well-mannered in an archaeological sense. They often chose to live in settlements known as rancherias with dispersed and nongeometrically arranged structures. To make matters worse, they constructed insubstantial, semisubterranean hovels until the Classic period (and usually even afterward). Consequently, surface survey has been much less definitive, more frustrating, and of secondary importance. Even with the most systematic methods, which are infrequently employed, the results are less productive and more ambiguous than in any other part of the Southwest.

Ethnographic analogs for the Hohokam are more problematic than Puebloan regions where a general and sometimes biological continuum can be traced to historic or modern times. Although Puebloan analogs cannot always be applied on a one-to-one basis, material culture correlates of social organization and belief systems can be applied down to specific furnishings of prehistoric kivas. The social significance of Hohokam ballcourts, mounds, and ritual paraphernalia cannot be clarified by similar observations among Pima and Papago, who are sometimes questioned as direct descendants (Ezell 1963; Di Peso 1956). Major ethnographies for these groups date no earlier than the turn of the century (Castetter and Bell 1942; Russell 1908; Underhill 1939) with relatively sparse and undetailed earlier Spanish accounts. By the period of close observation, even subsistence analogs are shaped by Old World crops and animals, participation in a cash economy, and population densities and distributions dissimilar to prehistoric ones.

## CULTURE HISTORY

Large and small excavation and survey projects occasioned by accelerated development throughout southern Arizona have caused a recent explosion of primary data. These projects reveal a degree of variability less and less easily fitted into schemes primarily established within one subregion and emphasizing one site. As the massive projects currently underway are reported and digested, existing perceptions of the "facts" of Hohokam prehistory are bound to be altered in important ways. However, contract restrictions and orientations have limited problem domains and have not produced comparable interregional data or satisfactory definition of local developments.

### Chronology

Trash levels superimposed in Snaketown mounds furnished a basic ceramic sequence (Gladwin et al. 1937: 248–249). The inapplicability of dendrochronology and lack of other chronometric techniques prevented direct absolute dating during earlier excavations. Dates for the Colonial and Sedentary periods were obtained by Mogollon and Anasazi intrusives with styles dated by tree rings. Pioneer phases were placed by a backward interpolation of estimated increments of 200 years. The early appearance of the Pioneer period according to traditional chronology (Fig. 4) made the Hohokam nonsynchronous with other southwestern ceramic traditions, thereby contradicting many popular and current views about regional interaction and social change (e.g., Plog 1980; LeBlanc 1982; Wilcox and Shenk 1977; Wilcox and Sternberg 1983; McGuire and Schiffer 1982).

Controversy surrounded the 1937 Snaketown chronology (e.g., Gladwin 1942, 1948; Di Peso 1956; Bullard 1962). Haury's (1976) return to the site in 1964 furnished new data interpreted as supporting the original chronology. Other investigators from Arizona State University (Ruppe 1966; Ives and Ophenring 1966) also undertook a reevaluation focusing on small sites with few components where Pioneer ceramics prevailed. Their series of radiocarbon dates supported the original phase sequence but strongly suggested temporal compression of Pioneer phases and a later initial date (Schiffer 1982:320–321). With one exception (Morris 1969), the Arizona State University research remains unreported or available only in very preliminary form.

Comprehensive presentation of the 1964 Snaketown chronological information has fueled reevaluation from numerous perspectives (Plog 1980; Schiffer 1982; LeBlanc 1982; Wilcox and Shenk 1977; Wilcox and Sternberg 1983). Aside from Plog (1980), these writers support the phase sequence advocated by Haury. A revisionist consensus, followed in this paper, begins the sequence at approximately A.D. 300, while compressing phase intervals through the Colonial period. Given the critical need to finally and firmly anchor the Hohokam chronology, reworking the 1964 Snaketown data needs to be replaced by focused research on the earlier phases. A proliferation of radiocarbon and archaeomagnetic dates can be expected for all portions of the Colonial, Sedentary, and Classic periods as major contract undertakings just completed or in progress are reported.

## The Sequence

### Late Archaic Transition (500 B.C. to A.D. 300)

The relationship of sedentism, agriculture, and ceramics remains undefined in the Hohokam area. Sites spanning the Archaic-to-Hohokam transition have not been identified or investigated in any subregion. Pollen and plant macrofossil information is available from a number of Late Archaic sites containing corn, all of which are south of the Salt and Gila Rivers (Martin 1963:32–36; Hemmings et al. 1968; Doelle 1985; Huckell 1984; Fish et al. 1986). These demonstrate nonsynchronous adoption of farming and ceramics in southern Arizona.

The rarity of Archaic sites in the floodplain has been cited as indicating an empty niche filled by the earliest Hohokam (Haury, in Weaver et al. 1978:8). However, a number of large Late Archaic sites in riverine contexts can be documented for the Sonoran Desert. Some are buried and much evidence points to the fact that depositional processes in desert river basins add to the apparent sparsity of Late Archaic and early Pioneer sites.

Two major interpretations have been advanced for the origin of the Hohokam. Haury (1976) believed that a Mesoamerican group characterized by sedentism, pottery, and irrigation settled a riverine niche of minor impor-

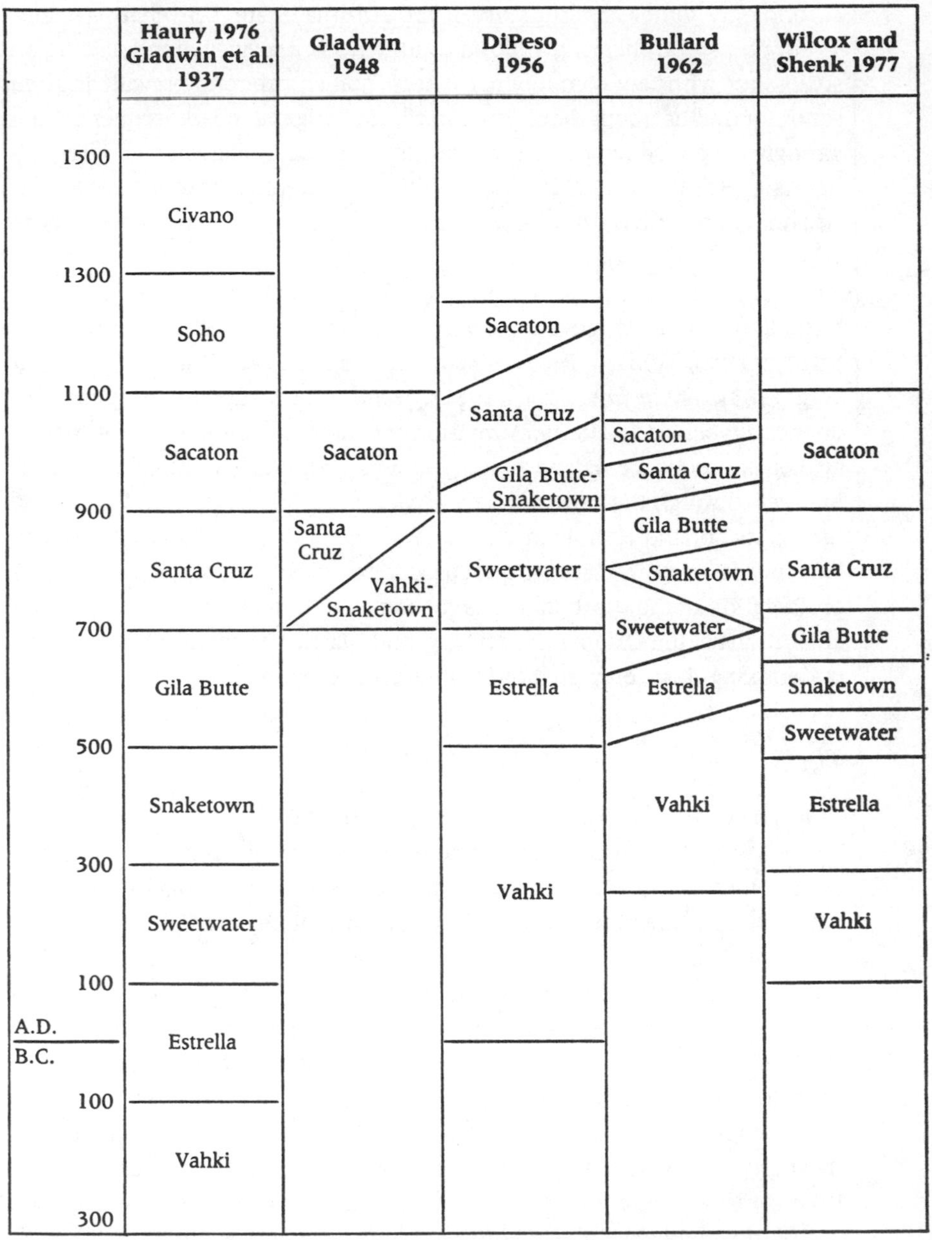

| | Haury 1976 Gladwin et al. 1937 | Gladwin 1948 | DiPeso 1956 | Bullard 1962 | Wilcox and Shenk 1977 |
|---|---|---|---|---|---|
| 1500 | | | | | |
| | Civano | | | | |
| 1300 | | | | | |
| | Soho | | Sacaton | | |
| 1100 | | | | | |
| | Sacaton | Sacaton | Santa Cruz | Sacaton | Sacaton |
| | | | Gila Butte-Snaketown | Santa Cruz | |
| 900 | | Santa Cruz | | Gila Butte | |
| | Santa Cruz | | Sweetwater | Snaketown | Santa Cruz |
| | | Vahki-Snaketown | | | |
| 700 | | | | Sweetwater | Gila Butte |
| | Gila Butte | | Estrella | Estrella | Snaketown |
| 500 | | | | | Sweetwater |
| | Snaketown | | | Vahki | Estrella |
| 300 | | | Vahki | | |
| | Sweetwater | | | | Vahki |
| 100 | | | | | |
| A.D. B.C. | Estrella | | | | |
| 100 | | | | | |
| | Vahki | | | | |
| 300 | | | | | |

Fig. 4. *Influential interpretations of the Hohokam chronological sequence are correlated with the model used in this volume.*

| | Plog 1980 | Schiffer 1982 | Le Blanc 1982 | Cable and Doyel, in press | Volume Model |
|---|---|---|---|---|---|
| | - - - - - - - | | | | Aggregation |
| | Civano | Civano | Classic | | |
| | Soho | Soho | | | Reorganization |
| | Sacaton | Sacaton | | | Differentiation |
| Vahki | Santa Cruz | Santa Cruz | Santa Cruz Sacaton | | Expansion |
| | | Gila Butte | | | |
| | | Snaketown | Snaketown/G.B. | | |
| | Snaketown | Sweetwater | Sweetwater | | |
| | | Estrella | Estrella | Snaketown | |
| | | Vahki | | Red-on-grey Horizon | Initiation |
| | Estrella | | Vahki | | |
| | | | | Vahki | |
| | | | | Red Mountain | |

tance to local hunters and gatherers. A native population already committed to initial forms of agriculture and sedentism has also been proposed. For Di Peso (1956) and Hayden (1970), these are the Ootam, and for Schroeder (1957, 1960, 1979), the Hakataya. According to these views, Late Archaic groups in the southern desert gradually incorporated features of Mesoamerican agricultural life. Thus, the Vahki phase originated by adoption of distinctive pottery styles and associated traits. This general model has been invoked more recently (LeBlanc 1982; Plog 1980; Wilcox and Shenk 1977; Wilcox 1979). With upward revision of Vahki dates, the beginning of the Hohokam sequence can be more readily reconciled with a larger pattern of contemporary southwestern acceptance of pottery and sedentary agriculture.

### Initiation of Pioneer Period (A.D. 300 to 700)

Traits characterizing the Pioneer period are recognized almost exclusively from the Salt and Gila valleys, largely from only three substantial excavated samples (Gladwin et al. 1937; Haury 1976; Morris 1969; Cable and Doyel 1987). Isolated sherds are reported for all subareas. The perception of an initial limited appearance in the Salt-Gila area may relate to intensity of investigation there and the rarity of diagnostic decorated pottery in early assemblages. For example, recent intensive survey and excavation in the Tucson Basin during a five year period has identified almost as many Pioneer sites as had been known previously for any subarea.

The earliest ceramics in a pre-Vahki Red Mountain phase from the Phoenix area, as proposed by Cable and Doyel (1987), are plain wares. Repeated associations of Archaic diagnostics and undecorated brown wares are also reported from survey in the vicinity of Tucson (Czaplicki et al. 1984; S. Fish, Fish, and Madsen 1985; Arizona State Museum Site Survey Files). The earliest distinctive pottery in the Vahki phase is thin, highly micaceous, and may be plain or polished red, but does not comprise the entire assemblage. Painted decoration in red appears in the succeeding Estrella phase, but it is only in the final Snaketown phase that a uniquely Hohokam red-on-buff combination is established. Incised decoration also begins in the Estrella phase, spanning the rest of the Pioneer period and ending in succeeding Gila Butte times. The red-on-buff combination and incision are ceramic traits not shared with other southwestern traditions.

A complex of ritual objects is present from early in the Pioneer period. These include figurines, palettes, and stone bowls. Figurines are a hallmark of this period, with over 90 percent of this age from dated contexts at Snaketown (Wilcox and Sternberg 1983:221). The first clearly public architecture begins with caliche-capped mounds in the Snaketown phase. Secondary pit and trench cremations and both flexed and extended inhumations show variety in interment practices. A widespread trade network is also in place, with the most abundant item being shell.

Pioneer subsistence is most often interpreted as emphasizing riverine habitats as the optimal agricultural locales for first farmers in desert basins. Floodwater farming from rivers often has been cited as the basic early technology (Gladwin et al. 1937; Wilcox 1979; Cable and Doyel 1987), but Haury (1976) reports a Vahki canal at Snaketown. During the Pioneer period in the Salt River Valley, Linda Nicholas and Jill Neitzel (1984) show two relatively simple canal systems capable of delivering water over ten miles from the river. More varied agriculture is suggested by nonriverine Pioneer sites, such as a large settlement with a diverse assemblage and trash mounds in the McDowell Mountains (Ophenring 1965) and several villages on bajada alluvial fans in the Tucson Basin (S. Fish, Fish, and Madsen 1985).

All Pioneer villages appear to have been small, even at Snaketown where Wilcox (Wilcox et al. 1981) estimates a maximum of 200 individuals through the Snaketown phase. Pioneer pithouses, among the largest floor areas in the Hohokam sequence, have been interpreted as containing larger family units (Haury 1976) and as representing communal structures (Wilcox et al. 1981; Cable and Doyel 1987). A plaza-oriented settlement plan at Snaketown (Wilcox et al. 1981) and courtyard groupings of houses (Cable and Doyel, 1987) may be present by the early Pioneer. Although a number of general house styles clearly distinguish the Hohokam at this time, overall village size and configuration appear to fit expectations established for intensively excavated and contemporary early farming villages in the Mogollon region (e.g., Lightfoot 1984; Anyon et al. 1981; Sayles 1945)

## Expansion/Differentiation or Colonial/Sedentary Period (A.D. 700 to 1150)

Hohokam ceramics become more abundant in a wider geographic area by the Gila Butte phase and continue that trajectory through the Sacaton phase of the Sedentary period. Aside from differences in ceramic style, the Colonial to Sedentary transition is marked in most other ways by few changes in orientation, culminating in the greatest extent and elaboration in Hohokam material culture. Red-on-buff ceramics, comprising substantial percentages of site assemblages by the Sedentary and reduced thereafter, define a succession of horizon styles reflected from Flagstaff to at least the Mexican border. Designs paralleling red-on-buff occur on local wares in limited amounts north of the Phoenix Basin, but in the Tucson area from a separate sequence from Gila Butte onward.

Ritual items, with the exception of figurines, become more elaborate, with highly decorated palettes, stone bowls, and censors. Specialized and well crafted projectile points, other stone items, and carved and etched shell are usually thought to have been produced by part-time specialists (Haury 1976:194, 205; Crabtree 1973; Doyel 1977a; Nelson 1981) and are regarded as components of a ritual complex occurring most often with cremation burials. Ballcourts with perhaps both ritual and integrative functions appear in the Gila Butte phase. These increase dramatically in number into the Sacaton phase (Wilcox and Sternberg 1983). From beginnings in the late Pioneer period, platform mounds become more and more formalized, occupying structured intrasite positions with respect to ballcourts and plaza areas. By the Sedentary period, palisades and post-reinforced adobe walls around mounds may be the precursors of later adobe compound arrangements. Both ritual artifact types and public architecture emphasized in Colonial and Sedentary periods are often seen as results of Mesoamerican influences (Di Peso 1956, 1974; Haury 1976; Hayden 1970; Gladwin et al. 1937; Schroeder 1966).

The extent of Hohokam horizon styles and wide occurrence of items and architecture with ritual association have been seen as evidence of outmigration from the core area and incorporation of a larger territory under some sort of Hohokam sway (Gladwin et al. 1937; Haury 1976; Schroeder 1960; Grebinger and Adam 1974; Masse 1980; Wood and McAllister 1980). The nature of interaction with adjacent regions may not be homogenous. Magnitudes of colonization and political incorporation are not well defined from archaeological evidence in any subarea. Review of kinds, quantities, and contexts of Hohokam items north of the core area suggests that extensive trade networks and participation in aspects of a widespread ritual complex account equally well for known distributions (Fish et al. 1980); similar interaction may account for an expanded Hohokam sphere in additional areas (Doyel 1980). The volume of trade in raw materials and finished items between Hohokam and outlying groups in all directions is a striking feature of late Colonial and Sedentary periods (Nelson 1981; Howard 1983; McGuire and Downum 1982; Haury 1976; Crown 1984a).

Stability and continuity in locations of larger settlements and zones of concentrated use in the Salt and Gila valleys are often linked to the fact that basic irrigation networks were established by the end of the Colonial period (Haury 1976:354; Masse 1981), although large increases in irrigated acreage occurred in the Sedentary (Nicholas and Neitzel 1984). Where adequate investigation of nonriverine locales has been undertaken throughout the Hohokam tradition, a wide variety of additional agricultural technologies and correlated settlement can be demonstrated (Crown 1984b; Doyel 1984; Dove 1984; Henderson and Rogers 1979). Full coverage survey across the northern Tucson Basin provides an opportunity to examine comprehensive nonriverine as well as riverine settlement pattern for these periods, revealing comparable continuity and stability in both settings (S. Fish, Fish, and Madsen 1985). Continuity is a feature of internal site structure also. Small courtyards or work areas uniting pithouse groups can be defined by the Colonial at a variety of Phoenix Basin sites other than Snaketown (Wilcox et al. 1981; Wilcox and Sternberg 1983; Howard 1982; Henderson 1987; Sires 1984), many of which are preserved in subsequent rebuildings. Rebuilding of houses and house groups in the same location is also seen at large numbers of other sites.

Complexity increases from Colonial to Sedentary in the sense of greater site differentiation in size and central function. Maximum site sizes increase dramatically beyond Pioneer levels; for example, a population of 500 is estimated for Snaketown by the Sacaton phase (Wilcox and Sternberg 1983). Sites with public architecture contain differing combinations, from one platform mound or ballcourt to multiples. This variability suggests site hierarchies, with differing magnitudes of integration. Regular spacing between ballcourt sites can be cited for the Phoenix (Wilcox and Sternberg 1983) and Tucson basins (Doelle et al. 1987), indicating some consistency in size of participating units. Hierarchy also exists among sites along canal systems, as measured by size and presence of public architecture (Doyel 1977a, 1980; Nicholas and Neitzel 1984; Wilcox and Sternberg 1983).

**Reorganization/Aggregation or Classic Period (A.D. 1150 to 1450)**
The geographic extent of anything that can be defined as a relatively uniform "Hohokam culture" contracts with the advent of the Classic period. The red-on-buff ceramic complex is reduced in the Salt and Gila heartland and becomes a rarity to the north. To the south, however, painted ceramics in the Tucson red-on-brown sequence continue to make up substantial percentages of assemblages and even expand areally. By late Classic, red-on-buff decoration virtually disappears in the core area. Low frequencies of Salado polychromes then represent the bulk of painted ceramics here, with higher percentages of these types to the east. Smudged and polished red wares rise to prominence throughout the maximal geographic extent of the Preclassic, in concert with a broader trend in the southern portion of the Southwest. Like buff wares, the distribution of Classic platform mounds has been used as a gauge of Hohokam tradition at this time (Fig. 5), to define more limited boundaries than previous ones encompassing ballcourts.

Previous artifacts with ritual use such as censors, elaborately carved stone bowls, and palettes cease to be made in the Classic. By the Soho phase, platform mounds assume residential as well as ritual functions.

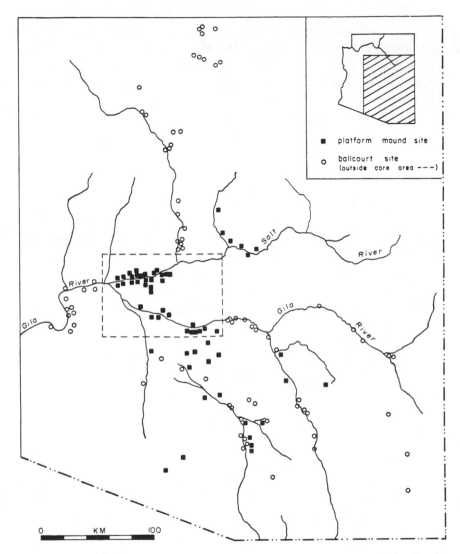

Fig. 5. *The distribution of sites with platform mounds contrasted with ones outside the Phoenix Basin with ballcourts (partly adapted from Gregory and Nials 1985 and Wilcox and Sternberg 1983).*

Adobe compounds surround mounds, with structures on the mound tops and within the walls. Regularity can be seen in the placement of mounds in compounds and in the spatial arrangement of these with respect to ball-courts (Gregory 1987). Careful excavation of one Civano phase platform mound and compound produced an estimate of storage function for half of the roofed area (Doyel 1974), suggesting a locus of redistribution. Late in the period, ballcourts are no longer constructed and a few new mounds, such as at Casa Grande, take the form of "big houses" with internal rooms.

Shell circulates more abundantly than ever for items of personal adornment, while stylistic standardization increases. Several writers (McGuire 1980; Di Peso 1974; Weigand et al. 1977:21) have seen a takeover of regional trade to the north by Casas Grandes, based largely on changing proportions of shell species supposedly unique to Casas Grandes or to the Hohokam. However, Nelson (1981:81) demonstrates that 95 percent of Hohokam shell overlaps in species and frequencies with those from Casas Grandes. Widespread trade in Salado polychromes, lithic raw materials, and the extent of copper bells document a vigorous trading network in both the Phoenix Basin and in peripheral areas. This dynamic exchange may have supported the rise of local specialists. Possible instances of this phenomenon are found in several areas of the northern and southern peripheries (Fish et al. 1980; Howard 1983).

The disappearance of red-on-buff pottery and absence of Classic platform mounds have figured prominently in a perception of inward collapse or contraction of the Hohokam system and population from outlying areas (Weaver 1972; Doyel 1977a, 1980; Wilcox et al. 1981, Wilcox and Sternberg 1983). The most comprehensive causal mechanism advanced for this shrinkage has been climatic deterioration, as interpolated from the Colorado Plateau evidence (Weaver 1972; Doyel 1977a, 1980; Masse 1982; Smith 1978). In only a very few instances can abandonment of outlying areas be demonstrated. Indeed, for the Flagstaff area (Pilles 1978), the Verde Valley (Fish and Fish 1977), Papagueria (Haury 1945), the Tucson Basin (Wallace and Holmlund 1984; P. Fish, Fish, and Madsen 1985), the San Pedro (Masse 1980), and other peripheral areas there is evidence for substantial population increase during the early Classic.

Canal systems reach a maximum extent in the Phoenix area during the Classic and become interconnected (Masse 1981; Nicholas and Neitzel 1984). Intensified nonriverine agriculture occurs at this time in the Tucson Basin and becomes more highly differentiated (S. Fish, Fish, Miksicek, and Madsen 1985). Expanded use of nonirrigated valley slopes is also apparent in much of southern Arizona (Debowski et al. 1976; Crown 1984b; Doelle 1976; Masse 1979).

Architecture undergoes change by the Soho phase, with adobe surface structures becoming common, sometimes in the form of contiguous rooms and sometimes associated with walled compounds. Pithouses continue to be constructed, and remain the dominant structural type at many sites. Regional architectural variability appears to be great, with emphasis on surface structures exemplified by the Salt, Gila, and Tonto basins. Introduction of compound architecture, combined with the dominance of new ceramic styles, has been interpreted as strong influence, migration, or invasion by Salado peoples (Gladwin 1957; Haury 1945), the Sinagua (Schroeder 1952, 1953), or Mexicans (Ferdon 1955; Di Peso 1956, 1974). Continuities in intrasite spatial arrangements (e.g., Howard 1982; Sires 1984:138), and Sedentary precursors for Classic domestic and public adobe architecture and red ware ceramics (Wasley 1966) have led to a current consensus for indigenous development of these trends (Doyel 1980; Wilcox 1979, 1980; Wasley and Doyel 1980).

On the major canal systems, sites with public architecture tend to be evenly spaced, with the largest frequently near the terminus (Nicholas and Neitzel 1984; Gregory and Nials 1985). More abundant sites along the canals indicate greater numbers of people interacting by proximity. Population aggregation and site differentiation in communities not focused on irrigation networks can be demonstrated for the Tucson (P. Fish, Fish, and Madsen 1985), Picacho (Wilcox 1984), and Tonto areas (Wood and McAllister 1984). Early in the Classic, public architecture in many sites is rebuilt and relocated (Gregory 1987; Gregory and Nials 1985; Wilcox and Sternberg 1983), in combination with wall construction for spatial demarcation or exclusion. A later Classic form of public architecture, the "big house" as at Casa Grande, emphasizes large multistoried adobe buildings on proportionally smaller mound bases. Sociopolitical reorganization involving more pronounced hierarchical relationships between sites and among their inhabitants are Classic developments.

Sometime after A.D. 1400, a cohesive Hohokam tradition ceases to exist. Population is sharply reduced at large sites, and at least some platform mounds seem to lose their focal role (Hammack and Sullivan 1981). A few small villages (Crown and Sires 1984; Robert Gasser, personal communication), individual post-mound structures at Las Colinas (Hammack and Sullivan 1981), and rooms at Escalante (Doyel 1974) have been dated to the post-1400 period by absolute techniques, but similar dates may be indicated by the frequent occurrence of Hopi Jeddito ceramics at a number of additional large sites such as University Indian Ruin (Hayden 1957) and Casa Grande (Wilcox and Shenk 1977). The precise timing and synchroneity of dissolution of the Hohokam tradition is even more poorly understood than its initiation. By the time of earliest Spanish observation in the seventeenth century, population size and distribution had changed significantly and more elaborated aspects of integration such as massive canal systems and public architecture had fallen into disuse. Descendant status of Pima, Papago, and other historic groups in the area remains a matter of debate.

## Local Developments and Regional-Scale Data: A Tucson Basin Example

Critical evaluation of the completeness and representativeness of available data is a continuing weakness at many levels in summary and interpretation of Hohokam culture history and process. This is an old problem of widely interpolated models formulated at few or single sites and a new problem in the integration of disjointed data from contract projects. The issue of data adequacy lacks rigorous consideration in reconstruction and interpretations of local sequences and in examinations of pan-Hohokam models. Efforts to compile data meeting consciously defined criteria for given problems are few to date, and represent the most challenging and promising avenues of research.

Within the Hohokam tradition, representative regional-scale data are almost universally lacking, and at the same time are a necessity for moving beyond speculation on the dynamics of culture history. The potential for insights offered by this kind of data is illustrated by full-coverage results from the northern Tucson Basin (P. Fish, Fish, and Madsen 1985; S. Fish, Fish, and Madsen 1985, 1989). Settlement distributions enhance understanding of local Hohokam development and furnish a concrete instance of Classic period reorganization.

Survey of 350 contiguous square kilometers at intervals of 30 meters has resulted in the identification of over 700 sites and thousands of scatters and isolated artifacts. These remains show that major patterns of land use began early and remained constant. Sites of all ceramic periods beginning with the initial Pioneer period parallel the Santa Cruz River. This concentration includes sites at the edge of the floodplain itself, and those on the lower edge of the adjoining bajada. Along the flanks of the eastern Tortolita Mountains, occupation is clearly indicated from the succeeding Colonial period onward. Longstanding preferred locations within river-oriented and mountain flank concentrations are attested by numerous multicomponent sites and clusterings of temporally discrete ones (See Fig. 6). Systematic examination of bajada and foothill areas contradict earlier reconstructions that these locales were settled secondarily in the Classic (Grebinger and Adam 1974) or used only for marginal resource extraction (Doyel 1977b).

The upland and riverine settlement groups appear to represent equally substantial and permanent occupations. Ballcourts and large trash mounds occur at the largest sites. A range in site sizes and topographic settings in each cluster suggests differentiation in functions and productive capacities. Agricultural complexes of stone features are present in both upper bajada

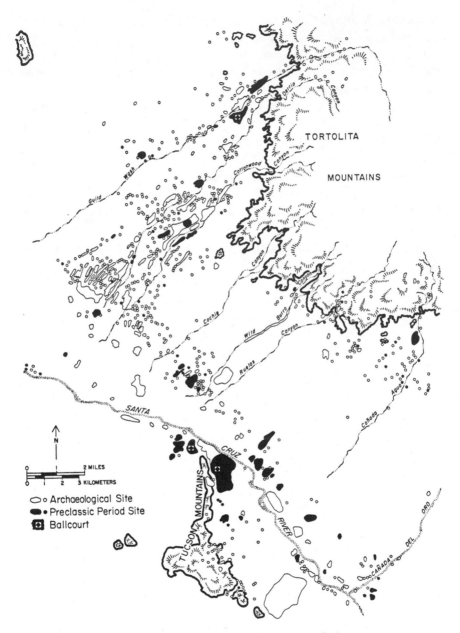

*Fig. 6. Distribution of Preclassic settlement in the northern Tucson basin.*

and riverine contexts. The variety of overall artifact classes is duplicated, including groundstone and shell. Year-round springs are the basis of year-round domestic water in the upland community. Locales of high water table on the floodplain provided opportunities for small reservoirs and shallow wells to supplement surface flows.

## The Classic Community

At about A.D. 1050, a dynamic settlement element is added to the longterm and persisting bands of occupation in riverine and mountain edge zones. The new locational orientation is evident in substantial remains upslope from a site containing a platform mound (Fig. 7). Dense sites span the previously unused middle portion of the bajada and are continuous to mountain flanks. Settlement also increases on the eastern lower bajada and adjacent floodplain.

Ballcourts fall into disuse at this time. A platform mound is constructed approximately midway between the two Preclassic villages with courts, and the new inclusive Classic Marana community encompasses both earlier site clusters. The new configuration appears to be a temporally restricted phenomenon (ca. A.D. 1050–1350), beginning in the late Rincon phase, fully developed in the early Classic and terminating prior to the advent of Gila or Tonto polychromes in the later Classic. The community incorporates multiple sites and environmental zones, extending from valley bottom to both eastern and western mountain flanks. A central site with platform mound and compounds near the present town of Marana, lesser sites with compounds, sites without compounds in a range of sizes, a trincheras site, large communal agricultural fields, small agricultural fields, and a variety of specialized activity sites are components of this highly differentiated complex. Classic reorganization is marked by a sharp increase in site density, in the elaboration of functionally and locationally specialized sites, and in an innovative, intensified use of the mid-bajada. The population level evident in the community seems only partially duplicated by settlements identified for preceding or succeeding periods. Depopulation of outlying areas and withdrawal of Hohokam groups to optimal riverine locations, often seen as reflecting early Classic environmental deterioration (Weaver 1972; Doyel 1977a, 1980), clearly is not evident in the Tucson Basin.

## Zonal Patterns in the Marana Community

Six zones of settlement can be defined within the larger Classic community of the Marana complex (Fig. 8). The first four pertain to the Tortolita bajada. Zone 1 sites, including the platform mound, occur in a more or less continuous band along the lower bajada. Coalescing alluvial fans in this zone create an active depositional environment. Abundant sherd, groundstone, and

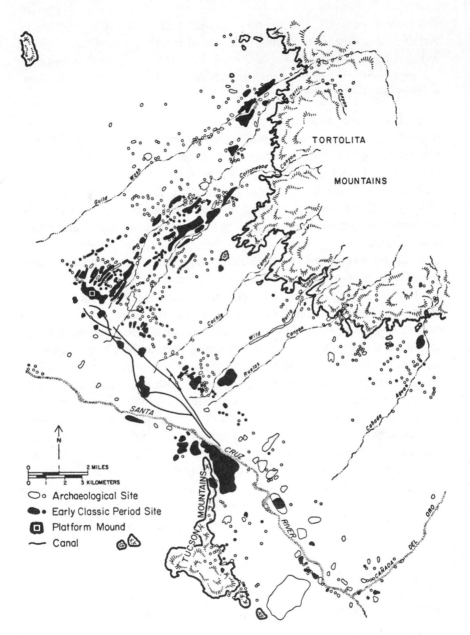

Fig. 7. Early Classic settlement in the northern Tucson basin.

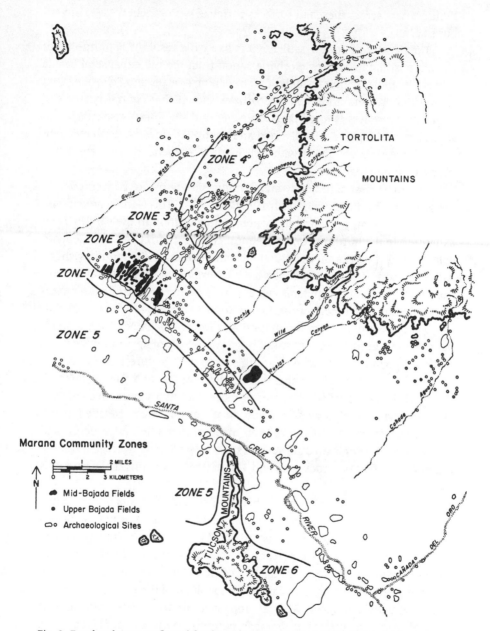

*Fig. 8. Zonal settlement configured for the early Classic in the northern Tucson basin.*

lithic scatters across these fan surfaces correlate with rancheria sites of various size.

The density of Zone 1 settlement is likely the result of opportunity for ak chin farming in an area receiving runoff from the full expanse of bajada slopes. Geomorphological studies and trenching (Katzer and Schuster 1984; Field 1985; Waters and Field 1986) have shown that central portions of large fans were less favored than fan edges and small fans associated with secondary drainages. Easily diverted and controlled flows in small channels would have renewed fields with rich loads of suspended sediment in the course of supplying water.

The most desirable floodwater farming situations are concentrated in the southern third of Zone 1 (Fish 1987:236–238). This is the segment with earliest settlement, predating study area reorganization in the Classic. Later expansion to the north in Zone 1 is almost certainly correlated with dependable water through canal construction from the river to the mound vicinity. Although Zone 1 inhabitants may have realized some agricultural benefits from this canal, topographic placement suggests maximal irrigation potential for floodplain inhabitants of sites in Zone 5 below.

Zone 2 is uphill from the mound and lower bajada edge sites. Dominant remains in this zone consist of huge complexes of agricultural features without habitations. Rock piles are the prominent feature type, accompanied by low cobble terrace alignments, check dams, and roasting pits (S. Fish et al. 1985). Over 485 hectares or more than two square miles of large (10–50 hectares) of rock pile fields have been located. Detailed maps, counts, and measurements have been made of rock piles, alignments, and check dams in sample areas of several sites. Interpolating average densities, a zonal total of 42,000 rock piles and 120,000 meters of linear alignments is estimated.

Zone 2 fields occur on ridges between secondary drainages on gentle bajada slopes. Sample collections involve several thousand artifacts, including over 400 stone tools. Tabular or "mescal" knives account for 9 percent of all stone artifacts, or 19.2 percent of retouched tools. Huge—up to 35 meter—roasting "areas" are in all large fields. These appear to have been seasonally reused over many years. Flotation at 20 of the pits at 14 sites has consistently yielded agave. Annual crops were probably attempted only in favorable years in the small drainage bottoms. With less predictable and abundant water than in other zones, drought-adapted agaves provided dependable harvests.

A third settlement zone (Zone 3), in the middle portion of the bajada, interfingers with the upper bajada nearer the foothills of the Tortolitas. A few small sherd and lithic scatters are widely dispersed in a rancheria pattern and are located in optimal situations for water diversion and utilization. Like Zone 2, Zone 3 is characterized by a scarcity of substantial habitation remains and the occurrence of unique and specialized sites.

Surface scatters of ceramics with few or no other artifact classes comprise the only other Zone 3 sites. Sometimes huge (approaching 1.0 kilometer in length), these tend to be linearly arranged along ridge tops. Relatively dense distributions of sherds number as high as the tens of thousands. Intensive backhoe trenching at one of the largest scatters confirmed the absence of subsurface features. The obviously specialized function of these sites is unknown, but location in high densities of saguaro cacti makes longterm seasonal resource gathering one possibility. Rock rings, usually associated with saguaro fruit procurement (Goodyear 1975; Raab 1973), are the only surface features and offer some support for this hypothesis.

Zone 3 settlement patterns intergrade with a fourth zonal type nearest the mountains and between the major Cottonwood, Derrio, and Guild drainages. Unlike the lower zones underlain by deep colluvial basin fill, Zone 4 corresponds with mountain pediment, where shallow bedrock prevents deep percolation of water originating on the Tortolita slopes. A relatively high and accessible water table is therefore maintained in the drainages. The proliferation of large and small habitation sites undoubtedly reflects the availability of water. The three major drainages and secondary ones appear to have supported cultivation. Agricultural features such as terraces, rock piles, and check dams occur in substantial numbers in Zone 4 in conjunction with large sites, small sites, and isolated structures, but never independent of habitation as in Zone 2.

The largest Zone 4 sites (a few approach or exceed one square kilometer) are found on ridges overlooking Derrio and Cottonwood floodplains. Structural remains at these include a number of architectural forms: compounds with house mounds, compounds exhibiting only cobble room outlines, dry-laid masonry structures, and isolated cobble outlined structures. The density of architectural remains at large sites indicates a high probability of pithouses as well.

The floodplain and terraces of the Santa Cruz constitute Zone 5. From the southern boundary of the study area to the end of the Tucson Mountains, the river channel and floodplain are more concisely delimited. Igneous intrusions near the end of the mountains force underground flow to the surface, creating an elevated water table and more persistent surface water. Large and small sites of all periods occur on both sides of the river as it parallels the mountains. Two of the largest long-term sites in the community, Los Morteros and the Huntington site, are located on either side of the mountain terminous. A ballcourt at Los Morteros and a probable one at the

Huntington site (Huntington 1910) identify focal sites for southern pre-Classic settlement.

To the north, surface flow in the river is more infrequent and of briefer duration. Terraces become poorly defined and the floodplain broadens substantially. Precision of site definition decreases on the broad northern floodplain due to extensive modern agriculture. However, maximum site size appears to be small and overall densities reduced.

The highly foreshortened bajada between the Tucson Mountains and the Santa Cruz compresses zonal topography equivalent with that in the eastern transbajada axis. Inhabitants of southern Zone 5 undoubtedly diverted flow from Tucson Mountain watersheds; some sites at the western floodplain edge seem oriented toward such floodwater situations. Riverine canals undoubtedly account for the denser populations and consistently favored locales. Multiple canals and shallow wells are reported from excavations at the site of Los Morteros (Bernard-Shaw 1988). Also drawing upon the optimal water table of this general locale was the intake of the canal to the mound vicinity. A number of historic gravity canals heading here and irrigating fields in the broad floodplain to the north probably duplicate earlier land use.

The Tucson Mountains define Zone 6. These form a low chain with maximum study area height of less than 130 meters above the floodplain. Dark volcanic hills are covered with a variety of cacti and leguminous trees, providing immediate access to upper bajada resources for inhabitants of the river edge.

Trincheras sites, characterized by terraces and walls of dry-laid masonry, occur on Tucson Mountain hillslopes as large and small groups of features (Wallace and Holmlund 1982). The largest concentration is immediately above Los Morteros. Some of the 250 terraces in this site yield evidence of agricultural function, and excavated pithouses in several other terraces have all the appearances of permanent habitations (S. Fish et al. 1984). A cobble-outlined compound and a few masonry surface structures are also present. A single radiocarbon date and design treatment on Tanque Verde ceramics suggest that some of the trincheras features may be somewhat later than the major occupation of the Marana community, although still predating the advent of Gila and Tonto polychrome.

## Classic Reorganization

Location of the Marana mound roughly midway between the river and the foothills signals an early Classic shifting of the center of gravity in settlement pattern away from the river. The continuous distribution of sites from floodplain to mountain flanks suggests a direct integration of greater environmental diversity in a single interactive unit than previously. Coordination of activities and products within the dense population distributed across this variable topography may have required a strengthening of organization ties, expressed through construction of the mound. Support of high community population levels in the Tucson Basin desert environment probably also entailed intensified production and an assurance of resource circulation among all zones. The linked fortunes of community inhabitants is demonstrated in simultaneous abandonment, as measured by archaeological time. Where at least partial settlement information is available across other desert basin slopes, similarities are apparent in Classic zonal patterns. Resemblances can be seen in the Tonto Basin (Wood and McAllister 1984) and the Florence area (Debowski et al. 1976; Crown 1984b).

The Marana Classic community appears to have been a relatively short-lived phenomenon within the span of Hohokam occupation in the northern Tucson Basin. Polychromes diagnostic of the later Classic are present at higher elevation sites in the adjacent Tortolita uplands, but only five small sites with such ceramics are recorded in the 350 square kilometer survey study area. Larger late Classic settlements to the north and south demonstrate the existence of persisting populations at that time, although regional settlement is reduced.


## TREND AND PERCEPTION IN HOHOKAM PREHISTORY

### Environmental Change

Following a general trend of the mid-1960s and 1970s in southwestern archaeology, environmental change became one of the most popular means of explaining cultural change in Hohokam prehistory. The evidence of environmental change remains almost entirely external. A deterministic super-structure based ultimately on the Colorado Plateau pollen chronology (Schoenwetter and Dittert 1968) has been perpetuated in the literature by continual cross-referencing. Reiteration has been supplemented by more current interpolated data from the Plateau and Mogollon Rim (Masse 1982:14, citing Euler et al. 1979; Miksicek 1984).

Donald Weaver (1972) presents the most influential scheme of Hohokam culture history as shaped by climatic trends. Effective moisture level on the Colorado Plateau affected flow in core-area rivers and thereby the success of irrigation. Toward the close of the eleventh century, moisture decreased, causing contraction into the most favorably supplied area. Subsequently, conditions improved, permitting population growth, expansion of irrigation, and instigation of a theocratic class structure. Reduced moisture around A.D. 1275 truncated these developments. At approximately A.D. 1325, strong increases in effective moisture were destructive to fields and canals.

Problems exist with simplified reconstructions of environment/climate on the Plateau itself. A number of palynologists have argued on floristic grounds and from modern analogs that archaeological pollen cannot be interpreted solely as a record of undisturbed vegetation (Bohrer 1971; Lytle-Webb 1978; Fish 1985). Independent lines of climatic evidence for the Plateau produce less than total consensus (Euler et al. 1979). Tree-ring data have suggested that climatic effects were probably not uniform across the Southwest (Dean and Robinson 1977), raising the question of synchroneity between plateau and desert, and perhaps even within upland portions.

The implicit assumption always seems to have been that high effective moisture in the uplands equaled greater stream flow and "good times" for the Hohokam. As early as 1965, Schroeder cited the complicating factor of temperature in the timing of snowmelt. An untested link between upland climate and Hohokam well-being lies in irrigation technology. Lightfoot and Plog (1984) have documented an inverse relationship between high rainfall years in the mountains and security of valley irrigation canals. Evidence of washouts and interruptions in canal use are reported in large systems on both the Salt (Masse 1981) and Gila (Haury 1976). Ethnohistoric data suggest serious flooding disasters as frequently as every five years (Russell 1908:66). Donald Graybill's (1985) reconstruction of Salt River streamflow between A.D. 800 and 1400 provides an exciting avenue to begin exploring the effects of this aspect of environmental variability.

Climatic change may not necessarily predict corresponding magnitudes of response in Hohokam culture. The variation within, as well as between, given increments of time was undoubtedly great. It has been observed that groups most vulnerable to climatic oscillation occupy the boundaries between arid and more favorable rainfall regimes (Sheridan 1981:4, Goodie and Wilkinson 1977:72–73). Inhabitants of truly arid lands accept environmental fluctuation as omnipresent. Maintenance of a comparatively stable trajectory for at least 1,000 years argues for a system which anticipated and could absorb large amounts of climatic variability through customary and effective patterns of response.

## Stability

As observed by Doyel (1977a, 1980), the incidence of long-term stability in site location for the Hohokam is unique among southwestern traditions. Snaketown is the best known example, but many others occur in the Salt and Gila basins and elsewhere. Full appreciation of temporal stability has usually come as the result of extensive excavation. Earlier components are commonly obscured in surface collections by overlying deposits, the abundance of later artifacts, or simply by more modest extent.

Within large settlements, continuity in layout over impressive timespans is becoming apparent. At Snaketown, David Wilcox (Wilcox et al. 1981) has defined house and mound arrangements around a central plaza maintained from late Pioneer through Sedentary times. A similar pattern has been recognized at Los Hornos (Howard 1982) and La Ciudad (Henderson 1987). The transition from Sedentary to Classic, touted as witnessing the most pronounced shifts in settlement (Schroeder 1940:111, 1952:331; Haury 1945:204; Masse 1980; Doyel 1980; Wilcox and Sternberg 1983:137) also provides illustrations of exceptional stability in site location and sometimes even in village layout. Continuity in some Sacaton-to-Soho sites is expressed in the superposition of individual structures from the two periods, as well as in overall site patterns. Particularly impressive examples of Soho houses superimposed onto Sacaton ones and almost precise continuity in village plan occur at Second Canyon Ruin (Franklin 1980, Fig. 2) and at AZ U:3:51 in the Roosevelt Lake area (Hohmann 1985).

Continuity in pattern is expressed at Second Canyon Ruin and AZ U:3:51 at the level of individual houses. Soho structures directly overlie Sacaton counterparts and are oriented similarly. In fact, general superpositioning of structures is a characteristic of Hohokam sites. The continual reuse of a specific house site, particularly within dispersed or rancheria patterns, implies continuity in residential rights. Such continuities recognized within communities may have been along family lines or may have followed some other structural principle.

## Subsistence

Most interpretations of Hohokam subsistence have been closely tied to ethnographic models from the extensive literature on Pima and Papago practices (e.g., Castetter and Bell 1942; Russell 1908). While ethnographic insights are of great value, points of almost certain divergence with the prehistoric situation have been neglected. An important example is the relative contribution of wild resources versus cultigens. A pivotal model was derived by Vorsila Bohrer (1970, 1971) from Pima analogy and botanical remains at Snaketown. This pioneering attempt to quantify and chronologically interpret Hohokam subsistence remains continues as a dominant force in the literature, although the model has not proved replicable (Gasser 1980) and the methodology of botanical analysis has been refined.

Size and density must have affected the ability of entire populations to fall back on wild resources. This alternative may have been feasible in poor agricultural years for sparser historic groups, but was less so during prehistoric population maxima. The Hohokam probably had greater impetus to develop storage, exchange, or political integration of larger areas to avoid population disasters. In one of the few approaches focusing on prehistoric conditions, Plog (1980) suggests that widespread agricultural clearing and overexploitation of wild resources by dense populations degraded the pre-Classic subsistence base.

Implications of historically absent large-scale canals have been discussed more frequently for analogs of social organization than for subsistence. In terms of subsistence implications, the canal networks may have both underwritten and required denser populations. Haury (1976:149) points out the ethnographic importance of large work parties for quickly repairing washout damage, and Lightfoot and Plog (1984) document equally critical recruitment needs for historic Mormons near Showlow.

Population densities and distribution not duplicated ethnographically are apparent from the abundance of settlement and nonirrigated agricultural features. These occur in many topographic situations used by historic Pimans for occasional hunting, if at all. Furthermore, the full diversity of prehistoric technology cannot be replicated historically. A wide variety of stone construction for agriculture are echoed only weakly by brush and earth features of more recent Indian groups.

A changing perception of Hohokam subsistence emphasizes their effectiveness as environmental managers rather than their vulnerability to a harsh climatic regime (Fish 1984a). Farming and gathering may not be properly defined as polar categories in Hohokam subsistence. Both ethnographic (Rea 1979; Nabhan et al. 1982; Crosswhite 1981) and archaeobiological data (Bohrer 1970; Fish 1984b, 1985; Szuter 1984) have illustrated increased variety and accessibility in useful flora and fauna occasioned by the supplemental water and diversified habitats of traditional desert agriculture. The conscious maximization of these opportunities by the Hohokam has been suggested by morphological and circumstantial evidence of directed manipulation or semidomestication in several "wild resources." These include little barley (Bohrer 1984; Adams 1987), chenopods, (Gasser and Miksicek 1985) and amaranth (Bohrer 1962), panic grass (Nabhan and Wet 1984), devil's claw (Nabhan et al. 1978), and cholla (Fish 1984b). Ubiquitous charred macrofossils of agave in sites outside natural distributions and in roasting pits at rockpile fields identify another manipulated plant grown on a large scale (S. Fish, Fish, Miksicek, and Madsen 1985).

Although progress has been made in describing canal systems and understanding the technology (Haury 1976; Masse 1981; Crown 1984b; Nicholas and Neitzel 1984), the form and yields of irrigated agriculture supported by the canals remain poorly known. Few analogs are available for evaluating many kinds of runoff features. Interest in these once neglected farming devices is increasing (Masse 1979; Henderson and Rogers 1979; Crown 1984b; Fish et al. 1984, S. Fish, Fish, and Madsen 1985; Doyel 1984), and they are now being studied in every region and topographic zone occupied by the Hohokam.

## Population

Population size estimates are more difficult and imprecise at any level for the Hohokam than for most periods in other southwestern culture areas. A formula for translating site extent on the surface to numbers of persons does not exist. Many Hohokam sites and most of the large ones were occupied over many ceramic periods. No surface indications of pre-Classic structures usually are present. Even for the Classic, the persistence of pithouse structures makes room counting inconclusive. The "rancheria" pattern of dispersed dwellings within overall site boundaries is characteristic. These factors combine to make population estimates from survey data very complex and questionable.

The conditions just described have led to totally unpredictable excavation results at large sites even after multistage testing. For example, competent and experienced Hohokam archaeologists recently developed two research designs around chronologically inappropriate populations in the Phoenix area. At Las Colinas, an anticipated scale of Classic occupation could not be located (Gregory 1982); major Sacaton remains were found. At La Ciudad, Pioneer, Sedentary, and primarily Colonial settlements were revealed where an exclusively Sedentary occupation was expected (Rice 1981).

With large excavated sites, population estimates are no closer to informed consensus. Snaketown is a good example. Haury (1976:75–77) estimated a maximum (Sacaton) population of 2,000. He inferred 7,000 houses, and based his estimate on a 25-year use-life for structures. Wilcox et al. (1981:185–197) considered differential distributions of houses in various precincts and reduced the total number of potential structures to 1,000. Invoking a use-life of between 25 and 100 years depending on intrasite location, Wilcox arrived at a population estimate between 600 and 1,000 for the Sacaton (Wilcox et al. 1981) and later even revised this downward to less than 500 (Wilcox and Sternberg 1983). Reviewing the pivotal and totally unresolved issue of pithouse use-life, Plog (1980:14) concluded that it was impossible to arrive at meaningful population estimates for even well excavated samples.

Density in large settlements never seems to have approached the compact patterns of Hopi pueblos, Chacoan towns, or Casas Grandes. Although boundaries for large settlements beneath Phoenix can no longer be defined, the total contemporary population at Snaketown is modest by any estimate. At one of the largest sites (Los Muertos) in the Salt River Valley where real extent can be examined, Plog (Martin and Plog 1973:314) estimates 500 rooms. On the other hand, the most favorable parts of the Salt-Gila basin may have been covered by continuous dispersed settlement (cf. Omar Turney's [1924] 1890 description of house outlines for miles about Pueblo Grande). The probability is that some collective regional densities were very high.

## Trade and Exchange

Most prominently cited as evidence of trade with external areas are Hohokam items of a Mesoamerican flavor. Easily identified in non-Hohokam assemblages, these artifacts have received disproportionate attention, partly because they include many specialized and artistically elaborated forms. Ceramic incision, life forms, and other distinctive decorative elements, and presumably Mesoamerican forms such as figurines and palettes cease by the Classic, when stylistic orientations are thought to become more pan-southwestern. Actual Hohokam interchange with Mexico can be poorly evaluated in virtual absence of archaeological knowledge for the adjacent areas south of the border. Tangible items of potential Mexican origin are always rare (McGuire 1980).

Much of the trade Hohokam goods probably took the form of down-the-line interchange. Widely dispersed artifacts have been interpreted as resulting from colonization and domination by pochtecalike traders. Quantitative analyses show that pre-Classic Hohokam artifact classes appear as highly varied packages, independently incorporated into local receptor assemblages (Fish et al. 1980). The exceptions where there are varied and large amounts of Hohokam items may represent resident traders (Stove Canyon, Winona) or involve extraction of valued raw materials by Hohokam peoples (Perkinsville, Walnut Creek Village). Expeditionary trade may be evidenced by Hohokam rock art along western Arizona shell routes (Hayden 1972) and Hohokam remains near turquoise sources near Las Vegas, Nevada and Kingman, Arizona (Johnson 1964). In the most active and regular trade, scheduling was probably coordinated.

Two quantified studies have demonstrated that certain exotic trade items were concentrated at larger sites in the Hohokam core area and in regions with which they traded (Fish et al. 1980; McGuire and Downum 1982). Where size is not a factor, sites with ball courts tend to have more trade goods than those without (Wilcox and Sternberg 1983). Based on rich burials and concentrations of prestige artifacts within a single precinct at Snaketown, Nelson (1981) proposed that elites controlled much of the trade, an argument elaborated by McGuire (1983). Similarly, Doyel (1980:31–35) concluded that homogeneity in prestige items reflects widespread exchange among elites.

Ethnographically, food and subsistence related items figured prominently in regional and interregional exchange in the southern deserts (Russell 1908:194; Underhill 1939:103). Established interregional exchange networks involving exotic items and finished products would have facilitated circulation of subsistence goods when surpluses and logistics allowed and when agricultural failure necessitated. Insurance functions of trade may have been important to even out the fluctuations of floodwater farming. Doelle (1980) suggested that the abundant shell-working remains and raw materials in Papaguerian sites are evidence of risk-minimizing trade with the Salt–Gila area. Food exchange is difficult to document archaeologically, however, and no substantial body of evidence has yet been presented.

## Social and Political Organization

Social organization of the Hohokam frequently has been viewed from the political sphere. Lack of easily demonstrable continuities between the Hohokam and Pimans comparable to those for Puebloans make social interpretations more difficult. In addition, the level of conscious resort to social structural (particularly kinship) principles seems less developed among the Pima and Papago. The dispersed informal rancheria settlement pattern of the Pima and Papago may relate to less highly structured interrelationships. This contrasts with the tightly clustered habitation conditions in pueblos and the attendant multiplicity of rules governing interactions.

The nature of Hohokam architecture has made it difficult to derive social structure from physical remains. The failure to systematically identify and compare assemblages from houses, burials, and other features has resulted in a neglect of a possible source of primary social data. Orientations of pithouses cannot be surmised from surface remains, and recovery of excavated site plans is made difficult by superimposed components. Recent research has begun to define house clusters with common courtyards persisting over time (Wilcox et al. 1981; Sires 1984; Howard 1982) and these clusters have sometimes been interpreted as work groups (Haury 1976:194–196).

The dispersed rancheria-type pattern of most Hohokam sites has influenced perceptions of political organization and complexity. In the Southwest, complexity often has been linked with aggregation. Less nucleated settlements may have produced dense populations at the scale of a square kilometer, however. Without living wall-to-wall, the continuous interactions of people in this kind of proximity could still generate occupational specialization and administration hierarchies.

Social inequalities as expressed by differential access to accumulated wealth or valuable items are poorly documented for the Hohokam. Some of the most extensive cemetery excavations took place prior to 1940 with proveniences poorly reported and collections often unavailable. Very rich cremations are known to have occurred in these and in pot-hunted burials (Nelson 1981), but only in anecdotal detail. Snaketown is one exception to the problem of poor records, and here 3 of 24 cremation areas contained the majority of prestige items (Nelson 1981:468). The social personae linked with such manifestations are unknown. Individuals, kinship groups, classes, or secular societies may have been involved.

Speculations on the causes of social/political inequality and complexity have been derived from general models of social function. The necessity to direct and adjudicate irrigation networks involving multiple villages is one such function (Doyel 1977a, 1980). Hierarchy within irrigation communities has been interpreted from ranges in site size and occurrence of public architecture along canal systems (Doyel 1980; Upham and Rice 1980; Gregory and Nials 1985; Nicholas and Neitzel 1984). Sophisticated outsiders also have been seen as fostering social differention in the pre-Classic (Di Peso 1956, 1979; Schroeder 1965; Hayden 1970) and Classic (Di Peso 1956; Schroeder 1965; Haury 1976). Other suggested bases for elites include Big Men roles in redistribution (Wilcox and Shenk 1977:188–197), trade entrepreneurs (Nelson 1981; Howard 1983), and religious specialization à lá the Mesoamerican calendric complex (Wilcox and Sternberg 1983).

By comparison with ethnographic groups within the Hohokam area, and generally in the Southwest and northern Mexico, a number of internal ethnic/political divisions would be expected. The concept of a monolithic Hohokam culture and concentrated study at Snaketown and near Phoenix have resulted in a core-periphery comparative methodology ineffective for defining subdivisions. Ceramic analysis has yielded a multitude of localized substyles for the Anasazi and Mogollon, but for the Hohokam has only produced recognition that sequences depart from core area standards more and more with distance. Papaguerian and Tucson sequences are the only locally named series. More refined analyses necessary to define local traditions have only recently been initiated in the Salt–Gila area (e.g., Neitzel 1985).

Two architectural features, interpreted as integrative facilities, have been examined as midpoints of interacting territorial units. Wilcox and Sternberg (1983:189) found approximately equal spacing of 5.5 km between pre-Classic ballcourt sites in the Phoenix Basin. Some regularity also has been discussed by Gregory and Nials (1985) for spacing of Classic period platform mounds in the Phoenix area. However, these studies are far from complete, with significant discovery of new instances of both feature types.

## HOHOKAM TRAJECTORIES

Development of complexity as expressed by settlement hierarchies and social linearization (Flannery 1972:409–414) can be seen as basically unidirectional through the Classic. Factors contributing to this perception of overall trend combine elements pertaining to belief systems and socio-political organization. The roles of these analytical categories are not easily separated, a confusion exacerbated by the lack of clear ethnographic analogs for these facets of Hohokam life. Material remains of ritual activity suggest that a pre-Classic dispersion of observance throughout the population begins to be replaced by the late Sedentary period. Figurines, palettes, censors, and other specialized artifacts with presumed ritual function are widely, if not uniformly, distributed within sites and among cremations. Such artifacts denoting noncentralized or individualistic participation become more elaborated into the Sedentary and then disappear abruptly.

A developmental sequence in public architecture overlaps later parts of the trend in ritual paraphernalia and reveals concurrent narrowing of participating segments within the society during the Classic period. Numbers of ballcourts increase rapidly throughout much of the Hohokam territory in the Colonial and Sedentary periods. Although Mesoamerican and southwestern ballgame analogies suggest that game participants were not themselves true specialists, court frequencies indicate greater and greater numbers of players and spectators into the Sedentary period. By the Classic only a few ballcourts were constructed anywhere and these apparently were restricted to the Phoenix Basin and the northern periphery.

A trend toward exclusion with indications of hierarchical specialists in later portions of the sequence is seen in mound architecture. The earliest adobe-capped Snaketown phase mounds are not secluded from the rest of the site in any way. Palisades are added during the Sedentary and are replaced by adobe compound walls by the late Sedentary or early Classic period. Structures atop mounds and within the surrounding compounds bespeak public-oriented activity by small numbers of socially differentiated actors. Storage, residential, and possibly ritual functions for these structures imply an overlay of administrative or redistributive roles for mound complex participants. Formalization in layout of public architecture during this time appears to correlate with crystalization of structured activity on behalf of the public.

At an intersite level, trends toward hierarchy and integration of larger units can also be discussed. No tangible evidence of such integration exists for the Pioneer period, but by the Colonial, larger sites on canal networks show a beginning of primacy. Later, sites with public architecture tend to be evenly spaced, with a Classic tendency for a principal site near the canal system terminus. Ballcourts begin earlier and are found at a larger number of sites than structured platform mound complexes. The size of units integrated by earlier ballcourts appear to be eclipsed by those of mounds with compounds. Sizes of territories associated with the latest expressions of public architecture, the "big houses," are as obscure as other aspects of the final stages of Hohokam prehistory. Truncation of the system prior to contact and interruption of impressive cultural stability is one of the most poorly understood and intriguing aspects of southwestern prehistory.

## ACKNOWLEDGMENTS

The primary data and many of the ideas in this paper are shared with Suzanne K. Fish. Funding for the Tucson Basin study has come from the National Science Foundation (BNS-8408141), the Bureau of Reclamation (4-CS-30-01380), and the Arizona State Historic Preservation Office (SP 8315-70). David Doyel, Gordon Ekholm, Emil Haury, Keith Kintigh, Steve LeBlanc, William Lipe, J. Jefferson Reid, Michael Schiffer, and David Wilcox made particularly helpful observations leading to a number of revisions in the manuscript.

## REFERENCES

Adams, Karen
    1987    Little Barley (*Hordeum pusillum* Nutt.) as a Possible New Wild Domesticate. In *Specialized Studies in Economy, Environment, and Culture of La Ciudad*, edited by J. Kisselburg, G. Rice, and B. Shears. Arizona State University Anthropological Field Studies 20. Tempe.

Anyon, Roger, Patricia Gilman, and Steven LeBlanc
  1981    A Reevaluation of the Mogollon-Mimbres Archaeological Sequence. *The Kiva* 46:209–225.

Bernard-Shaw, Mary
  1988    Hohokam Canal Systems and Late Archaic Wells: The Evidence from the Los Morteros Site. In *Recent Research on Tucson Basin Prehistory: Proceedings of the Second Tucson Basin Conference*, edited by W.H. Doelle and Paul Fish. Institute for American Research Anthropological Papers 10.

Bohrer, Vorsila
  1962    Nature and Interpretation of Ethnobotanical Materials from Tonto National Monument. In *Archaeological Studies at Tonto National Monument*, edited by Lewis Caywood. Southwest Monuments Association Technical Series 2.
  1970    Ethnobotanical Aspects of Snaketown, a Hohokam Village in Southern Arizona. *American Antiquity* 35.
  1971    Paleoecology of Snaketown. *The Kiva* 36:11–19.
  1984    Domesticated and Wild Crops in the CAEP Study Area. In *Prehistoric Cultural Development in Central Arizona: Archaeology of the Upper New River Region*, edited by P. Spoerl and G. Gumerman. Center for Archaeological Investigations Occasional Paper 4. Carbondale, Illinois.

Bullard, William R.
  1962    *The Cerro Colorado Site and Pithouse Architecture in the Southwestern United States prior to A.D. 900.* Papers of the Peabody Museum of American Archaeology and Ethnology 44. Harvard University, Cambridge.

Cable, John S., and David E. Doyel
  1987    Pioneer Period Village Structure and Settlement Pattern in the Phoenix Basin. In *The Hohokam Village*, edited by David Doyel. Southwest and Rocky Mountain Division of the American Association for the Advancement of Science. Glenwood Springs, Colorado.

Castetter, E. F., and W. H. Bell
  1942    *Pima and Papago Indian Agriculture.* University of New Mexico Press, Albuquerque.

Crabtree, Donald
  1973    Experiments in Replicating Hohokam Points. *Tebiwa* 16:10–45.

Crosswhite, Frank
  1981    Desert Plants, Habitat, and Agriculture in Relation to the Major Pattern of Cultural Differentiation in the O'otam People of the Sonoran Desert. *Desert Plants* 3:47–76.

Crown, Patricia
  1984a    Ceramic Vessel Exchange in Southwest Arizona. In *Hohokam Archaeology Along the Salt-Gila Aqueduct, Central Arizona Project*, volume 9: Synthesis and Conclusion, edited by Lynn S. Teague and Patricia Crown. Arizona State Museum Archaeological Series 150.
  1984b    Adaptation Through Diversity: An Examination of Population Pressure and Agricultural Technology in the Salt-Gila Basin. In *Prehistoric Agricul-*

*tural Strategies in the Southwest*, edited by Suzanne K. Fish and Paul R. Fish. Arizona State University Anthropological Research Papers 33.

Crown, Patricia, and Earl Sires
1984    The Hohokam Chronology and Salt-Gila Aqueduct Project Research. In *Hohokam Archaeology Along the Salt-Gila Aqueduct, Central Arizona Project*, volume 9: Synthesis and Conclusions, edited by Lynn Teague and Patricia Crown. Arizona State Museum Archaeological Series 150.

Czaplicki, Jon, Adrianne Rankin, and Christian Downum
1984    *An Intensive Archaeological Survey of the Lower Santa Cruz River Basin, Picacho Reservoir to Rillito, Arizona*. Arizona State Museum Archaeological Series 165.

Dean, Jeffrey, and William Robinson
1977    Dendroclimatic Variability in the American Southwest from A.D. 680 to 1970. Manuscript on file, Tree Ring Laboratory, University of Arizona, Tucson.

Debowski, Sharon, Anique George, Richard Goddard, and Deborah Mullon
1976    *An Archaeological Survey of the Buttes Reservoir*. Arizona State Museum Archaeological Series 93.

Di Peso, Charles C.
1956    *The Upper Pima of San Cayetano del Tumacacori: An Archaeological Reconstruction of the Ootam of Pimeria Alta*. The Amerind Foundation 7.
1974    *Casas Grandes*. Northland Press, Flagstaff.

Doelle, William
1976    *Desert Resources and Hohokam Subsistence: The CONOCO Project*. Arizona State Museum Archaeological Series 103.
1980    *Postadaptive Patterns in Western Papagueria: An Archaeological Study of Nonriverine Resource Use*. Ph.D. dissertation, University of Arizona, Tucson.
1985    *Excavations at the Valencia Site: A Preclassic Hohokam Village in the Southern Tucson Basin*. Institute for American Research Report 3.

Doelle, William, Fredrick Huntington, and Henry Wallace
1987    Rincon Phase Community Reorganization in the Tucson Basin. In *The Hohokam Village*, edited by David Doyel. Southwest and Rocky Mountain Division of the American Association for the Advancement of Science Monograph.

Dove, Donald E.
1984    *Prehistoric Subsistence and Population Change Along the Lower Agua Fria River, Arizona: A Model Simulation*. Arizona State University Anthropological Research Papers 32.

Doyel, David
1974    *Excavations in the Escalante Ruin Group, Southern Arizona*. Arizona State Museum Archaeological Series 37.
1977a   *Classic Period Hohokam in the Escalante Ruin Group*. Ph.D. dissertation, University of Arizona, Tucson.
1977b   Rillito and Rincon Period Settlement Systems in the Middle Santa Cruz Valley: Alternative Models. *The Kiva* 43:93–110.

1980    Hohokam Social Organization and the Sedentary to Classic Transition. In *Current Issues in Hohokam Prehistory: Proceedings of a Symposium*, edited by David Doyel and Fred Plog. Arizona State University Anthropological Research Paper 23.

1984    Sedentary Period Hohokam Paleo-economy in the New River Drainage, Central Arizona. In *Prehistoric Agricultural Strategies in the Southwest*, edited by Suzanne K. Fish and Paul R. Fish. Arizona State University Anthropological Research Paper 33.

Dunbier, Roger
1968    *The Sonoran Desert*. The University of Arizona Press, Tucson.

Euler, Robert, George Gumerman, Thor Karlstrom, Jeffrey Dean, and Richard Hevly
1979    The Colorado Plateau: Cultural Dynamics and Paleoenvironment. *Science* 205:1089–1101.

Ezell, Paul H.
1963    Is There a Hohokam-Pima Culture Continuum? *American Antiquity* 29:61–66.

Felger, Richard, and Gary Nabhan
1976    Deceptive Barrenness. *Ceres* 9:34–39.

Ferdon, Edwin N.
1955    *A Trial Survey of Mexican-Southwestern Architectural Parallels*. School of American Research, Museum of New Mexico Monographs 21.

Field, John
1985    *Depositional Facies and Hohokam Settlement Patterns on Holocene Alluvial Fans, Northern Tucson Basin*. M.S. thesis, University of Arizona, Tucson.

Fish, Paul R., and Suzanne K. Fish
1977    *Archaeology of the Verde Valley: Review and Perspective*. Museum of Northern Arizona Research Paper 7.

Fish, Paul R., Suzanne Fish, Austin Long, and Charles Miksicek
1986    Early Corn Remains from Tumamoc Hill, Southern Arizona. *American Antiquity* 51:563–571.

Fish, Paul R., Suzanne Fish, and John Madsen
1985    The Marana Platform Mound Community: Research Results and Recommendations. In *Addendum to a Class III Survey of the Tucson Aqueduct Phase A Corridor, Central Arizona Project*, edited by Jon Czaplicki. Arizona State Museum Archaeological Series 165.

Fish, Paul R., Peter Pilles, and Suzanne Fish
1980    Colonies, Traders and Traits: the Hohokam in the North. In *Current Issues in Hohokam Prehistory: Proceedings of a Symposium*, edited by David Doyel and Fred Plog. Arizona State University Anthropological Papers 23.

Fish, Suzanne K.
1984a    Agriculture and Subsistence Implications of the Salt-Gila Aqueduct Project Pollen Analyses. In *Hohokam Archaeology Along the Salt-Gila Aqueduct, Central Arizona Project*, vol. 7, Environment and Subsistence, edited by Lynn Teague and Patricia Crown. Arizona State Museum Archaeological Series 150.

1984b    The Modified Environment of the Salt-Gila Aqueduct Sites: A Palynological Perspective. In *Hohokam Archaeology Along the Salt-Gila Aqueduct, Central Arizona Project*, vol. 7: Environment and Subsistence, edited by Lynn Teague and Patricia Crown. Arizona State Museum Archaeological Series 150.

1985    Prehistoric Disturbance Floras of the Lower Sonoran Desert and Their Implications. In *Late Quaternary Vegetation and Climates in the Southwestern United States*, edited by B. F. Jacobs, R. Fall, and O. Davis. American Association of Stratigraphic Palynologists. Contribution Series 16.

1987    An Evaluation of Subsistence and Specialization at the Marana Sites. In *Studies of the Hohokam Community of Marana*, edited by Glen Rice, pp. 235–248. Arizona State University Anthropological Field Studies 15.

Fish, Suzanne K., Paul R. Fish, and Christian Downum
1984    Hohokam Terraces and Agricultural Production in the Tucson Basin. In *Prehistoric Agricultural Strategies in the Southwest*, edited by Suzanne Fish and Paul Fish. Arizona State University Anthropological Research Paper 33.

Fish, Suzanne K., Paul R. Fish, and John Madsen
1985    A Preliminary Analysis of Settlement and Agriculture in the Northern Tucson Basin. In *Proceedings of the 1983 Hohokam Symposium*, edited by A. E. Dittert and D. E. Dove. Arizona Archaeological Society Occasional Paper 2.

1989    Classic Period Hohokam Community Integration in the Tucson Basin. In *The Sociopolitical Structure of Prehistoric Southwestern Societies*, edited by Steadman Upham and Kent Lightfoot. Westview Press, Denver.

Fish, Suzanne K., Paul Fish, Charles Miksicek, and John Madsen
1985    Prehistoric Agave Cultivation in Southern Arizona. *Desert Plants* 7:107–112.

Flannery, Kent V.
1972    The Cultural Evolution of Civilizations. *Annual Review of Ecology and Systematics* 3:399–426.

Franklin, Hayward H.
1980    *Excavations at Second Canyon Ruin, San Pedro Valley, Arizona*. Arizona State Museum Contribution to Highway Salvage Archaeology in Arizona 60.

Gasser, Robert
1980    Exchange and the Hohokam Archaeobotanical Record. In *Current Issues in Hohokam Prehistory: Proceedings of a Symposium*, edited by David Doyel and Fred Plog. Arizona State University Anthropological Research Papers 23.

Gasser, Robert, and Charles Miksicek
1985    The Specialists: A Reappraisal of Hohokam Exchange and the Archaeobotanical Record. In *Proceedings of the 1983 Hohokam Symposium*, edited by A. E. Dittert and D. E. Dove. Arizona Archaeological Society Occasional Papers 2.

Gladwin, Harold S.
1942    *Excavations at Snaketown, III: Revisions*. Medallion Papers 30.
1948    *Excavations at Snaketown, IV: Review and Conclusions*. Medallion Papers 38.
1957    *A History of the Ancient Southwest*. Bond Wheelright, Portland.

Gladwin, Harold, E. W. Haury, E. B. Sayles, and N. Gladwin
  1937    *Excavations at Snaketown I: Material Culture.* Medallion Papers 25.

Gladwin, Winifred, and Harold Gladwin
  1929a    *The Red-on-buff Culture of the Gila Basin.* Medallion Papers 3.
  1929b    *The Red-on-buff Culture of the Papagueria.* Medallion Papers 4.
  1930    *The Western Range of the Red-on-buff Culture.* Medallion Papers 5.
  1935    *The Eastern Range of the Red-on-buff Culture.* Medallion Papers 16.

Goodie, Andrew, and John Wilkinson
  1977    *The Warm Desert Environment.* Cambridge University Press, Cambridge.

Goodyear, Albert
  1975    *Hecla II and III: An Interpretive Study of Archaeological Remains from the Lakeshore Project, Papago Indian Reservation, South-central Arizona.* Arizona State University Anthropological Research Paper 9.

Graybill, Donald
  1985    Paleoclimate of the Hohokam Area: Problems and Prospects. In *Proceedings of the 1983 Hohokam Symposium,* edited by A. E. Dittert and Donald Dove. Arizona Archaeological Society Occasional Paper 2.

Grebinger, Paul F., and David Adam
  1974    Hard Times? Classic Period Hohokam Cultural Development in the Tucson Basin, Arizona. *World Archaeology* 6:226–241.

Gregory, David A.
  1982    A Proposal for Data Recovery at Las Colinas. Ms. on file, Arizona State Museum, University of Arizona, Tucson.
  1987    The Morphology of Platform Mounds and the Structure of Classic Period Hohokam Sites. In *The Hohokam Village,* edited by David Doyel. Southwestern and Rocky Mountain Division of the American Association for the Advancement of Science. Glenwood Springs, Colorado.

Gregory, David, and Fred Nials
  1985    Observations Concerning the Distribution of Classic Period Hohokam Platform Mounds. In *Proceedings of the 1983 Hohokam Symposium,* edited by A. E. Dittert and D. E. Dove. Arizona Archaeological Society Occasional Paper 2.

Hammack, Laurens C., and Alan P. Sullivan
  1981    *The 1968 Excavations at Mound 8, Las Colinas Ruins Group, Phoenix, Arizona.* Arizona State Museum Archaeological Series 154.

Haury, Emil W.
  1945    *The Excavation of Los Muertos and Neighboring Ruins in the Salt River Valley, Southern Arizona.* Papers of the Peabody Museum of American Archaeology and Ethnology 24. Harvard University, Cambridge.
  1976    *The Hohokam: Desert Farmers and Craftsmen.* University of Arizona Press, Tucson.

Hayden, Julian D.
  1957    *Excavations, 1940, at University Indian Ruin.* Southwestern Monuments Association, Technical Series 5.
  1970    Of Hohokam Origins and Other Matters. *American Antiquity* 35:87–94.

1972          Hohokam Petroglyphs of the Sierra Pinacate, Sonora, and the Hohokam
              Shell Expeditions. *The Kiva* 37:74–84.

Hemmings, Thomas, M. D. Robinson, and R. N. Rogers
    1968      Field Report on the Pantano Site (Arizona EE:2:50). Ms. on file, Arizona
              State Museum, University of Arizona, Tucson.

Henderson, T. Kathleen
    1987      *Structure and Organization at La Ciudad.* Arizona State University Anthropo-
              logical Field Studies 3.

Henderson, T. Kathleen, and James B. Rodgers
    1979      *Archaeological Investigations in the Cave Creek Area, Maricopa County, South-
              central Arizona.* Arizona State University Anthropological Research Papers
              17.

Hohmann, John
    1985      *Hohokam and Salado Hamlets in the Tonto Basin, Site Descriptions.* Arizona
              State University Office of Contract Archaeology Report 64.

Howard, Ann V.
    1983      *The Organization of Interregional Shell Production and Exchange Within South-
              ern Arizona.* M.A. thesis, Department of Anthropology, Arizona State Uni-
              versity, Tempe.

Howard, Jerry B.
    1982      Hohokam Community Organization at La Ciudad de Los Hornos. Ms. on
              file, Department of Anthropology, Arizona State University, Tempe.
    1987      The Lehi Canal System: Organization of a Classic Period Irrigation Commu-
              nity. In *The Hohokam Village,* edited by David Doyel. Southwestern and
              Mountain Division of the American Association for the Advancement of
              Science. Glenwood Springs, Colorado.

Huckell, Bruce
    1984      *The Archaic Occupation of the Rosemont Area, Northern Santa Rita Mountains,
              Southeastern Arizona.* Arizona State Museum Archaeological Series 147.

Huntington, Ellsworth
    1910      Notebook 10A: The Journal of Ellsworth Huntington. Ms. on file, Yale
              University Library, New Haven.

Ives, John C., and Dan J. Ophenring
    1966      Some Investigations into the Nature of the Early Phases of the Hohokam
              Culture, Central Arizona. Ms. on file, Department of Anthropology, Ari-
              zona State University, Tempe.

Johnson, Alfred E.
    1964      Archaeological Excavations in Hohokam Sites of Southern Arizona. *Ameri-
              can Antiquity* 30:145–161.

Katzer, Keith, and Jeanette Schuster
    1984      *The Quaternary Geology of the Northern Tucson Basin.* M.S. thesis, University
              of Arizona, Tucson.

Kidder, Alfred V.
    1924      *An Introduction to Southwestern Archaeology.* Yale University Press, New
              Haven.

Kroeber, Alfred L.
　　1939　　*Cultural and Natural Areas of Native North America.* University of California Publications in American Archaeology and Ethnology 38.

LeBlanc, Steven A.
　　1982　　The Advent of Pottery in the Southwest. In Southwestern Ceramics: A Comparative Review, edited by Albert H. Schroeder. *The Arizona Archaeologist* 15:27–52.

Lightfoot, Kent
　　1984　　*The Duncan Project: A Study of the Occupation Duration and Early Settlement Pattern of an Early Mogollon Pithouse Village.* Arizona State University Anthropological Field Studies 6.

Lightfoot, Kent, and Fred Plog
　　1984　　Intensification Along the North Side of the Mogollon Rim. In *Prehistoric Agricultural Strategies in the Southwest,* edited by S. Fish and P. Fish. Arizona State University Anthropological Papers 33.

Lytle-Webb, Jamie
　　1978　　Pollen Analysis in Southwestern Archaeology. In *Discovering Past Behavior: Experiments in the Archaeology of the American Southwest,* edited by Paul Grebinger. Gordon and Breach, New York.

McGuire, Randall H.
　　1980　　The Mesoamerican Connection in the Southwest. *The Kiva* 46:3–38.
　　1983　　Breaking Down Cultural Complexity: Inequality and Heterogeneity. *Advances in Archaeological Method and Theory,* vol. 6, edited by M. Schiffer, pp. 91–142. Academic Press, New York.

McGuire, Randall H., and Christian E. Downum
　　1982　　A Preliminary Consideration of Desert-Mountain Trade Relations. *Mogollon Archaeology: Proceedings of the 1980 Mogollon Conference,* edited by Patrick H. Beckett and Kira Silverbird. Acoma Books, Ramona.

McGuire, Randall H., and Michael Schiffer
　　1982　　*Hohokam and Patayan: Prehistory of Southwestern Arizona.* Academic Press, New York.

Martin, Paul S.
　　1963　　*The Last 10,000 Years: A Fossil Pollen Record of the American Southwest.* University of Arizona Press, Tucson.

Martin, Paul S., and Fred Plog
　　1973　　*The Archaeology of Arizona: A Study of a Southwest Region.* Natural History Press, New York.

Masse, W. Bruce
　　1979　　An Intensive Survey of Prehistoric Dry Farming Systems Near Tumamoc Hill in Tucson, Arizona. *The Kiva* 45:141–186.
　　1980　　The Hohokam of the Lower San Pedro Valley and the Northern Papagueria: Continuity and Variability in Two Regional Populations. In *Current Issues in Hohokam Prehistory: Proceedings of a Symposium,* edited by David Doyel and Fred Plog. Arizona State University Anthropological Research Papers 23.

1981    Prehistoric Irrigation Systems in the Salt River Valley, Arizona. *Science* 214:408–415.

1982    Hohokam Ceramic Art: Regionalism and the Imprint of Societal Change. In Southwestern Ceramics: A Comparative Review, edited by Albert Schroeder. *The Arizona Archaeologist* 15.

Miksicek, Charles H.
1984    Historic Desertification, Prehistoric Vegetation Change, and Hohokam Subsistence in the Salt-Gila Basin. In *Hohokam Archaeology Along the Salt-Gila Aqueduct, Central Arizona Project*, Vol. 7, Environment and Subsistence, edited by Lynn Teague and Patricia Crown. Arizona State Museum Archaeological Series 150.

Morris, Donald
1969    Red Mountain: An Early Pioneer Period Hohokam Site in the Salt River Valley of Central Arizona. *American Antiquity* 34:40–53.

Nabhan, Gary P., Amadeo Rea, Karen Reichhardt, Eric Mellink, and Charles Hutchinson
1982    Papago Influences on Habitat and Biotic Diversity: Quitovac Oasis Ethnoecology. *Journal of Ethnobiology* 2:124–143.

Nabhan, Gary P., and J. M. J. de Wet
1984    *Panicum sonorum* in Sonoran Desert Agriculture. *Economic Botany* 38:65–82.

Nabhan, Gary P., A. Whiting, H. Dobyns, R. Hevly, and R. Euler
1978    Devil's Claw Domestication: Evidence from Southwestern Indian Fields. *Journal of Ethnobiology* 1:135–164.

Neitzel, Jill
1985    *Regional Organization of the Hohokam in the American Southwest*. Ph.D. dissertation, Arizona State University, Tempe.

Nelson, Richard S.
1981    *The Role of a Pochteca System in Hohokam Exchange*. Ph.D. dissertation, Department of Anthropology, New York University, New York.

Nicholas, Linda, and Jill Neitzel
1984    Canal Irrigation and Sociopolitical Organization in the Lower Salt River Valley: A Diachronic Analysis. In *Prehistoric Agricultural Strategies in the Southwest*, edited by Suzanne Fish and Paul Fish. Arizona State University Anthropological Research Paper 33.

Ophenring, Dan
1965    *The Herberger Site: A McDowell Mountain Hohokam Settlement*. M.A. thesis, Arizona State University, Tempe.

Pilles, Peter J.
1978    The Fieldhouse and Sinagua Demography. In *Limited Activity and Occupation Sites: A Collection of Conference Papers*, edited by Albert Ward. Contributions to Anthropological Studies 1.

Plog, Fred
1980    Explaining Culture Change in the Hohokam Preclassic. In *Current Issues in Hohokam Prehistory: Proceedings of a Symposium*, edited by David Doyel and Fred Plog. Arizona State University Anthropological Research Papers 23.

Raab, L. Mark
  1973      AZ AA:5:2, A Prehistoric Cactus Camp in Papagueria. *Journal of the Arizona Academy of Science* 8.

Rea, Amadeo
  1979      The Ecology of Pima Fields. *Environment Southwest* 484:8–13.

Rice, Glen
  1981      La Ciudad Archaeological Project: A Proposal for Data Recovery. Ms. on file, Department of Anthropology, Arizona State University, Tempe.

Ruppe, Reynold J.
  1966      A Survey of Hohokam Remains in the Salt River Drainage. Ms. on file, Department of Anthropology, Arizona State University, Tempe.

Russell, Frank
  1908      *The Pima Indians*. Twenty-sixth Annual Report of the Bureau of American Ethnology, 1904–1905. Smithsonian Institution, Washington D.C.

Sauer, Carl
  1934      The Distribution of Aboriginal Tribes and Languages in Northwestern Mexico. *Ibero-Americana* 5.

Sayles, Edwin B.
  1945      *The San Simon Branch Excavations at Cave Creek and in the San Simon Valley: Material Culture*. Medallion Papers 34.

Schiffer, Michael B.
  1982      Hohokam Chronology: An Essay on History and Method. In *Hohokam and Patayan: Prehistory of Southwestern Arizona*, edited by R. H. McGuire and M. B. Schiffer. Academic Press, New York.

Schoenwetter, James, and Alfred E. Dittert
  1968      An Ecological Interpretation of Anasazi Settlement Patterns. In *Anthropological Archaeology in the Americas*, edited by B. J. Meggers. Anthropological Society of Washington, Washington, D.C.

Schroeder, Albert H.
  1940      *A Stratigraphic Survey of Pre-Spanish Trash Mounds of the Salt River Valley, Arizona*. M.A. thesis, University of Arizona, Tucson.
  1952      The Bearing of Ceramics on Developments in the Hohokam Classic Period. *Southwestern Journal of Anthropology* 8:320–335.
  1953      The Problem of Hohokam, Sinagua and Salado Relations in Southern Arizona. *Plateau* 26:75–83.
  1957      The Hakataya Cultural Tradition. *American Antiquity* 23:176–178.
  1960      The Hohokam, Sinagua and Hakataya. *Society for American Archaeology, Archives of Archaeology* 5.
  1965      Unregulated Diffusion from Mexico into the Southwest Prior to A.D. 700. *American Antiquity* 30:297–309.
  1966      Pattern Diffusion from Mexico into the Southwest After A.D. 600. *American Antiquity* 31:683–704.
  1979      Prehistory: Hakataya. In *Handbook of North American Indians*, Vol. 9, Southwest, edited by Alfonso Ortiz. Smithsonian Institution, Washington, D.C.

Sheridan, David
    1981    *Desertification of the United States.* U.S. Government Printing Office, Washington, D.C.

Sires, Earl W.
    1984    Hohokam Architecture and Structure. In *Hohokam Archaeology Along the Salt-Gila Aqueduct, Central Arizona Project,* Vol. 9: Synthesis and Conclusions, edited by Lynn S. Teague and Patricia Crown. Arizona State Museum Archaeological Series 150.

Smith, Landon D.
    1978    Paleoenvironmental Factors Affecting Hohokam Small Site Settlement Patterns Peripheral to the Salt-Gila Drainages: 11th–14th Centuries. In *Limited Activity and Occupation Sites: A Collection of Conference Papers,* edited by Albert Ward. Contributions to Anthropological Studies 1.

Szuter, Christine
    1984    Faunal Exploitation and the Reliance on Small Animals. In *Hohokam Archaeology Along the Salt-Gila Aqueduct, Central Arizona Project,* Vol. 7, Environment and Subsistence, edited by L. Teague and P. Crown. Arizona State Museum Archaeological Series 150.

Turney, O. A.
    1924    *The Land of the Stone Hoe.* Arizona Republican Print Shop, Phoenix.

Underhill, Ruth M.
    1939    *Social Organization of the Papago Indians.* Columbia University Press, New York.

Upham, Steadman, and Glen Rice
    1980    Up the Canal Without a Pattern: Modeling Hohokam Interaction and Exchange. In *Current Issues in Hohokam Prehistory,* edited by David Doyel and Fred Plog. Arizona State University Anthropological Research Papers 23.

Wallace, Henry, and James Holmlund
    1982    The Mortars, Petroglyphs, and Trincheras on Rillito Peak. *The Kiva* 48.
    1984    The Classic Period in the Tucson Basin. *The Kiva* 49:167–194.

Wasley, William
    1966    Classic Period Hohokam. Ms. on file, Arizona State Museum, University of Arizona, Tucson.

Wasley, William, and David Doyel
    1980    The Classic Period Hohokam. *The Kiva* 45:337–352.

Waters, Michael, and John Field
    1986    Geomorphic Analysis of Hohokam Settlement Patterns on Alluvial Fans along the Western Flank of the Tortolita Mountains, Arizona. *Geoarchaeology* 1:29–345.

Weaver, Donald
    1972    A Cultural-Ecological Model for the Classic Hohokam Period in the Lower Salt River Valley, Arizona. *The Kiva* 38:43–52.

Weaver, Donald, Susan Burton, and Minnabel Laughlin
    1978    *Proceedings of the 1973 Hohokam Conference.* Acoma Books, Ramona.

Weigand, Phil C., Garman Harbottle, and Edward V. Sayre
  1977    Turquoise Sources and Source Analysis: Mesoamerica and the Southwestern U.S.A. In *Exchange Systems in Prehistory*, edited by Timothy Earle and Jonathan Ericson. Academic Press, New York.

Wilcox, David R.
  1979    The Hohokam Regional System. In *An Archaeological Test of Sites in the Gila Butte-Santan Region, South-Central Arizona*, edited by Glen Rice, David Wilcox, Kevin Rafferty, and James Schoenwetter. Arizona State University Anthropological Research Papers 18.
  1980    The Current Status of the Hohokam Concept. In *Current Issues in Hohokam Prehistory: Proceedings of a Symposium*, edited by David Doyel and Fred Plog. Arizona State University Anthropological Research Papers 23.
  1984    Research Problems. In *A Class III Survey of the Tucson Aqueduct Phase A Corridor, Central Arizona Project*, edited by John Czaplicki. Arizona State Museum Archaeological Series 165.
  1986    The Tepiman Connection: A Model of Mesoamerican-Southwestern Interaction. In *Ripples in the Chichimec Sea*, edited by Frances Mathien and Randall McGuire. Southern Illinois University Press, Carbondale.
  In Press *Site Structure and Maximum Extent of The Pueblo Grande Site*. Pueblo Grande Monograph Series 1.

Wilcox, David R., Thomas McGuire, and Charles Sternberg
  1981    *Snaketown Revisited: A Partial Cultural Resource Survey, Analysis of Site Structure, and an Ethnohistoric Study of the Proposed Hohokam-Pima National Monument*. Arizona State Museum Archaeological Series 155.

Wilcox, David R., and Lynette O. Shenk
  1977    *The Architecture of the Casa Grande and its Interpretation*. Arizona State Museum Archaeological Series 115.

Wilcox, David R., and Charles Sternberg
  1983    *Hohokam Ballcourts and Their Interpretation*. Arizona State Museum Archaeological Series 160.

Wood, Jon S., and Martin E. McAllister
  1980    Foundation and Empire: the Colonization of the Northeastern Hohokam Periphery. In *Current Issues in Hohokam Prehistory: Proceedings of a Symposium*, edited by David E. Doyel and Fred Plog. Arizona State University Anthropological Research Paper 23.
  1984    Second Foundation: Settlement Patterns and Agriculture in the Northeastern Hohokam Periphery, Central Arizona. In *Prehistoric Agricultural Strategies in the Southwest*, edited by Suzanne K. Fish and Paul R. Fish. Arizona State University Anthropological Research Paper 33.

# A Grasshopper Perspective on the Mogollon of the Arizona Mountains

The idea of a Mogollon people living in the mountains and adjacent deserts of Arizona and New Mexico began in controversy and continued in debate for over twenty years (Reid 1986). When proposed by Emil Haury in 1936, most southwestern archaeologists were reticent to accept the Mogollon as distinct from the neighboring Anasazi and Hohokam. Archaeologists working on the Colorado Plateaus were further annoyed by the suggestion that the Mogollon possessed ceramics earlier than their own Anasazi. As evidence accumulated, primarily through the prodigious field research of Haury and Paul Martin and the careful delineation of argument by Erik Reed, objection to the general notion of a Mogollon people gradually subsided. The invention of alternative cultural labels and the development of rather divergent working definitions of the Mogollon for different regions, however, continued to keep Mogollon studies in weakly disguised disarray. Although a biennial Mogollon conference ratifies broad acceptance of a cultural entity distinct from Anasazi and Hohokam, a commonly shared definition of Mogollon is unavailable (see Dean 1988; Haury 1988; Speth 1988; Wilcox 1988).

Starting with the perspective that the mountains required an adaptation distinct from either the desert or plateau, one establishes a baseline for exploring other behavioral differences that should, in time, lead to a more consistent picture of what it was to be Mogollon. The picture presented here, therefore, is one perception derived from a particular theoretical approach to the reconstruction of past behavior and from extensive research in the mountains of Arizona. It is a picture of a resilient, robust people skilled in the technology of hunting, gathering, gardening, and domestic crafts performed in a richly diverse and demanding environment; a people who, by the beginning of history, had become part of the uniquely southwestern pueblo agriculturalist pattern (see Martin 1979; Rice 1980; Cordell 1984b; see Haury 1985:406 on the Tarahumara connection).

## TOWARD A DEFINITION OF MOGOLLON

The Mogollon Culture defined by Emil Haury (1936; reprinted in Reid and Doyel 1986) was typified by people who lived in pithouse villages and made brown plain and red-slipped pottery throughout the mountains of Arizona and New Mexico until A.D. 1000. Haury envisioned a subsequent merging of Mogollon distinctiveness into a culture he felt owed much of its expression to the Anasazi (see Haury 1985:403–407, 1988). Throughout his career Haury stressed the similarities between these later pueblo-building descendants of the Mogollon and the influential Anasazi neighbors; Paul Martin, John Rinaldo, Joe Ben Wheat, and others concurred with this interpretation. On the other hand, Erik Reed (1950), while recognizing increasing similarities between Mogollon and Anasazi after A.D. 1000, preferred to emphasize the differences that continued to mark these two pueblo cultures of the northern Southwest. Reed introduced the names Mogollon Pueblo and Western Pueblo to distinguish what he regarded as Mogollon distinctiveness and continuity in the period after A.D. 1000. Recent research permits the ideas of Haury, Martin, Rinaldo, Wheat, and Reed to be incorporated in a more inclusive formulation of the Mogollon concept.

The period of Mogollon dominion in the central mountains of Arizona extends from around A.D. 200 until the abandonment in the A.D. 1400s. It has traditionally been divided at A.D. 1000 into the pithouse builders before that time and the pueblo builders afterward, a dateline that applies best to western New Mexico (see Anyon, Gilman, and LeBlanc 1981); this architectural transition occurs later as one moves west. Diagnostic characteristics indicative of particular behaviors for the pithouse-building era as defined by Haury (1936:79–126) include:

1. The manufacture of polished brown plain ware, red-slipped ware, and decorated red-on-brown pottery; use of smudging on the interior of

some vessels (corrugated pottery appears after A.D. 1000 in the Arizona mountains);

2. The construction of deep pithouses, which early were round or rounded and later were rectangular, entered through a lateral passageway;

3. An unpatterned arrangement of pit houses in a village (compare Lightfoot 1984:109–111); and

4. A strong emphasis on hunting and gathering as a subsistence complement to cultivation.

Behavioral characteristics isolated by Reed (1950; see also 1942, 1946, 1948a, 1948b) to distinguish the Mogollon Pueblo include:

1. The use of cradle boarding techniques that produced the vertical-occipital form of head deformation;

2. The manufacture and use of three-quarter groove axes;

3. The construction of rectangular ceremonial rooms or kivas within pueblo room blocks;

4. Mortuary practices that included positioning of the deceased on the back, fully extended; and

5. Pueblo architectural arrangement that focused inward on a plaza (Reed 1956).

It is clear that after A.D. 1000 there was an increase in the tempo of contact between the Anasazi and Mogollon; trade, population movement, and coresidence are evident in the archaeological record. In addition, one suspects a variety of more subtle mechanisms operating to exchange items and information. Even so, the descendants of the pithouse-building Mogollon retained behaviors that contrasted with their neighbors. Mogollon Pueblo can provisionally be retained as a useful label for many of the pueblo communities in the Arizona mountains.

## MOGOLLON LANDSCAPES

The maximum geographic extent of Mogollon in each cardinal direction is conveniently estimated by Reed (1950) to include the mountains and adjacent deserts in the vast area bounded by the Verde on the west, the Little Colorado River on the north, the Pecos River in the east, and an uncharted extension southward into the northern Mexican states of Chihuahua and Sonora (see Sayles 1936; Gladwin 1936; Lister 1958). Within Arizona four regions serve as reference points on the landscape of the mountain

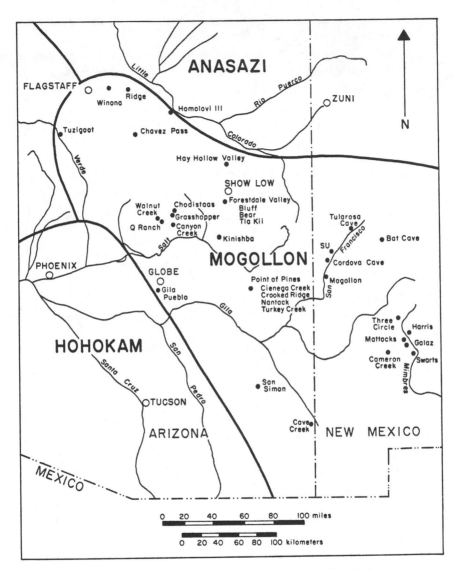

*Fig. 9. Prehistoric sites in the Mogollon area of Arizona and western New Mexico.*

Mogollon—Point of Pines, Forestdale, Grasshopper, and Q Ranch (Fig. 9). Although these regions share environmental characteristics common to the central mountains, they are not comparable at all levels of behavioral inference. Furthermore, these regions are geographic units rather than cultural branches, even though region labels may coincide with published branch labels (for example, Wheat 1955; Martin 1979).

The Mogollon Rim forms the northern limit of Arizona's central mountains, a transition zone running diagonally between the basin and range deserts to the south and the Colorado Plateaus. Geologic faulting and vulcanism in this zone have resulted in a heavily dissected terrain of high elevations, steep canyons, and narrow valleys. Vegetation is characterized by Ponderosa Pine above 6,000 feet; evergreen woodlands of pinyon, juniper, and oak, and chaparral in intermediate elevations; and Sonoran desert shrubbery and cactus below 3,500 feet. This variegated landscape exhibits a high diversity of native plant, animal, and mineral resources in a zone marginal to agriculture. Similar environmental conditions in the past would have encouraged mixed subsistence strategies and residential moves as solutions to the problem of adjusting population to resources.

The Point of Pines region (Fig. 9), an area of roughly 175 square miles, is marked by pine and mixed evergreen woodland surrounding a large grassland known as Circle Prairie. Elevations range around 6,000 feet. The growing season is estimated at 165 to 170 days; annual precipitation at 18 to 19 inches. A high water table was tapped with surface wells throughout the prehistoric occupation beginning in Late Archaic times (Wendorf 1950:13–19).

Forestdale (Fig. 9) is a narrow mountain valley immediately below the Mogollon Rim with plant life typical of the setting—pine, juniper, and manzanita on the slopes; juniper, oak, and walnut on the floor. Valley floor elevations are near 6,500 feet. The growing season is estimated at 140 days; annual rainfall at 20 inches. Domestic water supplied by Forestdale Creek, probably a perennial stream prehistorically, was augmented by numerous springs along the margin of the valley (Haury 1940:10–16; reprinted in Haury 1985; see Rose 1980).

The Grasshopper and Q Ranch regions (Fig. 9) are adjacent mountain plateaus and their contiguous canyons; they are roughly bounded by the Salt River on the south and the Mogollon Rim to the north. Within this combined area of approximately 550 square miles, vegetation ranges from Ponderosa Pine to evergreen woodland, thick chaparral brush, and grasslands. Sonoran Desert plants emerge as elevations approach Salt River. Records at Cibecue provide an estimate of 140 days for the growing season and 19 inches annual rainfall (Holbrook and Graves 1982:5–11; Ciolek-Torello and Lange 1979:109–119).

The portion of the Mogollon homeland in Arizona remains a vast and rugged region of environmental diversity and behavioral variability. It has also been the scene of extensive archaeological research, largely through archaeological field schools by the University of Arizona (Forestdale, 1939–1941; Point of Pines, 1946–1960; Grasshopper, 1963 to present) and Arizona State University (Vosberg, 1967–1970). Additional information has been provided through contract sponsored research by the Arizona State Museum at the University of Arizona, the Office of Cultural Resource Management at Arizona State University, the Museum of Northern Arizona, and the Tonto National Forest. These investigations spawned a series of regional culture sequences that permit prehistoric remains to be ordered into phases, which in practice connote blocks of time. These phase sequences, though occasionally useful, are collapsed here into a scheme consistent with the synthetic theme of this volume.

## MOGOLLON INITIATION (A.D. 200 TO A.D. 600)

It is generally agreed that the Mogollon developed out of the Cochise Culture, the Archaic lifeway of southern Arizona and New Mexico (Haury 1943; Haury and Sayles 1947; Martin, Rinaldo, and Antevs 1949). At the Cienega Site in the Point of Pines region, Haury (1957; reprinted in Reid and Doyel 1986) uncovered remains, especially stone tools, that provided evidence for continuity between these Archaic people and the pottery-producing Mogollon. The addition of pottery with pithouses distinguishes the earliest Mogollon from Late Archaic people. Pithouse villages of this Mogollon period, however, are infrequent in the archaeological record of Arizona.

The earliest dated settlement is the Bluff Village in the Forestdale Valley where Haury and Sayles (1947; reprinted in Haury 1985) uncovered pithouses ranging in shape from circular and oval to square with rounded corners. Pottery was not plentiful, and was almost exclusively brown plain ware (Alma Plain). During the earliest dated occupation, estimated to immediately after A.D. 300, circular pithouses were dug into the fractured bedrock of the bluff. The larger structures contain hearths, suggesting their use for habitation (House 10 = 29 m² versus an average of 18 m²). The size of Structure 5 (83 m²) led Haury to suggest communal and possibly religious functions in addition to habitation. The smaller circular structures may also have served as places of habitation, although the absence of hearths and the presence of grinding equipment suggest storage and food processing activities. The presence of exterior hearths indicates that cooking was not restricted to houses. It is unknown how many of the circular houses were in use at any time. Subsequent occupations by people who built the oval houses and later the square houses indicate a continuing selection of this bluff-top location with its panoramic view of the valley floor. Without the benefit of tree-ring dates, Haury estimates that the occupation of the bluff extended to A.D. 600. The paucity of artifacts suggests part-time habitations.

The subsistence routine is unclear from the scant food remains found. Haury recovered few animal bones and, except for charred black walnut hulls, no plant remains. The presence of knives, projectile points, and grinding equipment argues for a mixed subsistence strategy of hunting and gathering. In addition, Haury suspects the cultivation of corn on the basis of developed milling stones.

## Summary of Trends

The paucity and ambiguity of information restrict reconstruction of the Mogollon lifeway in the Arizona mountains during this period to general impressions, which are bolstered by remains in the Arizona desert (Lightfoot 1984) and in New Mexico (Martin 1940, 1943; Martin and Rinaldo 1947; Anyon, Gilman, and LeBlanc 1981; LeBlanc 1983). The impression is of a lifeway essentially unchanged from the Late Archaic except for the addition of ceramic pots; stone tools are little changed. Small pithouse villages located on high landforms, when contrasted with later valley floor locations, suggest a defensive posture in response to social or economic uncertainty. The presence of a large pithouse, perhaps a great kiva, at the Bluff Village marks it as a focal settlement in the protracted process of increasing residential stability through extended occupation of a base camp. Residential moves served as the principal means of adjusting small populations to the availability of resources. The proceeds of hunting and gathering dominate the diet, though small garden plots probably contributed. In fact, selection of settlement locations near lands suitable for gardens may have had the effect, over time, of localizing separate occupations into the clusters of houses that appear in the archaeological record as unstructured villages. In any event, the Mogollon appear to have been less committed to plant food production at this time than their contemporary Hohokam and Anasazi neighbors.

## MOGOLLON EXPANSION AND DIFFERENTIATION (A.D. 600 TO A.D. 1150)

This period in the Arizona mountains is characterized by pithouse villages contemporaneous with the Harris and Mogollon Villages initially excavated in New Mexico by Haury (1936; reprinted in Reid and Doyel 1986). In the Point of Pines region the Crooked Ridge Village (Wheat 1954) contains approximately 100 pithouses, of which 24 houses and two great kivas were excavated. Revision of Wheat's (1954: 167–175) ceramic dating and phase associations suggest occupations from the beginning of this period to A.D. 900 (see Breternitz 1959:69–71). At Nantack Village (Breternitz 1959), the 11 pithouses and one great kiva excavated represent occupations after A.D. 900. Architectural features suggesting the transition to above-ground structures as well as later above-ground rooms are present at Nantack. No tree-ring dates are available for either of these villages.

In the Forestdale Valley, the Bear Village reflects behavioral patterns only partially documented by tree-ring dates (Haury 1940; reprinted in Haury 1985). Bear is a pithouse village where 17 houses, about half of the total present, were excavated. Several pithouses yielded dates indicating construction in the late A.D. 600s, while ceramic cross-dating suggests occupation extending into the 800s. Alma Plain remained the dominant ceramic in association with indigenous smudged and red-slipped pottery. Anasazi derived ceramics included Lino Gray, Lino Black-on-gray, White Mound Black-on-white, and some later types, all in low frequency.

The village is on the valley floor near Forestdale Creek, with pithouses dug deep into the alluvial clays. Though three rectangular houses were excavated, the majority were round; all houses exhibit mixed architectural features, some characteristic of the Mogollon, others of the Anasazi. Habitation structures possess hearths, food processing equipment, and internal storage pits in higher frequency than the two excavated structures interpreted as storage rooms. Animal remains indicate substantial hunting of deer, while milling equipment attests to the processing of plant foods. Although only one charred corn cob was recovered, it is reasonable to infer that corn was a component of the diet.

The remains from the Bear Village suggest a hunting-gathering-horticultural economy pursued by groups of households, some of which (or individual members) derived from different ethnic traditions. This suggestion of ethnic coresidence is supported by architectural features and different forms of cradleboard-produced head deformation consistent with types found characteristic of the later Anasazi and Mogollon. The coming together of different people is compatible with perceptions of population movements throughout the Southwest during this period and may in part account for the movement of villages down from more defensible bluff-top locations and the construction of great kivas as corporate ceremonial structures. It is not easy to distinguish the results of trade or information exchanges from those representing occupation by people of different traditions. It is equally difficult to distinguish contemporaneous from sequential occupations, though information from Bear suggests the direction that interpretation may take.

At the Bear Village, Haury (1940:64–67; reprinted in Haury 1985) notes a mixing of mortuary characteristics common among the Anasazi and Mogollon, including variability in head deformation and its absence. Instances of vertical-occipital deformation, the form hypothesized to be associated with the Mogollon, are present, and Haury's field appraisal of the poorly preserved crania led him to estimate that the bulk of the burial population was of this type (Haury 1940:138). Lambdoidal deformation, hypothesized to be associated with the Anasazi, and an undeformed skull are also present. The clearest cases are three males, each exhibiting one of the three categories. Represented at Bear, therefore, are three adult males whose mothers employed different cradleboards (or techniques of infant restraint). One suggests that these mothers were of different cultural traditions, at least Anasazi and Mogollon. If so, one may assume that the men belonged to the tradition of their mothers, though this need not necessarily be the case. Pursuing this line of thought further, one may suggest that the different house types and houses with mixed architectural features represent what one might expect if people of different house-building traditions cooperated in construction. Although I favor the implication that Anasazi lived side-by-side with a larger number of Mogollon at the Bear Village, the possibility of pithouse remodeling by sequential occupants cannot be eliminated. The great kiva at Bear, and large structures in other Mogollon villages such as Crooked Ridge and Nantack, may have served to bring members of dispersed communities and of different cultural traditions together in a culturally neutral, unthreatening communal setting, oftentimes to participate in ritual. The long history and widespread distribution of these large structures may reflect the fluid demographic and social patterns that are thought to characterize the mountain Mogollon (see Anyon and LeBlanc 1980; Anyon 1984).

This coming together of different people that is glimpsed at the Bear Village foreshadows what we see much more clearly 600 years later at the large Point of Pines and Grasshopper Pueblos. One long-term result of ethnic coresidence would have been the exchange of ideas and the overlay of archaeological remains that produced the material similarities observed for the centuries after A.D. 1000. In this light, the different viewpoints of Haury and Reed concerning Anasazi influence on the Mogollon become more congruent.

Moving further west in the Arizona mountains, one finds that information for this period is more complete for the Q Ranch region than for Grasshopper. Occupation of the Vosberg Valley, beginning around A.D. 700, is characterized by pithouses in isolation or in scattered, small clusters (Cartledge 1976, 1977). The number of pithouses at a settlement tends to increase through time, though it is difficult to separate the intensification of contemporary occupations from sequential occupations of the same locality (see Whittlesey 1982). Site location is associated with diabase-derived soils, a pattern found throughout the occupation of the Q Ranch region and one inferred to mark these as agricultural soils (Tuggle 1982; see Wood 1980). The dominant settlement system is characterized by residential moves among settlements occupied only part-time, although full-time, but not long-term, habitations occurred. Artifact assemblages and biological remains indicate subsistence based on hunting, gathering, and horticulture (Tuggle 1982; Whittlesey and Reid 1982).

It is interesting that only during this period in the Q Ranch region do we find red-on-buff decorated ceramics (Hohokam), plain ware ceramics with micaceous temper (suggesting Hohokam), and greatest use of the local steatite sources for bead manufacture. Although Morris (1970) has suggested ethnic coresidence at the Walnut Creek Village in the Vosberg Valley to account for the variability in pithouses and ceramics, unsolved problems of contemporaneity similar to those at the Bear Village make this inference tentative. The bulk of the locally produced utility ceramics were the brown plain ware, characteristic of the mountains. The sudden cessation of a Hohokam ceramic presence at the end of this period suggests a shift in patterns of contact between groups or in the joint use of the region (see Tuggle 1982).

In the Grasshopper region, the only substantial evidence for occupation during this period is one excavated, burned pithouse at a small settlement that may possess additional houses. One tree-ring date of A.D. 921vv accords with the brown plain ware pottery. Lack of domesticates among the plant remains and ample quantities of animal bone suggest part-time occupation devoted to hunting and gathering.

## Summary of Trends

The highly visible occupation during this period indicates population expansion and regional differentiation in material categories, all of which can be seen as variations on the Mogollon theme catalogued by Wheat's (1955) classic synthesis. There is a tendency for villages to be located on a valley floor or on low ridges adjacent to land suited to cultivation. This move from higher, more defensible locations of the previous pattern suggests both the growing significance of cultivation in settlement decisions and a relaxation of economic and social uncertainties. Residential mobility characterized adjustment to much of the mountains while in areas of local resource advantage more stable settlements developed. The presence of great kivas suggests continuation of focal communities. Evidence exists for either coresidence or joint use and certainly multiple use of the mountain zone by people of different traditions as well as an increase in the tempo of communication between the Mogollon and their Hohokam and Anasazi neighbors.

Subsistence needs were still met through hunting, gathering, and gardening. Domesticated plants contributed to the diet in proportion to highly localized growing conditions; horticulture was more important at Point of Pines and Forestdale than at Grasshopper or Q Ranch. In all regions the reliance upon plant food production increased during this period, yet continued to lag behind the Hohokam and Anasazi.

## MOGOLLON PUEBLO REORGANIZATION (A.D. 1150 TO A.D. 1300)

This was a time of change among the Mogollon, brought about by an increase in contact with people to the north and in the experimentation required to adjust subsistence and social organization to diverse mountain environments. Evidence suggests that experiments with building above-ground structures of stone began around A.D. 1000. This shift was well established by the early A.D. 1100s with the appearance of small pueblos at Forestdale and Point of Pines; these appear later at Grasshopper and Q Ranch. Small pueblos dot the landscape of the Point of Pines region, suggesting favorable environmental conditions for early agriculturalists experimenting with plant varieties and the technology of dry-farming in environments that were also profitable for hunting and gathering. The appearance is one of elaborating earlier economic and organizational patterns.

During the A.D. 1200s increasingly larger pueblos sprang up in the Point of Pines region. The 335-room Turkey Creek Pueblo, estimated to have been founded around A.D. 1240, appears to have been the first large pueblo community there (Johnson 1965; Lowell 1986). Toward the last quarter of this century, Point of Pines Pueblo attracted a group of emigrants from the Anasazi region (Haury 1958, reprinted in Reid and Doyel 1986). Many of the 70 rooms identified as theirs were intentionally burned. A D-shaped kiva located away from the burned rooms is thought to have been used by this Anasazi population. The burning-out of these people, an undated event thought to have occurred before A.D. 1300, provokes speculation on the possibility of social tension in the mountains during the late A.D. 1200s.

In the Forestdale Valley, Haury (1985) excavated the Tla Kii Ruin, a small pueblo of 21 habitation and storage rooms, a detached small kiva, and a great kiva. Tree-ring dates place the occupation of this pueblo between A.D. 1100 and A.D. 1150. Although Tla Kii is earlier than the beginning of this reorganization period, it may be taken as one example of life in a small mountain pueblo that owed much of its character to an Anasazi tradition. Utility ceramics include the ubiquitous brown pottery, both plain and corrugated ware, along with vessels with red-slipped exteriors and vessels with smudged interiors. Decorated ceramics include McDonald Painted Corrugated, Wingate Black-on-red, and black-on-white designs in Wingate, Puerco, and Snowflake styles.

Tla Kii represents a small agricultural community with fields on the valley floor. Hunting and gathering continue to provide a portion of the diet. Contact and exchange between groups of Mogollon and Anasazi can be suggested from architectural and ceramic styles and from mortuary practices. The presence of a great kiva, in addition to a small kiva, suggests activities involving more people than those who inhabited the 21-room pueblo, and further supports the continuing pattern of a focal community serving a dispersed, local population. Use of the fertile Forestdale Valley by members of different cultural traditions is suggested and may represent continued flexibility in group membership.

Architectural change moved more slowly in the backwoods of Grasshopper and Q Ranch. At the beginning of this period appeared cobble habitation structures—three or four low-wall surface rooms of stacked cobbles early in the period, and dressed stone masonry toward the end. Surface rooms probably do not replace pithouses until much later, and cobble rooms continue throughout the succeeding period as an alternative architectural form coeval with masonry pueblos. There is no evidence for true masonry pueblos (full-standing walls) being built before A.D. 1300 in either the Grasshopper or Q Ranch regions, although individual rooms, especially those used for storage, may have had full-standing walls.

Cobble structures occur singly and in clusters with limited contiguity; occasionally, enclosure walls join groups of rooms to define courtyards, giving an impression of village plan. Although settlements are larger, contain more people, and are occupied with greater redundancy than in the previous period, habitation was part-time (Whittlesey and Reid 1982). The dispersed configuration characterized by residential moves continued, and there is evidence that the territory encompassed by these moves is sufficiently broad along a north-south axis (20 to 40 miles) to include areas outside of the Q Ranch and Grasshopper regions (see Graybill and Reid 1982; compare Goodwin 1942: Map VI). There is a tendency for settlements in the late A.D. 1200s to cluster in both the Q Ranch and Grasshopper regions (Tuggle 1970, 1982; Graves, Holbrook, and Longacre 1982).

The local ceramic assemblage is characterized by an increase in brown corrugated utility ceramics and in red-slipped pottery (including Roosevelt Red Ware); and by the importation from areas to the northeast of decorated ceramics, which are almost exclusively Cibola White Ware types (Puerco, Snowflake, Reserve, and Tularosa Black-on-white). White Mountain Redware types occur late in this period and in low numbers.

During the period of the Great Drought (A.D. 1276–1299), population increased in the Grasshopper and Q Ranch regions with evidence suggesting a growing sense of community and increased residential stability resulting in full-time habitation toward the end of the century. Settlements were small, up to 20 rooms, more numerous than before, and loosely clustered near agricultural land. Behavior appears as an elaboration of long established settlement, subsistence, and organizational patterns that contrast with the highly visible behavioral shifts that occur around A.D. 1300. Chodistaas Pueblo is the only excavated representative of this pattern in the Grasshopper region.

## Chodistaas Pueblo

Chodistaas is located on a bluff overlooking the largest expanse of agricultural soil in the region, one mile north of Grasshopper Pueblo. It is an 18-room pueblo constructed of dressed stone laid into low walls (at least for most rooms) and a plaza which identifies Chodistaas as the focal community for a cluster of settlements and special-use localities (Fig. 10). Sixteen rooms have been excavated; nine of these and the ceramic assemblage are discussed by Crown (1981). Room construction began in A.D. 1263 and continued through the A.D. 1270s, with at least four rooms added in A.D. 1280 (Rooms 4, 7, 6, 10) and another four in the mid A.D. 1280s (Rooms 3, 5, 8, 9). Before A.D. 1300, Chodistaas was burned and abandoned, leaving systemic inventories of nonperishable artifacts on room floors. Based on a pervasive habitation pattern also found in the Q Ranch region, Chodistaas was occupied part-time, at least initially. This generalization does not preclude brief periods of year-round habitation nor increased habitation through time resulting in full-time occupancy toward the end. A provisional reconstruction envisions part-time occupation from A.D. 1263 until the A.D. 1280s, the height of the Great Drought, when the addition of storage space (Rooms 3, 5, 8, and 9) suggests an increase in the length of habitation.

With regional population increase it is likely that the previously broad territory of exploitation and movement shrank under competition pressures resulting in fewer residential moves and a concomitant shift in procurement behavior. A subsistence strategy based in hunting, gathering, and horticul-

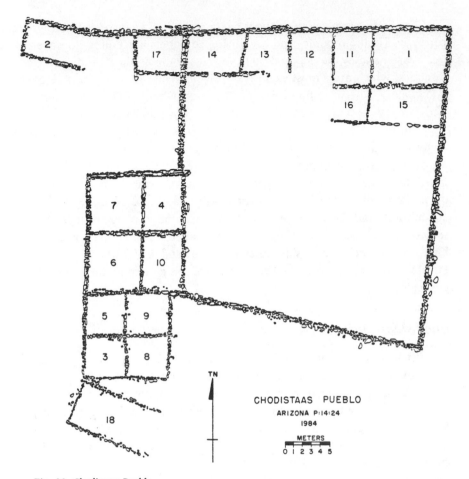

*Fig. 10. Chodistaas Pueblo.*

ture may have become more dependent upon the cultivation of corn and beans with dry farming techniques. It is unclear whether the burning of Chodistaas and two nearby, contemporary pueblos was intentional, and, thus, related to density-dependent competition that may have arisen in response to the widespread drought conditions.

Recent work on the household indicates that the partitioning of domestic space at Chodistaas differs from that at the later Grasshopper Pueblo; larger rooms (29 m² versus 16 m² at Grasshopper) were paired; habitation, storage, and manufacturing activities were less rigidly assigned; and there was a greater use of outdoor space. The impression is one of households sharing domestic space and activities in a more informal arrangement than at Grasshopper Pueblo (see Ciolek-Torrello 1978, 1984, 1985).

The Chodistaas ceramic assemblage of 307 whole vessels contrasts with the Grasshopper assemblage in having a higher frequency of white wares, which are broadly labeled Pinedale Black-on-white (Crown 1981). An interesting feature of the black-on-white assemblage is the "Snowflake Phenomenon"—the occurrence of different styles of design at the same settlement (see Tuggle and Reid 1982). At Chodistaas these include Red Mesa, Puerco, Snowflake, Tularosa, Kayenta, Pinedale, and Roosevelt styles (Crown 1981:296–308, Fig. 14). It is unclear to what behavioral mechanisms this stylistic variability may be attributed. Results of the unreported x-ray florescence study and the limited petrographic analysis did not permit Crown (1981:375) to make conclusive statements concerning whether vessels were made locally, though the petrographic analyst observed that the vessels were manufactured by different potters in different localities (Wheeler in Crown 1981:433). In the Q Ranch region, trace-element identification by neutron activation indicates an external source for black-on-white ceramics typologically identical to those at Chodistaas (Tuggle, Kintigh, and Reid 1982). Thus, there is reason to believe that black-on-whites found in the Grasshopper region during this period were also manufactured elsewhere.

The mechanisms for the movement of vessels into Chodistaas are unclear. Trade in large, black-on-white jars to small communities scattered throughout the mountains seems improbable, since the occurrence of only three St. Johns Polychrome bowls among 97 decorated vessels on room floors indicates that Chodistaas was not participating in the network that distributed this ceramic type widely throughout Arizona and New Mexico (Carlson 1970:30, Fig. 14). Chodistaas and similar, contemporary settlements in the Grasshopper and Q Ranch regions possessed neither the residential stability nor the population mass to attract long-distance ceramic trade. The contrast between Chodistaas and Grasshopper Pueblo in this regard is dramatic; clearly, Grasshopper possessed the stability and mass to attract items from distant sources. Given that white-firing clays are scattered and scarce in the mountains, trade in clays or household procurement of clays or household manufacture of pots at other encampments nearer these clays may have occurred. The variability in the Chodistaas ceramic assemblage is best accounted for by the movement of people; ethnic coresidence cannot be discounted.

## Summary of Trends

The period is characterized by the elaboration of the mountain adaptive pattern and the continuation of regional differences, an aspect of which is the realignment of contacts with neighboring peoples. Most noticeable is the shift to surface architecture and larger settlements that develop into aggregated pueblos before the mid A.D. 1200s at Point of Pines, but not until A.D. 1300 at Grasshopper and Q Ranch. The relatively accelerated development at Point of Pines was largely due to its sustained contact with people to both the north and south, a result of which led Johnson (1965) to view the material culture of Turkey Creek Pueblo as a mixture of Mogollon, Hohokam, and Anasazi. Grasshopper and Q Ranch, on the other hand, exhibit fewer indicators of contact with the Hohokam, fewer even than in the period prior to A.D. 1150, and more indicators of an increasingly northern orientation, which is pronounced after A.D. 1300.

Further adaptation of dry farming techniques to mountain environments is suspected, though it is apparent that hunting and gathering continued as prominent components of the subsistence routine. The ceramic assemblage of locally produced brown plain ware was steadily augmented with brown corrugated pottery, which at Point of Pines was extremely well made and profusely patterned in a manner strikingly reminiscent of baskets. Decorated ceramics were most commonly black-on-white types brought into the mountains. Chodistaas Pueblo is considered broadly representative of the material and adaptive pattern that characterized much of the mountain zone during this period.

## MOGOLLON PUEBLO AGGREGATION (A.D. 1300 TO THE A.D. 1400s)

The A.D. 1300s mark a unique period of prehistory in the Arizona mountains, when the majority of the population lived in pueblo communities of 100 to 800 rooms. For some people, like those in the Grasshopper and Q Ranch regions, aggregation occurred for the first time. Aggregation and a sudden population increase are in part a product of demographic shifts on the Colorado Plateaus that brought people of an Anasazi tradition into the mountains to live with the Mogollon and also to establish separate pueblo communities. This joint occupation of the mountains contributed to the consolidation of the Southwest pueblo pattern and obscures the ethnic identification of unexcavated pueblo sites in the mountains.

Aggregation into large pueblo communities at different times throughout the mountains was probably the result of different sets of conditions producing a similar response. The Grasshopper case provides insight into the aggregation process under one set of local conditions, which may not have been unique. During the latter half of the A.D. 1200s the Grasshopper region was characterized by the following relevant factors.

1. Population density increased as a result of movement into the mountains by people from both the desert and plateau areas, an increase in residential stability of long-time inhabitants, and the spatial clustering of settlements around scarce agricultural soils.

2. The three excavated sites of this period were burned.

3. Large pueblo communities developed earlier to the north and east of the Grasshopper region.

These conditions fit a scenario where people in the Grasshopper region, living in small, vulnerable communities at a time of demographic change and economic uncertainty, come together in response to the potential threat posed by already aggregated communities. That a threat was an initial and continuing settlement consideration is suggested by the location of smaller pueblos in the first half of the A.D. 1300s on vantage points along the perimeter of the Grasshopper Plateau and after A.D. 1350 on high, defensible landforms. One may infer that organizational and economic benefits of collective behavior reinforced the aggregation process.

The Arizona mountains' final and most dramatic prehistoric occupation is best documented for the Grasshopper region, even though the Grasshopper perspective may not characterize the full range of behaviors found from Point of Pines to Chavez Pass (see Upham, Lightfoot, and Feinman 1981; Upham 1982; Plog 1983; Cordell 1984a, 1984b; Kintigh 1985).

## Settlement Pattern and System in the Grasshopper Region

The earlier settlement system based largely in residential moves comes to an end by A.D. 1300 with population aggregation and the rapid growth of the pueblo communities at Grasshopper and Q Ranch; each the largest in its region and located in the middle of the broadest continuous expanse of agricultural land.

The Grasshopper Plateau hosts 10 pueblos of greater than 35 rooms, an estimated total of 1,300 rooms out of the nearly 2,000 pueblo rooms assigned to the A.D. 1300s. Of these 10 pueblos, six have from 35 to 100 rooms, three have from 120 to 150 rooms, and Grasshopper has 500 rooms. Their location is interpreted to be a function of proximity to agricultural land (Tuggle, Reid, and Cole 1984) and positioning along the plateau perimeter. Size differences are a product of two closely related settlement processes. One is differential growth due to regional population expansion, a niche-filling phenomenon; the second is a return by at least some of the regional population to a dispersed settlement system based in residential moves.

Support for the niche-filling process comes from the relationship between settlement size and agricultural land within areas measured by Thiessen polygons. The relationship runs from a density of 16 rooms per square mile of agricultural soil for a 45-room pueblo to 65 rooms per square mile for a pueblo of 129 rooms. Grasshopper Pueblo, with a density of 92 rooms per square mile, suggests a maximum density figure for this area as well as the probability that the true relationship is nonlinear.

The best documented growth of a satellite community is at Canyon Creek, a cliff-dwelling of over 100 rooms (Haury 1934; Reynolds 1981; Graves 1982, 1983). Graves's analysis indicates an initially temporary occupation beginning in A.D. 1327, with pueblo growth reaching its maximum shortly after A.D. 1340. All other cliff-dwellings in the region date after A.D. 1340.

The second process, that of a partial return to residential mobility is glimpsed in small masonry pueblos throughout the Grasshopper and Q Ranch regions that are situated on high landforms and in cliffs, and that were used for part-time habitation and unobtrusive storage (Whittlesey and Reid 1982). These small pueblos may have functioned as a specialized component of the aggregated system before the region was abandoned.

## Subsistence in the Grasshopper Region

In the agriculturally limited environment of the Grasshopper region the Mogollon managed to grow corn, beans, squash, and cotton using a rainfall-dependent technology; agricultural productivity was supplemented by hunting and gathering. Preliminary analysis suggests a dietary contribution for cultivated plants of approximately 75 percent and that this contribution increased during the occupation (Decker 1986). The quantity of animal bone and the proliferation of projectile points suggests an initial emphasis upon hunting, especially mule deer, far in excess of contemporary populations in the desert or on the Colorado Plateaus (Olsen 1980). (The amount of animal bone is in part the result of preservation and a procurement strategy whereby proceeds of the hunt were brought back to the pueblo for processing.) The simple agricultural technology comprised only water and soil conservation features in the form of check dams and contour terraces, and no devices for water diversion.

Whatever may have been the pressure on resources, the difficulties with the agricultural base, or the specific factors leading to abandonment, there is no evidence that any effort was made toward increasing agricultural productivity through changes in technology. It is unclear whether runoff agriculture in the Grasshopper region could have produced greater yields, but the system as a whole could have been upgraded through a shift to simple irrigation as demonstrated by the later Apache occupants of the region.

## Grasshopper Pueblo

Grasshopper Pueblo (Fig. 11) comprised approximately 500 rooms distributed among 13 room blocks and 15 smaller habitation units situated on either side of the old channel of Salt River Draw and on the surrounding low hills. The main pueblo consists of one- and two-story rooms concentrated in the flat land along the draw; the outliers are low-wall structures, often with only three walls, scattered around the periphery of the main pueblo. Reconstruction of pueblo growth and rainfall variability provide the framework for discussing community and regional organization (Reid 1973; Reid and Shimada 1982; Longacre 1975, 1976; Longacre, Holbrook, and Graves 1982; Graves, Holbrook, and Longacre 1982; Graves, Longacre, and Holbrook 1982; Dean and Robinson 1982).

### Pueblo Growth

*Establishment Phase (A.D. 1275 to A.D. 1300).* Although wall segments beneath the present ruin and ceramics indicate initial occupation of the Grasshopper locality during this time, there is no evidence for assessing the architectural or behavioral character of this occupation. Grasshopper is located near a spring, near abundant construction materials and firewood, and in the midst of the largest continuous expanse of local agricultural land. Establishment at Grasshopper coincides with the occupation of the nearby Chodistaas and Grasshopper Spring Pueblos, and with the Great Drought. It is probable that this initial settlement functioned as a focal community similar to Chodistaas and Grasshopper Spring.

*Expansion Phase (A.D. 1300 to A.D. 1330).* Construction on all three major room blocks of Grasshopper Pueblo began around A.D. 1300. Growth rapidly accelerated with the addition of multiple-room construction units. The rapid rate of initial growth suggests immigration (Longacre 1975, 1976), and the later addition of single and double room construction units suggests subsequent expansion of resident households. A cluster of tree-ring dates indicates that the southern corridor joining Room Blocks 2 and 3 was roofed in A.D. 1320; the eastern corridor exiting Plaza II was probably roofed shortly afterward. Plazas 1, 2, and 3 were in use throughout this period of rapid growth and, by the late A.D. 1320s, Plaza 3 was enclosed, roofed, and transformed into the Great Kiva. Following Eighmy's (1979) method, architectural growth closely describes a logistic curve, reaching a plateau around

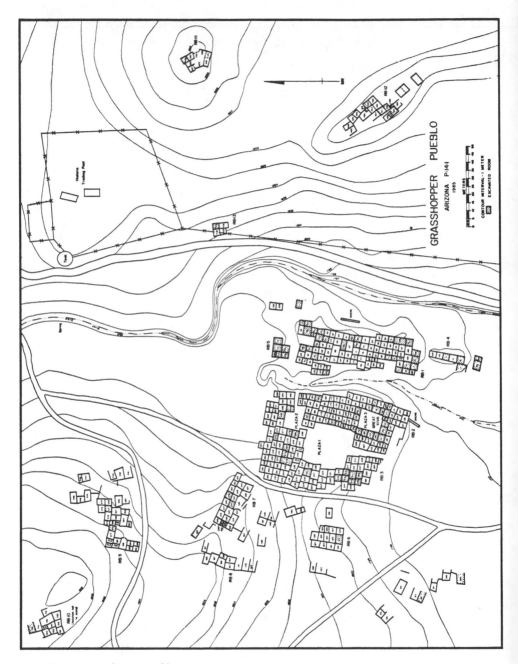

*Fig. 11. Grasshopper Pueblo.*

A.D.1330 (Ciolek-Torrello 1978:81, Fig. 5). Although there is no evidence for a composite village plan being implemented from the beginning, there are indications of an informal design for linking isolated, multiple-room construction units into an architectural whole that included internal plazas and roofed corridors. Rainfall is significantly higher for the first two decades of this expansion phase (Dean and Robinson 1982).

*Dispersion Phase (A.D. 1330 overlapping with Abandonment Phase).* Reasonably strong evidence exists for a portion of the last occupation of the pueblo to have been on a part-time basis. The low-wall outliers that surround the main pueblo have floor assemblages and archaeomagnetic dates indicating late abandonment. The compression of all indoor domestic activities into these less substantial structures suggests temporary habitation, perhaps during the summer, while residual households continued year-round occupation of the main pueblo. It is inferred that during this Dispersion phase Grasshopper households began moving to the temporary occupation of satellite settlements.

*Abandonment Phase (overlapping Dispersion phase to around A.D. 1400).* Although it is uncertain how many Grasshopper households moved temporarily to satellite settlements, it is clear that they and the rest of the communities in the region did eventually abandon the area, and that some smaller communities were established prior to this gradual abandonment. At Grasshopper Pueblo there is evidence for limited new construction after A.D. 1350 and for the acquisition of additional domestic space through reoccupation of abandoned rooms. The reoccupation of rooms in a no-growth community supports an interpretation of gradual abandonment, which is estimated to have been complete by A.D. 1400.

## Community Structure and Organization

The reconstruction of community structure and organization is based on two sets of data; the large mortuary collection and the room-floor artifact assemblages. Identification of household variability and ritually linked household groups precedes discussion of features reconstructed from the mortuary data.

*Households.* Building upon earlier household studies (Reid 1973, 1978; Ciolek-Torrello and Reid 1974), and Ciolek-Torrello's (1978, 1984, 1985) identification of functional room types, nine room types are identified (Reid and Whittlesey 1982). Two broad categories of households existed at Grasshopper—those that occupied two or more rooms and those that occupied only one room. The general form of the multiple room household in the main pueblo comprised a specialized habitation room plus one or two rooms for storage and manufacturing. The largest households occupied three rooms that included a specialized habitation room, one storage room, and one manufacturing room. Two-room households approximate the traditionally recognized pueblo pattern of one specialized habitation room and one room combining storage and manufacturing activities. In contrast to the main pueblo, multiple-room households in the outliers consist of two rooms, a specialized habitation room and a manufacturing room; no storage rooms have been identified in the outliers, although sharing of storage rooms with households of the main pueblo remains a strong possibility.

Single-room households, on the other hand, combine habitation, storage, and manufacturing activities in one room. In the main pueblo they consist of a generalized habitation room and its associated roof; in the outliers they consist only of a generalized habitation room since the roofs were of pole and brush. Household size and space allocation variability is broadly interpreted to reflect stages in the developmental cycle of domestic groups, change in the occupation of the Grasshopper Pueblo, and wealth-prestige factors.

Households may have been ritually linked through the sharing of ceremonial rooms and kivas. Proceeding from the ratio of three households to a ceremonial room and six households to a kiva, we infer that households, ceremonial groups, and kiva groups formed a hierarchy of kin-related social units structuring major divisions of the community. Households also contributed personnel to sodalities that presumably cross-cut kin, residence, and ethnic boundaries.

*The Individual in Death.* The mortuary collection (674 individuals) permits the reconstruction of the modal mortuary pattern to have been a single, primary, extended inhumation in a simple rectangular pit lacking elaborations. One-third of all burials lack any associated burial goods. The average number of associated artifacts is slightly under four per burial, and the average number of ceramic vessels is two per individual. Ceramic vessels are the most common artifact type found in mortuary context, ornaments follow, then ritually significant items. A few individuals, all adult males, were buried with tool kits or paraphernalia suggesting skilled flintknappers or ceremonial specialists. Domestic tools and equipment (such as manos, metates, and large utility vessels) were never included with burials (Whittlesey 1978, 1984:282–284).

Children differ from adults and males differ from females in mortuary treatment. Most children were buried without associated artifacts, although after age nine both the number of associated artifacts and the burial locale shift to a pattern more typical of adults. By age 15 adult status was achieved. Male individuals were provided with twice as many burial offerings as women, both ceramic vessels and other items. Artifacts suggesting special skills or roles, especially ritual items, are found exclusively with deceased men. Some ornaments are also gender-specific (Whittlesey 1984).

*Sodalities.* About half of the adult males belonged to sodalities or ceremonial societies. Four societies are identified by stylized ornaments, presumably worn as part of the ceremonial costume in which a male was buried. Three societies were mutually exclusive in male membership; they were marked by glycymeris shell pendants, conus shell tinklers, and bone hairpins. The fourth group, represented by clusters of arrows at the left shoulder, drew its membership from males affiliated with each of the three other societies. Less clearly identified are two possible societies, one symbolized by conus shell rings and restricted to females, the other by glycymeris shell bracelets with both men and women (Reid and Whittlesey 1982; Whittlesey 1984).

Authority was apparently vested in leadership of societies. Burial 140, a Mogollon male of 40 to 45 years of age (Griffin 1967), presumed to be the leader of the community, was a member of societies marked by arrows, bone hairpins, and glycymeris shell bracelets. We infer a community leadership role and interpret this position to have been a product of his multiple society memberships and his probable leadership of the arrow society (Reid and Whittlesey 1982; Whittlesey 1984).

*Residence Groups.* The three largest room blocks forming the main pueblo may reflect kinship and residence identifications that are also exhibited in the plaza inferred to be associated with each (Room Block 1–Plaza 2, Room Block 2–Plaza 3, Room Block 3–Plaza 1). This distinction among room block-plaza sets appears to have been marked by a variety of characteristics, one of which was gender. Another was decorated pottery wares; Room Block 1 with Grasshopper Ware, Room Block 2 with Roosevelt Red Ware (Pinto, Gila, and Tonto), and Room Block 3 with White Mountain Redware. At least one function of room block identification may have been the regulation of marriage.

*Ethnic Coresidence.* Another dimension of group identification was along ethnic lines. Two and possibly three ethnic groups resided at Grasshopper, each identified by a characteristic form of cranial deformation—vertical-occipital deformation associated with the Mogollon, lambdoidal associated with the Anasazi, and no deformation. The group with the largest constituency is identified as Mogollon and the authority figure (Burial 140) discussed above was a member. An Anasazi enclave is represented in the mortuary collection by 28 individuals. Unlike Point of Pines Pueblo (Haury 1958), there is no evidence at Grasshopper to indicate from where the nonlocal people migrated, nor is there evidence to suggest that their existence at Grasshopper was threatened. In fact, the supposed Anasazi enclave was distinguished by greater wealth and prestige than the average Mogollon, though not greater than the most prominent members of the Mogollon community.

## Social Inequality and Complexity

One supposes, given the pattern of scattered community clusters prior to A.D. 1300, that few of the Grasshopper households had prior experience with living in a large aggregated community. Aggregation is presumed to have had major implications for these participants. The principal social adjustments probably occurred in the restructuring of households and their contribution to the performance of social, economic, and religious activities. The role of sodalities, presumably cross-cutting kinship and ethnic boundaries, is thought to have been a major component of the organizational adjustment. The level of social inequality and complexity inferred for Grasshopper accords with ethnographic accounts of historic Pueblo village organization (see Jorgensen 1980:226–240).

Johnson's (1983; n.d., this volume) sequential hierarchy is an especially appealing model for the organization of Grasshopper Pueblo, quite apart from the recurrence of social units in groups of six. (An estimated six households shared a kiva, and six sodalities cross-cut the community.) Within this model consensual community decision-making can be maintained under conditions of population increase through basal social units, the global mean for which is six per community. Furthermore, that politically egalitarian groups typically maintain their fission option as basal units increase in number and consensus becomes unwieldy is also consistent with the evidence of satellite community formation in the Grasshopper region. The implication is that Grasshopper social organization is an example of a prehistoric sequential hierarchy with community decision-making vested in sodalities.

## Exchange

Grasshopper, like other large communities, attracted nonlocal goods in varying quantities and probably exchanged these items with other, smaller pueblo communities throughout the region (Tuggle 1970). Imported goods that traveled a considerable distance include macaws (20), copper bells (3), finished shell ornaments, and ceramics such as White Mountain Redwares (Whittlesey 1974). It is unclear by what process nonlocal products reached Grasshopper; except for ceramics, the frequency of occurrence of these items is sufficiently low for them to have been transferred by rather informal mechanisms. No evidence exists for the importation of foodstuff into the region.

Prior to A.D. 1300 the importation of decorated ceramics is most parsimoniously accounted for as a result of population movement. After A.D. 1300 the abundance and widespread distribution of imported ceramics to sedentary agricultural communities cannot be accounted for by population movement. Solely on the basis of impressions, it is hypothesized that Grasshopper was involved in a network of exchange whose most conspicuous elements were the southward movement of White Mountain Redware and the northward movement of shell. The only evidence for manufacturing items for potential export involves turquoise, although the possibility exists for the export of ceramics (Mayro, Whittlesey, and Reid 1976), salt, hematite, and chert. The prominent manufacturing component that has been identified at Grasshopper appears to be restricted to community domestic and ceremonial requirements (see Whittaker 1984). The Mogollon of the Grasshopper region appear to have been self-sufficient in food and raw materials until immediately prior to their abandonment of the mountains.

## Abandonment of the Grasshopper Region

At its peak, probably in the mid-1300s, the people in the Grasshopper region may have been near the maximum carrying capacity for their agricultural technology, and no evidence exists to indicate attempts at agricultural intensification. Defensible locations of several major pueblos, networks of small, butte-top pueblos in defensible positions, as well as the extensive use of cliffs for unobtrusive storage, all suggest an increase in economic and social uncertainty. The correlation of this expansion in settlement pattern with the precipitation regime is suggestive. The most recent dendroclimatological data upon which the construction is based are analyzed by Donald A. Graybill (Reid and Graybill 1984). After a period of ample precipitation extending from A.D. 1300 to A.D. 1325, the Grasshopper region experienced about 30 years of below-average precipitation. Settlement at the satellite community of Canyon Creek in A.D. 1327, preceded by stockpiling construction timbers, points to an anticipation of recurrent environmental changes and a short response time for adjustments to agricultural shortfalls. Increased physiological stress among subadults during the late period of occupation at Grasshopper Pueblo supports an inference of periodic subsistence shortages (Hinkes 1983).

Around A.D. 1400, the Mogollon occupation of the mountains came to an end. The threads of continuity that run throughout Mogollon prehistory, even through the pueblo building era, become vague and the traces of their movement difficult to follow. Erik Reed (1949, 1950) has discussed similarities between historic pueblo groups and the Mogollon, suggesting movement to Hopi, Zuni, and the Rio Grande. The evidence is only suggestive at this point. Experimentation with alternative subsistence and organizational forms was played against the background of an environment that was agriculturally limited, one not heavily farmed today. One suspects that these experiments in living continued until it was generally recognized by a growing population that the central mountains of Arizona were ill suited to dependable agriculture, at which time the Mogollon moved away.

The Mogollon always hunted, and from the amount of animal bone recovered, we presume them to have been skilled. They were not given to flamboyant displays of projectile point artistry, preferring in the post-A.D. 1000 period small triangular points manufactured by the thousands. Late Mogollon settlements yield vastly more projectile points and deer bone than contemporaneous settlements in the desert or the plateau. Since the technology of the hunt was also that of warfare, one suspects the Mogollon to have been a potentially disturbing presence for neighbors disposed to more sedentary, agricultural pursuits. From the mountains the Mogollon moved where they pleased. In any event, the mountain homeland was abandoned, never to be occupied again by large pueblo communities.

## ACKNOWLEDGMENTS

The University of Arizona Archaeological Field School at Grasshopper continues through the cooperation and encouragement of the White Mountain Apache Tribal Council. The analysis of Grasshopper data presented here was supported in part by a grant from the National Science Foundation (BNS 74–23724–A01) to the author. Information on the Q Ranch region was collected as part of Cholla Project contract research sponsored by Arizona Public Service Company through the Arizona State Museum. Valuable comments were provided by Jeffery S. Dean, Keith W. Kintigh, Barbara K. Montgomery, William J. Robinson, Michael B. Schiffer, H. David Tuggle, and Stephanie M. Whittlesey.

## REFERENCES

Anyon, Roger
    1984    *Mogollon Settlement Patterns and Communal Architecture.* Unpublished M.A. thesis. Department of Anthropology, University of New Mexico.

Anyon, Roger, Patricia A. Gilman, and Steven A. LeBlanc
    1981    A Reevaluation of the Mogollon-Mimbres Archaeological Sequence. *The Kiva* 46(4):209–225.

Anyon, Roger, and Steven A. LeBlanc
    1980      The Architectural Evolution of Mogollon-Mimbres Communal Structures. *The Kiva* 45(3):253–277.

Breternitz, David A.
    1959      *Excavations at Nantack Village, Point of Pines, Arizona.* Anthropological Papers of the University of Arizona 1.

Carlson, Roy L.
    1970      *White Mountain Redware: A Pottery Tradition of East-central Arizona and Western New Mexico.* Anthropological Papers of the University of Arizona 19.

Cartledge, Thomas R.
    1976      Prehistory in Vosberg Valley, Central Arizona. *The Kiva* 42(1):95–104.
    1977      *Human Ecology and Changing Patterns of Co-residence in the Vosberg Locality, Tonto National Forest, Central Arizona.* USDA Forest Service Southwestern Region Cultural Resources Report 17.

Ciolek-Torrello, Richard S.
    1978      *A Statistical Analysis of Activity Organization, Grasshopper Pueblo, Arizona.* Ph.D. dissertation, University of Arizona. University Microfilms, Ann Arbor.
    1984      An Alternative Model of Room Function from Grasshopper Pueblo, Arizona. In *Intrasite Spatial Analysis in Archaeology,* edited by Harold Hietala, pp. 127–153. Cambridge University Press, New York.
    1985      A Typology of Room Function at Grasshopper Pueblo, Arizona. *Journal of Field Archaeology* 12:41–63.

Ciolek-Torrello, Richard S., and Richard C. Lange
    1979      The Q Ranch Study Area. In *An Archaeological Survey of the Cholla-Saguaro Transmission Corridor,* Vol. 1, assembled by L. S. Teague and L. L. Mayro, pp. 109–174. Arizona State Museum Archaeological Series 135.

Ciolek-Torrello, Richard S., and J. Jefferson Reid
    1974      Change in Household Size at Grasshopper. *The Kiva* 40(1–2):39–47.

Cordell, Linda S.
    1984a    Southwestern Archaeology. *Annual Review of Anthropology* 13:301–332.
    1984b    *Prehistory of the Southwest.* Academic Press, New York.

Crown, Patricia L.
    1981      *Variability in Ceramic Manufacture at the Chodistaas Site East-central Arizona.* Ph.D. dissertation, University of Arizona. University Microfilms, Ann Arbor.

Dean, Jeffrey S.
    1988      The View from the North: An Anasazi Perspective on the Mogollon. *The Kiva* 53(2):197–199.

Dean, Jeffrey S., and William J. Robinson
    1982      Dendrochronology of Grasshopper Pueblo. In *Multidisciplinary Research at Grasshopper Pueblo, Arizona,* edited by W. A. Longacre, S. J. Holbrook, and M. W. Graves, pp. 46–60. Anthropological Papers of the University of Arizona 40.

Decker, Kenneth W.
1986    Isotopic and Chemical Reconstruction of Diet and its Biological and Social Dimensions at Grasshopper Pueblo, Arizona. Paper presented at the 1986 meeting of the Society for American Archaeology, New Orleans.

Eighmy, Jeffrey L.
1979    Logistic Trends in Southwest Population Growth. In *Transformations: Mathematical Approaches to Culture Change,* edited by C. Renfrew and K. L. Cooke, pp. 205–220. Academic Press, New York.

Gladwin, Harold S.
1936    Discussion. In *An Archaeological Survey in Chihuahua, Mexico,* by E. B. Sayles, pp. 89–105. Medallion Papers 22.

Goodwin, Grenville
1942    *The Social Organization of the Western Apache.* University of Arizona Press, Tucson.

Graves, Michael W.
1982    Anomalous Tree-ring Dates and the Sequence of Room Construction at Canyon Creek Ruin, East-central Arizona. *The Kiva* 47(3):107–131.
1983    Growth and Aggregation at Canyon Creek Ruin: Implications for Evolutionary Change in East-central Arizona. *American Antiquity* 48(2):290–315.

Graves, Michael W., Sally J. Holbrook, and William A. Longacre
1982    Aggregation and Abandonment at Grasshopper Pueblo: Evolutionary Trends in the Late Prehistory of East-central Arizona. In *Multidisciplinary Research at Grasshopper Pueblo, Arizona,* edited by W. A. Longacre, S. J. Holbrook, and M. W. Graves, pp. 110–121. Anthropological Papers of the University of Arizona 40.

Graves, Michael W., William A. Longacre, and Sally J. Holbrook
1982    Aggregation and Abandonment at Grasshopper Pueblo, Arizona. *Journal of Field Archaeology* 9:193–206.

Graybill, Donald A., and J. Jefferson Reid
1982    A Cluster Analysis of Chipped Stone Tools. In *Cholla Project Archaeology: Introduction and Special Studies,* edited by J. J. Reid, pp. 47–50. Arizona State Museum Archaeological Series 161(1).

Griffin, P. Bion
1967    A High Status Burial from Grasshopper Ruin, Arizona. *The Kiva* 33(2):37–53.

Haury, Emil W.
1934    *The Canyon Creek Ruin and the Cliff Dwellings of the Sierra Ancha.* Medallion Papers 14.
1936    *The Mogollon Culture of Southwestern New Mexico.* Medallion Papers 20.
1940    Excavations in the Forestdale Valley, East-central Arizona. *University of Arizona Bulletin* 11(4), *Social Science Bulletin* 12.
1943    A Possible Cochise-Mogollon-Hohokom Sequence. *Proceedings of the American Philosophical Society* 86(2):260–263.
1957    An Alluvial Site on the San Carlos Indian Reservation, Arizona. *American Antiquity* 23(1):2–27.

1958 Evidence at Point of Pines for a Prehistoric Migration from Northern Arizona. In *Migrations in New World Culture History*, edited by R. H. Thompson, pp. 1–6. University of Arizona Social Science Bulletin 27.

1985 *Mogollon Culture in the Forestdale Valley, East-Central Arizona.* University of Arizona Press, Tucson.

1988 Recent Thoughts on the Mogollon. *The Kiva* 53(2):195–196.

Haury, Emil W., and Edwin B. Sayles
1947 An early pit house village of the Mogollon Culture, Forestdale Valley, Arizona. *University of Arizona Bulletin* 18(4), *Social Sciences Bulletin* 16.

Hinkes, Madeleine J.
1983 *Skeletal Evidence of Stress in Subadults: Trying to Come of Age at Grasshopper Pueblo.* Ph.D. dissertation, University of Arizona. University Microfilms, Ann Arbor.

Holbrook, Sally J., and Michael W. Graves
1982 Modern Environment of the Grasshopper Region. In *Multidisciplinary Research at Grasshopper Pueblo, Arizona*, edited by W. A. Longacre, S. J. Holbrook, and M. W. Graves, pp. 5–11. Anthropological Papers of the University of Arizona 40.

Johnson, Alfred E.
1965 *The Development of the Western Pueblo Culture.* Ph.D. dissertation, University of Arizona. University Microfilms, Ann Arbor.

Johnson, Gregory A.
1983 Decision-making Organization and Pastoral Nomad Camp Size. *Human Ecology* 11(2):175–199.

n.d. *System Scale and Decision-making Organization: Implications for Ethnology and Archaeology.* Proceedings of the Second USSR-USA Archaeological Symposium.

Jorgensen, Joseph G.
1980 *Western Indians.* Freeman, San Francisco.

Kintigh, Keith W.
1985 *Settlement, Subsistence, and Society in Late Zuni Prehistory.* Anthropological Papers of the University of Arizona 44.

LeBlanc, Steven A.
1983 *The Mimbres People.* Thames and Hudson, London.

Lightfoot, Kent G.
1984 *The Duncan Project: A Study of the Occupation Duration and Settlement Pattern of an Early Mogollon Pithouse Village.* Arizona State University Anthropological Field Studies 6.

Lister, Robert H.
1958 *Archaeological Excavations in the Northern Sierra Madre Occidental, Chihuahua, and Sonora Mexico.* University of Colorado Studies, Series in Anthropology 7.

Longacre, William A.
1975 Population Dynamics at the Grasshopper Pueblo, Arizona. In *Population Studies in Archaeology and Biological Anthropology: A Sympo-*

sium, edited by A. C. Swedlund. *Society for American Archaeology, Memoir* 30:71–74.

1976    Population Dynamics at the Grasshopper Pueblo, Arizona. In *Demographic Anthropology: Quantitative Approaches*, edited by E. B. W. Zubrow, pp. 169–184. University of New Mexico Press, School of American Research Advanced Seminar Series, Albuquerque.

Longacre, William A., Sally J. Holbrook, and Michael W. Graves (editors)
1982    *Multidisciplinary Research at Grasshopper Pueblo, Arizona.* Anthropological Papers of the University of Arizona 40.

Lowell, Julie C.
1986    *The Structure and Function of the Prehistoric Household in the Pueblo Southwest: A Case Study from Turkey Creek Pueblo.* Ph.D. dissertation, University of Arizona. University Microfilms, Ann Arbor.

Martin, Paul Sidney
1940    *The SU Site: Excavations of a Mogollon Village, Western New Mexico, 1939.* Field Museum of Natural History Anthropology Series 32(1).

1943    *The SU Site, Excavations at a Mogollon Village, Western New Mexico. Second Season, 1941.* Field Museum of Natural History Anthropology Series 32(2).

1979    Prehistory: Mogollon. In *Handbook of North American Indians*, vol. 9, Southwest, edited by A. Ortiz, pp. 61–74. W.G. Sturtevant, general editor. Smithsonian Institution, Washington, D.C.

Martin, Paul S., and John B. Rinaldo
1947    *The SU Site, Excavations at a Mogollon Village, Western New Mexico. Third Season, 1946.* Field Museum of Natural History Anthropology Series 32(3).

Martin, Paul S., John B. Rinaldo, and Ernst Antevs
1949    Cochise and Mogollon Sites, Pine Lawn Valley, Western New Mexico. *Fieldiana: Anthropology* 38(1).

Mayro, Linda L., Stephanie M. Whittlesey, and J. Jefferson Reid
1976    Observations on the Salado Presence at Grasshopper Pueblo. *The Kiva* 42(1):85–94.

Morris, Donald H.
1970    Walnut Creek Village: A Ninth-Century Hohokam-Anasazi Settlement in the Mountains of Central Arizona. *American Antiquity* 35(1):49–61.

Olsen, John W.
1980    *A Zooarchaeological Analysis of Vertebrate Faunal Remains from the Grasshopper Pueblo, Arizona.* Ph.D. dissertation, University of California, Berkeley. University Microfilms, Ann Arbor.

Plog, Fred
1983    Political and Economic Alliances on the Colorado Plateaus, A.D. 400–1450. In *Advances in World Archaeology*, edited by Fred Wendorf, pp. 289–330. Academic Press, New York.

Reed, Erik K.
1942    Implications of the Mogollon Concept. *American Antiquity* 8(1):27–32.
1946    The Distinctive Features and Distribution of the San Juan Anasazi Culture. *Southwestern Journal of Anthropology* 2(3):295–305.

1948a    The Dating of Early Mogollon Horizons. *El Palacio* 55(12):382–387.
1948b    The Western Pueblo Archaeological Complex. *El Palacio* 55(1):9–15.
1949    Sources of Upper Rio Grande Pueblo Culture and Population. *El Palacio* 56(6):163–184.
1950    Eastern-central Arizona archaeology in Relation to the Western Pueblos. *Southwestern Journal of Anthropology* 6(2):120–138.
1956    Types of Village-Plan Layouts in the Southwest. In *Prehistoric Settlement Patterns in the New World,* edited by Gordon R. Willey, pp. 11–17. Viking Fund Publications in Anthropology 23.

Reid, J. Jefferson
1973    *Growth and Response to Stress at Grasshopper Pueblo, Arizona.* Ph.D. dissertation, University of Arizona. University Microfilms, Ann Arbor.
1978    Response to Stress at Grasshopper Pueblo, Arizona. In *Discovering Past Behavior: Experiments in the Archaeology of the American Southwest,* edited by Paul Grebinger, pp. 195–228. Gordon and Breach, New York.
1986    Historical Perspective on the Concept of Mogollon. In *Mogollon Variability,* edited by Charlotte Benson and Steadman Upham, pp. 1–8. New Mexico State University Museum Occasional Papers 15.

Reid, J. Jefferson, and David E. Doyel (editors)
1986    *Emil W. Haury's Prehistory of the American Southwest.* University of Arizona Press, Tucson.

Reid, J. Jefferson, and Donald A. Graybill
1984    Paleoclimate and Human Behavior in the Grasshopper Region, Arizona. Paper presented at the 1984 meeting of the Society for American Archaeology, Portland.

Reid, J. Jefferson, and Izumi Shimada
1982    Pueblo Growth at Grasshopper: Methods and Models. In *Multidisciplinary Research at Grasshopper Pueblo, Arizona,* edited by W. A. Longacre, S. J. Holbrook, and M. W. Graves, pp. 12–18. Anthropological Papers of the University of Arizona 40.

Reid, J. Jefferson, and Stephanie M. Whittlesey
1982    Households at Grasshopper Pueblo. *American Behavioral Scientist* 25(6):687–703.

Reynolds, William E.
1981    *The Ethnoarchaeology of Pueblo Architecture.* Ph.D. dissertation, Arizona State University. University Microfilms, Ann Arbor.

Rice, Glen E.
1980    An Analytical Overview of the Mogollon Tradition. In *Studies in the Prehistory of the Forestdale Region, Arizona,* edited by C. R. Stafford and G. E. Rice, pp. 9–40. Arizona State University Anthropological Field Studies 1.

Rose, Martin
1980    A Topographic-Climatological Summary of the Corduroy Creek area. In *Studies in the Prehistory of the Forestdale Region, Arizona,* edited by C. R. Stafford and G. E. Rice, pp. 374–424. Arizona State University Anthropological Field Studies 1.

Sayles, Edwin B.
   1936    *An Archaeological Survey of Chihuahua, Mexico.* Medallion Papers 22. Globe.

Speth, John D.
   1988    Do We Need Concepts Like "Mogollon," "Anasazi," and "Hohokam" Today? A Cultural Anthropological Perspective. *The Kiva* 53(2):201–204.

Tuggle, H. David
   1970    *Prehistoric Community Relationships in East-central Arizona.* Ph.D. dissertation, University of Arizona. University Microfilm, Ann Arbor.

   1982    Settlement Patterns in the Q Ranch Region. In *Cholla Project Archaeology: the Q Ranch Region,* edited by J. J. Reid, pp. 151–175. Arizona State Museum Archaeological Series 161(3).

Tuggle, H. David, Keith W. Kintigh, and J. Jefferson Reid
   1982    Trace-element Analysis of White Wares. In *Cholla Project Archaeology: Ceramic Studies,* edited by J. J. Reid, pp. 22–38. Arizona State Museum Archaeological Series 161(5).

Tuggle, H. David, and J. Jefferson Reid
   1982    Cross-Dating Cibola White Wares. In *Cholla Project Archaeology: Ceramic Studies,* edited by J. J. Reid, pp. 8–17. Arizona State Museum Archaeological Series 161(5).

Tuggle, H. David, J. Jefferson Reid, and Robert C. Cole, Jr.
   1984    Fourteenth Century Mogollon Agriculture in the Grasshopper Region of Arizona. In *Prehistoric Agricultural Strategies in the Southwest,* edited by S. F. Fish and P. R. Fish, pp. 101–110. Arizona State University Anthropological Research Papers 33.

Upham, Steadman
   1982    *Polities and Power: An Economic and Political History of the Western Pueblo.* Academic Press, New York.

Upham, Steadman, Kent G. Lightfoot, and Gary M. Feinman
   1981    Explaining Socially Determined Ceramic Distributions in the Prehistoric Plateau Southwest. *American Antiquity* 46(4):822–833.

Wendorf, Fred
   1950    A Report on the Excavation of a Small Ruin Near Point of Pines, East-central Arizona. *University of Arizona Bulletin* 21(3), *Social Science Bulletin* 19.

Wheat, Joe Ben
   1954    Crooked Ridge Village. *University of Arizona Bulletin* 25(3), *Social Science Bulletin* 24.

   1955    Mogollon Culture Prior to A.D. 1000. *Memoirs of the American Anthropological Association* 82, *Memoirs of the Society for American Archaeology* 10.

Wheeler, Jane A.
   1981    Chodistaas Site Petrographic Analysis of Sherds. In *Variability in Ceramic Manufacture at the Chodistaas Site, East-central Arizona,* by Patricia L. Crown, pp. 405–435. Ph.D. dissertation, University of Arizona. University Microfilms, Ann Arbor.

Whittaker, John C.
  1984    *Arrowheads and Artisans: Stone Tool Manufacture and Individual Variation at Grasshopper Pueblo.* Ph.D. dissertation, University of Arizona. University Microfilms, Ann Arbor.

Whittlesey, Stephanie M.
  1974    Identification of Imported Ceramics Through Functional Analysis of Attributes. *The Kiva* 40(1–2):101–112.
  1978    *Status and Death at Grasshopper Pueblo: Experiments Toward an Archaeological Theory of Correlates.* Ph.D. dissertation, University of Arizona. University Microfilms, Ann Arbor.
  1982    Examination of Previous Work in the Q Ranch Region: Comparison and Analysis. In *Cholla Project Archaeology: The Q Ranch Region,* edited by J. J. Reid, pp. 123–150. Arizona State Museum Archaeological Series 161(3).
  1984    Uses and Abuses of Mogollon Mortuary Data. In *Recent Research in Mogollon Archaeology,* edited by Steadman Upham, Fred Plog, David G. Batcho, and Barbara E. Kauffman, pp. 276–284. New Mexico State University Museum Occasional Papers 10.

Whittlesey, Stephanie M., and J. Jefferson Reid
  1982    Cholla Project Settlement Summary. In *Cholla Project Archaeology: Introduction and Special Studies,* edited by J. J. Reid, pp. 205–216. Arizona State Museum Archaeological Series 161(1).

Wilcox, David R.
  1988    Rethinking the Mogollon Concept. *The Kiva* 53(2):205–209.

Wood, J. Scott
  1980    The Gentry Timber Sale: Behavioral Patterning and Predictability in the Upper Cherry Creek Area, Central Arizona. *The Kiva* 16(1–2): 99–119.

GEORGE J. GUMERMAN AND
JEFFREY S. DEAN 4

# Prehistoric Cooperation and Competition in the Western Anasazi Area

## INTRODUCTION

Archaeologists' perception of the character of Anasazi society has changed dramatically in the last five years. Oddly, this is not so much in response to new data, although there are a great deal of those, as it is to new ways of looking at the data.

The 1960s and early 1970s in Anasazi archaeology were devoted to the development of local sequences. This was in large part a result of increasing knowledge about local variation. In addition, there was frustration over the inability to structure local developmental sequences into the Pecos Classification stages and the geographical divisions based on the major drainage systems, largely unchanged since Kidder's (1924, 1927) formulations.

Traditional temporal and spatial categories have been deemed inadequate for years (Martin and Plog 1973; F. Plog 1981), and pleas have been made for schemes that permit the use of continuous rather than categorical measurements. Unfortunately, in very few localities is either the chronological control or the understanding of behavioral nuances and environmental perturbations sufficiently detailed to structure a continuous dynamic model. The result of the construction of local sequences was a tendency to view the Anasazi area as made up of discrete, relatively autonomous social and economic entities that changed periodically at what are considered phase boundaries.

Somewhat in reaction to this discrete temporal and spatial packaging have been recent attempts to demonstrate that the Anasazi engaged in large-scale social and economic interaction, which included economic interdependence and, in some cases, complex political organization and social ranking (Lightfoot and Feinman 1982; F. Plog 1983b; Upham, Lightfoot, and Feinman 1981; Upham 1982). While these scholars have addressed the excesses of past parochial views, we suggest they may be erring in the opposite direction. There was, as many chemical, physical, and stylistic analyses indicate, much greater interaction and information flow among localities than previously supposed; however, this was not necessarily accomplished through an elite class, a hierarchical social system, or even a formally organized network.

We contend that (1) the Anasazi were for the most part egalitarian, except for short periods in certain areas; (2) minute social, technological, and demographic adjustments were made partly in response to spatial and temporal changes in the natural environment; (3) these adjustments, sometimes over a distance of only a few kilometers, produced variations on the Anasazi pattern that are much more localized and distinctive than previously realized; (4) interaction networks expanded and contracted, and cooperation and competition between localities increased and decreased depending, in part, on demography and on spatial and temporal patterning of the environment; (5) cooperation between social entities and relative absence of environmental circumscription hindered the development of more complex socially hierarchical forms; and (6) the generally egalitarian nature of Anasazi societies was partially responsible for the persistence of the culture for some two millennia. If these propositions are correct, the Anasazi concept should be reevaluated.

The main thrust of this paper is that the basic behavioral mechanism of Anasazi adaptation is cooperation (Fig. 12). Cooperation is effected by the coordination of activities and the flow of information, sometimes restricted, sometimes faulty, which conditions decision making. This coordination can be accomplished through one of several levels of social organization: egalitarianism, ranking, or stratification, which may represent a continuum of variation rather than discrete categories. In addition, social interaction involving phenomena such as exchange, the development of cultural boundaries, and other kinds of information flow facilitates adaptation.

This scheme provides a framework for understanding the connectivity and interaction of horizontally organized social entities. Change in the system results from changing relationships among behavioral, demographic, and environmental variables (Dean 1988; Dean et al. 1985). When change in any

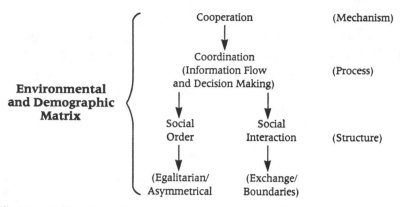

Fig. 12. *A model for the mechanism, process, and structure by which the Anasazi adapted to environmental and demographic variation.*

component of the system crosses a systemic boundary, it triggers major adaptive change in other components. These transformations make certain information obsolete and may require changes in the intensity and form of cooperation and competition, in the nature of the social order, and in the rate, direction, and form of social interaction.

## Cooperation and Competition

Our theoretical stance is that in the heterogeneous but relatively uncircumscribed environment of the Colorado Plateaus there is a distinct adaptive advantage to behavior that (1) initiates and reciprocates cooperation; (2) provokes easily and quickly retaliates against aggressive behavior; and (3) forgives aggressive behavior after retaliation. This proposition runs counter to the common anthropological belief that conflict, warfare, and inequality are in large part the cause of, or co-occur with, social ranking and stratified societies (R. Adams 1975; Carneiro 1970, 1978; Haas 1982). It does appear that stratified, aggressive societies tend to coincide with the development of chiefdoms and the pristine state; therefore, ranking, stratification, and aggressive behavior are seen as attributes of these evolutionary stages. While these stages are conceived as advances in evolutionary form, however, individual societies within them are usually unstable and fall to competing entities. As Wright (1977:385) has observed, chiefdoms and simpler states exist in networks ever-changing in scale, intensity, and direction regulated by competition and alliance. It cannot be assumed, however, that in the absence of systemic circumscription, nonegalitarian societies are in the long run more evolutionarily "fit," or that chiefdoms or states based on political centralization, warfare, and competition for resources necessarily have adaptive characteristics superior to those of more egalitarian or tribal entities. In fact, just the opposite may be the case.

Adaptation based on cooperation as opposed to competition has been studied using game theory and computer simulation based on the iterated Prisoner's Dilemma game, which models ecological adaptation (Axelrod and Hamilton 1981; Axelrod 1983). A strategy that combined cooperation with other entities, retribution when acted against, followed by a rapid return to cooperative behavior proved most successful against competing strategies when run for a great many generations of encounters. Interestingly, this cooperation-retribution-cooperation (CRC) strategy did not defeat a single rival in the many generations of encounters that have been run; the best result it produced was a tie, and often it lost to competition by a slight margin. The CRC strategy is successful for the entire system because it elicits behavior that permits *all* strategies to do well. Aggressive strategies that attempt to exploit more cooperative programs often did well for many generations of encounters but, in closed system environments, proved to be self-defeating in the long run. Practitioners of aggressive strategies eventually eliminated the subordinate programs on which they depended for their existence. Thus, the character of the environment in which the game is played is important for understanding the efficacy of a specific adaptive strategy. The CRC strategy's strength is its ability to adapt to a great variety of environments by perpetuating cooperation among a variety of more-or-less equal practitioners (societies).

Lessons from the iterated Prisoner's Dilemma game seem to be especially useful in understanding the long range adaptive stance of the Anasazi, the generally conservative nature of Anasazi culture, and the occasional and short-lived emergence of possibly stratified societies exemplified by complex entities such as the "Chaco Phenomenon."

## Coordination

In order for social entities to cooperate, coordination is necessary. Social systems are in part arenas of interaction that coordinate and disseminate information, usually on a selective basis. Articulation of the constituent parts of the social system depends on information flow about human-human and human-environment interactions that can vary in direction, frequency, and intensity (Johnson 1978; Root 1983). In egalitarian societies, comparatively unrestricted information flow promotes relatively equal access to critical resources with the result that no major economic or political advantage occurs through control of those resources (Fried 1967). Information flow integrates and coordinates components of the social system, and institutionalized social relationships are the channels through which the information flows (Van der Leeuw 1981; Root 1983).

In a heterogeneous environment, such as that of the Western Anasazi area, the unregulated flow of information through institutionalized social relationships would mitigate potential differential access to resources caused by spatial and temporal variability in those resources.

Anthropologists have sometimes assumed that decisions based on received information are made under conditions of omniscient rationality by individuals striving for economic optimization. There has been a widespread failure to recognize that decisions are made in social contexts that may or may not involve economic optimization. As Moore (1983:183) has noted, "In reality, decisions are based on a mix of information, ignorance, error, and lies."

In sum, archaeologists should not expect a one-to-one correspondence between environmental change and human optimizing behavior, even if there is equal access to information and critical resources. However, archaeologists have to assume that coordination and information flow existed on some level, or the society would cease to function.

## THE STUDY AREA

Because the success of a CRC strategy depends in part on the environment, it is important to understand in some detail the natural environment of the study area. The "Western Anasazi" study area corresponds neither to a distinct environmental zone nor to a single previously described "culture" zone. The study area extends from Chinle Wash to southern Nevada and includes southern Utah and Arizona as far south as the Little Colorado River. Named cultural manifestations grouped under the Western Anasazi rubric include the Kayenta, Tusayan, Winslow, and Virgin branches (Fig. 13). Western Anasazi extends in time from Basketmaker II, which began around 500 B.C., to the Hopi villages occupied during the Spanish Entrada.

Archaeologists have given differential treatment to the study area. The cultural and natural data base for northeastern Black Mesa is unparalleled in the Southwest. Intensive work in the Glen Canyon area provides considerable detail for the northern and western parts of the Kayenta district. Less well known are the Tusayan and Winslow branches, with little recent work having been done there. The Virgin branch currently is receiving much attention by a number of investigators. These regional traditions are used as referents for describing the study area. Because of the spotty nature of both

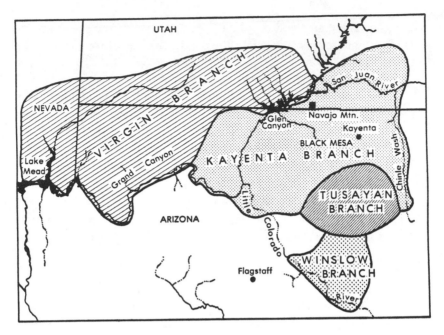

*Fig. 13. Local traditions in the Western Anasazi region.*

the cultural and environmental records, our discussion is focused mostly on the Kayenta, Tusayan, and Winslow branches.

The value of the area for the purposes of this study is that the scale of social integration ranges from small, relatively independent farmsteads to communities composed of many functionally differentiated components. The study area, however, does not include regional systems of the scale exemplified by that centered on Chaco Canyon. The relatively low level of complexity in the western area may color our interpretation of social scale throughout the Colorado Plateaus. On the other hand, this view counterbalances the tendency to overestimate Anasazi social complexity that naturally arises from a focus on Chaco Canyon and the more complex aspects of Mesa Verde.

## THE WESTERN ANASAZI

"Western Anasazi" comprises at least three archaeologically recognizable and geographically circumscribed variants of the Anasazi cultural tradition. Ceramic technology (clays, temper, firing atmosphere, color of slip, and pigment medium) and design styles distinguish the Western Anasazi from other Anasazi manifestations and differentiate the Western Anasazi variants from one another. Architectural differences among Anasazi subtraditions are less definitive because of considerable overlap in the ranges of variability. In general, Western Anasazi architecture tends to be less massive, spectacular, and esthetically pleasing than that of the Chaco and Mesa Verde branches. Western Anasazi sites are smaller, less formally structured, and less internally differentiated than those of their eastern counterparts.

In addition to the material attributes that set the Western Anasazi apart are more inferential divergences. Differences in the scale and configuration of settlement and community patterning, in social organizational scale and complexity, and in range and intensity of interaction with other populations attest to the simpler sociocultural attainments of the Western Anasazi. While Jennings's (1966:63) characterization of the Kayenta branch peoples as "backwoods Anasazi" may be somewhat extreme, it does convey the lesser complexity and elaboration of the Western Anasazi. Nevertheless, the time depth and geographic extent of Western Anasazi archaeological materials reflect successful adaptations to extensive, varied, and harsh congeries of habitats. Perhaps simplicity and adherence to the basics of survival underlay these adaptive attainments.

The Tusayan branch on southern Black Mesa (Fig. 14) is distinguished from the Kayenta branch largely on the basis of minor technological differences in ceramics, and for most purposes the two can be combined. We retain the distinction here merely for the sake of geographical specificity. The Virgin branch, which is not recognizable much before A.D. 500 and lasts until around 1150, appears to be an attenuated version of the Kayenta branch. Ceramic technology and generally small sites that appear to lack kivas differentiate the Virgin branch from the Kayenta–Tusayan and Winslow branches. The Winslow branch of the Little Colorado Desert, which is recognizable from about A.D. 1000 to 1250, has a distinctive tradition of ceramic technology and design and is architecturally different in the occurrence of distinctive pithouse forms, of a central ceremonial center, and, late in the sequence, of extremely large pueblos.

## The Environment of the Western Anasazi Area

The modern environment of the area is as varied as might be expected for so large a region. Space limitations prohibit an exhaustive consideration of this complex topic here. Adequate summaries of the area in general and of various localities within it are provided in the archaeological literature (Dean 1969, 1970; Dean, Lindsay, and Robinson 1978; Gumerman 1986; Jennings 1966; Lindsay 1969; Lindsay, Ambler, Stein, and Hobler 1968; Lipe 1970).

*Fig. 14. Major sites in the vicinity of Black Mesa.*

Environmental conditions varied substantially in response to natural processes that can be characterized as either low or high frequency (Dean 1988; Dean et al. 1985; Gumerman 1988). Low frequency processes (LFP) have periodicities, either regular or irregular, of more than one human generation (approximately 25 years). Such processes are responsible for fluctuations in alluvial groundwater levels, episodes of floodplain aggradation and erosion, and long-term changes in the composition and distribution of plant communities. Low frequency natural processes can cause abrupt and severe environmental transformations, such as the rapid development of integrated arroyo systems, when LFP variability exceeds systemic boundary conditions. Low frequency processes establish the general conditions to which human societies adapt, and LFP regulated environmental conditions probably are perceived as stability by human groups.

High frequency natural processes (HFP) have periodicities of less than 25 years and are responsible, among other things, for seasonal and annual variations in climate and other environmental factors. Such processes determine the environmental variability around long-term "means" established by low frequency processes. Human groups are cognizant of most HFP environmental changes, and many behavioral buffering mechanisms (Clarke 1978:135; Jorde 1977) function to adapt societies to HFP environmental variability.

Intensive chronostratigraphic research on the Colorado Plateaus (Cooley 1962; Euler et al. 1979; Hack 1942; Hevly and Karlstrom 1974; T. Karlstrom 1981; E. Karlstrom 1983) has empirically established the sequence of depositional and erosional changes represented in the aggradation curve (Figure 15A, heavy line), which is extrapolated from data presented by Euler et al. (1979, Figs. 4, 5) and by Dean et al. (1985:Fig. 1). The curve (Figure 15A, light line; Euler et al. 1979, Figs. 4, 5; T. Karlstrom 1981) superimposed on the aggradation curve depicts general trends in alluvial groundwater levels that cause the depositional and erosional events illustrated by the aggradation curve. These fluvial changes are well documented for the Kayenta area and probably apply to the entire Western Anasazi area.

Several different kinds of HFP variability are presented in Figure 15. The amplitude plots of Tsegi Canyon, Black Mesa, Navajo Mountain, and Hopi Mesas tree growth departures (Fig. 15B–E) indicate relative variability in annual precipitation in these localities. The series are plotted in standard deviation units with values lying outside ± 1.1 units considered to be of potential significance for plant, animal, and human populations (Dean 1982). During most periods, all three dendroclimatic records exhibit low temporal variability; that is, transitions from high to low values took place fairly gradually over extended intervals of time. In contrast, the A.D. 750–1000 interval in the Tsegi Canyon and Navajo Mountain areas exhibits high temporal variability; that is, oscillations from high to low values are fairly rapid. This pattern is far less evident in the Black Mesa and Hopi Mesas series. Spatial variability in climate across the Colorado Plateaus (Fig. 15F) has little direct effect on local populations but is an important facilitating variable with regard to interaction among areas (Dean et al. 1985; Plog 1983a; Plog et al. 1988). Local and general demographic trends in the Western Anasazi area (Fig. 15G) are depicted because relative population sizes and densities are major independent variables in the process of adaptive behavioral stability and change.

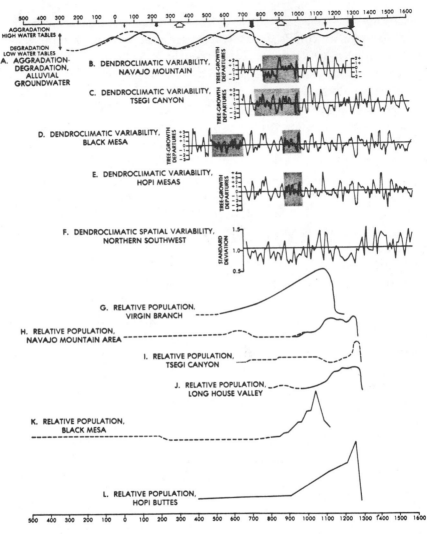

Fig. 15. Environmental and demographic trends in Hopi Country. Nonlobed solid arrows indicate minor LFP environmental stress. Lobed solid arrows indicate major LFP stress. The size of the arrow is proportional to severity as determined by human population. Open upward pointing arrows indicate release of stress (after Euler 1988). Periods of high temporal variability stippled. (A) Alluvial hydrology derived mainly from Black Mesa (Karlstrom 1981); (B) Navajo Mountain dendroclimatic variability; (C) Tsegi Canyon dendroclimatic variability; (D) Black Mesa dendroclimatic variability; (E) Hopi Mesas dendroclimatic variability; (F) Dendroclimatic spatial variability across the Colorado Plateaus (Plog 1983a; Dean et al. 1985); (G) Relative population, Virgin Branch area (Euler 1988); (H) Relative population, Navajo Mountain area (after Ambler et al. 1983); (I) Relative population, Tsegi Canyon; (J) Relative population, Long House Valley; (K) Relative population, Black Mesa (Layhe 1981; S. Plog 1986; Powell and Nichols 1983); (L) Relative population, Hopi Buttes area.

The various kinds of environmental variability illustrated in Figure 15 have different effects on human adaptive behavior depending on their relationships to one another and to human population levels. Behavioral responses to various kinds of environmental variability and archaeological data expectations for the recognition of such responses are delineated elsewhere (Dean et al. 1985; Plog et al. 1988). It is our goal here to consider the degree to which Western Anasazi adaptive behavior conforms to or departs from these expectations.

## Adaptive History of the Western Anasazi A.D. 1–1500

The following discussion is organized chronologically but not in terms of phases or the traditional Pecos Classification periods. Rather, the continuum is treated in terms of successive subsistence-settlement configurations that are thought to represent distinct and persistent patterns of behavioral adaptation to demographic and environmental processes and circumstances. Such "stable" adaptations are not viewed as representing equilibrium in a systemic sense as it seems unlikely that the Western Anasazi ever achieved prolonged equilibrium with their social and physical environments. Too many variables—behavioral, demographic, and environmental—were in continuous flux to permit stable equilibria to develop and persist. As was probably true of other groups on the Colorado Plateaus, the Western Anasazi story is one of nearly continual change in one or more aspects of the adaptive system.

A strong correspondence is evident between the subsistence-settlement configurations of the Western Anasazi sequence and the stages of southwestern prehistory delineated in the initial chapter of this volume. Western Anasazi conformity with regional patterns of development probably is a consequence of three factors: (1) general synchroneity in environmental variability throughout the Southwest; (2) similar traditions of behavioral response to environmental and culture change among southwestern populations; and (3) interactions among the populations of the region. The following discussion of Western Anasazi prehistory, therefore, reflects the regional patterning exemplified in Figure 16.

### Basketmaker II (Initiation): 560 B.C.–A.D. 700
A large number of excavated sites document the BMII occupation of the Western Anasazi area. Earliest are the "classic" rockshelter sites in the Marsh Pass area, which have produced radiocarbon dates on maize that cluster in the first few centuries B.C. Somewhat later are 35 open sites in the interior of Black Mesa that yielded radiocarbon dates placing the bulk of the

| | | Kayenta | Northeastern Black Mesa | Winslow Tradition | Virgin Tradition |
|---|---|---|---|---|---|
| | A.D. 1600 | | | | |
| | A.D. 1500 | | | | |
| Aggregation | A.D. 1400 | | | | |
| | A.D. 1300 | | | | |
| | | Tsegi | | | |
| Reorganization | A.D. 1200 | Transition | | McDonald | |
| | A.D. 1100 | | Toreva | | Mesa House |
| Differentiation | | Pueblo II | Lamoki | Holbrook | |
| | A.D. 1000 | | Wepo | | |
| Expansion | A.D. 900 | Pueblo I | Dinnebito | | Lost City |
| | A.D. 800 | | Tallahogan | | |
| | A.D. 700 | B.M. III | Dot Klish | | |
| | A.D. 600 | | | | |
| | A.D. 500 | | | | |
| Initiation | A.D. 400 | | | | |
| | A.D. 300 | B.M. II | | | |
| | A.D. 200 | | | | |
| | A.D. 100 | | | | |
| | A.D. 1 | | Lolomai | | |

Fig. 16. Stages and phases for the Western Anasazi.

occupation between A.D. 150 and 250. Matson and Lipe (1978) document a BMII occupation of the Cedar Mesa–Grand Gulch area between A.D. 200 and 400. An apparent late third-century site near the north rim of the Grand Canyon is rendered equivocal by the possible association of ceramics with the C-14 dated pithouses (Thompson 1983). A single radiocarbon date of A.D. 435 ± 75 from Tsé Yaa Tsoh (Carlson 1982: 209) and tree-ring dates from Tsé Yaa Tsoh, Mummy Cave (Bannister et al. 1966), the Sonic Boom site, and an unnamed storage site attest to fourth-, fifth-, and sixth-century occupations in the Canyon de Chelly area. Tree-ring dates from Sand Dune Cave near Navajo Mountain (Harlan and Dean 1968:380–381; Lindsay et al. 1968:41) indicate that the BMII lifeway persisted until A.D. 700 in the Western Kayenta branch uplands.

BMII subsistence was based on a mixture of gathering, hunting, and horticulture with emphasis on the components undoubtedly varying with circumstances. Gathering and hunting probably exploited the full range of upland and lowland habitats, while farming probably was concentrated on the aggrading floodplains of lowland and upland drainages. The occurrence of maize at all but one of the dated and excavated Black Mesa BMII sites and at the Marsh Pass rockshelters marks the earliest securely dated maize agriculture on the Colorado Plateaus, with a substantial commitment to agriculture by 600 B.C. This indicates a late dispersal of the crop from Mexico and a rapid spread throughout the Anasazi Southwest (Berry 1982; Ford 1975; Smiley 1985; Smiley and Andrews 1983; Smiley et al. 1986; Wills 1985). Ford (1982, 1984) suggests that the wild plant resources of Black Mesa were too widely dispersed and too unpredictable in yield to support a permanent population, and therefore, the introduction of cultigens made the mesa suitable for permanent occupation. Once farming was accepted on northeastern Black Mesa, the mix of domesticated and gathered products remained relatively constant from around A.D. 100 to the abandonment of the locality about A.D. 1150 with probably a slight increase in the agricultural component after BMII.

In some areas settlement seems to have been seasonal, with fairly substantial winter habitation sites in the uplands (Powell 1983) and summer activity loci in both the uplands and lowlands. Habitation of the Navajo Mountain uplands is evident at Sand Dune Cave (Lindsay et al. 1968:30–101) and is suggested by the presence on Paiute Mesa of surface remains that resemble the circular houses with slab-lined entries excavated by Matson and Lipe (1978:2–6; Berry 1982, Fig. 4) on Cedar Mesa and by Sharrock et al. (1963:151–161) at Lone Tree Dune on Castle Wash. The uplands of the Tsegi–Marsh Pass area have yet to yield much evidence for BMII habitations, although survey in these areas has been sparse. The abundance of such sites on Black Mesa suggests that more will be found in other upland areas. Occupation of topographic lowland localities is documented for the Grand Gulch, Tsegi–Marsh Pass, and Canyon de Chelly areas. Throughout the Western Anasazi area, the aggrading floodplains were avoided for nonsubsistence activities. Although a large number (35) of BMII sites has been excavated, archaeological evidence indicates that population remained low during this period.

Site patterning varies with the function of the activity locus, and a wide variety of settlement types exist (Smiley 1985). Black Mesa habitation sites range from small camps consisting of a hearth and a few artifacts to permanently occupied hamlets consisting of up to a score of shallow pit structures with associated storage pits and other features (Smiley 1985). Many of the rockshelters may have been occupied in connection with farming on nearby floodplains. These sites usually contain outdoor work areas, hearths, "beds" (Kidder and Guernsey 1919:86; Lindsay et al. 1968:41), and numerous slab-lined cists for the storage of agricultural and wild food products and seed stock for future planting. Many of the cists were used secondarily for human interment. Evidence from Three Fir Shelter (Smiley et al. 1986) supports the inference that rockshelters supported a full range of habitation activities in contrast to earlier views on the limited functions of these loci (Kidder and Guernsey 1919; Lockett and Hargrave 1953).

BMII material culture reflects the general lifeway of the people and the function of the sites. The portable and durable nature of containers, hide and twined bags and baskets, is consistent with the degree of mobility inferred for these groups. Food procurement and processing implements specify a gathering-hunting-horticulture subsistence economy. The common occurrence on lowland sites of fist-sized chunks of limestone probably indicates that stone boiling was a common cooking technique. Roasting pits are abundant at sites on Black Mesa.

The archaeological data provide only tantalizing glimpses of BMII social structure and organization. Certainly, the fairly rapid adoption of maize agriculture "generated a whole series of scheduling, labor input, settlement, and demographic possibilities and constraints" (Smiley and Andrews 1983:52), which in turn transformed whatever organizational pattern had characterized the preceding, nonagricultural Archaic period. Replacement of the mobile Archaic subsistence-settlement system with a biseasonal pattern of winter residence in small, fairly permanent communities with summer forays into nearby farming localities undoubtedly required new mechanisms of social integration and control. What these mechanisms were is unknown; however, there is no evidence for the types of community or higher levels of ceremonial organization that developed later on.

BMII burials reveal degrees of "personal wealth" incommensurate with the "egalitarianism" usually inferred for such societies. In fact, these interments possess attributes often taken to indicate status differentials characteristic of the social stratification of tribal and chiefdom levels of organization. In the Western Anasazi area, the richest burials in terms of the quality and quantity of "luxury" goods, such as turquoise and shell ornaments, occur in the BMII period. Furthermore, there seem to be differences within sites and between localities in the amounts of richness of grave goods. The amount of nonutilitarian material interred with individuals seems to decrease from east to west with Canyon de Chelly being a locus of particularly rich burials.

An unusual aspect of BMII culture is indicated by the frequent postinterment removal of heads and long bones from corpses, apparent attempts to protect the heads of the deceased from vandalism (Lockett and Hargrave 1953), by the occurrence in the burial of a young woman of a "scalp" made from the skin of a human head (Kidder and Guernsey 1919:81), and by the common association of fires and burned human bones in BMII burial caves (Lockett and Hargrave 1953; Guernsey and Kidder 1921). It is possible that these somewhat bizarre, though not uncommon, occurrences reflect some sort of witchcraft, a possibility not incongruent with societies of the general level of development of BMII.

Despite the relatively simple nature of the BMII adaptive system, evidence exists for interaction within the area and with nearby areas. The ubiquity on Tsegi–Marsh Pass lowland sites of flakes of a white baked shale that occurs only on Black Mesa (Green 1986) testifies to contact between the populations of these localities. The utilization of lithic raw materials from localized sources, such as the gravels of the San Juan River, indicates interaction among early BMII local groups. Exchange on a broader scale is indicated by the relative abundance of marine shell from the Pacific Ocean and the Gulf of California. In contrast, consistent differences between western BMII and more easterly BMII expressions—such as those in the Durango, Navajo Reservoir, and Chaco areas—bespeak barriers to communication and emphasize the time depth of the schism between the Western and Eastern Anasazi populations.

## Basketmaker III (Initiation): A.D. 550–825

BMIII is fairly well represented in the sample of excavated sites, and survey reveals such sites to be abundant. Canyon and valley sites in the Red Rock (Morris 1980), Chinle (Bannister et al. 1968:67–68), Laguna Creek (Haury 1928), and Klethla (Ambler and Olson 1977) Valleys, in Canyons del Muerto (Morris 1925, 1936) and de Chelly, in Tsegi and Navajo Canyons, along middle reaches of the Tusayan Washes on Black Mesa (Klesert 1982a,

Linford 1982; Ward 1976), and on Antelope (Daifuku 1961) and Second Mesas (Sebastian 1985) provide information on Western Anasazi BMIII. The earliest date for a western BMIII site is A.D. 550 at NA—8163 in the Klethla Valley (Ambler and Olson 1977:6). The earliest dated BMIII structures, however, fall in the 620s, and are located in the Prayer Rock District—Red Rock Valley sites on the eastern periphery of the area (Morris 1980:49—50). Farther west, BMIII dates cluster between A.D. 675 and 825, but whether this apparent temporal disjunction reflects a developmental lag or merely nonrepresentative archaeological sampling is unknown. Population, though growing, remained comparatively low and localized throughout the span of the BMIII adaptive mode.

BMIII subsistence emphasized farming much more than the BMII adaptation, and the settlement pattern reflects a high degree of sedentism attendant on increased farming. A major shift in settlement occurred as essentially permanent habitation sites, many of them quite large, were established along the margins of lowland alluvial floodplains, which had begun aggrading again around A.D. 350 (Fig. 15). Apparently, groundwater farming of the adjacent floodplains was carried out from the permanently occupied settlements. The large number of limited activity sites away from the villages indicates that gathering and hunting had assumed a more logistic mode than had been the case in BMII. The BMIII focus on lowland agriculture is underscored by the fact that the uplands appear to have been virtually abandoned as living areas, although burial in alluvium may obscure such sites. Rock shelters near alluvial bottomlands became the loci of more or less permanent habitation as indicated by the presence of domiciles and storage facilities. Thus, the strong seasonal patterning characteristic of the BMII subsistence-settlement system seems to have given way to year-round residence in medium sized to large hamlets and villages concentrated in more favorable loci—those with deeper alluvium, longer growing seasons, and higher water tables.

Site structure also underwent major changes that reflect increasing sedentism. Domiciles consisted of stone slab-lined pithouses with single or double ventilators and sometimes with antechambers. These houses possess a fairly standard set of floor features including fire and ash pits, low clay ridges delineating functionally specific areas of the floor, small intramural storage pits, and sometimes grinding equipment. Commonly, one to three circular slab-lined storage cists were set into the ground behind each pithouse. These pithouse-cist units were organized into "villages" that ranged from fewer than five to scores of such units. The larger sites were formally structured, the domestic units laid out according to topographic features or arranged in parallel rows. Apart from a problematic feature in

Broken Flute Cave on the eastern margin of the area (Morris 1980:40–41), the Juniper Cove site (Cummings 1953; Haury 1928) near Marsh Pass possesses the only "great kiva" known for the western area, a structure that probably served several nearby communities in addition to Juniper Cove itself.

BMIII artifact assemblages also reflect greater residential permanence than that existing during BMII times. Ceramic vessels augmented or supplanted baskets as containers. The common occurrence of limestone chunks on BMIII sites indicates the survival of stone boiling, whether in baskets or pots. The bow replaced the atlatl as the primary projectile delivery implement, and the skill and care lavished on the production of stone arrow points attests to a continuing heavy reliance on hunting.

Western BMIII populations maintained wide contacts both within the area and with groups in other parts of the Colorado Plateaus. Continued general reliance on a few localized lithic raw material sources testifies to exchange or visitation within the area. The importation of marine shell indicates long distance trade relationships similar to those of the BMII period. In addition, Western Anasazi populations were involved in the general adoption of ceramics, bows and arrows, stone axes, and pithouse architecture that characterized the transition to BMIII throughout the Plateaus. Western Anasazi potters also participated in the widespread Lino style of painted ceramic decoration, although this stylistic horizon could be due more to the application of technologically determined basketry designs to pottery than to the direct sharing of ceramic design principles. The construction by several eastern BMIII groups of "great houses" or "great kivas" may represent interaction with the Mogollon area where such structures have a much longer history. If this phenomenon represents the adoption by the Anasazi of a Mogollon pattern of intervillage ceremonial organization, it was a localized and ephemeral experiment among the Western Anasazi.

Habitation site size and configuration indicate a fairly high level of social organization. Individual residential units, consisting of a pithouse and associated storage facilities, were integrated into large villages, which, in one locality, were organized into a multisettlement community through participation in great kiva ceremonialism. The sedentism promoted by reliance on horticulture under favorable environmental conditions undoubtedly fostered the degree of social integration evidenced by BMIII sites.

## Pueblo I (Initiation): A.D. 825–1000

Recent excavations on Black Mesa (Nichols and Smiley 1984) flesh out an incomplete picture of lowland PI in the Western Anasazi area. Although PI sites are abundant in the lowlands, only a few have been excavated, most notably in the Laguna Creek Valley (Bannister et al. 1968:64–5; Taylor 1954). The initial date of A.D. 825 for the PI pattern is based on tree-ring dates from NA-8300, a site near Kayenta (Bannister et al. 1966:64–65) where bowls with Kana-a Black-on-white designs on the interior and Lino Black-on-gray designs on the exterior occur. The terminal date is derived from sites where both Kana-a and Black Mesa Black-on-white sherds appear together. A number of sites on Black Mesa that conform to the PI pattern have produced tree-ring dates between these extremes with a strong cluster in the A.D. 840–900 range. The number and apparent size of PI sites indicate a substantial increase in population over that of the BMIII period.

Clearly, the PI adaptive pattern is a continuation and elaboration of the BMIII pattern. Subsistence remained firmly anchored in farming, even though gathering and the hunting of large and small game remained important. Settlement continued to be concentrated along lowland drainages, especially in the Tsegi–Marsh Pass locality; however, increasing permanent occupation of villages adjacent to major upland drainages is evident on Black Mesa (S. Plog 1984), probably as a result of range expansion due to population growth. On Black Mesa, limited activity sites are situated close to secondary drainages in upland wooded zones. In sharp contrast to the BMIII avoidance of the floodplains, PI villages both in the lowlands and on Black Mesa (Gumerman, Westfall, and Weed 1972:37–46) occur on or adjacent to the floodplains of major drainages. Agglomeration into sizable communities on the lowland floodplains probably reflects increased dependence on farming combined with the restriction of farmland and stabilization of alluvial surfaces caused by low groundwater levels and arroyo development (Fig. 15A). PI habitation sites are rare in uplands other than Black Mesa, although limited activity sites do occur in these localities.

Site structure is difficult to comprehend due to the large size of the sites and to the fact that many of them are buried beneath seven or more meters of alluvium. PI pithouses are similar to their BMIII counterparts in possessing single and double ventilator complexes and a comparable range of floor features and artifacts. They differ in their lack of antechambers. PI pithouses are accompanied by surface storage facilities—circular slab-lined cists or rectangular jacal, slab-lined, or masonry rooms—and outdoor work areas. PI sites *seem* less highly structured than BMIII sites, but this impression may be a function of sampling deficiencies. If PI villages were integrated into larger communities, it apparently was by some mechanism other than "great kiva" ceremonialism, for these structures are absent from PI sites. In fact, no PI ceremonial structures have yet been identified in the Western Anasazi area.

PI material culture is virtually identical to that of the BMIII period, although ceramic and projectile point manufacturing procedures and styles are different. The quality of PI projectile points bespeaks the continuing importance of large game hunting during this period. The absence of limestone chunks from PI sites probably marks the demise of stone boiling as a food preparation technique.

Local and regional interchange played important roles in the PI adaptive system. Marine shells and shell artifacts attest to the perpetuation of the extraregional interaction and exchange networks that had existed in BMII and BMIII times. Exotic chipped stone raw materials and trade pottery denote resource procurement in other areas as well as exchange with the inhabitants of these areas (Green 1986). Similarly, large amounts of San Juan Red Ware pottery were imported from southeastern Utah or southwestern Colorado into the Tsegi–Marsh Pass–Black Mesa area (Hantman and Plog 1982).

Western Anasazi potters participated in the Kana-a (or Red Mesa) style of ceramic design that specifies interaction among the ninth- and tenth-century populations of the Colorado Plateaus. S. Plog (1984) suggests that the apparent extent of PI exchange systems may reflect a need for expanded marriage networks among localities with low populations, although the Black Mesa trade network seems too extensive for this purpose alone. At the same time, the characteristic isolation of Western Anasazi populations from other southwestern groups continued. At the time western PI people were living in pithouse villages, their Mesa Verde and Chaco counterparts, by and large, inhabited surface pueblos. It is instructive to remember that around A.D. 900, when the Western Anasazi PI manifestation was at its peak, Pueblo Bonito was already in existence.

## Pueblo II (Expansion): A.D. 1000–1150

Many Western Anasazi sites representative of the PII pattern have been excavated, and their temporal range is securely dated dendrochronologically. The large number and ubiquitous distribution of PII sites testify to an increased and growing population. During this period population levels and densities probably reached magnitudes sufficient to affect adaptive behavior throughout the entire area. In some upland areas, notably Black Mesa (Gumerman and Euler 1976; S. Plog 1986), population levelled off and began to decline around A.D. 1100.

Farming remained the basis of subsistence. The expansion of settlement undoubtedly curtailed gathering and hunting as humans appropriated habitats formerly occupied by wild plants and animals. Gathering in arid lowland areas, such as the Hopi Buttes, probably emphasized wild grasses more than that of upland areas where pinyon nuts were abundant. Reduced exploitation of large game and increased emphasis on small animals is symptomatic of the changing resource mix.

Settlement underwent a major transformation as the large, localized PI villages characteristic of the Kayenta heartland and other nuclear areas were supplanted by small "homesteads" distributed through all the habitats of the area. All upland and lowland localities, except those intrinsically uninhabitable, were occupied during this period as rapid population growth fueled range expansion. Empty and sparsely populated parts of nuclear areas were filled, and the growing Western Anasazi populations expanded outward from these localities to attain their greatest geographical distribution. In the south, the first permanent occupation of the Hopi Buttes area coincided with the differentiation of the Winslow expression from the Kayenta branch (Gumerman and Skinner 1968). Settlements were small and dispersed over the landscape to take advantage of arable plots and localized floral resources (Gumerman 1986, 1975). Kayenta people expanded into the country north of the San Juan and moved westward into the Grand Canyon area. Beyond the Canyon, the Virgin branch achieved the apogee of its development with populations inhabiting small to medium sites throughout the area, especially along the margins of drainage channels. The large, complex community at Lost City on the Muddy River in southern Nevada was occupied during this period. In the Kayenta nuclear area, PII habitations occupied virtually every conceivable spot. Only the aggrading surfaces of the floodplains were shunned, although even brief interruptions of sediment accumulation induced habitation construction on the floodplains. On Black Mesa, a trend toward habitation site location on interfluves away from major drainages developed early in the period. By the latter half of the period, however, this trend was reversed, and habitation sites were situated closer to the major streamcourses. Limited activity loci were located primarily in the parts of the uplands that were not suitable for farming.

Site patterning became highly uniform during this period. Habitation sites typically consist of a roomblock of masonry storage rooms and masonry or jacal living chambers, one or more kivas, and a trashmound arranged in the front-oriented fashion of the "unit pueblo." Semisubterranean mealing rooms are found in some of the sites, as are residential pithouses. Such "unit pueblos" rarely possess more than a dozen rooms. Large agglomerations of contiguous surface units are common only at Lost City in southern Nevada where linear roomblocks reminiscent of those in earlier PI sites, such as Alkali Ridge in southeastern Utah, occur. The absence of kivas from some small residential sites indicates that sites with kivas sometimes served the ceremonial needs of the inhabitants of other, nearby habitation loci as well as of their own residents (Phillips 1972). Despite such cases, the discrete, self-contained nature of PII residential loci indicates a large measure of independence in terms of the everyday survival of their inhabitants.

Functionally complete artifact assemblages at habitation sites also reflect the general economic self-sufficiency of these hamlets. About the only notable change in material culture is the abrupt decline in the quantity, and especially the quality, of stone projectile points. This change probably reflects the diminishing importance of big game hunting as populations of large game animals were displaced or depleted by human expansion into previously sparsely occupied habitats.

A fairly high level of intercommunity interaction involving the procurement or exchange of lithic (Green 1986) and ceramic raw materials and finished products (Braun and Plog 1982; Deutchman 1980; S. Plog 1980) prevailed throughout the area during the early part of the period. This development, however, was characterized by increasing localization and decreasing spatial extent of interaction networks. A.D. 1000 marks the development of localized traditions in ceramics, architecture, and in some cases subsistence strategies. The Winslow tradition and others, such as the Virgin branch, are the result of information sharing on local levels. Aspects of domestic architecture, such as the morphology and ratio of pithouses to surface structures, pattern distinctively for the area immediately north of Black Mesa (Bliss 1960), northeastern Black Mesa (Bagley-Baumgartner 1984), the Piñon region (Linford 1982), the Hopi Buttes (Gumerman 1986), and the Virgin branch area (Aikens 1966). Beginning around A.D. 1000 on northeastern Black Mesa, lithic raw materials were procured from many different sources; however, distance to the utilized sources decreased (Green 1986, 1984). It is at this time also that the frequency of San Juan Red Ware decreases dramatically, and Tsegi Orange Ware increases in frequency (S. Plog 1986). Lithic raw material trade networks on northeastern Black Mesa appear to break down around A.D. 1100, after which lithic raw material came from the mesa itself (Green 1986, 1984). This corresponds to the settlement shift to lower elevations along streamcourses. Both patterns are reversions to earlier configurations.

Reflecting the increasing localization of interchange and resource procurement, interaction with other Colorado Plateaus populations appears to have declined as Western Anasazi adaptations became even more differentiated from those of their eastern neighbors. The incidence of trade items and materials from outside the western area—shell, ceramics, raw materials—falls off abruptly. Except for participation in the widespread Dogoszhi style of black-on-white pottery decoration, the Kayenta Black-on-white and Red Ware ceramic design traditions continued to develop along lines different from those of other Anasazi populations. Farther east, this period was marked by the florescence of the Chaco phenomenon where road and communication networks linked large pueblos and population concentrations into some sort of regional interaction complex. While many other Colorado Plateaus groups were involved in the Chacoan interaction sphere, the Western Anasazi *seem* to have been immune to such influences. Thus we appear to have somewhat contradictory trends during PII toward increasing parochialism at a time of rapid population growth and geographic expansion and of widespread structured interaction in other Plateaus areas.

Social organization underwent a number of changes during this period in response to increasing localization in an ameliorating environment. Although population fluctuated locally, the overall trend was upward, and areas not previously suitable for permanent habitation were occupied. Relatively high economic self-sufficiency reduced the need for long-distance interaction; consequently, localized stylistic traditions developed. This parochialism does not mean a lack of change. During this period, the change from semisubterranean to above ground habitation structures, the replacement of large villages by smaller, dispersed homesteads, and the introduction of kivas indicates a major organizational restructuring. Various combinations of masonry and jacal were tried for both habitation and storage structures, and a rapid transition to the almost exuberant decoration of both the necks and bodies of plain gray ceramics occurred. The dispersed population in the Hopi Buttes was integrated by a large ceremonial site unlike anything in the Kayenta or Virgin areas, suggesting a different type of social integration for the lower and dryer Little Colorado Desert (Gumerman 1986, 1975).

### Transition (Differentiation): A.D. 1150–1250

This critical period in Western Anasazi prehistory is poorly known due to a paucity of excavated sites. Fewer than a dozen Kayenta sites, most of them in the Navajo Mountain locality (Ambler, Lindsay, and Stein 1964:21–9, 58–83), and along Arizona Highway 98 linking Shonto and Page (Anderson 1980; Bannister, Dean, and Robinson 1968:71–3), have been thoroughly examined; others are known only through survey (Dean, Lindsay, and Robinson 1978, Fig. 2). Temporal placement is based primarily on the tree-ring dating of the preceding and following periods. Although Kayenta and Hopi Buttes populations remained high and probably continued to increase, rates of growth appear to have slackened in both areas (Fig. 15). By the beginning of this period peripheral Western Anasazi populations declined precipitously, probably as a result of emigration.

Subsistence was even more firmly based on agriculture than previously. Agricultural soil and water control features made their initial appearance in many localities and became particularly abundant around Navajo Mountain (Lindsay 1961; Lindsay et al. 1968:136–50, 184–8; Sharrock, Dibble, and Anderson 1961). The appearance and proliferation of such field systems may indicate an agricultural intensification response to adaptive stress caused by high populations and LFP and HFP environmental deterioration. Gathering staged something of a resurgence in some areas (Dean, Lindsay, and Robinson 1978) as populations withdrew from many locales that had been occupied in the preceding period. Hunting, especially of large game, seems to have continued its decline. The first intimations of concern for domestic water supplies are seen in the form of site concentrations around natural water sources and the initial appearance of reservoirs (Dean, Lindsay, and Robinson 1978).

Western Anasazi settlement underwent a drastic and sudden change at the beginning of this period. Range expansion ceased, and populations withdrew from peripheral areas and returned to the Kayenta–Tusayan–Winslow nuclear areas. At the same time, the Virgin branch came to an end. Major population rearrangements characterized the Kayenta nuclear area as well. Except in the vicinity of Navajo Mountain, the uplands were virtually abandoned as places of habitation. Northern Black Mesa, the Shonto Plateau, and lesser upland localities in the Tsegi–Marsh Pass locality were vacated as the population congregated along lowland drainages in locations where alluvial farmland and water were available. Laguna, Long House, and Klethla Valleys experienced major population influxes (Fig. 15) as did the lower, southern areas of Black Mesa. In the lowlands, an up-drainage population movement began, a trend that characterized the remaining history of the Kayenta Anasazi. In headwater locales such as Long House Valley, the PII pattern of residential sites distributed evenly around the valley floor disappeared as habitation collapsed into less than half the valley area (Dean, Lindsay, and Robinson 1978, Figs. 1, 2). One result of these trends was the development of a discontinuous occupational distribution in which centers of dense population were separated by nearly empty areas. In the Hopi Buttes area, a fairly dispersed population continued to be organized around a central ceremonial site (Gumerman 1975, 1986).

Kayenta branch site patterning underwent a transformation comparable in magnitude to that seen in settlement patterning as the PII "unit pueblos" were replaced by sites of at least two different configurations. One type consists of more or less randomly scattered pithouses associated with masonry-lined kivas. The second type is of a more traditional pueblo configuration with a masonry roomblock facing an open or enclosed plaza containing one or more kivas. Within these roomblocks habitation and storage rooms coexisted, perhaps grouped into units equivalent to the later Tsegi phase room cluster. While the pithouse–kiva sites seem to have been fairly small but numerous, some of the pueblos probably were quite large, having as many as 50 rooms. Both types are abundant in the Tsegi-Marsh Pass and Klethla Valley localities, while the pueblo configuration predominates in the vicinity of Navajo Mountain.

Artifact assemblages reflect a growing isolation and parochialism. Communities seem to have remained fairly self-sufficient economically. Projectile point technology declined in quality as local, sometimes poor, sources of raw material were substituted for more distant sources of better material. This, coupled with declining projectile point workmanship, underscores the continuing trend away from large game hunting and the increased reliance on small game.

Increasing isolation of the Kayenta Anasazi is apparent in the reduced evidence for interaction with other Kayenta local groups and other Anasazi populations. Trade within and outside the Kayenta area seems to have declined as populations became more localized and separated by "empty areas." Exotic imports such as shell, lithic raw materials, and trade pottery seem to be rare, although the apparent dearth of imported materials could be a function of the poor sample of Transition sites. At the same time, all Kayenta local groups continued to participate in unified traditions of black-on-white, black-on-red, and polychrome ceramic production and design that differed from Eastern Anasazi ceramic traditions. Furthermore, the Dogoszhi horizon style persists into this period.

Lack of excavated sites limits what can be said about social organization. Obviously, there was a great deal of variability in this regard. The Kayenta pithouse sites may represent individual family residential units integrated by ceremonies performed in the kivas. The more "traditional" pueblos may have been similarly organized or may have been more tightly integrated by religious and secular social mechanisms. The occurrence in the Hopi Buttes area of a central ceremonial site suggests an intercommunity level of social integration not yet evident in the Kayenta area.

## Pueblo III (Reorganization): A.D. 1250–1300

Without doubt, Pueblo III (Tsegi phase) is the best understood period in Kayenta branch prehistory. Numerous sites in the Navajo Mountain (Ambler, Lindsay, and Stein 1964; Cummings 1945; Lindsay et al. 1968) and Tsegi–Marsh Pass (Dean 1969; Judd 1930; Fewkes 1911; Kidder and Guernsey 1919) areas have been intensively studied. Secure dating is provided by hundreds of tree-ring dates that fall between A.D. 1250 and 1286. Population, though concentrated in a few rather small localities, probably attained the highest absolute levels and local densities in Kayenta prehistory, just before abandonment of the area and termination of the Kayenta cultural tradition. To the south, in the Little Colorado River Valley, populations centered in lowland areas where water is relatively plentiful, although as Upham (1982) indicates, not all localities that could have supported population were occupied.

During this period of falling alluvial water tables and progressive arroyo cutting, Western Anasazi subsistence achieved an unprecedented degree of reliance on agriculture. Agricultural intensification, as indicated by water and soil control devices, was more prevalent and widespread in both the Kayenta and Little Colorado River areas than during the preceding interval. Extensive agricultural systems—consisting of terraces, check dams, linear borders, and often ditches—are most abundant in the Navajo Mountain locality, where surface and subsurface water is more dispersed than in the eastern Kayenta lowlands. Water and soil control devices are uncommon in eastern Kayenta lowlands, probably because the natural concentration of surface runoff and alluvial groundwater rendered such facilities unnecessary.

Gathering probably diminished in importance. Adverse and worsening LFP and HFP conditions probably combined to reduce the productivity of natural plant communities. The small number of Tsegi phase nonagricultural limited activity sites (Dean and Lindsay 1978; Dean, Lindsay, and Robinson 1978) emphasizes the reduced contribution of gathering to the economy. Hunting probably contributed even less than it had in the preceding period. Both faunal remains and low quality weaponry suggest that large game hunting had become relatively unimportant.

The Tsegi phase was a period of heightened concern for water. Reservoirs for the collection and storage of domestic water are abundant. The concern for domestic water seems greater in the eastern lowlands than around Navajo Mountain, perhaps because falling alluvial water tables would have had a greater effect on domestic supplies in the former locality. Many lowland sites are located with reference to natural water sources, such as springs (Dean 1969:22–3; 1970) and tanks (Dean, Lindsay, and Robinson 1978), and artificial sources such as reservoirs (Dean, Lindsay, and Robinson 1978; Kidder and Guernsey 1919, p2.23a).

Tsegi phase settlement behavior, which was the culmination of processes set in motion around A.D. 1150, was complex. The movement toward the upper reaches of drainage systems and the agglomeration of populations in large sites concentrated in a few restricted localities continue trends begun in the previous period. In Long House, Klethla, and Kayenta Valleys a settlement hierarchy of at least two and perhaps three levels developed. The lowest level comprises small habitation sites located adjacent to farmable alluvial bottomland. The highest level consists of a very few "central pueblos" that appear to have had special, extraresidential functions related to the maintenance of multipueblo communities. Among such functions are the storage (and redistribution?) of communal water and food supplies, communication, and perhaps refuge in times of strife. Large sites that lack the specialized attributes of central pueblos may constitute an intermediate level in the settlement hierarchy, or they may merely be exceptionally large members of a single lowest level. In these valleys, habitation sites are organized into localized communities, each consisting of a number of residential sites clustered around a central pueblo situated on an eminence above the valley floor and the other units of the cluster. An even higher level of interaction is suggested by the fact that in Long House Valley (Dean, Lindsay, and Robinson 1978), and probably also in segments of the Klethla and Kayenta Valleys, the central pueblos are situated so that each can be seen from all the others, which suggests that the multisite communities were integrated into even larger interaction systems.

The distribution of Tsegi phase site groups in the eastern lowlands is highly clustered. Each group is situated adjacent to an area of alluvial bottomland that, because of particular hydrologic or topographic features, can be farmed under conditions of depressed water tables and arroyo cutting. In general, these are localities where outwash fans inhibit arroyo cutting and force alluvial groundwater toward the surface. Few habitation sites occur in the spaces between the clusters. Limited activity loci are comparatively scarce and fall into two main types (Dean and Lindsay 1978): "fieldhouses," which are located near farmable land away from the habitations, and "gathering camps" near upland wild food resources.

Settlement pattern in the eastern (Tsegi) and western (Navajo and Paiute) canyons *appears* to lack the organizational structure of the valley site agglomerations. In canyons, functionally complete habitation sites are located near farmable locations where tributary canyons join the main stems. A few cases exist, notably Kiet Siel, where a large cliff dwelling may have served as a locus of some activities, principally ceremonial, shared with residents of nearby small sites. As a rule, however, cliff dwellings have few of the special attributes of central pueblos and seem to have functioned as residential loci where the full range of secular and ceremonial activities was performed.

The Navajo Mountain settlement patterns are less well known. Here, also, large sites located on eminences and possessing some or all of the attributes of central pueblos occur. Little is known, however, about the grouping of lower order sites around these possible central pueblos. Thus, the Navajo Mountain upland pattern may resemble the canyon pattern more than it does the more structured eastern valley configuration. In the Hopi area and along the Little Colorado River, populations also aggregated into large communities, some of which achieved sizes rarely attained in the Kayenta area.

Expectably, Tsegi phase site patterning is complex, with considerable formal and functional differentiation of units within sites. The basic structural unit of Tsegi phase sites is the room cluster (Dean 1969:34–5; 1970; Lindsay 1969:363), which consists of one or two living rooms, one to several storage chambers, and sometimes a grinding room grouped around an unroofed courtyard. Occasionally, especially in the Navajo Mountain locality, several room clusters are grouped around a single large courtyard to form courtyard complexes (Dean 1969:35; Lindsay 1969:363). Other components of Tsegi phase habitation sites include circular and rectangular kivas and communal grinding and storage facilities.

Three types of residential site are recognized. *Plaza-oriented sites* consist of masonry roomblocks situated on one to four sides of an open or enclosed plaza that contains one or more kivas. Most large open sites and nearly all central pueblos are of the plaza type. In addition, most central pueblos have reservoirs, communal food storage facilities, and occasionally features designed to restrict access to the pueblo interior. "Defensive" features of this sort may be more common in the Navajo Mountain locality. Plaza-oriented sites are abundant throughout the Kayenta nuclear area and are characteristic of the Hopi and Little Colorado areas. *Room cluster sites* lack central plazas. Instead, the room clusters are grouped around single or multiple courtyards, or are oriented along formal walkways or "streets." All Tsegi phase cliff dwellings are room cluster sites for the simple reason that rock shelters cannot accommodate plazas. Open sites of the room cluster type are common, especially in the vicinity of Navajo Mountain, and some are quite large. *Pithouse sites,* consisting of loose agglomerations of rather informal subterranean habitation structures often grouped around a central pueblo, are fairly abundant in the Klethla Valley (Haas and Creamer 1985), less so elsewhere.

The organizational implications of Tsegi phase settlement and site patterns are not terribly obvious (Dean 1970). Room clusters probably represent some sort of residential household unit (Dean 1969: 36–39; 1970), while courtyard complexes may represent larger multihousehold units. Such units were the basic components of village organization. Plaza orientation may denote a higher order of social integration than room cluster sites. The fact that nearly all central pueblos are of the former type may indicate that plaza site residents were organized differently than the inhabitants of room cluster sites. On the other hand, the different site patterns may reflect alternative village layouts, the choice of which is based more on topography or historical factors than on social organization. Several supravillage levels of organization or interaction are indicated for the eastern valleys. Each group of habitation sites and its central pueblo probably constituted a formally organized community, and clusters of such communities may have formed larger, valley level communities. Whether intervalley communication represents integration or merely interaction is unknown.

Western Anasazi Pueblo III artifact attributes and assemblages indicate a strong reliance on agriculture. Corn grinding equipment is an important component of room clusters and occurs also in communal mealing rooms. Projectile point industries remained technologically indifferent and dependent on local, inferior raw materials. In contrast, ceramic technology and design blossomed, and differences between the centers of population are minimal.

Tendencies toward greater regional divergence on the one hand, and increased internal uniformity on the other, characterize Pueblo III interactional dynamics. As the Western Anasazi agglomerated into small locales, the unoccupied areas between population centers grew larger. At the same time, interaction among local groups, at least in the Kayenta area, apparently increased in intensity. Ceramic production and design identity throughout the area attests to a high level of interaction between Kayenta population centers.

Considerable evidence also exists for Kayenta interaction with other southwestern groups. The importation of pottery from the Mesa Verde and Tusayan areas and the occurrence of Kayenta pottery in these and other areas implies widespread exchange. Particularly close relationships with the Tusayan area are denoted by the near identity of Kayenta and Tusayan ceramic design styles. The relative abundance of Mesa Verde pottery in Tsegi phase sites and the Kayenta adoption of Mesa Verde architectural forms, such as towers (Dean 1969:138–139, 187) and granary construction standards (Dean 1969:125–6), identify particularly close relationships with Mesa Verde populations. Even more distant contacts are suggested by the Kayenta adoption of white outlining of design motifs on polychrome pottery, a practice that probably originated in the White Mountain Redware tradition of the Mogollon Rim area. Further evidence of long range southern contacts is provided by similarities in Kayenta and White Mountain ceramic design styles and by the Kayenta migration to Point of Pines (Haury 1958).

Relatively long distance trade, especially in "luxury" goods, is evident in the Little Colorado and Hopi areas toward the end of this period (Upham 1982, 1983), which suggests an economic network linking the few large sites in this area. Turquoise, shell, ceramics, and even copper bells were involved in this network, which apparently did not extend northward into the Kayenta area.

## Abandonment of the Northern Areas: A.D. 1300

Like other parts of the San Juan drainage basin, the Kayenta area was abandoned by the Anasazi at the end of the thirteenth century. Tree-ring dates and ceramic type distributions indicate that the Kayenta emigration must have occurred between A.D. 1286 and 1300. This exodus took place in an orderly fashion. Most portable items were removed from the sites, mealing bins and metates were destroyed, and in some places doorways were sealed, probably in anticipation of a return to the area. There is no evidence that the Kayenta Anasazi were driven from their homes by other humans, nor did other groups replace them until centuries after they had gone. Undoubtedly, the Kayenta Anasazi moved south to join closely related groups on the southern fringes of Black Mesa.

Momentum undoubtedly was an important factor in the final abandonment of the Kayenta area. Once emigration had proceeded far enough, population would have fallen below the upper threshold of what the area could support, and further departures would have been unnecessary. Once people began leaving, however, the process of withdrawal probably reached a point at which others left in order to maintain social relationships and to fulfill sociocultural obligations that had been translocated to the south. In order to maintain the community organization that had been achieved by the Tsegi phase, whole communities had to move. Eventually this process totally depopulated the Kayenta nuclear area.

## Pueblo IV (Aggregation): A.D. 1300–1600

Except for the Arizona State Museum's Homolovi Project little recent work has been done in Pueblo IV villages north of the Little Colorado River. The most ambitious effort, the Awatovi Project (Brew 1941), undertaken in the late 1930s, is still largely unreported except for the ceramics (Gifford and Smith 1978; Smith 1971) and some architectural aspects (Smith 1952, 1972). Excavations at Walpi (Adams 1981, 1982) involve materials too recent to provide much information on the early protohistoric period. Earlier work in the 1800s and early 1900s produced large amounts of beautiful pottery but little in the way of information (Fewkes 1895, 1896, 1897, 1898, 1904; Hodge 1907; Hough 1903).

Subsistence probably was little changed from earlier periods; however, with population even more concentrated than in earlier periods, there may have been greater agricultural intensification and other forms of capital development such as reservoirs. Population was concentrated in only a few locations—on the Hopi Mesas and Jeddito Valley and along the Little Colorado River. All these isolated areas of habitation are located where water is plentiful, although not all suitable areas were occupied (Upham 1982). The lack of arable land in proximity to water may have precluded settlement of some localities.

Recorded sites are large, consisting of at least several hundred rooms. Most sites appear to comprise large roomblocks enclosing plazas, or consist of parallel rows of rooms separated by spaces that may have served the same functions as plazas.

Basic changes and additions occur in material culture, which is a reflection of a major shift in world view (Adams 1981, 1983). These changes are most striking in ceramics and kiva mural painting. The designs of Sikyatki Polychrome and the kiva murals at Awatovi and Homolovi express an "artistic and cultural virility" (Smith 1952:322–323). While earlier artistic forms were simple, repeated geometric designs, the new tradition stressed complex, asymmetrical curvilinear forms of both abstract and life-form configurations (Smith 1952:261). Often forms identical to contemporary katchina figures are depicted, and it is presumed that the katchina cult was adopted by the Hopi about this time (Adams 1983). The katchnia cult, which became pervasive in Western Anasazi society, probably originated to the south or southeast of the Western Anasazi area. Adams (1981, 1983) speculates that its roots may be in the Mimbres–El Paso–Casas Grandes region.

The continued constriction of population and the adoption of the katchina cult, both of which must have had profound political and social consequences, have been attributed to environmental conditions by Adams (1981, 1983). He posits that the degradation of the environment described for the period preceding Pueblo IV continued and perhaps even increased. Low water tables, arroyo cutting, and diminishing farm land produced subsistence stress, which might have allowed for the easy assimilation of the katchina cult with its emphasis on rainmaking and fertility. This in turn may have strengthened the power of religious specialists.

Upham (1982) views the Pueblo IV period of Western Anasazi as an economically and politically linked system of villages. He sees a hierarchically organized system based on elite trade. Long-distance trade linking the larger sites included turquoise, shell, ceramics, and copper bells. He posits the development of this system as the result of interplay between agricultural intensification, organization of labor, and surplus production. Upham's supposition of a hierarchically organized society is counter to traditional interpretations of Pueblo IV social organization and to a major thesis of this paper. Nevertheless, his model offers interesting alternatives to environmentally based explanations.

By the time of the Spanish Entrada, all the Arizona communities had been abandoned except for the Hopi villages at the south end of Black Mesa, where springs still flow today.

## WESTERN ANASAZI ADAPTATION TO ENVIRONMENTAL VARIABILITY

As expected, LFP environmental variability seems to have had the greatest impact on human adaptive behavior. Both lowland and upland floodplains generally were shunned as places of residence during intervals of rising water tables and aggradation (Fig. 15:A.D. 1–250, 350–750, 925–1275). Conversely, residence on the floodplain occurred during most primary and some secondary intervals of low water tables and erosion. This pattern is absent during the A.D. 250–350 period, probably because the BMII groups were not fully committed to horticulture and because populations were low. During the A.D. 750–925 erosional interval, lowland and upland alluvial floodplains were the most densely populated habitats in the area. Residence directly on stable floodplain or terrace surfaces was not common during the Tsegi phase, perhaps because every available bit of potential farmland had to be used to support the large population. However, except in the Navajo Mountain locality, Pueblo III was a time when populations vacated the uplands and congregated adjacent to lowland floodplains, on which are found numerous fieldhouses but few residences. Even some secondary dips in the aggradation and hydrologic curves allowed brief occupations of temporarily stabilized floodplain surfaces.

Alluvial aggradation, accompanied by high and growing populations, fostered range expansion into upland areas. This movement actually began during the A.D. 750–925 erosional interval, when population pressures alone probably triggered the PI expansion into the uplands, but accelerated rapidly during the A.D. 1000–1150 PII range expansion. Finally, populations tended to aggregate near locally farmable areas of the floodplains when low water tables and arroyo cutting drastically reduced the number, distribution, and size of arable locales. The agglomerative tendency was strongest when populations were high (Tsegi phase), but even the relatively low populations of the PI period seem to have localized around suitable floodplain farming localities.

Direct effects of HFP environmental variability are more difficult to recognize than are the results of LFP fluctuations. Most storage responses to HFP variability in the amount of precipitation are likely to be so brief, coinciding with the interval of stress, as to be detectable in the archaeological record only when extremely high resolution chronological controls are available. Analysis of temporal changes in room dimensions and in room cluster composition at Kiet Siel shows a marked increase in storage capacity relative to living space during the Great Drought, but this shift could be due in whole or in part to the worsening LFP conditions of the time. The effects on storage behavior of high vs. low temporal variability in climate cannot be assessed because too few data on storage capacities are available. Developments contrary to expectations based on the model may be denoted by a trend on Black Mesa toward increasing storage capacity that begins at the time of the shift from high to low temporal variability around A.D. 1000 (Powell and Nichols 1983, Fig. 8). Spatial variability in climate seems to have had considerable effect on the Western Anasazi. As shown by F. Plog (1983a, 1983b), during intervals of increasing or high spatial variability, most occupants of the Colorado Plateaus were linked in interaction networks marked in the archaeological record by widespread black-on-white ceramic design horizon styles. Conversely, interaction diminished and localization increased during periods of low spatial variability. As yet, the nature of the broad interaction networks is poorly known (S. Plog 1986); however, it is clear that the Western Anasazi participated in those networks that arose under conditions of high spatial variability in climate.

Even more impressive are the almost one-to-one correspondences between the events of Western Anasazi prehistory and the relative magnitudes of behavioral responses on the one hand, and the potential impact of various population-environment circumstances on the other. The greatest potential for negative impact occurred when adverse LFP and HFP environmental conditions coincided with high population levels and densities near the end of the thirteenth century. It probably is no coincidence that the Kayenta area was vacated at this time. Situations of the second most severe type should have developed, at least locally, whenever populations reached levels high enough to approach carrying capacity limits. Population relocations in several upland areas in the early A.D. 1100s (S. Plog 1986) may have resulted from local populations nearing carrying capacity boundaries. Apparently, however, the population of the western area as a whole never became large enough by itself to cause major adaptive changes.

A population environment situation of third order severity is identified for the middle of the twelfth century when high populations accompanied a secondary LFP environmental disruption and a severe and prolonged HFP drought. Initiation of withdrawal from peripheral areas occupied between A.D. 1000 and 1150, major population dislocations within the area as a whole, settlement relocations within many localities, and major changes in community patterning testify to the severity of the adaptive situation. Behavioral responses to pre-A.D. 1100 third order environmental stress are less obvious because low populations would have mitigated the impact of such fluctuations. Even so, the differences between BMIII and PI subsistence-settlement behavior seem to be related to the primary LFP degradation of the A.D. 750–925 period.

The correlation of Western Anasazi behavior with favorable conditions is less impressive than that with unfavorable circumstances. Release from LFP environmental constraint should have occurred during the A.D. 350–525, 625–750, 925–1125, and 1175–1275 intervals; therefore, these periods should have been characterized by general range expansion and reduction of behavioral variation. The A.D. 625–750 period marked the expansion of BMIII populations and the development of uniform settlement and community patterns. Similarly, the A.D. 1000–1150 interval was characterized by rapid population growth, the extensive PII geographic expansion, and fairly uniform settlement and community patterns. Furthermore, when population levels became high after A.D. 1100, LFP environmental amelioration had little effect in reducing behavioral variation. Thus, the post A.D. 1150 interval was characterized by high behavioral variability within the western area and within individual localities. The uniformity of a satisfactory adaptation to LFP environmental stress appears only in the PI adaptive system, which was fairly widespread and uniform. A successful adaptation to LFP and HFP environmental stress was not achieved by Pueblo III populations, at least in the Western Anasazi area.

## SOCIAL ORDER AND INTERACTION

As stated in the introductory section, cooperation is hypothesized to be the basic behavioral mechanism for adaptation in the Western Anasazi area. It ensured the relatively unrestricted flow of information, and facilitated decisions necessary to mediate the unequal distribution of natural resources in the heterogeneous environment. This is not to say that at some times and places competition over important resources did not restrict the flow of critical information. In addition, interaction, in terms of exchange and other forms of social interchange, shifted in direction, duration, and intensity in relation to demographic, environmental, and behavioral variables.

Recent provocative publications have suggested that at certain times and places asymmetrical, nonegalitarian societies developed in the Southwest (Lightfoot and Feinman 1982; Upham et al. 1981, Upham 1982). Further, it has been suggested there were periods and areas when populations coalesced into formal political and economic "alliances" in contrast to a simpler "resiliant" pattern, characterized by small, relatively autonomous farmsteads or seminomadic groups (Upham 1982; F. Plog 1983b; Cordell and Plog 1979; Stuart and Gauthier 1981).

These studies have provided an important awareness of spatial and temporal variability in social organization and interaction. They have forced archaeologists to consider information flow, social order, and interaction in a non-normative way. There are, however, several alternative explanations for the patterning observed in the archaeological record.

Some studies (Lightfoot and Feinman 1982; Upham et al. 1981; Upham 1982) do not view egalitarian and asymmetrical societies as social entities along a continuum, but rather, like classical evolutionary categorizations, which viewed culture change in broad stages. This is in spite of the fact that some of the authors themselves caution against the use of nonscalar concepts (Lightfoot and Feinman 1982). The authors often appear to view *any* evidence of social status difference as proof of a nonegalitarian society. No human society is completely egalitarian if that term is taken to mean the absence of status differences. Even simply organized societies like those of the Shoshoneans, which most anthropologists agree were egalitarian, had "talkers" and "rabbit chiefs" who acted as headmen at certain times in order to accumulate, process, and transmit information about subsistence resources and to organize collection and hunting activities (Steward 1938).

Attempts have been made to rationalize models of a hierarchical social order in prehistory by emphasizing the inequities that exist in present Western Pueblo society (Upham 1982; Upham et al. 1981). Indeed, inequities do exist, even in those aspects of society that control access to vital resources. Such inequities, however, are based less on the accumulation of material wealth than on ritual knowledge (Smith 1983). Commonly, ritual knowledge is widely apportioned throughout the society and is, therefore, diffused rather than accumulated. Smith (1983:42) goes on to state that "the distinction, then, between egalitarian, ranked, and stratified societies may, at best have only narrow analytical utility, particularly if it rests on such ethnocentrically materialistic criteria as access to real goods."

Nevertheless, a scale of asymmetry is useful for understanding degrees of social complexity and can be used effectively to describe and understand culture change. Furthermore, it matters little for our purpose whether or not access to ritual power results in the accumulation of material wealth or whether the two are concomitant or independent.

For our purposes, an appropriate definition of egalitarian society is one whose members have essentially equal access to critical resources and to a relatively unrestricted flow of information about those resources. This definition allows for the development of leadership through achievement, personal abilities, and even hereditary status, so long as that status does not convey the right to restrict the access of others to critical resources. To confine the term *egalitarian* to less than this definition excludes most, if not all, human societies. The ideal is, of course, to consider degrees of egalitarianism and asymmetry—difficult to do in an archaeological situation.

Within the Western Anasazi area there is no archaeological evidence for the existence of an asymmetrical social order, at least until the late fourteenth century; there is no evidence of surplus labor, large capital investment, or great specialization of production. Furthermore, there is no indication that the need to process information about resources was so enormous that it required asymmetry in the social order, structuring the flow of information to reduce production or procurement costs.

There is no need to invoke the nuances of environmental or demographic variability to explain the egalitarian nature of Western Anasazi society prior to the fourteenth century. In spite of the vagaries of environmental and demographic pressure or release, the most effective strategy for dealing with most situations would have been one of cooperation and access to information and resources necessary for survival. During the late fourteenth century, however, population density and capital investment at large communities may have increased tendencies toward a conscriptive society.

Prior to the fourteenth century evidence for "central places" is minimal. Klesert (1982b) proposes that Standing Fall House, a cliff structure at the extreme northeastern edge of Black Mesa dating just prior to abandonment of the area about A.D. 1150, served as a central storage and redistribution center, although the evidence for this is minimal.

The Plaza site in the Hopi Buttes was almost certainly a "central place" (Gumerman 1975, 1986). The Plaza site, in contrast to the surrounding small (three to eight room) habitation sites, is distinguished by a high ratio of public to nonpublic space. There is no evidence, however, to suggest that the Plaza site restricted access to critical information or resources as there are no qualitative or quantitative differences in artifact inventory from the contemporaneous small habitation sites in the immediate vicinity. On the contrary, the Plaza site's main function was probably to enhance accumulation and dissemination of information and facilitate the distribution of critical resources, thus mediating the effects of a heterogeneous and high risk environment.

A dispersed population, dwelling in numerous small sites, was economically most efficient for food production and procurement in the Hopi Buttes area. Nevertheless, with an expanding population in a heterogeneous environment, a mechanism to ensure an unrestricted information flow had to be developed to monitor the environmental situation for effective cooperation. The Plaza site provided that function.

Tsegi phase communities of the Klethla, Laguna Creek, and Long House Valleys also appear to have been internally differentiated, with the central pueblos functioning as "central public places." Although data pertaining to this issue are scant, central pueblos probably served as loci of information exchange among inhabitants of the villages clustered around them. The mutual intervisibility of central pueblos in Long House Valley suggests that intercommunity information exchange, perhaps regulated in some fashion, also existed.

Northeastern Black Mesa had no need for a "central place" to monitor information because the physiography (unlike the Hopi Buttes) is dominated by a dendritic drainage system where deep alluvium and water are arranged in linear fashion. Relatively small sites could maintain the majority of social, economic, and religious functions. Because most sites had equal access to all critical resources, it was not necessary to establish a central place for the monitoring of environmental information over a large area. In contrast, the dispersion of population throughout a heterogeneous environment stimulated the sharing of information and coordination of effort over the entire area. The discontinuous distribution of usable farmland under the conditions of alluvial degradation that prevailed during the Tsegi phase may account in part for the development of "central places" in the eastern Kayenta area.

There is evidence in the study area for greater social complexity after the Hopi Buttes and Kayenta areas were abandoned. Upham (1982) disputes the egalitarian nature of the Western Pueblo during Pueblo IV (ca. A.D. 1300–1450), suggesting that "hereditary oligarchies" controlled ritual and other knowledge resulting in a much more asymmetrical social order in the Upper and Middle Little Colorado River than previously supposed; certainly more than existed at the time of European contact. Upham's evidence consists largely of the "central place" spacing of contemporaneous sites, which suggests a network of what could be called power systems, and the differential distribution of certain artifacts, which may reflect the restricted access to commodities attendant on status differences.

Several arguments can be marshalled against the supposition that a ranked, hereditary elite exercised control over the system of communities. First, the existence of interaction or regulated exchange among large communities does not necessarily specify a nonegalitarian society. On the contrary, the evidence for interaction among smaller, earlier sites indicates that such relationships should be expected for the later, larger sites—even if the distance between individual sites is much greater. If there are fewer sites, interaction will be maintained or even augmented in spite of increased distances between the sites. Second, and more important, there is no *neces-*

*sary* correlation between the differential distribution of artifacts and the denial of access to those artifacts on status grounds.

As Plog and Upham themselves state, archaeologists probably cannot distinguish situations where access to resources is based on preference or opportunity rather than differential power (Plog and Upham 1983:208–209). It is our contention that in spite of deteriorating environmental conditions, demographic pressure, and capital investment, the advantages of cooperation in a process of unrestricted information flow and equal access to resources outweighed the advantages of hereditary asymmetrical social organization. That may be why asymmetrical social order along the Little Colorado River was so emphemeral, if it existed at all.

There can be little question that there was a great diversity in the manner in which Anasazi societies were organized, and some were certainly more complex than Western Pueblo societies or those that existed at the time of Spanish contact. Some of this complexity, evidenced for example by Chacoan road systems and great public architecture, must have required a ranked or even stratified society, based on competition and on control of information flow, as well as preferential access to resources. We do not intend to discuss the origins of these manifestations, except to note that characteristically they are short lived.

The short-lived phenomena of an aggressively exploitative strategy in a social environment of cooperation is precisely what is expected in the iterated Prisoner's Dilemma game. One of the fascinating results of the game is that a group of cooperating entities can successfully resist aggressively exploitative strategies if the cooperating entities continue to interact with one another. This demonstrates how an egalitarian cooperation strategy can successfully adapt in an environment of social exploitation, whether or not that exploitation derived from external social systems, such as Mesoamerica, or was internally derived.

In sum, the Western Anasazi area provides no concrete evidence for the development of an asymmetrical social system, with the possible exception of late in the prehistoric period when, for a short time, environmental circumscription, high population, and the capital expenditure of labor may have encouraged social ranking along the Little Colorado River. Outside the Western Anasazi area, evidence for short-lived ranked or stratified societies exists, but cooperation and egalitarianism were the primary adaptive modes.

Considerably more archaeological evidence exists for the degree, direction, and intensity of social interaction than for any determination of the social order (Dean et al. 1985). Social interaction in an archaeological sense includes such traditional spheres as exchange and "cultural boundaries" as well as recently articulated concepts of provinces and alliances.

The direction, degree, and intensity of interaction changed dramatically several times in the Western Anasazi area. These changes are evidenced by either shared or distinctive styles in ceramics and architecture, and in the results of chemical and physical material analyses (Deutchman 1980; Green 1984; S. Plog 1980; Upham 1982). The stage names proposed in the first chapter of this volume are largely indicative of variations in interactive behavior.

The interpretation of changing interaction as periods of alliances and breakdowns of alliances by F. Plog (1983b, 1984) and Upham and Plog (1983) appears to be too narrow an interpretation of the data. Alliances are usually considered to be formal, political, highly organized arrangements among elite segments of large social entities. Alliance behavior, however, is only one extreme in a continuum of interactional options that can produce shared styles or materials. Interactional forms range from episodic contacts between individuals to highly structured, continuing, formal relationships between large social and political entities. Interaction between individuals or small groups of individuals is more consistent with our views of the Western Anasazi. However, it is also evident that the extent and formality of relationships varied through time. For example, at times there is a sense of great parochiality when architecture and, to some extent, ceramic style were consistent over only a few kilometers on Black Mesa and in the Hopi Buttes. At other times, especially early and late in the sequence, there is evidence of intensive and continuing pan-Western Anasazi interaction.

The Western Anasazi archaeological record suggests regional interactive behavior far less complex than that implied by the concept of formal political alliances. The alternation of periods of widespread interaction with intervals of more localized interchange may be explained as reflections of cooperational-retribution-cooperation (CRC) behavior rather than of participation in formal political alliances. The same sort of environmental variability that is thought to have triggered alliance-forming behavior in other areas may have stimulated CRC behavior among the Western Anasazi. Thus, high spatial variability in climate may have enhanced interareal information exchange (i.e., increased cooperation), while periods of uniform climatic conditions reduced the need for information exchange and cooperation, exacerbated intersocietal differences, and stimulated competition and retributive behavior that persisted until environmental conditions once again favored cooperation. The CRC response to ecological diversity suggested by the iterated Prisoner's Dilemma game provides an alternative to the political alliance explanation of archaeological evidence for intermittent increases in interactive behavior. While the CRC model seems to better account for the nature of this evidence in the Western Anasazi prior to A.D. 1300, the alliance model may be more applicable to other areas or other time periods. Evaluation of both models in particular instances of interactive behavior undoubtedly will increase resolution and the explanatory power of each, and thereby enhance understanding of southwestern prehistory.

The recent dialogues over the nature of the social order and the degree and form of interaction have provided a more realistic understanding of Western Anasazi social behavior. In spite of differing points of view, all scholars paint a much more variegated portrait of Anasazi society than had previously been observed. Of especially great value is that the discussion centers not on whether the Anasazi were hierarchically organized or the exact form of social interaction, but on what these social conditions tell us about changing Anasazi behavior.

# REFERENCES

Adams, E. Charles
    1981    A View from the Hopi Mesas. In *The Protohistoric Period in the North American Southwest, A.D. 1450–1700*, edited by David R. Wilcox and W. Bruce Masse, pp. 321–335. Anthropological Research Papers 24. Arizona State University.
    1982    *Walpi Archaeological Project: Synthesis and Interpretation.* National Endowment for the Humanities and the Museum of Northern Arizona, Flagstaff.
    1983    The Appearance, Evolution, and Meaning of the Katsina Cult to the Pre-Hispanic Pueblo World of the Southwestern United States. Paper presented at the XI International Congress of Anthropological and Ethnological Sciences, Vancouver.

Adams, Richard N.
    1975    *Energy and Structure: A Theory of Social Power.* University of Texas Press, Austin.

Aikens, C. Melvin
    1966    *Virgin-Kayenta Cultural Relationships.* University of Utah Anthropological Papers 79. University of Utah Press, Salt Lake City.

Ambler, J. Richard, Helen C. Fairly, and Phil R. Geib
    1983    Kayenta Anasazi Utilization of Canyons and Plateaus in the Navajo Mountain Area. Paper presented at the Second Anasazi Symposium, Bloomfield, New Mexico.

Ambler, J. Richard, Alexander J. Lindsay, Jr., and Mary Anne Stein
    1964    *Survey and Excavations on Cummings Mesa, Arizona and Utah, 1960–1961.* Glen Canyon Series No. 5. Museum of Northern Arizona Bulletin No. 39. Flagstaff.

Ambler, J. Richard, and Alan P. Olson
    1977    *Salvage Archaeology in the Cow Springs Area.* Museum of Northern Arizona Technical Series No. 15. Flagstaff.

Anderson, Keith M.
  1980    *Highway Salvage on Arizona State Highway 98: Kayenta Anasazi Sites Between Kaibito and the Klethla Valley.* Arizona State Museum Archaeological Research Series No. 140. Tucson.

Axelrod, Robert
  1983    *The Evolution of Cooperation.* Basic Books, New York.

Axelrod, Robert, and William D. Hamilton
  1981    The Evolution of Cooperation. *Science* 211:1390–1396.

Bagley-Baumgartner, Kathy
  1984    Toward a Functional Classification of Nonceremonial Structures on Black Mesa, Northeastern Arizona. In *Papers on the Archaeology of Black Mesa Arizona,* vol. 2, edited by Stephen Plog and Shirley Powell, pp. 47–86. Center for Archaeological Investigations Publications in Archaeology. Southern Illinois University Press, Carbondale.

Bannister, Bryant, Jeffrey S. Dean, and Elizabeth A.M. Gell
  1966    *Tree-Ring Dates from Arizona E: Chinle-de Chelly-Red Rock Area.* Laboratory of Tree-Ring Research, University of Arizona, Tucson.

Bannister, Bryant, Jeffrey S. Dean, and William J. Robinson
  1968    *Tree-Ring Dates from Arizona C–D: Eastern Grand Canyon-Tsegi Canyon-Kayenta Area.* Laboratory of Tree-Ring Research, University of Arizona, Tucson.

Berry, Michael S.
  1982    *Time, Space, and Transition in Anasazi Prehistory.* University of Utah Press, Salt Lake City.

Braun, David P., and Stephen Plog
  1982    Evolution of "Tribal" Social Networks: Theory and Prehistoric North American Evidence. *American Antiquity* 47 (3):504–525.

Brew, J. O.
  1941    Preliminary Report of the Peabody Museum Awatovi Expedition of 1939. *Plateau* 13:37–48.

Brew, John Otis
  1946    *Archaeology of Alkali Ridge, Southwestern Utah: With a Review of the Prehistory of the Mesa Verde Division of the San Juan and Some Observations on Archaeological Systems.* Papers of the Peabody Museum of American Archaeology and Ethnology 21. Harvard University, Cambridge.

Carlson, Roy L.
  1982    The Polychrome Complexes. In *Southwestern Ceramics: A Comparative Review,* edited by Albert H. Schroeder, pp. 201–234. The Arizona Archaeologist, No. 15. Arizona Archaeological Society, Phoenix.

Carneiro, Robert L.
  1970    A Theory of the Origin of the State. *Science* 169:733–738.
  1978    Political Expansion as an Expression of the Principle of Competitive Exclusion. *Origins of the State,* edited by Ronald Cohen and Elman R. Service, pp. 205–224. Institute for the Study of Human Issues, Philadelphia.

Clark, David L.
  1978     *Analytical Archaeology.* Second Edition. Columbia University Press, New
           York.

Cooley, Maurice E.
  1962     Late Pleistocene and Recent Erosion and Alluviation in Parts of the Colo-
           rado River System, Arizona and Utah. In *Geological Survey Research 1962:
           Short Papers in Geology, Hydrology, and Topography, Articles 1–59,* pp. 48–50.
           United States Geological Survey Professional Paper 450–B. Washington.

Cordell, Linda S., and Fred Plog
  1979     Escaping the Confines of Normative Thought: A Reevaluation of Puebloan
           Prehistory. *American Antiquity* 44:405–429.

Cummings, Byron
  1945     Some Unusual Kivas Near Navajo Mountain. *The Kiva* 1(4):30–35.
  1953     *First Inhabitants of Arizona and the Southwest.* Cummings Publication Coun-
           cil, Tucson.

Daifuku, Hiroshi
  1961     Jeddito 264: A Report on the Excavation of a Basketmaker III-Pueblo I
           Site in Northeastern Arizona, with a Review of Some Current Theories in
           Southwestern Archaeology. *Reports of the Awatovi Expedition, Report No. 7.*
           Papers of the Peabody Museum of American Archaeology and Ethnology
           33(1). Harvard University, Cambridge.

Dean, Jeffrey S.
  1966     The Pueblo Abandonment of Tsegi Canyon, Northeastern Arizona. Paper
           presented at the 31st Annual Meeting of the Society for American Archae-
           ology, Reno, Nevada.
  1969     *Chronological Analysis of Tsegi Phase Sites in Northeastern Arizona.* Papers of
           the Laboratory of Tree-Ring Research No. 3. The University of Arizona
           Press, Tucson.
  1970     Aspects of Tsegi Phase Social Organization. In *Reconstructing Prehistoric
           Pueblo Societies,* edited by William A. Longacre, pp. 140–174. School of
           American Research, University of New Mexico Press, Albuquerque.
  1982     Dendroclimatic Variability on Black Mesa A.D. 385 to 1970. Paper pre-
           sented at the School of American Research Advanced Seminar, Culture
           Change on Black Mesa, Santa Fe.
  1988     A Model of Anasazi Behavioral Adaptation. In *The Anasazi in a Changing
           Environment,* edited by G. J. Gumerman. School of American Research
           and Cambridge University Press, Cambridge.

Dean, Jeffrey, S., Robert C. Euler, George J. Gumerman, Fred Plog, Richard H. Hevly, and
Thor N.V. Karlstrom
  1985     Human Behavior, Demography and Paleoenvironment on the Colorado
           Plateaus. *American Antiquity* 50:537–554.

Dean, Jeffrey S., and Alexander J. Lindsay, Jr.
  1978     Special Use Sites in Long House Valley, Northeastern Arizona: An Analy-
           sis of the Southwestern Anthropological Research Group Data File. In
           *Limited Activity and Occupation Sites: A Collection of Conference Papers,* edited

by Albert E. Ward, pp. 109–117. Contributions to Anthropological Studies No. 1. Center for Anthropological Studies, Albuquerque.

Dean, Jeffrey S., Alexander J. Lindsay, Jr., and William J. Robinson
1978    Prehistoric Settlement in Long House Valley, Northeastern Arizona. In *Investigations of the Southwestern Anthropological Research Group: The Proceedings of the 1976 Conference,* edited by Robert C. Euler and George J. Gumerman, pp. 25–44. Museum of Northern Arizona, Flagstaff.

Deutchman, Haree L.
1980    Chemical Evidence of Ceramic Exchange on Black Mesa. In *Models and Methods in Regional Exchange,* edited by Robert E. Fry, pp. 119–133. Society for American Archaeology No. 1. Washington, D.C.

Euler, Robert C.
1988    Demography and Cultural Dynamics on the Colorado Plateaus. In *The Anasazi in a Changing Environment,* edited by George J. Gumerman. The School of American Research and Cambridge University Press, Cambridge.

Euler Robert C., George J. Gumerman, Thor N.V. Karlstrom, Jeffrey S. Dean, and Richard H. Hevly
1979    The Colorado Plateaus: Cultural Dynamics and Paleoenvironment. *Science* 205:1089–1101.

Fewkes, Jesse Walter
1895    *Preliminary Account of an Expedition to the Cliff Villages of the Red Rock Country and the Tusayan Ruins of Sikyatki and Awatobi.* Annual Report for 1895, 1896. Smithsonian Institution, Washington, D.C.
1896    *Archaeological Explorations.* Annual Report for 1896. Smithsonian Institution, Washington, D.C.
1897    *Tusayan Migration Tradition.* Bureau of American Ethnology, Annual Report 19(2). Washington, D.C.
1898    *Archaeological Expedition to Arizona in 1895.* Bureau of American Ethnology, Annual Report, 17(2). Washington, D.C.
1904    *Two Summer's Work in Pueblo Ruins.* Bureau of American Ethnology, Annual Report 22(1). Washington, D.C.
1911    *Preliminary Report on a Visit to the Navajo National Monument, Arizona.* Bureau of American Ethnology Bulletin 50. Washington, D.C.

Ford, Richard I.
1975    Re-excavation of Jemez Cave, New Mexico. *Awanyu* 3:12–37.
1982    People and Plants on Prehistoric Black Mesa. Paper presented at the School of American Research Advanced Seminar, Culture Change on Black Mesa. Santa Fe.
1984    Ecological Consequences of Early Agriculture in the Southwest. In *Papers on the Archaeology of Black Mesa, Arizona,* Vol. 2, edited by Stephen Plog and Shirley Powell, pp. 127–138. Center for Archaeological Investigations Publications in Archaeology. Southern Illinois University Press, Carbondale.

Fried, Morton H.
1967    *The Evolution of Political Society: An Essay in Political Anthropology.* Random House, New York.

Gifford, James C., and Watson Smith
1978     *Gray Corrugated Pottery from Awatovi and Other Jeddito Sites in Northeastern Arizona.* Papers of the Peabody Museum of American Archaeology and Ethnology 69. Harvard University, Cambridge.

Green, Margerie
1986     *Chipped Stone Raw Materials and the Study of Interaction on Black Mesa, Arizona.* Center for Archaeological Investigations, Occasional Paper No. 11. Southern Illinois University, Carbondale.
1984     The Relationship of Source Distance to Conservation of Chipped Stone Raw Materials. In *Papers on the Archaeology of Black Mesa, Arizona*, Vol. 2, edited by Stephen Plog and Shirley Powell, pp. 173–188. Center for Archaeological Investigations Publications in Archaeology. Southern Illinois University Press, Carbondale.

Guernsey, Samuel James
1931     *Explorations in Northeastern Arizona: Report on the Archaeological Fieldwork of 1920–1923.* Papers of the Peabody Museum of American Archaeology and Ethnology 12(1). Harvard University, Cambridge.

Guernsey, Samuel James, and Alfred Vincent Kidder
1921     *Basket-Maker Caves of Northeastern Arizona: Report on the Explorations, 1916–17.* Papers of the Peabody Museum of American Archaeology and Ethnology 8(2). Harvard University, Cambridge.

Gumerman, George J.
1986     *Archaeology of the Hopi Buttes District, Arizona.* Center for Archaeological Investigations Research Paper No. 49. Southern Illinois University, Carbondale.
1975     Alternative Cultural Models for Demographic Change: Southwestern Examples. In Population Studies in Archaeology and Biological Anthropology: A Symposium, edited by Alan C. Swedlund, pp. 104–105. *Memoirs of the Society for American Archaeology* 30.

Gumerman, George J. (editor)
1988     *The Anasazi in a Changing Environment.* The School of American Research and Cambridge University Press, Cambridge.

Gumerman, George J., and Robert C. Euler
1976     Black Mesa: Retrospect and Prospect. In *Papers on the Archaeology of Black Mesa*, edited by George J. Gumerman and Robert C. Euler, pp. 162–170. Southern Illinois University Press, Carbondale.

Gumerman, George J., and S. Alan Skinner
1968     A Synthesis of the Prehistory of the Central Little Colorado Valley, Arizona. *American Antiquity* 33:185–199.

Gumerman, George J., Deborah Westfall, and Carol S. Weed
1972     *Black Mesa: Archaeological Investigations on Black Mesa: The 1969–1970 Seasons.* Prescott College Press, Prescott, Arizona.

Haas, Jonathan
1982     *The Evolution of the Prehistoric State.* Columbia University Press, New York.

Haas, Jonathan, and Winifred Creamer
1985    Warfare and Tribalization in the Prehistoric Southwest: Report on the First Season's Work—1984. Report submitted to The Harry Frank Guggenheim Foundation, New York. School of American Research, Santa Fe, New Mexico.

Hack, John T.
1942    *The Changing Physical Environment of the Hopi Indians of Arizona.* Papers of the Peabody Museum of American Archaeology and Ethnology 35(1), Reports of the Awatovi Expedition No. 1. Harvard University, Cambridge.

Hantman, Jeffrey L., and Stephen Plog
1982    The Relationship of Stylistic Similarity to Patterns of Material Exchange. In *Context for Prehistoric Exchange,* edited by Jonathon E. Ericson and Timothy K. Earle, pp. 237–263. Academic Press, New York.

Harlan, Thomas P., and Jeffrey S. Dean
1968    Tree-Ring Data for Several Navajo Mountain Region Sites, Appendix II. In *Survey and Excavations North and East of Navajo Mountain, Utah, 1959–1962,* by Alexander J. Lindsay, Jr., J. Richard Ambler, Mary Anne Stein, and Philip M. Hobler, pp. 379–82. Museum of Northern Arizona Bulletin No. 45, Glen Canyon Series No. 8. Flagstaff.

Haury, Emil W.
1928    *The Succession of House Types in the Pueblo Area.* M.A. thesis, the University of Arizona, Tucson.
1958    Evidence at Point of Pines for a Prehistoric Migration from North Arizona. In Migrations in New World Culture History, edited by Raymond H. Thompson, pp. 1–6. *University of Arizona Bulletin* 29(2), *Social Science Bulletin* 27. Tucson.

Hevly, Richard H.
1981    Prehistoric Exploitation of Biotic Resources, Paleoclimates, and Human Demography on the Colorado Plateaus. Paper presented at the School of American Research Advanced Seminar, Anasazi Cultural Developments and Paleoenvironmental Correlates. Santa Fe.

Hevly, Richard H., and Thor N.V. Karlstrom
1974    Southwest Paleoclimate and Continental Correlations. In *Geology of Northern Arizona with Notes on Archaeology and Paleoclimate: Part I—Regional Studies,* edited by Thor N.V. Karlstrom, Gordon A. Swann, and Raymond L. Eastwood, pp. 257–295. Geological Society of America, Flagstaff.

Hodge, F. W.
1907    *Awatobi.* Bureau of American Ethnology Bulletin, No. 30. Smithsonian Institution, Washington, D.C.

Hough, W.
1903    Archaeological Field Work in Northeastern Arizona: The Museum-Gates Expedition, 1901. *Annual Report for 1901.* United States National Museum, Washington, D.C.

Jennings, Jesse D.
   1966      *Glen Canyon: A Summary.* University of Utah Anthropological Papers No.
              81. University of Utah Press, Salt Lake City.

Johnson, Gregory A.
   1978      Information Sources and the Development of Decision-making Organiza-
              tions. In *Social Archaeology: Beyond Subsistence and Dating,* edited by C.
              Redman, M. J. Berman, E. V. Curtin, W. T. Langhorne, Jr., N. M.
              Versaggi, and J. C. Wanswer, pp. 89–112. Academic Press, New York.

Jorde, Lynn B.
   1977      Precipitation Cycles and Cultural Buffering in the Prehistoric Southwest.
              In *For Theory Building in Archaeology,* edited by Lewis R. Binford, pp. 385–
              396. Academic Press, New York.

Judd, Neil Merton
   1930      *The Excavation and Repair of Betatakin.* Proceedings of the United States
              National Museum, Vol. 77, Article 5, Washington.

Karlstrom, Eric T.
   1983      Soils and Geomorphology of Northern Black Mesa. In *Excavation on Black
              Mesa 1981: A Descriptive Report,* edited by F. E. Smiley, D. L. Nichols, and P.
              P. Andrews, pp. 317–348. Center for Archaeological Investigations Re-
              search Paper No. 36. Southern Illinois University, Carbondale.

Karlstrom, Thor N. V.
   1981      Alluvial Chronology and Environmental Change, Colorado Plateaus. Pa-
              per presented at the School of American Research Advanced Seminar,
              Anasazi Cultural Developments and Paleoenvironmental Correlates.
              Santa Fe.

Kidder, Alfred V.
   1924      *An Introduction to the Study of Southwestern Archaeology, With a Preliminary
              Account of the Excavations at Pecos.* Papers of the Phillips Academy South-
              western Expedition, No. 1. Yale University Press, New Haven.
   1927      Southwestern Archaeological Conference. *Science* 66:489–491.

Kidder, Alfred Vincent, and Samuel J. Guernsey
   1919      *Archaeological Explorations in Northeastern Arizona.* Bureau of American Eth-
              nology Bulletin 65. Washington.

Klesert, Anthony L.
   1982a     Foreword. In *Kayenta Anasazi Archaeology on Central Black Mesa, Northeast-
              ern Arizona: The Pinon Project,* edited by Laurence D. Linford, unpaginated.
              Navajo Nation Papers in Anthropology, No. 10. Navajo Nation Cultural
              Resource Management Program, Window Rock.
   1982b     Standing Fall House: An Early Puebloan Storage and Redistribution Cen-
              ter in Northeastern Arizona. *The Kiva* 48:39–61.

Layhe, Robert W.
   1981      *A Locational Model for Demographic and Settlement System Change: An Exam-
              ple from the American Southwest.* Ph.D. dissertation, Department of Anthro-
              pology, Southern Illinois University, Carbondale. University Microfilms,
              Ann Arbor.

Lightfoot, Kent G., and Gary M. Feinman
    1982    Social Differentiation and Leadership Development in Early Pithouse Villages in the Mogollon Region of the American Southwest. *American Antiquity* 47:64–86.

Lindsay, Alexander J., Jr.
    1961    The Beaver Creek Agricultural Community on the San Juan River, Utah. *American Antiquity* 27:174–87.
    1969    *The Tsegi Phase of the Kayenta Cultural Tradition in Northeastern Arizona.* Ph.D. dissertation, University of Arizona, Tucson. University Microfilms, Ann Arbor.

Lindsay, Alexander J., Jr., and J. Richard Ambler
    1963    Recent Contributions and Research Problems in Kayenta Anasazi Prehistory. *Plateau* 35:86–92.

Lindsay, Alexander J., Jr., J. Richard Ambler, Mary Anne Stein, and Philip M. Hobler
    1968    *Survey and Excavations North and East of Navajo Mountain, Utah, 1959–1962.* Museum of Northern Arizona Bulletin No. 45, Glen Canyon Series No. 8. Flagstaff.

Linford, Laurance D. (editor)
    1982    *Kayenta Anasazi Archaeology on Central Black Mesa, Northeastern Arizona: The Pinon Project.* Navajo Nation Papers in Anthropology, No. 10. Navajo Nation Cultural Resource Management, Window Rock.

Lipe, William D.
    1970    Anasazi Communities in the Red Rock Plateau, Southeastern Utah. In *Reconstructing Prehistoric Pueblo Societies,* edited by William A. Longacre, pp. 84–139. School of American Research, University of New Mexico Press, Albuquerque.

Lockett, H. Claiborne, and Lyndon L. Hargrave
    1953    *Woodchuck Cave, a Basketmaker II Site in Tsegi Canyon, Arizona.* Museum of Northern Arizona Bulletin 26, Flagstaff.

Martin, Paul S., and Fred Plog
    1973    *The Archaeology of Arizona: A Study of the Southwest Region.* Doubleday/Natural History Press, Garden City, New York.

Matson, R. G., and W. D. Lipe
    1978    Settlement Patterns on Cedar Mesa: Boom and Bust on the Northern Periphery. In *Investigations of Southwestern Anthropological Research Group, Proceedings of the 1976 Conference,* edited by R. C. Euler and G. J. Gumerman, pp. 1–12. Museum of Northern Arizona, Flagstaff.

Moore, James A.
    1983    The Trouble with Know-It-Alls: Information as a Social and Ecological Resource. In *Archaeological Hammers and Theories,* edited by James A. Moore and Arthur S. Keene, pp. 173–191. Academic Press, New York.

Morris, Earl H.
    1925    Exploring in the Canyon of Death. *The National Geographic Magazine* 48(3):263–300.

1936        Archaeological Background of Dates in Early Arizona Chronology. *Tree-Ring Bulletin* 2(4):34–36.

Morris, Elizabeth Ann
1980        *Basketmaker Caves in the Prayer Rock District, Northeastern Arizona.* Anthropological Papers of the University of Arizona No. 35. The University of Arizona Press, Tucson.

Nichols, Deborah L., and F. E. Smiley
1984        A Summary of Prehistoric Research on Northern Black Mesa. In *Excavations on Black Mesa, 1982: A Descriptive Report,* edited by Deborah L. Nichols and F. E. Smiley, pp. 89–107. Center for Archaeological Investigations Research Paper No. 39. Southern Illinois University, Carbondale.

Phillips, David A.
1972        Social Implications of Settlement Distribution on Black Mesa. In *Archaeological Investigations on Black Mesa: The 1969–1970 Seasons,* by George J. Gumerman, Deborah J. Westfall, and Carol S. Weed, pp. 199–210. Prescott College Press, Prescott, Arizona.

Plog, Fred
1981        *Cultural Resources Overview: Little Colorado Area, Arizona.* United States Department of Agriculture, Forest Service, Southwest Region, Albuquerque.
1983a       Human Responses to Environmental Variation: The Anasazi Case. Paper presented at the Second Anasazi Conference, Farmington, New Mexico.
1983b       Political and Economic Alliances on the Colorado Plateaus, A.D. 400–1450. In *Advances in World Prehistory,* edited by Fred Wendorf and Angela Close, pp. 289–302. Academic Press, New York.
1984        Exchange, Tribes, and Alliances: The Northern Southwest. *American Archaeology* 4:217–223.

Plog, Fred, George J. Gumerman, Jeffrey S. Dean, Robert C. Euler, Thor N. V. Karlstrom, and Richard Hevly
1988        Anasazi Adaptive Strategies: The Model, Predictions, and Results. In *The Anasazi in a Changing Environment,* edited by George J. Gumerman. School of American Research and Cambridge University Press, Cambridge.

Plog, Fred, and Steadman Upham
1983        The Analysis of Prehistoric Political Organization. In *The Development of Political Organization in Native North America: 1979 Proceedings of the American Ethnological Society,* edited by Elisabeth Tooker, pp. 199–213. American Ethnological Society, Washington, D. C.

Plog, Stephen
1980        Village Autonomy in the American Southwest: An Evaluation of the Evidence. In *Models and Methods in Regional Exchange,* edited by Robert E. Fry, pp. 135–146. SAA Papers, No. 1. Society for American Archaeology, Washington, D.C.

Plog, Stephen
1984        Regional Perspectives on the Western Anasazi. *American Archaeology* 4:162–170.

Plog, Stephen (editor)
  1986    *Spatial Organization and Exchange: Archaeological Survey on Northern Black Mesa.* Center for Archaeological Investigations and Southern Illinois University Press, Carbondale.

Powell, Shirley L.
  1983    *Mobility and Adaptation: The Anasazi of Black Mesa, Arizona.* Center for Archaeological Investigations Publications in Archaeology, Southern Illinois University Press, Carbondale.

Powell, Shirley, and Deborah L. Nichols
  1983    Physical Environment, Technology, and Cultural Change: The Black Mesa Anasazi. Paper presented at the Second Anasazi Symposium, Farmington, New Mexico.

Root, Dolores
  1983    Information Exchange and the Spatial Configurations of Egalitarian Societies. In *Archaeological Hammers and Theories,* edited by James A. Moore and Arthur S. Keene, pp. 193–219. Academic Press, New York.

Schoenwetter, James
  1962    The Pollen Analysis of Eighteen Archaeological Sites in Arizona and New Mexico. In *Chapters in the Prehistory of Eastern Arizona, I,* by Paul S. Martin, John B. Rinaldo, William A. Longacre, Constance Cronin, Leslie G. Freeman, Jr., and James Schoenwetter, pp. 168–209. Fieldiana: Anthropology 53. Chicago Natural History Museum, Chicago.
  1970    Archaeological Pollen Studies of the Colorado Plateau. *American Antiquity* 35:35–47.

Sebastian, Lynne
  1985    *Archaeological Excavation Along the Turquoise Trail: The Mitigation Program.* Office of Contract Archaeology, University of New Mexico, Albuquerque.

Sharrock, Floyd W., Kent C. Day, and David S. Dibble
  1963    *1961 Excavations, Glen Canyon Area.* University of Utah Anthropological Papers, No. 63. University of Utah Press, Salt Lake City.

Sharrock, Floyd W., David S. Dibble, and Keith M. Anderson
  1961    The Creeping Dune Irrigation Site in Glen Canyon, Utah. *American Antiquity* 27:188–202.

Smiley, Francis Edward, IV
  1985    *The Chronometrics of Early Agricultural Sites in Northeastern Arizona: Approaches to the Interpretation of Radiocarbon Dates.* Ph.D. dissertation, Department of Anthropology, University of Michigan, Ann Arbor. University Microfilms, Ann Arbor.

Smiley, F. E., and Peter P. Andrews
  1983    An Overview of Black Mesa Archaeological Research. In *Excavations on Black Mesa, 1981: A Descriptive Report,* edited by F. E. Smiley, Deborah L. Nichols, and Peter P. Andrews, pp. 45–60. Center for Archaeological Investigations, Research Paper No. 36. Southern Illinois University, Carbondale.

Smiley, F. E., William J. Parry, and George J. Gumerman
  1986    Early Agriculture in the Black Mesa/Marsh Pass Region of Arizona: New

Chronometric Data and Recent Excavations at Three Fir Shelter. Paper presented at the Society of American Archaeology meeting.

Smith, M. Estellie
1983    Pueblo Councils: An Example of Stratified Egalitarianism. In *The Development of Political Organization in Native North America: 1979 Proceedings of the American Ethnological Society*, edited by Elisabeth Tooker, pp. 32–44. The American Ethnological Society, Washington, D.C.

Smith, Watson
1952    *Kiva Mural Decoration at Awatovi and Kawaika-a, with a Survey of Other Wall Paintings in the Pueblo Southwest*. Papers of the Peabody Museum of American Archaeology and Ethnology 37. Harvard University, Cambridge.
1971    *Painted Ceramics of the Western Mound at Awatovi*. Papers of the Peabody Museum of American Archaeology and Ethnology 38. Harvard University, Cambridge.
1972    *Prehistoric Kivas of Antelope Mesa, Northeastern Arizona*. Papers of the Peabody Museum of American Archaeology and Ethnology 39(1). Harvard University, Cambridge.

Steward, Julian H.
1938    *Basin-Plateau Aboriginal Sociopolitical Groups*. Bureau of American Ethnology Bulletin 120. Smithsonian Institution, Washington, D.C.

Stuart, David E., and Rory P. Gauthier
1981    *Prehistoric New Mexico: Background for Survey*. Historic Preservation Bureau, State Department of Finance and Administration and Tularosa, Human Systems Research, Inc. Santa Fe.

Taylor, Walter W.
1954    An Early Slabhouse Near Kayenta, Arizona. *Plateau* 26:109–116.

Thompson, Richard
1983    A Consideration of Virgin Anasazi Subsistence and Settlement. Paper presented at the Second Anasazi Symposium, Bloomfield, New Mexico.

Upham, Steadman
1982    *Polities and Power: An Economic and Political History of the Western Pueblo*. Academic Press, New York.
1983    Intensification and Exchange: An Evolutionary Model of Non-egalitarian Socio-political Organization for the Prehistoric Plateau Southwest. In *Ecological Models in Economic Prehistory*, edited by Gordon Bronitsky, pp. 219–245. Anthropological Research Papers, No. 29. Arizona State University, Tempe.

Upham, Steadman, Kent G. Lightfoot, and Gary M. Feinman
1981    Explaining Socially Determined Ceramic Distributions in the Prehistoric Plateau Southwest. *American Antiquity* 46:822–833.

Van der Leeuw, S. E.
1981    Information Flows, Flow Structures and the Explanation of Change in Human Institutions: The Case of Early States. In *Archaeological Approaches to the Study of Complexity*, edited by S. E. Van der Leeuw, pp. 229–329. Universiteit van Amsterdam, Amsterdam.

Ward, Albert E.
   1976    Black Mesa to the Colorado River: An Archaeological Traverse. In *Papers on the Archaeology of Black Mesa, Arizona,* edited by George J. Gumerman and Robert C. Euler, pp. 3–105. Southern Illinois University Press, Carbondale.

Wills, Wirt Henry, III
   1985    *Early Agriculture in the Mogollon Highlands of New Mexico.* Unpublished Ph.D. dissertation. Department of Anthropology, University of Michigan.

Wright, Henry T.
   1977    Recent Research on the Origin of the State. In *Annual Review of Anthropology,* Vol. 6, edited by Bernard J. Siegel, pp. 379–398. Annual Reviews, Inc., Palo Alto.

ARTHUR H. ROHN **5**

# Northern San Juan Prehistory

Although the Mesa Verde has often been viewed as the nucleus of the northernmost prehistoric Puebloan occupation, it more accurately represents one subdivision within the Northern San Juan Region. Such a cultural region occupies the drainages of the northern tributaries of the San Juan River from Comb Ridge in southeastern Utah to the upper San Juan Valley in southwestern Colorado. It extends from the valley of the San Juan River on the south to the arc of mountains stretching from the Abajos in the west to the La Plata and San Juan Mountains in the east. During some stages, Puebloan occupation expanded westward beyond Comb Ridge into the large rugged triangle bounded by the San Juan and Colorado Rivers. Other boundaries fluctuated less markedly.

An eastern subregion is well watered by permanent streams such as the San Juan, Piedra, Pine, Animas, and La Plata flowing from high mountain sources through wooded mesa land. A western subregion is drained by ephemeral stream channels such as the McElmo, Yellow Jacket, Monetzuma, Recapture, and Cottonwood that were cut before their mountain headwaters were pirated by the Dolores River or that flow out of the relatively dry Abajo Mountains. Frequently, such channels have become deeply incised, steep-sided canyons that impede movement.

The Mancos River offers a transition between the two subregions. It originates on the western slopes of the La Plata Mountains and flows through the relatively moist Mancos Valley before bisecting the progressively more arid Mesa Verde and the sparse desert grassland south of Ute Mountain. Ute Mountain, an eroded laccolithic stock of andesite porphyry (Wanek 1959), stands almost as a sentinel visible from all portions of the western subregion.

Vegetation zones reflect available moisture and vary primarily according to elevation. Open ponderosa pine forests occupy the flanks of the mountains, especially those in the east. Pinyon-juniper woodland covers many of the higher mesas and canyon slopes, intermingled with hardwood brush and oak thickets. Occasional local conditions of cold air drainage cause localized inversions of woodland and chaparral, and together with north-facing slopes, allow pockets of Douglas fir to exist. Extensive sage flats and high desert grasslands cover most of the lower elevations, especially in the broad Montezuma Valley in the western subregion. Some cottonwoods and other moisture-loving vegetation grow along watercourses and around springs.

Elevation also governs precipitation and the duration of summer's frost-free days. As farmers might seek longer growing seasons in lower elevations, they must sacrifice moisture. Hence, a somewhat delicate balance between adequate moisture and the length of growing season annually threatens the yields from dry farming.

Running upland streams provide an obvious source of domestic water unless they are choked with runoff sediments and debris. The absence of such streams in the western subregion does not mean the absence of potable water, however. The deep canyon-dissected, nearly horizontal beds of Cretaceous sandstones and shales have created numerous opportunities for springs and seeps to develop.

The vast majority of archaeological remains within the Northern San Juan have been left by prehistoric Pueblos, often called Anasazi. At one time or another, these people inhabited virtually all of the region. Archaeological investigations have concentrated much more heavily in some districts than others, leading to a quite uneven knowledge of prehistoric cultural developments within the region. Currently, government agencies such as the Bureau of Land Management and the Office of the Colorado State Archaeologist are developing comprehensive regional plans for managing archaeological resources within their domains.

While the extent of prehistoric Pueblo occupancy has essentially delineated the Northern San Juan Region, earlier and later archaeological remains have been encountered. Neither fit the bounds of the region in terms of cultural pattern distributions.

## CHRONOLOGY

Numerous phase sequences have been proposed for the Northern San Juan or its subregions, especially in recent years. However, because virtually all of them have been generated through investigations within a single district, or even locality, it is simpler to synthesize the cultural chronology through a modified Pecos Classification (Kidder 1927), using the classificatory units primarily as stages of development rather than periods of time (Fig. 17).

Most archaeological studies have emphasized changes in material culture through time, essentially describing seriations of development in architecture, ceramics, and lithic technology. Consequently, most of these seriations provide remarkably utilitarian and sensitive chronological indicators.

Pre-Basketmaker remains have so far been recognized primarily from projectile point styles such as San Juan, Pinto, and Jay, most often seen in private collections or recovered as isolated finds. Some have even been recovered from later archaeological contexts where they probably served as heirlooms. Mohr and Sample (1959) defined a La Sal complex from the region's northern edge, but no clearly excavated components have yet been defined. Presumably, the makers of these point styles were typical desert Archaic-style hunters and gatherers who lived in rather ephemeral camps. Several probable sites are known, but none have been excavated.

During the five Basketmaker-Pueblo stages, housing units shifted from semisubterranean earth-covered lodges with associated outdoor storage units and hearths to contiguous room blocks with associated kivas. Timber and brush superstructures covered with earth gave way first to jacal construction (upright poles interwoven with wattles and covered with mud) during the eighth century and ultimately to stone masonry in the tenth and eleventh centuries. Techniques for facing sandstone building blocks shifted from bifacially flaking a wedge-shaped face in the eleventh century to pecking and grinding flat faces in the twelfth and thirteenth centuries. Kivas supplanted earlier pithouses around A.D. 900 and then underwent a seriation of attributes (cf. Lancaster and Pinkley 1954).

Ceramic seriations are continuously undergoing refinement (e.g., Abel 1955; Breternitz, Rohn, and Morris 1974; Lister and Lister 1969; Rohn 1977; Blinman 1984) in terms of formally named types, individual attributes, and site assemblages. Even subregional variability can be discovered (e.g., Dittert et al. 1961; Eddy 1966). Other items that possess some seriational value include projectile points, manos and metates, stone axe heads, sandals, cradles, and source animals for bone awls. Still other items such as tcamahias, bone humerus scrapers, elk antler tools, baked clay figurines, and cotton textiles have known limited periods of popularity and use.

| Northern San Juan Stages | Southwest terminology (this book) |
|---|---|
| Pre-Basketmaker | |
| 500 B.C. ————————————————————— | Preceramic |
| Basketmaker II | |
| A.D. 450 ————————————————————— | |
| Basketmaker III | Initiation |
| 750 ————————————————————— | |
| Pueblo I | |
| 900 ————————————————————— | Expansion |
| Pueblo II | |
| 1050 ————————————————————— | |
| 1100 ————————————————————— | Differentiation |
| 1150 ————————————————————— | |
| Pueblo III | Reorganization |
| 1300 ————————————————————— | |
| Post Pueblo | Aggregation |
| 1550 ————————————————————— | |
| 1776 ————————————————————— | |
| Historic | Historic |

*Fig. 17. Northern San Juan cultural-historical stages in relation to the periods used in this volume.*

During the Puebloan culture history, the basic subsistence economy changed very little. Basketmaker II peoples combined the growing of maize and squash with the hunting of deer and small game and the collection of many edible wild plant parts. However, by Basketmaker III, cultigens including common beans replaced products of hunting and collecting as the most prominent subsistence resources. While the proportion of gathered plant foods and hunted animal meats declined, the range of species exploited remained the same. The most significant change in subsistence came with the development of water management capabilities by the tenth century in early Pueblo II. This allowed fuller exploitation of lower elevations with longer growing seasons (cf. Herold 1961; Rohn 1963).

Increasingly detailed paleoecological studies (e.g., Schoenwetter and Eddy 1964; Erdman et al. 1969; Petersen 1983; Petersen et al. 1985) and the tree-ring record (Schulman 1946) can identify some very minor swings in climatic conditions during the Puebloan occupation. However, none of these climatic variations would have required more adjustment than slight changes in elevation for field locations. They do not adequately explain the drastic changes in observable material culture and inferred social organization. Southwestern Colorado has not generally reflected the effects of low and high frequency climatic variability seen elsewhere in the Southwest (Gumerman and Dean, this volume).

With the refinements in chronology and seriations in aspects of material culture, plus a better understanding of the paleoenvironment, interpretations of the evolution of Puebloan society and demographic shifts within the Northern San Juan Region have become feasible. Such interpretations require the analyses of settlements in terms of size and arrangement, plus the broad survey data derived recently from cultural resource management surveys and contract archaeological activities associated with the rapidly expanded energy resource exploitation of the Four Corners. A survey of changing settlement and demographic patterns is presented in the following sections.

Post-Pueblo habitation in the Northern San Juan is almost as difficult to discern as the Pre-Basketmaker. Puebloan peoples abandoned the region around A.D. 1300. Early explorations by Spanish and later Anglo-Americans recorded the presence of nomadic Ute bands that subsisted by hunting and gathering. Ute sites seem to be as ephemeral as the earlier desert Archaic ones, so only a few have been tentatively identified. Whether Utes were present at the time of the Pueblo abandonment, or how soon afterwards they arrived, remain unanswered questions.

Historic references to features in the Northern San Juan begin with the travels and journals of the Spanish missionaries Escalante and Dominguez in 1776. Later, Spaniards began to mine silver from the La Plata Mountains, but permanent colonization began in the mid-1800s with miners and then homesteaders. Both Ute and Navajo sites have been recognized from historic times with Navajo and Spanish-American phases described from the Navajo Reservoir (Dittert et al. 1961; Eddy 1966).

## PUEBLOAN SETTLEMENTS THROUGH TIME

A survey of existing literature and ongoing projects produces considerable evidence concerning recognizable settlements for each of the Puebloan cultural stages. Let us examine these data for possible trends reflecting social and political developments within Puebloan society.

Basketmaker II remains are scarce and poorly reported relative to the other stages. However, Morris and Burgh (1954) described two groups of pithouses from a pair of adjacent rock shelters and from a talus slope situation in the Falls Creek Valley, north of Durango. Similar clusters of pithouses at Valentine Village and the Power Pole site in the Navajo Reservoir have been encompassed within a Los Pinos phase by Eddy (1961). Although none of these four villages was excavated totally, we can estimate their sizes from 6 to 11 pithouses plus associated features (Rohn 1983b).

In the extreme west, Basketmaker II materials have been encountered in Butler and Comb Washes, the Grand Gulch, and on Cedar Mesa. Only in the last case does the reporting suggest houses clustered into somewhat "dispersed villages," although none have been specifically delineated (Matson et al. 1983). Many of the Cedar Mesa sites also represented small camps and limited activity sites obviously used occasionally by the inhabitants of the more permanent dwellings.

While no one Basketmaker II settlement has been investigated in its entirety, we can observe a pattern of clusters of pithouses numbering perhaps as many as 11 together, with both interior and outside hearths and storage cists. Temporary camps and limited activity sites in the open and in caves reflect forays away from the home village for hunting, food gathering, and perhaps resource collection and even trade.

Deceased members of society were regularly buried in abandoned storage cists, crevices in rock shelters, beneath house floors, or in general refuse areas. The pattern of folding the legs and arms against the body and adding as accompaniments items of clothing and adornment plus utilitarian utensils presaged a tradition of burial practices that changed very little throughout Puebloan prehistory.

Over two centuries of transition between Basketmaker II and III are very poorly represented, in most places nonexistent, in the archaeological record. Dittert and associates have defined a Sambrito phase from the Navajo Reservoir producing an early brown pottery, but remains so identified never occur independently and have always been factored out from larger and later site assemblages (Eddy 1966). Several early Basketmaker III structures have recently been reported from the San Juan River valley near Mexican Hat (Robert Neily, personal communication).

Most excavated Basketmaker III sites date to the seventh and early eighth centuries. Even though most archaeologists have tended to excavate single pithouses, several villages have been clearly recognized. In the Yellow Jacket district, the Gilliland site consists of four pithouses plus associated outdoor ramadas, work areas, and storage units all surrounded by a wooden stockade (Rohn 1975), and the Payne site presented three houses, slab-lined storage rooms, outdoor ramadas and work areas with a stockade (Rohn 1974).

On the Mesa Verde, Lancaster and Watson (1942, 1954) recognized the existence of two clusters of pithouses in the Twin Trees locality, even though they only excavated one from each. The intensive survey of Chapin Mesa clearly indicated the clustering of Basketmaker III pithouses into villages of up to 8 in number (Rohn 1977). Presumably, extramural storage and work features would be discovered in these clusters through thorough excavation. Nusbaum's 1926 excavations in Step House Cave revealed three pithouses (Nusbaum 1981), to which the Wetherill Mesa Archeological Project work added three more. Thus, Step House Cave arched over a village of six pithouses plus associated structures built close to A.D. 600. Other Wetherill Mesa excavations exposed two pithouses in a cluster of several at the Badger House community (Hayes and Lancaster 1975).

Elsewhere in the region, some investigators have suggested that dispersed settlements of several pithouses occur— Cedar Mesa (Matson et al. 1983), Ridges Basin (Phillip Duke, personal communication), Navajo Reservoir (Dittert et al. 1961)—while others present the occurrence of individual pithouses as separate hamlets—Falls Creek (Carlson 1963), Dolores Archaeological Project's Sagehen phase (Kane 1983, 1984), Yellow Jacket district (Wheat 1955). It would seem that most Basketmaker III peoples lived in villages of at least three to eight pithouses plus associated features, while a few inhabited more rural hamlets. Presumably, they too ventured away from their year-round residences for farming, hunting, gathering, resource acquisition, and trade; at least some limited activity areas have been identified (e.g., Matson et al. 1983).

A distinctive structure makes its first appearance in several Basketmaker III settlements. Unusually large pithouses have been reported from Yellow Jacket (Wheat 1955), Wetherill Mesa (Hayes and Lancaster 1975), and upper Recapture Canyon, northeast of Blanding. Another large, probably nonresidential, pit structure located directly between the two successive settlements at Twin Trees locality on Chapin Mesa was partially excavated in 1941 (Jennings 1968). Any or all of these have frequently been mentioned as forerunners or prototypes of the widespread later great kivas. The structure at Twin Trees, probably serving two successive settlements of eight houses each, would most readily fit such a model.

Pueblo I residential arrangements mark the beginnings of a major change in settlement size and layout. Early excavations in the Piedra district (Roberts 1930), La Plata district (Morris 1939), Ackmen (Yellow Jacket) district (Martin 1939), and on Alkali Ridge (Brew 1946) firmly established the existence of villages made up of arcing rows of dwelling and storage rooms flanking the north and west sides of rows of deep pithouses. More recently, this pattern has been replicated through both excavation and survey data from Navajo Reservoir (Dittert et al. 1961; Eddy 1966), Chapin Mesa (O'Bryan 1950; Rohn 1977), Wetherill Mesa (Hayes 1964; Hayes and Lancaster 1975), Dolores River valley (Kane 1983, 1984), Yellow Jacket, and Nancy Patterson site in Montezuma Canyon (Janetski and Hurst 1984).

In many cases, the groups of living and storage rooms are not contiguous, verifying the oft-suggested concept of a unitary grouping of functionally distinct features analogous to Prudden's (1903, 1914, 1918) seminal recognition of the unit-type pueblo for later times. Each unit consists of a surface room block standing a short distance north (or northwest or even northeast) of a deep, squarish pithouse with wingwall partitions and a ventilator. Within the room block, storage rooms lined the north side, opening through their south walls into living rooms containing hearths. These in turn opened southward into porticoed or outdoor work spaces, frequently with hearths. The above ground rooms normally sported jacal walls often with upright sandstone slabs lining the room interiors. Some crude stone masonry makes its appearance in late Pueblo I in places like the Dolores River valley (Lipe and C. Breternitz 1980).

While most Pueblo I people lived in villages of a dozen or more such units, single units or small groups of two or three units located in places relatively isolated from the villages may represent small rural hamlets. Although no firm dates are yet in hand, I suspect the various size villages and hamlets were interwoven into larger sociopolitical units through the presence of clearly recognizable great kivas at several of the larger villages where their inhabitants may have gathered for major ceremonies. Hayes and Lancaster (1975:63) believe the Badger House community great kiva continued to be used into the Pueblo I occupation of that settlement, which probably consisted of about 20 units. Lister has excavated a Pueblo I great kiva in Morfield Canyon on the Mesa Verde without exploring its residential context. The Dolores Archaeological Project has excavated portions of great kivas on Grass Mesa and at Singing Shelter on House Creek (Kane 1984; Nelson and Kane 1986). Unexcavated great kivas in apparent Pueblo I contexts are presently known from Nancy Patterson site (Janetski and Hurst 1984) and from the point where Comb Ridge crosses the San Juan River. Undoubtedly, others will be recognized as awareness of Pueblo I vintage great kivas increases. Perhaps some of the larger pithouses, such as Pithouse B at Site 13 on Alkali Ridge and oversized pit structures in the Dolores River valley, may be reinterpreted as either great kivas, or more likely, as structures with some analogous functions on a smaller scale.

Limited activity sites and temporary camps on localities such as White Mesa (Davis 1983), again indicate the conduct of numerous activities away from the home village. Pueblo I ceramics and other material culture reflect a great deal of experimentation and contact with neighbors in regions to the south.

Pueblo II settlements have, for far too long, been characterized by the unit pueblo as if each unit constituted a separate settlement. Thus, Pueblo II peoples are still often seen as inhabiting hamlets or farmsteads widely dispersed over the landscape. Separate unit pueblos have been all too easily selected out of clusters for excavation as contained units. However, any intensive survey data (e.g., Rohn 1977; Hayes 1964) show definite patterns of clustering. Can we imagine a group of 8 to 12 contemporaneously inhabited unit pueblos grouped within a total distance of one-quarter mile as 8 to 12 separate settlements? One such small settlement of six kivas and four room blocks has been excavated at the Ewing site in Yellow Jacket (cf. Rohn 1983b), and perhaps a dozen such settlements were identified from Chapin Mesa survey results ranging from 8 to 36 units (Rohn 1977). Unfortunately, the recorded cases end there, but examination of the later Pueblo III towns and villages in the Montezuma Valley reveal Pueblo II components underlying many settlements and individual buildings within settlements. The best recorded instance of this may be seen in the Far View locality on Chapin Mesa (Rohn 1977:275–280).

Great kivas clearly belonging to Pueblo II settlements have not yet been identified. However, there is a strong possibility that many Pueblo III great kivas were first built during Pueblo II and either continued in use or were remodeled by Pueblo III descendents living in the same settlements. I would expect to find evidence for this occurrence at one or more of Lowry, Cahone, Yellow Jacket, or Goodman Point Ruins, among others.

Because Pueblo II settlements have been so neglected by archaeologists, and because many of the larger ones appear to have been obscured by later Pueblo III constuction on top of them, we cannot yet adequately estimate their maximum size. I would not be surprised if we someday tally settlements up to 30 or 40 units (each including a kiva) in size. Certainly the Mummy Lake II settlement from Chapin Mesa with at least 35 units (Rohn 1977) suggests this. Consequently, we can postulate a continued increase in maximum settlement size from Pueblo I through Pueblo II, rather than a decrease resulting from so-called dispersed farmstead settlement.

At the same time, we can further postulate that smaller villages and hamlets, such as the Ewing site and isolated unit pueblos, formed rural hinterland populations linked to the postulated larger settlements through systems of ritual and resource sharing. In other words, I believe the complex pattern of settlement we are now beginning to discern for Pueblo III populations had its roots in Pueblo II settlement.

Early Pueblo II room blocks continue to be constructed of jacal over much of the region, although crude masonry begins to appear in some districts, such as the Mesa Verde (O'Bryan 1950:32–33). Jacal does persist well into the eleventh century at the Ewing site and other Yellow Jacket sites (Wheat, personal communication). Stone masonry walls, one stone thick, appear quite regularly in the late tenth and early eleventh centuries in many districts, frequently existing side-by-side with jacal construction. The stone mason's technique of facing masonry blocks by bifacially flaking the long sides into wedge-shaped loaflike stones provides a useful horizon marker for eleventh-century architecture (cf. Lancaster and Pinkley 1954; Rohn 1977).

Specialized semisubterranean rooms with either jacal or stone masonry superstructure have been encountered in the Yellow Jacket district at several sites (Wheat, personal communication), including the Ewing site. Many of these features contain sets of grinding bins and must have functioned as specialized milling rooms. Deep bell-shaped storage pits, extramural hearths, and wooden stockades also occur (Wheat, personal communication; Gould 1982, Ewing site).

Kivas in early Pueblo II usually employed native earth walls like the earlier pithouses, although they now assumed a circular form, and roof support posts were placed in the edge of a banquette. Through time, stone masonry lining steadily covered more and more of the side walls, and masonry columns or pilasters, replaced the wooden post roof supports. The seriation of kiva modification has been well illustrated by Lancaster and Pinkley (1954) from excavated examples on the Mesa Verde.

Pueblo III settlements represent the agglomeration of once separate residence units into larger buildings, some with multiple stories. Actually, this process of agglomeration really began in late Pueblo II when two or three units merged into contiguous room blocks—e.g., at Ewing site and on Chapin Mesa (Rohn 1977:Table 7; Lister 1965, 1966). Nor did the process of agglomeration engulf all Pueblo III unit pueblos, for many single units have been reported (e.g., Prudden 1918; Fewkes 1923; Lancaster and Van Cleave 1954; Lister 1964, 1965; Gould 1982).

Despite this process of agglomeration, the kiva seems to remain an integral part of the residence unit, probably still linked to the kinship based lineage segment. Hence, the number of kivas—reflecting the number of residence units—probably provides a quite accurate representation of population. Only very late in the thirteenth century do we note evidence of some kivas losing their close relationships to the residence unit, in sites such as Mug House and Long House on Wetherill Mesa (Rohn 1971; Cattanach 1980). This change may reflect a shift in responsibility for some ceremonials from kinship groups to religious societies.

Circular towers, one to two stories high, make their appearance by early Pueblo III. They may be associated with a single unit pueblo or with a block of several contiguous units. Under these circumstances, towers are situated adjacent to the south (southwest or southeast) side of one or more kivas. They frequently connect by tunnels with the kivas (e.g., Lancaster and Van Cleave 1954; Gould 1982; Luebben 1982; Lister 1964). Some towers and kivas stand alone as apparent shrinelike structures apart from residences (cf. Rohn 1977; Fewkes 1921, 1922, 1923). In still other circumstances, towers seem to be situated near springs and/or artificial reservoirs, around which settlements are arranged. Several of the Hovenweep ruins, including both circular and rectangular towers, exemplify this association (Fewkes 1919; Winter 1975, 1976, 1977).

Virtually all buildings during Pueblo III were constructed using flat-faced stone blocks one stone thick, two stones thick, or more than two stones thick. Several rubble core walls have been reported (e.g., Lowry, Martin 1936; Far View House, Fewkes 1917). Many Pueblo III stone masons dressed the building stones by pecking the faces flat, creating a dimpled effect, and sometimes by grinding them. Pecked stone faces provide a useful horizon marker for Pueblo III architecture. Some jacal walls persist into the late thirteenth-century Mesa Verde cliff dwellings, but rarely (cf. Cattanach 1980; Fewkes 1916b).

During Pueblo III, large specialized ceremonial structures took two somewhat different forms. The great kiva flowered at many of the larger settlements and some smaller ones. In open valley or mesa top settings it took a circular form, while in the rock shelters of the Mesa Verde it took a more rectangular form, like Fire Temple (Fewkes 1916b, 1921; Cassidy 1960) and at Long House (Cattanach 1980). Features typical of great kivas have been clearly identified at those few excavated examples (Lowry, Martin 1936; Aztec, Morris 1921; Morfield Canyon, Lister, personal communication).

Concentric wall structures in circular or D plans also occur at many of the larger settlements. These buildings consist of two or three concentric walls encircling a kiva built above ground level. Perhaps the best known and best preserved such structure is the Hubbard site at Aztec. Three concentric circular walls surround a kiva, while a second subterranean kiva lies immediately to the south (Vivian 1959). A modified version of such a structure stands among the Cliff-Fewkes Canyon cliff dwelling group at Mesa Verde. The Sun Temple consists of two above-ground kivas inside a D-shaped court enclosed by two concentric D-shaped walls (Fewkes 1916a). Smaller versions of this plan with only two walls around an above-ground kiva constitute the "horseshoe houses" of many villages in the Hovenweep district (Fewkes 1919).

Once again, Pueblo III sites have consistently been misconstrued as residential settlements occupied by communities of people. Brew (1946) recognized a village of 17 kivas (residence units) at Site 1 on Alkali Ridge, while Morris referred to, but did not delineate, similar settlements in the La Plata district and at Aztec (Morris 1939, 1924, 1928). On Chapin Mesa, clusters of both early Pueblo III mesa top sites and late Pueblo III cliff dwellings could be readily delineated as settlements sharing water sources and access routes to arable land (Rohn 1977). However, the clearest picture of Pueblo III settlement arrangements seems to be emerging among the numerous sites of the Montezuma Valley between the Mesa Verde and the Abajo Mountains.

## MONTEZUMA VALLEY TOWNS

By far the most distinctive feature of Pueblo III settlements in the Montezuma Valley is the presence of sizeable towns housing 1,200 to 2,500 people. Even though these sites had been known for many decades (e.g., Newberry 1876; Holmes 1878; Fewkes 1919), only recently has anyone attempted to estimate their size (Rohn 1972, 1983a). As relatively precise mapping has now been started on several towns and villages and their hinterlands, we can begin to postulate a pattern of settlement.

My earliest estimates of settlement size employed visible kiva depressions as reflections of residence room blocks (whether contiguous, tightly clustered, or loosely clustered), and hence population. Apparently, three kinds of Pueblo III settlements can be recognized in terms of sheer size and the presence or absence of public buildings and/or water management devices. Towns boast 60 or more kivas (residence units), one or more large specialized ceremoi.ial structures, evidence of a managed domestic water supply, and a surrounding hinterland population residing in villages and hamlets. At least some towns also contain features such as streets, plazas, and shrines. Villages range in size between 17 and 40 kivas (residence units), occasionally include a specialized ceremonial structure, frequently employ domestic water management, and often have small hamlets clustered near them. Hamlets consist of one to six kivas (residence units), often not contiguous, and generally lack any other more specialized features.

To date, at least eight towns have been confirmed through mapping and ground inspection in the Montezuma Valley (Rohn 1983a). The largest, Yellow Jacket Ruin, has more than 160 kivas (residence units), two definite plazas, a great kiva, two streets and several narrower lanes, several shrines, a possible concentric wall structure, and a reservoir with a dam and spillway

(Ferguson and Rohn 1987:129). While not all of these units need have been inhabited at the same time, none were tallied that could possibly have overlapped others—hence juxtaposition alone argues for contemporaneous occupation. I would estimate it contained 1,800 rooms and housed possibly 2,500 people or more. Lowry, Goodman Point, and Sand Canyon Ruins each have slightly more than 100 kivas (residence units) and are deployed around springs that appear to have been enhanced by dams and reservoirs. Lowry and Goodman Point each have a great kiva while Sand Canyon has a concentric wall structure. Lowry shows evidence of three internal roads or streets, two probable plazas, and several shrines (Ferguson and Rohn 1987:41). The towns of Yucca House, Mud Springs, and Lancaster Ruin all have 80 or more kivas (residence units), while the Wilson or Monument Ruin on Bug Point has 70 to 74 kivas. All were built around or adjacent to springs and show evidence of some artificial water management construction. Mud Springs and Wilson Ruins (Leh 1940) each have a concentric wall structure; Yucca House has a definite great kiva; and Lancaster Ruin has a large unnatural depression among its buildings that could be a great kiva.

Many informants, professional and lay alike, have called attention to a number of large ruins as possible towns. Actual field examination has shown most of these fall in the village size range of 17 to 40 kivas (residence units), housing from 200 to 500 persons. Undoubtedly, a few more towns will eventually be recognized when adequate field assessments are completed.

The many ruins in the Hovenweep district belong to the village size class—Ruin Canyon (Square Tower) group, Cajon, Keeley Canyon (Holly), Hackberry, Cutthroat, Pedro Point, and Cannonball (Ferguson and Rohn 1987:135–153; Morley 1908). All focus on springs whose flows had been artificially enhanced through reservoir construction or clearing choking debris. Concentric wall horseshoe houses are present at four villages. The unpublished surveys for the Bureau of Land Management have located additional villages in the Sacred Mountain planning unit. Other villages include Westwater and Edge-of-the-Cedars Ruins near Blanding, a sizeable pueblo excavated under Cummings's direction (Kidder 1910) and Site 1 on Alkali Ridge (Brew 1946), sites at the mouths of Coalbed and Monument Canyons in the Montezuma Canyon (Swift, personal communication), Nancy Patterson site (Janetski and Hurst 1984), several sites on Squaw Point, Cahone Ruin with a great kiva, eight villages in the hinterland of the Yellow Jacket town, and at least three sites northeast of Cortez. Many more villages will undoubtedly be identified as additional investigations are reported.

Many villages and hamlets seem to form hinterlands inhabited by relatively rural populations for the larger towns. Luebben (1982) has excavated several single unit hamlets near Yucca House. Gould (1982) reports a single unit dated by tree-rings at A.D. 1231 near Goodman Point Ruin. I have recently attempted to survey the hinterland of the Yellow Jacket Ruin. To date we have identified eight villages of 18 or more kivas (residence units) and at least 17 hamlets, totalling 25 residence units with kivas. The hinterland also contains farming terraces, field houses, reservoirs, a walled pair of kivas with a tower, and a cluster of pottery kilns (Hibbets and Harden 1982; Bradley 1982).

It would seem likely that this distribution of towns, villages, hamlets, and other features were once interwoven with systems of communication such as roadways. While detailed investigations have not yet begun, several lines of evidence suggest they will be found. Both Lowry and Yellow Jacket towns have internal streets. At Yellow Jacket, the main north-south avenue definitely leads out of the settlement, and a short road segment is visible between two of the Yellow Jacket hinterland villages. Two of Lowry's three avenues almost certainly lead out of the settlement, one toward a major shrine and nearby farming zone about a mile away. Several suggestive straight lines show in the vegetation on Goodman Point. Possible line-of-sight communication may also be inferred from the occurrence of a small subterranean structure at the one point on Aztec Ridge between Yucca House and Mud Springs where both towns can be seen.

Positive evidence for trade or exchange has so far been limited to items clearly recognizable as exotic within the Northern San Juan. One copper bell of west Mexican origin has been recovered from a burial at a hinterland site of the Goodman Point Ruin (Cliff Chappell, personal communication). Obsidian tools and flakes, probably from the southern San Juan Mountains, east of Pagosa Springs, or from New Mexico, have been collected from Yellow Jacket and Lancaster towns, and from Cahone and Stevenson villages. A burial from the Dominguez Ruin overlooking the Dolores River valley contained a large cache of turquoise, most likely imported from New Mexico (Reed 1979). Potsherds of Tsegi Orange Ware from the Kayenta region and White Mountain Redware from the Chaco and Zuni regions occur regularly on Montezuma Valley settlements. Even several specimens of Tusayan White Ware and Chaco Black-on-white have been identified. Occasionally, trade pottery sherds have been worked into ornaments.

Elsewhere in the Northern San Juan region, two definite towns can be identified. On the Mesa Verde, the Cliff-Fewkes Canyon settlement consisted of some 60 kivas, 530–545 rooms, a great kiva, a concentric wall structure, a managed domestic water supply, nearby farming terraces, and an estimated population between 600 and 800 (Rohn 1977:282–285). Residents of 33 cliff-dwelling sites shared a common water supply, common farmland, two communal ceremonial buildings, and about eight trails out of their common canyon setting. Four smaller (village size) settlements focused on Spruce Tree House, Square Tower House, Balcony House, and Pool Canyon formed the hinterland population for this town (Rohn 1977). The cliff dwellings in Johnson Canyon (Nickens 1981) probably constitute a village that could also have belonged to the Cliff-Fewkes Canyon town's hinterland. Other settlements cluster around the great kiva at Long House on Wetherill Mesa (Hayes 1964; Rohn 1971; Cattanach 1980).

The other town would be Aztec Ruin, consisting of the excavated pueblo, several unexcavated structures, the great kiva, the Hubbard site concentric tri-wall structure, and reported irrigated field areas (Morris 1921, 1924, 1928; Vivian 1959). Rather than a Chacoan site like Salmon Ruin (Irwin-Williams 1983), later reoccupied by Mesa Verde peoples, Aztec more reasonably resembles a Northern San Juan town, into which a small Chacoan site-unit intrusion occurred. After the Chacoans left, or were assimilated, the indigenous population remodeled the Chacoan barrio.

It has become popular for some writers to see a "Chacoan presence" in the Northern San Juan from about A.D. 1050 to 1150, possibly even triggering the "Mesa Verde florescence." However, some of the features cited as Chacoan, such as great kivas and rubble core walls, are equally indigenous to the Northern San Juan. Others, such as roadways and line-of-sight positions, were very likely common to all Anasaziland, just best preserved in the arid Chaco Basin. Without doubt, large Chacoan rooms with distinctive Chacoan masonry and some Chacoan kiva features, such as subfloor ventilators, occur sporadically at sites in the Northern San Juan, but they better fit the model of site unit intrusions than one of an overlord class.

## POPULATION DYNAMICS

The archaeological record in the Northern San Juan reveals a steady increase in both maximum size of settlements and in their complexity. Variability in contemporary settlements also increases through time. While these settlement changes reflect changes in Puebloan social and political structure, our emerging knowledge on the distribution of settlements through time reflects shifting populations.

Individual studies have detailed population shifts within localities or districts. A progressive upstream drift can be seen along the San Juan River in the Navajo Reservoir from Rosa phase (Basketmaker III), through Piedra phase (Pueblo I), into Arboles phase (early Pueblo II), followed by virtual abandonment (Dittert et al. 1961). Almost constant population shifting in response to local factors has been described on Chapin Mesa (Rohn 1977) and on Wetherill Mesa (Hayes 1964; Cordell 1972). Herold (1961) suggests a population drift from higher elevations to lower elevations in the Montezuma Valley as water management techniques developed. The Dolores Archaeological Project suggests the most dramatic part of this drift, between Pueblo I and Pueblo II, had an environmental cause (Petersen 1983; Orcutt 1986). On White Mesa in Utah, Puebloan peoples seem to have utilized seasonal habitations for resource exploitation to varying degrees of intensity from Basketmaker III through Pueblo II (Davis 1983). Matson and associates (1983) have described the movements of Puebloan peoples onto Cedar Mesa during Grand Gulch (Basketmaker II) and Mossbacks (Basketmaker III) phases with an abandonment during Pueblo I and most of Pueblo II. Puebloan populations reappear about A.D. 1060 in late Pueblo II and inhabit the district through A.D. 1260.

These few examples of localized population movements contribute to an overall view of population dynamics for the Northern San Juan Region. Progressing by stages from early to late, projectile points of all desert Archaic styles occur sporadically throughout the entire region. Presumably, these pre-Puebloan hunters and gatherers were wandering from camp to camp to exploit a variety of available resources. However, this generalized picture does not really say much without numerous excavated and dated sites.

Basketmaker II settlements have been documented from Falls Creek north of Durango, the Pine River valley at Navajo Reservoir in the eastern part of the region, and from the Grand Gulch–Cedar Mesa–Comb Ridge zones in the west. Similar materials have been described from the Tabeguache Caves on the lower Dolores River to the north of the region and could represent an incoming population (cf. Hurst 1957). Even though some Basketmaker II style projectile points do occur in the Montezuma Valley and on the Mesa Verde, this east-west-north distribution on and toward the margins of the later population concentrations could reflect initial selective colonization of immigrating semisettled horticultural groups. The earlier dates of the Falls Creek sites have suggested to some a southward movement during Basketmaker II to lower elevations represented by the Los Pinos sites.

During Basketmaker III, virtually all of the Northern San Juan seems to be settled. The rarity of such sites predating A.D. 600 may reflect continuation of the earlier colonization process. By A.D. 600, Basketmaker III peoples are settled in permanent villages everywhere but in the lower elevations of the lower Montezuma Valley canyons. By A.D. 700 they have also penetrated the Dolores River valley.

Pueblo I population seems to increase dramatically over that of Basket-maker III. Pueblo I settlements are both larger and more numerous through-out the region, although the lands west of Comb Ridge have been emptied. People have moved into the lower elevations of the Montezuma Valley establishing sizeable settlements at Nancy Patterson and at the mouth of Recapture Creek, although the Hovenweep district contains very few sites at this time. Populations peak during Pueblo I in the Dolores Valley and in the districts east of the La Plata River.

Intriguingly, while utilitarian ceramics reflect the Pueblowide adoption of broad neck-banding, decorated ceramics and some other elements of material culture exhibit a distinctive regional flavor. Piedra Black-on-white continues the patterns and designs of the preceding Chapin Black-on-white on unslipped vessel surfaces. The use of lead glaze paint reaches its peak popularity, especially in the eastern subregion. Oxidized red pottery—Abajo Red-on-orange and Bluff Black-on-red—dominates in the western subre-gion. Axeheads are made from stream-worn cobbles notched for hafting. Evidence for trade appears scant.

By Pueblo II several major relocations have occurred. Virtually all of the territory east of the La Plata River has been abandoned except for a small remnant population represented by the Arboles and Chimney Rock phases along the upper San Juan River in Colorado's section of the Navajo Reser-voir. The Dolores River valley is almost abandoned except for its southern rim along Summit Ridge, just south of the town of Dolores. The lower elevations of the Montezuma Valley, especially in the Hovenweep district, are now occupied. Many districts in the western subregion, such as the Mesa Verde, show marked increases in population. Comb Ridge continues to act as a western frontier, perhaps while Kayenta region peoples are exploiting the triangle formed by it and the Colorado and lower San Juan Rivers.

This is also the time of strongest incursion of Puebloan cultural attributes northward into sites of Fremont affiliation—masonry wall construction, black-on-gray painted pottery, etc. Concurrently, the incidence of obvious trade items in Northern San Juan settlements increases. Ceramics have been identified from the Kayenta, Little Colorado, and Chaco Regions, while jew-elry made from Pacific coast shells and turquoise is relatively more common. Even though hard evidence is lacking, I get a feeling of more frequent inter-course among neighboring Puebloan peoples during Pueblo II and early Pueblo III than either before or afterwards.

By A.D. 1050–60, Northern San Juan peoples are again moving into the lands west of Comb Ridge. By about 1150, Puebloan influences on the Fremont seem to cease. Pueblo III populations are clearly concentrated in the Montezuma Valley between the Mesa Verde and Abajo Mountains, where some 30,000 people can be conservatively estimated. Another 2,500 to 3,000 inhabited the Mesa Verde with additional groups in the Mancos Valley, La Plata district, and San Juan valley near Farmington and Aztec. By 1125, even the Chimney Rock population had moved out of the upper San Juan Valley.

During late Pueblo II and early Pueblo III, several small groups of Chacoan people seem to migrate into the Northern San Juan. Salmon Ruin on the San Juan River near Bloomfield, New Mexico, was an apparent outlier of the Chaco Canyon settlements (Irwin-Williams 1983). A colony constructed one corner of the excavated pueblo at Aztec Ruin (Morris 1919). Eddy (1977) interprets the 35 rooms and two kivas of Chimney Rock Pueblo as the residences of a group of Chacoan men (priests?) who took indigenous wives. Other small colonies may have inhabited portions of Lowry's western wing (Martin 1936) and the Wallace Ruin near Cortez (Bradley 1974). All these migrant groups either retreated after a short time (50 years or less), or they were assimilated into native Northern San Juan society.

Abrupt abandonment of the Northern San Juan by Puebloan peoples at the end of the thirteenth century was a remarkable event. Even if the exodus had begun early in the century and dragged out over an extended time period, this relocation of more than 30,000 people marks a major migration. Without extensive excavation, we cannot judge when the Montezuma Valley towns and their hinterlands were vacated. Tree-ring construction dates at 1211 and 1231 argue for continued occupation into the early thirteenth century at least. Mesa Verde's cliff dwellings exhibit intensive building activities through the 1270s with some dates even in the 1280s. Consequently, the total absence of late Tsegi phase ceramics from the Kayenta region argues instead for a cessation of trade contacts rather than for an earlier abandonment. The identical nature of architectural and ceramic attributes between the settlements of the Montezuma Valley and the Mesa Verde argues for sustained occupations in both zones followed by a rather sudden and short-lived out-migration.

Estimated population curves for the Montezuma Valley and Chapin Mesa show increasing growth rates into Pueblo III (Rohn 1983b, 1977). Even though extensive portions of the region were abandoned during Pueblo II and III, the population density within the Montezuma Valley grew to dominate the region's statistics. Thus, even without thorough sampling, a similar curve reflecting steady population growth from Basketmaker II through Pueblo III can be suggested for the whole region.

## RELATIONSHIPS TO THE ENVIRONMENT

Obviously, Pueblo people found the Northern San Juan a suitable environment for their culture and its development, settling there for more than thirteen centuries. Not only did their culture develop markedly, their numbers increased dramatically. They actually exploited only a portion of the available resources, never making use of fish, lizards, or snakes for food; coal for fuel; or metal ores for tools or ornaments. Yet, their livelihood depended on a balance between arable soils, adequate growing season (usually dependent on elevation), sufficient moisture to mature crops, and a domestic water supply. Several excellent studies have grown out of the Navajo Reservoir, Wetherill Mesa, Cedar Mesa, and Dolores Projects relating the prehistoric Pueblos to their environment. Several have invoked changes in past climatic conditions to explain major and minor population shifts and the changes in Pueblo culture.

Perhaps the most consistent and potentially useful indicator of past climatic conditions is the tree-ring record. It provides reflections of available moisture for tree growth for more than 2,000 years, including all of the time Puebloan peoples inhabited the Northern San Juan. While considerable fluctuation occurs from year-to-year and several periods of drought may be observed, none of these appear to have been significant enough, nor do they occur at appropriate times, to explain the major happenings in Puebloan culture history. Even the Great Drought of 1276 to 1299 need not have caused total abandonment.

A well-coordinated program comparing the pollen record with cycles of alluviation and erosion in the Navajo Reservoir led Schoenwetter and Eddy (1964) to reconstruct cyclical shifts in storm patterns that they then correlated with periods of variable human exploitation. Their reconstruction totally ignored the tree-ring record, however. Peterson (1983) has correlated a variety of evidence to suggest minor changes in mean annual temperature would more severely affect length of growing season and hence the elevations at which farmers could hope to mature crops of maize.

There are really many excellent studies (e.g., Euler et al. 1979; Dean et al. 1985) of the paleoenvironmental context in which prehistoric peoples subsisted. A lesson can be taken from them. While a variety of environmental factors influenced the lives of prehistoric Puebloan peoples, and even subtle changes in these factors could evoke adaptive responses, such responses fit readily into the Puebloan cultural pattern and did not require major changes or relocations. The considerable environmental diversity available in the Northern San Juan allowed minor adjustments to solve the minor problems posed by environmental fluctuations. The truly major problem facing the resident peoples was economic adaptation of a steadily growing population to their erratic natural context.

This basic problem most likely led to the development of techniques to manage water supplies and develop supplemental croplands (Steward 1940; Stewart and Donnelly 1943a, 1943b; Herold 1961; Rohn 1963, 1977). Systems of check-dams built across ravines or along hillsides produced terraces by capturing eroding topsoil. Such terraces not only provided additional tillable acreage, but also stored moisture trapped from runoff.

Artificial reservoirs to collect and store water for domestic use took several forms. Some had been pecked into bedrock in runoff channels or below springs. Stone-faced earthen dams occasionally held pools at or just below springs. Other dams in natural drainage channels just above canyon pouroffs trapped rainwater runoff and fed it into the underlying bedrock from which it would then emerge in a spring (Rohn 1972, 1983a). Still other reservoirs caught water through artificial channels and held it in relatively flat mesa top situations, like Mummy Lake (Rohn 1963). Many reservoirs had overflow spillways and sediment traps.

Some ditches for transporting water either to reservoirs or to fields have been reported (e.g., Stewart 1940). Unconfirmed rumor suggested ditches once existed in the Animas River valley near Aztec Ruin (Moorehead 1908).

The precise dating of the origin of water and soil management techniques is unknown. Chronological evidence from Chapin Mesa indicates both terracing and reservoirs were in operation by early Pueblo II and may have begun earlier (Rohn 1963, 1977). Herold (1961) has suggested the population drift from higher elevations, such as the Dolores River valley, to the lower and warmer zones of the Montezuma Valley, such as Hovenweep, reflected technological capabilities to enhance water supplies in drier settings. This drift began about A.D. 900 but continued into Pueblo III.

Paleoclimatic changes seem to have had far less effect on population movements and cultural change than did social or cultural factors. While the Dolores Valley Pueblo I occupants moved to lower elevations by Pueblo II, the Navajo Reservoir residents were steadily shifting to higher elevations, and much of the eastern subregion at all elevations was abandoned. While local conditions such as arroyo cutting and increased cold air drainage undoubtedly affected local communities somewhat, these population movements more readily fit explanations of response to new technological developments, such as water management techniques, or to changing frontiers in the face of a neighboring non-Puebloan human cultural environment (early Utes or Athabascans?).

None of these speculations nor the new evidence of recent years provides any more satisfactory explanations for the biggest event in Puebloan prehistory—abandonment of the San Juan. We now realize environmental diversity would allow satisfactory adaptive responses to the so-called Great Drought for at least much of the populace. Our newer population estimates make it even more difficult to envision a broad scale retreat from the threats of wandering bands of proto-Utes or Navajos. We are thus left with only two viable possibilities: (1) the reasons for extensive Pueblo migrations out of the San Juan were purely social, political, or religious, or (2) burgeoning populations in such places as the Montezuma Valley caused total ecological collapse. We can never hope to uncover sound evidence for the former reasons without written documents or astounding artistic depictions. However, total ecological collapse should be detectable if it ever occurred, and current dendrochronological and palynological records fail to support this prospect. Further, a deteriorating environment could be offset by elaborating trade networks. Conversely, evidence for trade to the Mesa Verde actually declines from the eleventh through the thirteenth centuries. Consequently, I am increasingly inclined to accept purely cultural factors to explain the great Pueblo migration.

## DIRECTIONS FOR FUTURE RESEARCH

An obvious direction in which to focus future research would be the filling of gaps in our knowledge of chronological developments and geographic distribution. Indeed, several such gaps need attention. (1) Sites of pre-Basketmaker affiliation need to be identified and carefully investigated with full attention to obtaining sound dates and useful paleoecological information. It should be possible to develop a picture of changing culture history and environmental adaptation that would provide a more understandable background for the development of Puebloan culture. (2) A fuller picture of Basketmaker II occupation of the Northern San Juan is needed, in terms of their full geographic distribution, chronological changes within this relatively lengthy stage, and the precise nature of their subsistence balance between horticulture and hunting and collecting. (3) The most pronounced changes in subsistence and material culture took place between A.D. 300 and 600—rapid growth in the importance of agriculture, dominating the diet; appearance of domesticated beans and turkeys; construction of substantial semisubterranean houses in year-round villages according to clear patterns; replacement of the atlatl and dart by the bow and arrow; and extensive adoption of ceramic utensils for cooking and eating. Yet archaeological remains from this time are virtually unknown. An especially concerted effort needs to be made to find these remains if they exist.

Several other knowledge gaps also exist in our general understanding of Northern San Juan culture history. (1) The growth of large towns probably began at least in Pueblo II and possibly earlier. This development needs to be documented by explorations in several large settlements of Pueblo II and III vintage; (2) The history of several architectural features needs documentation, especially in terms of their functional values. These would include great kivas, concentric wall structures, towers, shrines, plazas, streets and roadways, and stockades. For example, the plaza could have originated as an open space free of both structures and refuse situated on the southeast side of Basketmaker III villages, often within a stockade line.

The explosive archaeological activity within the Northern San Juan resulting from contract projects to salvage information threatened by the nearly frantic explorations for energy and other resources has drawn attention to the need for archaeologists to establish broad-based research plans with priorities for investigative problems. These priorities will also affect cultural resource management plans about what resources to preserve and how. At the same time, resource surveys and mitigation projects have produced and continue to produce masses of largely unconnected data.

It seems to me we could greatly improve our data collection and understanding, as well as aid cultural resource management, if we refocused our attention on the specific human social groups responsible for the archaeological remains we see. This means deemphasizing the significance of the "site" to a handy provenience label for notes and artifacts. The basic unit of study should be the settlement and its various segments. By definition, settlements constitute the material remains that were (are) inhabited by communities of people who recognize their specific identity. Segments of communities also had specific social identities. Many nonresidential features served particular functions for the community, for segments of the community, or for several communities. Cultural behavioral patterns can only be described from the range of variation within each level of settlement organization.

The significance of any specific archaeological site, be it a permanent habitation, temporary camp, limited activity area, abandoned material culture, refuse deposits, or various disruptions of the natural landscape for farmlands, waterworks, roadways, and the like, stems from its information value about prehistoric human communities. Only when we understand the nature of such prehistoric communities and their social and political organization can we define adequate universes for sophisticated sampling. The most advanced archaeological techniques produce worthless data when misapplied, as they so often are. Statistical manipulations will become much more appropriate when applied to units of actual human settlement rather than to units of convenient archaeological recording.

# REFERENCES

Abel, Leland J.
> 1955    *San Juan Red Ware, Mesa Verde Gray Ware, Mesa Verde White Ware, and San Juan White Ware.* Museum of Northern Arizona Ceramic Series 3B. Flagstaff.

Blinman, Eric
> 1984    Dating with Neckbands: Calibration of Temporal Variation in Moccasin Gray and Mancos Gray Ceramic Types. In *Dolores Archaeological Program: Synthetic Report 1978–1981*, supervised by David A. Breternitz. Bureau of Reclamation, Denver.

Bradley, Bruce A.
> 1974    Preliminary Report of Excavations at Wallace Ruin, 1969–1974. *Southwestern Lore* 40(3 and 4):63–71.
> 1982    *Cultural Resource Monitoring of a Shell Oil Company CO² Well Pad and Significant Evaluation of 5MT7525, Montezuma County, Colorado.* Complete Archaeological Service Associates, Cortez.

Breternitz, David A., Arthur H. Rohn, and Elizabeth A. Morris
> 1974    *Prehistoric Ceramics of the Mesa Verde Region.* Museum of Northern Arizona Ceramic Series No. 5. Flagstaff.

Brew, John D.
> 1946    *Archaeology of Alkali Ridge, Southeastern Utah.* Peabody Museum Papers Vol. 21. Cambridge.

Carlson, Roy L.
> 1963    *Basket Maker III Sites Near Durango, Colorado.* University of Colorado Studies, Series in Anthropology No 8. Boulder.

Cassidy, Francis
> 1960    Fire Temple, Mesa Verde National Park. In *The Great Kivas of Chaco Canyon and Their Relationships* by Gordon Vivian and Paul Reiter. Monographs of the School of American Research No. 22. Santa Fe.

Cattanach, George S., Jr.
> 1980    *Long House, Mesa Verde National Park, Colorado.* National Park Service Archaeological Research Series No. 7-H. Washington.

Cordell, Linda S.
> 1972    *Settlement Pattern Changes at Wetherill Mesa, Colorado: A Test Case for Computer Simulation in Archaeology.* Unpublished Ph.D. dissertation, Department of Anthropology, University of California, Santa Barbara.
> 1981    The Wetherill Mesa Simulation: A Retrospective. In *Simulations in Archaeology*, edited by Jeremy A. Sabloff. School of American Research, University of New Mexico Press. Albuquerque.

Davis, William E.
    1983    *1981 Excavations on White Mesa, San Juan County, Utah*. Plano Archaeological Consultants and Abajo Archaeology, Bluff.

Dean, Jeffrey S., Robert C. Euler, George J. Gumerman, Fred Plog, Richard H. Hevly, and Thor N. V. Karlstrom
    1985    Human Behavior, Demography, and Paleoenvironment on the Colorado Plateaus. *American Antiquity* 50(3):537–554.

Dittert, Alfred E., Jr., James J. Hester, and Frank W. Eddy
    1961    *An Archaeological Survey of the Navajo Reservoir District, Northwestern New Mexico*. Monographs of the School of American Research No. 23. Santa Fe.

Eddy, Frank W.
    1961    *Excavations at Los Pinos Phase Sites in the Navajo Reservoir District*. Museum of New Mexico Papers in Anthropology No. 4. Santa Fe.
    1966    *Prehistory of the Navajo Reservoir District, Northwestern New Mexico* (2 parts). Museum of New Mexico Papers in Anthropology No. 15. Santa Fe.
    1977    *Archaeological Investigations at Chimney Rock Mesa: 1970–1972*. Memoirs of the Colorado Archaeological Society No. 1. Boulder.

Erdman, James A., Charles L. Douglas, and John W. Marr
    1969    *Environment of Mesa Verde, Colorado*. National Park Sevice Archaeological Research Series No. 7-B. Washington.

Euler, Robert C., George J. Gumerman, Thor N. V. Karlstrom, Jeffrey S. Dean, and Richard H. Hevly
    1979    The Colorado Plateaus: Cultural Dynamics and Paleoenvironment. *Science* 205(4411):1089–1101.

Ferguson, William M., and Arthur H. Rohn
    1987    *Anasazi Ruins of the Southwest In Color*. University of New Mexico Press, Albuquerque.

Fewkes, Jesse W.
    1916a    *Excavation and Repair of Sun Temple, Mesa Verde National Park*. Department of the Interior, Washington.
    1916b    The Cliff Ruins in Fewkes Cañon, Mesa Verde National Park, Colorado. In *Holmes Anniversary Volume*, edited by F. W. Hodge, pp. 96–117. Washington.
    1917    A Prehistoric Mesa Verde Pueblo and Its People. *Annual Report of the Smithsonian Institution—1916*, pp. 461–488. Washington.
    1919    *Prehistoric Villages, Castles, and Towers of Southwestern Colorado*. Bureau of American Ethnology Bulletin No. 70. Washington.
    1921    Field-Work on the Mesa Verde National Park. *Smithsonian Miscellaneous Collections: Explorations and Field-Work for 1920* 72(6):75–94. Washington.
    1922    Archaeological Field-Work on the Mesa Verde National Park. *Smithsonian Miscellaneous Collections: Explorations and Field-Work for 1921* 72(15):64–83. Washington.
    1923    Archaeological Field-Work on the Mesa Verde National Park. *Smithsonian Miscellaneous Collections: Explorations and Field-Work for 1922* 74(5):90–115. Washington.

Gould, Ronald
   1982    *The Mustoe Site: The Application of Neutron Activation Analysis in the Interpretation of a Multi-component Archaeological Site.* Ph.D. dissertation, University of Texas at Austin.

Hayes, Alden C.
   1964    *The Archeological Survey of Wetherill Mesa.* National Park Service Archeological Research Series No. 7-A. Washington.

Hayes, Alden C., and James A. Lancaster
   1975    *Badger House Community, Mesa Verde National Park.* National Park Service Archeological Research Series No. 7-E. Washington.

Herold, Joyce
   1961    *Prehistoric Settlement and Physical Environment in the Mesa Verde Area.* University of Utah Anthropological Papers No. 53. Salt Lake City.

Hibbets, Barry N., and Patrick L. Harden
   1982    *Archeological Monitoring of Celcius Energy Corporation's Woods Unit 1-S Well Pad and Access Road, and a Report of the Excavation and Evaluation of Site 5MT7143, Montezuma County, Colorado.* La Plata Archeological Consultants, Dolores, Colorado.

Holmes, William H.
   1878    Report on the Ancient Ruins of Southwestern Colorado. *U.S. Geological and Geographic Survey of the Territories for 1876, 10th Annual Report,* pp. 383–408. Washington.

Hurst, Blanche H.
   1957    A Comparative Study of the Peripheral Excavations of C. T. Hurst. *Southwestern Lore* 23(2):14–31. Boulder.

Irwin-Williams, Cynthia
   1983    Socio-economic Order and Authority Structure in the Chacoan Community at Salmon Ruin. Paper presented at the Anasazi Symposium, Farmington, New Mexico.

Janetski, Joel C., and Winston Hurst
   1984    *The Nancy Patterson Village Archaeological Research Project, Field Year 1983—Preliminary Report.* Brigham Young University Department of Anthropology Technical Series No. 84–7.

Jennings, Calvin H.
   1968    Archaeological Excavations at Site 60, Chapin Mesa. In *Contributions to Mesa Verde Archaeology: V, Emergency Archaeology in Mesa Verde National Park, Colorado, 1948–1966,* edited by Robert H. Lister. University of Colorado Studies, Series in Anthropology No. 15. Boulder.

Kane, Allen E.
   1983    The Sagehen Flats Archaeological Locality. In *Dolores Archaeological Program: Field Investigations and Analysis—1978,* supervised by David A. Breternitz. Bureau of Reclamation, Denver.
   1984    The Prehistory of the Dolores Project Area. In *Dolores Archaeological Program: Synthetic Report 1978–1981,* supervised by David A. Breternitz. Bureau of Reclamation, Denver.

Kidder, Alfred V.
1910    Explorations in Southeastern Utah in 1908. *American Journal of Archaeology* 14(3):337–360. Norwood.
1927    Southwestern Archaeological Conference. *El Palacio* 23(22):554–561. Santa Fe.

Lancaster, James A., and Jean M. Pinkley
1954    Excavation at Site 16 or Three Pueblo II Mesa-top Ruins. In *Archeological Excavations in Mesa Verde National Park, Colorado, 1950.* National Park Service Archeological Research Series No. 2. Washington.

Lancaster, James A., and Philip F. Van Cleave
1954    The Excavation of Sun Point Pueblo. In *Archeological Excavations in Mesa Verde National Park, Colorado, 1950.* National Park Service Archeological Research Series No. 2. Washington.

Lancaster, James A., and Don Watson
1942    Excavation of Mesa Verde Pithouses. *American Antiquity* 9(2):190–198.
1954    Excavation of Two Late Basketmaker III Pithouses. In *Archeological Excavations in Mesa Verde National Park, Colorado, 1950.* National Park Service Archeological Research Series No. 2. Washington.

Leh, Leonard L.
1940    A Prehistoric Population Center in the Southwest. *Southwestern Lore* 6(2):21–25. Gunnison.

Lipe, William D., and Cory D. Breternitz
1980    Approaches to Analyzing Variability Among Dolores Area Structures, A.D. 600–950. *Contract Abstracts and CRM Archeology* 1(2):21–28. Albuquerque.

Lister, Robert H.
1964    *Contributions to Mesa Verde Archaeology: I, Site 499, Mesa Verde National Park, Colorado.* University of Colorado Studies, Series in Anthropology No. 9. Boulder.
1965    *Contributions to Mesa Verde Archaeology: II, Site 875, Mesa Verde National Park, Colorado.* University of Colorado Studies, Series in Anthropology No. 11. Boulder.
1966    *Contributions to Mesa Verde Archaeology: III, Site 866, and the Cultural Sequence at Four Villages in the Far View Group, Mesa Verde National Park, Colorado.* University of Colorado Studies, Series in Anthropology No. 12. Boulder.

Lister, Robert H., and Florence C. Lister
1969    *The Earl H. Morris Memorial Pottery Collection.* University of Colorado Studies, Series in Anthropology No. 16. Boulder.

Luebben, Ralph A.
1982    The Grinnell Site: A Small Ceremonial Center Near Yucca House, Colorado. Ms. on file at Anthropology Department, Grinnell College.

Martin, Paul S.
1936    *Lowry Ruin in Southwestern Colorado.* Field Museum of Natural History Publications No. 356, Anthropological Series 23(1):1–216. Chicago.
1939    *Modified Basket Maker Sites, Ackmen-Lowry Area, Southwestern Colorado,*

*1938*. Field Museum of Natural History Anthropological Series 23, no. 3. Chicago.

Matson, R. G., William D. Lipe, and William R. Haase
1983    Adaptational Continuities and Occupational Discontinuities: The Anasazi Occupation on Cedar Mesa. The 1983 Anasazi Symposium, Farmington, New Mexico.

Mohr, Albert and L. L. Sample
1959    San Jose Sites in Southeastern Utah. *El Palacio* 66(4):109–119. Santa Fe.

Moorehead, W. K.
1908    Ruins at Aztec and on the Rio La Plata, New Mexico. *American Anthropologist* 10(2):255–263. Lancaster.

Morley, Sylvanus G.
1908    The Excavation of Cannonball Ruins in Southwestern Colorado. *American Anthropologist* 10(4):596–610. Lancaster.

Morris, Earl H.
1919    The Aztec Ruin. *American Museum of Natural History Anthropological papers* 26(1).
1921    The House of the Great Kiva at the Aztec Ruin. *American Museum of Natural History Anthropological Papers* 26(2):109–138. New York.
1924    Burials in the Aztec Ruin: The Aztec Ruin Annex. *American Museum of Natural History Anthropological Papers* 26(3 & 4):139–225, 227–257.
1928    Notes on Excavation in the Aztec Ruin. *American Museum of Natural History Anthropological Papers* 26(5):257–420. New York.
1939    *Archaeological Studies in the La Plata District, Southwestern Colorado and Northwestern New Mexico*. Carnegie Institution of Washington Publication No. 519. Washington.

Morris, Earl H., and Robert F. Burgh
1954    *Basket Maker II Sites Near Durango, Colorado*. Carnegie Institution of Washington Publication No. 604. Washington.

Nelson, G. Charles, and Allen E. Kane
1986    Excavations at Singing Shelter (Site 5MT4683), A Multicomponent Site. In *Dolores Archaeological Program: Anasazi Communities at Dolores: Middle Canyon Area*, compiled by Allen E. Kane and Christine K. Robinson. Bureau of Reclamation, Denver.

Newberry, J. S.
1876    Geological Report. In *Report of the Exploring Expedition from Santa Fe, New Mexico, to the Junction of the Grand and Green Rivers of the Great Colorado of the West in 1859* by J. N. Macomb. Government Printing Office. Washington.

Nickens, Paul R.
1981    Pueblo III Communities in Transition: Environment and Adaptation in Johnson Canyon. *Memoirs of the Colorado Archaeological Society* No. 2. Boulder.

Nusbaum, Jesse L.
1981    *The 1926 Re-excavation of Step House Cave, Mesa Verde National Park*. Mesa Verde Research Series Paper No. 1.

O'Bryan, Deric
    1950      *Excavations in Mesa Verde National Park, 1947–1948.* Medallion Papers No. 39. Globe.

Orcutt, Janet D.
    1986      Climate, Population, and Resource Supply in the Middle Canyon Area. In *Dolores Archaeological Program: Anasazi Communities at Dolores: Middle Canyon Area,* compiled by Allen E. Kane and Christine K. Robinson. Bureau of Reclamation, Denver.

Petersen, Kenneth L.
    1983      Reconstruction of Droughts and Summer Warmth for the Dolores Archaeological Project Area, Southwest Colorado: A.D. 550 to 950. Paper presented to the Second Anasazi Symposium, Bloomfield, New Mexico.

Petersen, Kenneth L., Vicki L. Clay, Meredith H. Matthews, and Sarah W. Neusius (compilers)
    1985      *Dolores Archaeological Program: Studies in Environmental Archaeology.* Bureau of Reclamation, Engineering and Research Center. Denver.

Prudden, T. Mitchell
    1903      The Prehistoric Ruins of the San Juan Watershed in Utah, Arizona, Colorado, and New Mexico. *American Anthropologist* 5(2):224–288. Lancaster.
    1914      The Circular Kivas of Small Ruins in the San Juan Watershed. *American Anthropologist* 16(1):33–58. Lancaster.
    1918      A Further Study of Prehistoric Small House Ruins in the San Juan Watershed. *American Anthropological Association Memoirs* 5(1). Lancaster.

Reed, Allen D.
    1979      *The Dominguez Ruin: A McElmo Phase Pueblo in Southwestern Colorado.* Bureau of Land Management Cultural Resource Series No. 7, Part I.

Roberts, Frank H. H., Jr.
    1930      *Early Pueblo Ruins in the Piedra District, Southwestern Colorado.* Bureau of American Ethnology Bulletin 96. Washington.

Rohn, Arthur H.
    1963      Prehistoric Soil and Water Conservation on Chapin Mesa, Southwestern Colorado. *American Antiquity* 28(4):441–455. Salt Lake City.
    1971      *Mug House, Mesa Verde National Park, Colorado.* National Park Service Archeological Research Series No. 7-D. Washington.
    1972      Budding Urban Settlements in the Northern San Juan. Paper presented to the American Anthropological Association Annual Meeting. New York.
    1974      Payne Site Investigations. *Southwestern Lore* 40(3 & 4):50–52.
    1975      A Stockaded Basketmaker III Village at Yellow Jacket, Colorado. *The Kiva* 40(3):113–119.
    1977      *Cultural Change and Continuity on Chapin Mesa.* Regents Press of Kansas, Lawrence.
    1983a     Budding Urban Settlements in the Northern San Juan. *Proceedings of the Anasazi Symposium 1981,* edited by Jack E. Smith. Mesa Verde Museum Association.
    1983b     Pueblo Indian Social History Seen from the Northern San Juan. Paper presented to the Second Anasazi Symposium, Bloomfield, New Mexico.

Schoenwetter, James and Frank W. Eddy
    1964    *Alluvial and Palynological Reconstruction of Environments, Navajo Reservoir District.* Museum of New Mexico Papers in Anthropology No. 13. Santa Fe.

Schulman, Edmund
    1946    Dendrochronology at Mesa Verde National Park. *Tree-Ring Bulletin* 12(3):18–24.

Stewart, Guy R.
    1940    Conservation in Pueblo Agriculture. *The Scientific Monthly* 51:201–220, 329–340.

Stewart, Guy R., and Maurice Donnelly
    1943a    Soil and Water Economy in the Pueblo Southwest, I. Field Studies at Mesa Verde and Northern Arizona. *The Scientific Monthly* 56:31–44.
    1943b    Soil and Water Economy in the Pueblo Southwest, II. Evaluation of Primitive Methods of Conservation. *The Scientific Monthly* 56:134–144.

Vivian, R. Gordon
    1959    *The Hubbard Site and Other Tir-wall Structures in New Mexico and Colorado.* National Park Service Archeological Research Series No. 5. Washington.

Wanek, Alexander A.
    1959    Geology and Fuel Resources of the Mesa Verde Area, Montezuma and LaPlata Counties, Colorado. *Geological Survey Bulletin* 1072-M. Washington.

Wheat, Joe Ben
    1955    MT-1, A Basketmaker III Site near Yellow Jacket, Colorado (A Progress Report). *Southwestern Lore* 21(2):18–26.

Winter, Joseph C.
    1975    *Hovenweep 1974.* San Jose State University Archeological Report No. 1. San Jose.
    1976    *Hovenweep 1975.* San Jose State University Archeological Report No. 2. San Jose.
    1977    *Hovenweep 1976.* San Jose State University Archeological Report No. 3. San Jose.

STEVEN A. LeBLANC 6

# Cultural Dynamics in the Southern Mogollon Area

The Mogollon cultural area is one of the three generally recognized major traditions in the Southwest. The area can be conveniently subdivided into a northern or mountain Mogollon, and a southern, valley or desert Mogollon. These divisions represent not only topographic variability but important differences in culture history.

The southern Mogollon encompasses all of the Mimbres branch in southwestern New Mexico, the San Simon branch in southeastern Arizona, and the Viejo period occupation in northern Chihuahua, which seems to represent another Mogollon branch. The Jornada "Mogollon" is considered in only a tangential way because it seems that its western part is an extension of the Mimbres branch, while the eastern area is not really Mogollon.

Several prefatory remarks are in order concerning the relative state of our knowledge of these areas. By far, the best known area is the Mimbres. Information is available on at least 45 excavation projects, which involved the excavation of 100+ pithouses and 400+ Classic Mimbres surface rooms. While this body of work is substantial, almost all of it concentrates on the period A.D. 650–1150, and much was undertaken in the 1920s and 1930s. Relatively less survey work has been undertaken. The archaeology of the area has been reviewed (LeBlanc and Whalen 1980), and the chronology reevaluated (Anyon et al. 1981; LeBlanc 1980a).

179

The San Simon area has seen little additional work since the pioneering efforts of Sayles (1945), and most of the later relevant work has been on late sites, for example, the Kuykendall and Curtis sites (Mills and Mills 1969, n.d.) and the Ringo site (Johnson and Thompson 1963). No recent synthesis exists. Except for some early research, our knowledge of northern Chihuahua comes almost exclusively from the work of DiPeso (1974) at Casas Grandes and its environs. As a consequence, we know a great deal about this site, but little about the area as a whole. In contrast to the above area, our knowledge of the Jornada area (Lehmer 1948) is largely based on survey information. Research in this area has been synthesized (LeBlanc and Whalen 1980).

Because our knowledge of the Mimbres area is more extensive than for these adjacent areas, and because the author has been conducting research in this area, the focus of this paper will be on the Mimbres. However, the region as a whole will be considered wherever possible.

## DEVELOPMENTAL BACKGROUND

The current focus is on the seven hundred year interval between A.D. 750 and 1450 (Fig. 18), but a very brief recap of previous events beginning with the Late Archaic is pertinent. Archaic sites predating A.D. 200 are known from most of the southern Mogollon area. They were occupied by a nonsedentary population with an economy predominantly based on hunting and gathering. Most sites are found in open desert areas and are not associated with well-watered floodplains. Whether this reflects a true cultural pattern or is a product of archaeological visibility is unknown.

It has been proposed (LeBlanc 1980b, 1983) that the years between A.D. 200 and 300 witnessed a marked shift in adaptation over the entire area. Fully permanent, or at least much more permanent, villages were first built during this interval. They are almost always found adjacent to good farm land and the use of more xeric areas seems greatly diminished. Villages are sometimes large, with perhaps 50 or more pithouse depressions, and are usually defensively located (LeBlanc 1980b, 1983). This pattern exists in all parts of the southern Mogollon region for which we have any information.

This change in settlement pattern seems to reflect a shift to an economy based predominantly on agriculture. Around A.D. 550 the defensive locations are abandoned and new village sites are founded adjacent to good farm land, primarily along well-watered river valleys. Where we have good survey information, there seem to have been relatively few special activity sites. The first production of painted pottery occurs a bit after this time, and several surveys in the Mimbres area indicate significant population growth

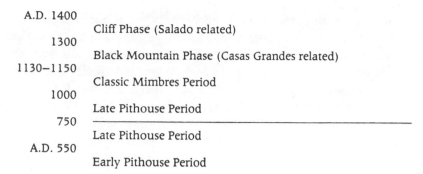

Fig. 18. *Southern Mogollon sequence based on Mimbres sequence. Other nearby sequences are primarily dated by cross-reference to the Mimbres branch, and do not provide additional information.*

(Minnis 1980; Blake et al. n.d.). The period A.D. 200–750 corresponds to the interval and concept defined by this volume as the Initiation period, discussed in Chapter 1. However, there does seem to be a significant set of changes that occurred around A.D. 550, which are not reflected in the pan-southwestern schema, but which do mark an equivalent period change.

It should be noted that the periods defined in this chapter were not used to conform to the chronology defined by the volume, but were developed prior to the School of American Research seminar. The fact that this new sequence fits the southern Mogollon data far better than any previous overall southwestern construct implies a level of interaction between regions in the Southwest not generally recognized. While I strongly support this chronologic scheme, I am not particularly comfortable with the terms used to label the intervals, and I use them only to conform with the rest of the volume.

## THE EXPANSION PERIOD (A.D. 750–1000)

The subsequent interval A.D. 750–1000 is basically similar over the entire area and a reasonably good characterization of it can be developed. This interval corresponds to the Three Circle phase (Haury 1936), the Pilon and Convento phases (DiPeso 1974), and the Mesilla phase in part (Lehmer 1948), and the Encinas, Cerros, and probably Galiuro phases (Sayles 1945).

### Villages and Settlement Patterns

Southern Mogollon settlement patterns are interesting in several ways. Village sites range in size from a single pithouse up to about 150 pithouses.

Although sites such as the Galaz in the Mimbres Valley had approximately 125–150 pithouses, when adjustments are made for period length and the life span of habitations (Anyon and LeBlanc 1984; Blake et al. 1986), the actual number of contemporaneous houses is greatly reduced. The largest villages at the beginning of the period probably had no more than 22 houses and at the end no more than 60. Most moderate-sized villages had a ceremonial or communal structure. These structures, often referred to as great kivas, were in use by the A.D. 500s, and underwent an evolution in size and form (Anyon and LeBlanc 1980; Anyon 1983; Haury 1950).

There is evidence, although weak, that there was some degree of village planning. The great kivas opened onto areas devoid of structures or "plazas." There is no evidence that the layout of domestic pithouses was patterned. In particular, there is no supporting evidence, and some negative evidence, for the presence of suites of pithouses or patio groups opening onto a central shared space, the case for Snaketown (Wilcox et al. 1981) and other Hohokam sites. Sites consist of pithouses, great kivas, a few more specialized structures of unknown use, and bell-shaped storage pits. There are no well-defined trash areas or burial areas and minimal patterning to village layouts.

It is possible that in some areas settlements were more dispersed. In some locales, single pithouses or groups of two or three pithouses appear to be scattered over several square kilometers. A common great kiva, either isolated or adjacent to only a few domestic houses, frequently accompanies these dispersed collections of pithouses. Areas where such a pattern seems to occur are relatively more marginal for floodplain agriculture than areas in which the large villages were located.

Pithouses went through an evolution in shape (Haury 1936), but for this interval they were rectangular with ramp entranceways and averaged about 15 sq m in floor area. It is hard to believe that they housed more than a nuclear family. The only community-based construction activities, besides the great kivas, might have been the building of irrigation canals in some of the valleys, although evidence for such canals is lacking at this time and population size/carrying capacity estimates (Minnis 1985; Anyon and LeBlanc 1984) suggest they were not needed, except perhaps at the end of the interval.

Villages, then, seem to have been comprised of individual households sharing a communal structure with little overall planning for spatial organization. Almost all villages fall below the demographic requirements for endogamy (Wobst 1974), and hence they were probably exogamous.

Regional settlement patterns are known in a useful way only for the Mimbres area and selected areas of the Jornada. Villages seem to be located near small river floodplains, which served as good farmland. More xeric areas and more mountainous areas have few villages and must have been exploited on a very ephemeral basis. There are sites, for example, one excavated by Minnis (1982) near Deming, which seem to represent seasonal procurement locations. The Deming site is on the western slope of the Florida Mountains and is surrounded by rather flat xeric areas. The site was apparently repeatedly occupied over many, if not hundreds, of years but had no permanent structures. Based on survey, other examples of this type of site exist, but they are not abundant.

A good case can be made (Hard 1982) that in the area east of the Rio Grande seasonal transhumance was practiced and agriculture did not provide the dietary staples, at least for part of the year. This does not seem to be the case for the rest of the southern Mogollon. The vast majority, if not all, of the population was relying on an agricultural economy.

It can be argued that the southern Mogollon area at this time consisted of tribally organized, egalitarian societies. This inference is based on several lines of reasoning. Burial practices are commensurate with such an interpretation. Burials are both intramural and extramural, no special cemetery areas are known. The Mimbres area burials seem to produce the greatest number of grave goods, but there is no evidence for sumptuous burials. No evidence for craft specialization has been produced, although the quality of some goods is high. The interpretation of these goods in terms of trade and cultural boundaries is considered later. Besides burials, few caches are known and most of these involve stone "hoes," which are not valuable trade goods nor hard to make. While there is variability in home size, it is difficult to build a convincing argument for elite residences, Lightfoot and Feinman (1982) not withstanding. There are no unusually large, extra-fancy houses, no unique houses in central locations, or other manifestations of social dichotomies. The question of whether there was political organization beyond a single village is best considered for the following period.

## Regional Interaction

Interaction between regions can be inferred from some indirect lines of evidence. The Mimbres, San Simon, and northern Chihuahua branches seem to have produced painted pottery with similar, but distinctive, styles. If there was local stylistic variability within any of these areas, it has yet to be recognized. Variation in the stylistic attributes of other artifact categories between southern Mogollon regions has never been observed, but no serious look has ever been made. There does seem to have been significant differences in communal structures among these areas of a magnitude greater than that seen within each area. Thus a case can be made, although inadequately documented, that these three divisions represent some form of ethnicity or culturally distinct groups.

The relationship of the Jornada to the rest of the Mogollon is less clear. No painted ceramics were being produced during this interval and no great kivas have been found. The area of the highest potential population density, the Rio Grande Valley, is poorly known, but was probably within the Mimbres branch. In the desert area to the east, population was sparse and may have only been seasonal in nature. Whether this was a culturally distinct area at this time or only a marginal area remains unknown.

Of particular interest with respect to later events was the nature of interaction between the Mimbres and the Hohokam. What is said for the Mimbres probably also applies to the San Simon area, but information is too scant to make a parallel argument.

Between A.D. 750 and 1000, and in particular between A.D. 800 and 900, there was a level of interaction between the Mimbres and the Hohokam never equalled again. This inference is drawn almost exclusively from the stylistic similarity in a number of artifact categories. There is little evidence of actual trade in some of these artifact types or of movement of people. Little evidence of Mimbres pottery exists in the Hohokam area, and even less Hohokam pottery in the Mimbres. A few Mimbres burials are cremations, perhaps suggesting some actual movement of people, but these are so rare as to be insignificant.

On the other hand, the ceramic similarity is striking (Brody 1977; LeBlanc 1983). The naturalistic elements are closely paralleled, as are some vessel forms, design layouts, and geometric motifs. These parallels are so close that there are vessels indistinguishable to area on the basis of design alone.

Shell goods are quite common in the Mimbres with large sites, for example, the Galaz site, yielding hundreds of pendants and bracelets and thousands of beads (Anyon and LeBlanc 1984). The shell objects seem to have been manufactured in the Hohokam area. A variety of stone goods were locally produced, closely paralleling Hohokam forms. This is especially true of the stone palettes that, while not as elaborate as some Hohokam examples, are very similar. Both the Mimbres and Hohokam stone axes are ¾ grooved. Some of the Mimbres axes have raised ridges adjacent to the groove like many Hohokam axes. There is a large stone disk from the Galaz site essentially identical in form and dimension to one from Snaketown (Haury 1976), but this may represent trade rather than stylistic sharing. Bas-relief carving of animal and human forms on stone bowls is another example of shared decorative styles between the two areas.

During the interval A.D. 800–900, for each class of objects that there is a shared style, the Hohokam examples are better made and more elaborate than the Mimbres counterparts. After this period, the Mimbres pottery develops in a unique direction, and stone palettes drop out of the Mimbres inventory.

The higher quality of the Hohokam artifacts suggests that the Hohokam exerted stylistic influence on the Mimbres area during the late Colonial period (A.D. 750–900) and not the reverse. Subsequently, this influence declined significantly and Mimbres styles seemed to evolve in greater isolation.

## Demography

Demographic trends are hard to typify for the southern Mogollon area as a whole, due to a lack of adequate systematic surveys. The most comprehensive information comes from the Mimbres Valley (Blake et al. 1986) and the adjacent, desert areas around Deming (Blake and Narod 1977). Minnis (1980) compared these surveys with surveys undertaken in other parts of the Mimbres area, including the upper Mimbres (Graybill 1975), the Redrock area (Lekson 1978), the Cliff area along the Gila (Fitting 1972), the Arenas Valley (Herrington 1979), and other more localized surveys. While neither methodology nor terminology are fully comparable between surveys, overall patterns seem to be generally similar with a few pertinent exceptions. Other than impressionistic assessments, no other meaningful demographic information exists for the other southern Mogollon branches. Consequently, this discussion of demography will focus on the Mimbres area and in particular on the Mimbres Valley.

It is currently estimated that the Mimbres Valley population grew at a rate of about 0.3 percent annually between A.D. 200 and A.D. 1000 (Blake et al. 1986). This resulted in a five-fold increase in population over that of A.D. 200. Absolute estimates are more difficult to make, but a total of 1,600 people for the Mimbres Valley and tributaries (900 sq km) at A.D. 900 seems to be reasonable based on several lines of evidence. This works out to a density of about two people per square kilometer. As will be argued below, the Mimbres Valley population was well below the effective carrying capacity at this time, and by extrapolation, this was probably the case for the southern Mogollon region as a whole.

These data can be used to estimate the population for the entire southern Mogollon area. The Mimbres Valley is one of the best agricultural areas in the entire region. If we assume it had a density of about twice the average, and if we estimate the entire southern Mogollon area includes 70,000 sq km, then we have a total population of 70,000 people at A.D. 900. This seems high. We must either conclude that there were far more people in the Southwest at A.D. 900 than we are prepared to admit, or that the Mimbres Valley population density was many times higher than the area as a whole. Demographic change and changes in settlement distribution within the Mimbres Valley, as an example of the region, will be considered below in comparison with later periods.

In summary, at about A.D. 900 the southern Mogollon area was occupied by basically egalitarian, horticultural societies, living in small (under 200 people), exogamous villages. Ethnic boundaries are possibly reflected by the three branches of the southern Mogollon. Trade or interaction is more in evidence by shared design styles than by goods actually traded. There was little in the way of village planning, and communal construction efforts were probably restricted to building great kivas.

## THE DIFFERENTIATION PERIOD (A.D. 1000–1150)

The period between A.D. 1000 and 1150 witnessed the development of the Classic Mimbres period and probably paralleled less well known developments in the other branches. The interval ends with the most major cultural change witnessed in the entire sequence. Change is so great that the concept of Mogollon is no longer applicable after A.D. 1150. This interval again conforms to the Differentiation period as defined in Chapter 1.

In the Mimbres area, three major developments took place during the A.D. 1000s: a shift to above ground dwellings, the florescence of the Mimbres pottery style, and the expansion of population into increasingly marginal areas. In the past, these changes were perceived as the consequence of Anasazi influence. Today, there is little doubt that we have a cultural continuum. Most of the changes seen in the Mimbres Classic period have precursors in the Three Circle phase. Nevertheless, there is a component of change that can be attributed to interaction with the north. This is seen mainly in ceramics. The previous similarity between Mimbres and Hohokam ceramics wanes as does actual trade. It is replaced by trade and/or copying of designs and texturing techniques between the Mimbres and Reserve areas. While there is not a great deal of evidence for interaction at this time, the data indicate that north to south communication predominated over contacts to the west.

The most archaeologically visible change is the shift to above-ground rooms. During the late Three Circle phase, there are semisubterranean rooms or pithouses, which have cobble walls. These rooms also have a posthole pattern of three major posts running down the central axis of the room. The shift to above-ground construction simply involved the construction of equivalent rooms without placing them in a pit. It did not represent any new construction technique.

What is of more interest is that the rooms were made in contiguous groups or roomblocks. Even the earliest surface rooms were contiguous. Classic period roomblocks range in size from a few rooms to 50 rooms, although most had no more than 20 rooms. Large villages were comprised of up to six of these roomblocks. Similar sites, probably dating to the same time period, are known from the San Simon area and northern Chihuahua (DiPeso 1974).

Several other architectural changes, not as well understood, also took place at this time. First, great kivas were in use at the beginning of the period, but seem to have been abandoned before the end (in a pattern very similar to the disuse of ballcourts in the Hohokam area). Second, roomblocks may have been arranged to define plaza areas, serving the role previously held by the great kiva. There is also evidence for ceremonial or special use in rooms that were small. One form of these rooms was a semisubterranean room with air shafts, similar to Anasazi kivas. These seem to be associated with roomblocks, with only one such room per block. Some unusually large, above-ground rooms may have also served a special ceremonial role, perhaps developing late in the period.

Habitation rooms show specialization for the first time. Large living rooms were constructed with a hearth, air vents, and multiple roof support posts with well-prepared floors. Smaller rooms without hearths and more irregular floors served as storage rooms. Roomblocks are comprised of both living and storage rooms with perhaps two living rooms to one storage room. However, distinctions in room function are not as clear-cut as the Anasazi area, and the roomblocks themselves are haphazardly arranged. There are few doorways between rooms and little regularity in the relative placement of living versus storage rooms.

What patterning there is to room location is little more than that governed by simple practical considerations. Storage rooms are most frequently on the colder, northern side of the roomblocks, and ramada areas are on the south. While the shift to above-ground rooms does not represent a major technological change, and the roomblocks seem unplanned, these changes may reflect a major social change. This is considered below.

The development of the Mimbres painted ceramics is the next most obvious change from the preceding period. Pottery painting reaches a peak of artistic achievement, and the use of naturalistic elements is unparalleled. Considerable efforts have been expended to find intervillage and intravillage patterning in designs, to look for trade in the ceramics, and to identify the work of individual painters. Full discussion of these efforts is beyond the scope of this chapter, but several points can be made. The association of motifs with particular villages or even roomblocks is very slight, and petrographic analysis has shown no differences in temper between villages in the Mimbres Valley. This is a difficult attribute to assess, especially considering the local geology, and future studies may yet show differences. Some individual painters can be recognized, but no other evidence for craft specialization exists. Both geometric and naturalistic designs show regular stylistic changes beginning in the Three Circle phase, and the Classic Mimbres painted pottery does not seem to be the result of outside influence. The implications of these findings are considered below.

Traditionally the typical Classic period burial has been considered to have one painted bowl as a grave good. However, slightly over half of all burials have no associated bowls, and about 5 percent of the burials have over five vessels. Sixteen percent of the Classic burials contain shell, turquoise, or other items. On average there was one turquoise bead and one-sixteenth of a turquoise pendant per burial. There were also about three shell beads and one-fifth of a shell bracelet per individual. While these figures are higher than many other areas of the Southwest (Anyon and LeBlanc 1984), they are not evidence for significant trade or social complexity.

Current evidence, then, provides little support for significant social stratification or more than tribal level organization. Based on architecture and funerary practices, there is significantly less evidence than Chaco, the Hohokam, or Casas Grandes. A related issue is the degree of social/political integration beyond a single village. There is the possibility that the basic village community consisted of a main village along a major drainage, nearby small "fieldhouse" type sites, and sites removed from main drainages where agriculture was undertaken in marginal locales. How then, did these communities articulate? On the one hand, throughout most of the sequence, biological considerations imply village exogamy at least in part, and the degree of similarity in great kivas, building technologies, and ceramics between sites all suggest very high levels of interaction, probably including mate exchange.

However, there does not seem to be evidence for macrovillage organization. Irrigation was probably employed at this time, but based on today's irrigation canals and the nature of the floodplains, canal systems, unlike those of the Hohokam, would have been short and not involved more than the land of a single village. The major villages were of rather equal size and evenly spaced along water courses. No exceptionally large sites exist, nor do any have great kivas larger or more elaborate than others. None have markedly different amounts of exotic materials such as shell and turquoise. No site seems to have had preeminence. Thus, any political integration beyond that of a single community must have been weak, at best.

## Demography, Environment, and Subsistence

Changes in settlement patterns and demography are marked during the period. First, there was considerable population growth, resulting in the highest population densities for the valley prehistorically or historically (Table 1). This was accompanied by population relocation into increasingly marginal areas and agricultural intensification (Table 2). Minnis (1985) argues that the long-term carrying capacity was reached or even exceeded by the end of the period. There was also an increase in maximal site size at this time (Table 3).

A series of interrelated long-term developments in environment and subsistence strategy occurred in the Mimbres Valley culminating in this period. These changes are probably mirrored throughout the area, although not necessarily to the same degree. As the population grew, there was increased exploitation of the riverine environment and faunal resources resulting in a negative impact on these natural communities. The riverine area was progressively denuded of tree and understory cover, resulting in the need to travel further for wood supplies. The normal fauna were replaced by species better adapted to an open habitat. At the same time, exploitation of large fauna, primarily deer, reduced the yield of this resource in terms of absolute amounts or at least on a per capita basis.

Minnis (1985) argues that at this time there was inadequate farm land and river water to supply the agriculturally derived food requirements of the valley's population, even assuming that irrigation was being employed. We see considerable population movement into marginal areas at this time. Simultaneously, there were efforts to increase the productivity of these marginal areas through the construction of check dams. "Fieldhouses" were also built along the river margins between villages (Nelson et al. 1978), presumably to increase the efficiency of valley bottom farming. Similarly, waffle garden-like features have been noted along the Gila River to the east of Safford. If these in fact date to this time range, then this pattern, and possibly the presumed cause, would be widespread over much of the southern Mogollon.

Another response to food provisioning stress may have been the shift to above-ground architecture. For the first time above-ground rooms had large areas dedicated to food storage. Moreover, such storage would have been hidden and not measured by one's neighbors. Beyond this, the roomblocks may represent a shift in family structure. The fundamental economic unit

**Table 1. Population
Estimates for the
Mimbres Valley**

| Time | Population |
|------|-----------|
| A.D. 200 | 290 |
| A.D. 550 | 830 |
| A.D. 1000 | 3,200 |
| A.D. 1130 | 5,133 |
| A.D. 1275 | 1,145 |
| A.D. 1400 | 240 |

*(estimates from Blake et al. 1986)*

may have changed from the nuclear family to a larger corporate group, for example, an extended family or minimal lineage. Different members of the unit may have been responsible for the exploitation of different resources or fields in different areas, pooling the results. In fact, it can be argued that at least some of the sites established away from the river were not permanent, but were seasonally used by some of the inhabitants of the large villages in the Mimbres Valley to increase overall productivity.

At a more speculative level, this period may have witnessed a shift from patrilocal to matrilocal residence. If we accept that the Archaic bands, like most bands, were patrilocal, and that the pithouse villages were structurally similar to Archaic camps with their dispersed houses, then we might infer a continuation of the patrilocal pattern. The use of roomblocks after A.D. 1000 is a pattern like that found in the matrilocal historic Western Pueblo villages (Eggan 1950). We see the architectural shift just when farm land becomes a particularly scarce resource and the importance of hunting wanes. This may have been a further response to these changed subsistence strategy needs.

It can be argued that these responses were to a large degree successful, at least into the A.D. 1100s. Sites in marginal areas continued to be occupied throughout the span. New construction took place on the major pueblos as late as A.D. 1117 (based on over 200 tree-ring samples), and there seems to be no degeneration in the pottery painting tradition or in any other artifact categories. Minnis (1985) suggests that this successful response was due to particularly good rainfall patterns during the 1000s, which allowed for the utilization of marginal areas. When conditions returned to normal, or perhaps a bit below average during the 1100s, production was markedly reduced, leading to nutritional stress and perhaps to a breakdown of the existing society.

It was at this time that the Casas Grandes society had an impact on the

**Table 2. The Percentage of the Number of Sites and the Numbers of Rooms Located on Three Classes of Arable Land**

| Time | Primary | | Secondary | | Tertiary | |
|------|---------|---------|-----------|---------|----------|---------|
| | *Sites* | *Rooms* | *Sites* | *Rooms* | *Sites* | *Rooms* |
| A.D. 200–550 | 86% | 98.5% | 14% | 2% | 0% | 0% |
| A.D. 550–1000 | 62 | 95 | 38 | 5 | 0 | 0 |
| A.D. 1000–1130 | 33 | 52 | 38 | 41 | 29 | 6 |
| A.D. 1150–1300 | 91 | 95 | 6 | 5 | 0 | 0 |
| A.D. 1300–1450 | 100 | 100 | 0 | 0 | 0 | 0 |

*(Primary land consists of major river valleys and major side drainages with well-developed floodplains. Secondary land consists of drainages with poor floodplains. Tertiary land is that with very limited agricultural potential [from Minnis et al. n.d.].)*

**Table 3. The Proportion of Total Site Floor Area for Five Time Periods Occurring on Sites of Different Sizes**

| Time | Site Size Ranges (number of rooms) | | | | |
|------|-------------|-------|-------|--------|---------|
| | *Less than 10* | *10–24* | *25–49* | *50–124* | *125–200* |
| A.D. 200–550 | 24% | 45% | 31% | 0% | 0% |
| A.D. 550–1000 | 5 | 16 | 19 | 60 | 0 |
| A.D. 1000–1130 | 3 | 23 | 13 | 27 | 34 |
| A.D. 1150–1300 | 5 | 32 | 10 | 52 | 0 |
| A.D. 1300–1450 | 0 | 24 | 27 | 49 | 0 |

*(from Blake et al. 1986)*

Mimbres area, and the relative importance of the two factors on the demise of the Mimbres system are difficult to determine. Arguments for the relative importance of these two factors are considered below.

We have no comparable information on the San Simon or northern Chihuahua areas for the degree of population growth, the responses to it, or any resultant cultural change. We do know that architectural changes seen in the Mimbres area were paralleled by architectural changes in these other areas.

In summary, the cultural traditions that began about A.D. 200 resulted in an unbroken, continuous development for over 900 years in the southern Mogollon area. Population grew, settlement size grew, painted ceramics began to be produced, great kivas evolved, trade increased, and toward the end, new social institutions may have evolved to deal with larger population aggregates and new resource procurement strategies. To a large degree these responses were successful into the A.D. 1100s, at which point the southern Mogollon, in any analytic sense, ceased to exist.

## THE DEVELOPMENT OF THE CASAS GRANDES INTERACTION SPHERE

The subsequent developments in the southern Mogollon area cannot be understood except in reference to the development of a sphere of interaction centered at Casas Grandes. Although there is some debate about the timing of this development (DiPeso 1974; LeBlanc 1980a; Wilcox and Shenk 1977), the generally accepted position is that it began in the early to mid A.D. 1100s.

The interaction sphere was in many ways parallel to that of Chaco. There was a major center, Casas Grandes, with outlying communities, in northern Chihuahua (Brand 1943; Carey 1931; Lister 1946; Sayles 1936), northeastern Sonora (Pailes n.d.), Hidalgo County, New Mexico (Kidder et al. 1949; McCluney 1962), Mimbres (LeBlanc 1977, 1980a), and southeastern Arizona (Mills and Mills n.d.; Johnson and Thompson 1963). It is also possible that sites in the southern part of the Jornada area represent part of the interaction sphere (Brook 1965, 1966). Thus, this sphere seems to have covered most of the southern Mogollon area, with the exception of the extreme northern periphery of the Mimbres branch and part of the Jornada area. It comprised an area of approximately 100,000 sq km, which made it similar in size to that of the Chaco interaction sphere.

There seems to be little doubt that the Casas Grandes interaction sphere was sociopolitically unlike what preceded it in the area. It can probably be best described in sociopolitical terms as a chiefdom (Service 1962). There is evidence for most of the expected archaeological manifestations of such nonegalitarian, hierarchical organizations. The population at Casas Grandes must have been in the thousands, a population size associated with chiefdoms rather than egalitarian societies (Sahlins 1958). There is considerable evidence for community building efforts in the form of platform mounds, ballcourts, and aqueducts. There is evidence for craft specialization in the localization of production (e.g., macaw raising areas and groundstone production areas), the quantities of stored goods (e.g., a room with several million shell beads), and in the quality of the goods themselves (e.g., the extremely well-made stone altar at the Mound of the Offerings and the copper artifacts) (DiPeso 1974).

Further evidence for an elite stratum at Casas Grandes comes from burial and residential structures. Crypts in the Mound of the Offerings seem to have been elite burial areas, which were looted prehistorically. Bodies, all of adults, were secondarily interred in extra-large polychrome jars, but were not cremated. They were placed in small room-like crypts, which were not filled in, allowing access to the rooms after interment. These rooms were connected with a room that had a stone feature, which must have been ceremonial, and onto a small courtyard. Thus, we have a burial mode different from the rest of the population. These burials were located in a public area; considerable energy was expended on the graves themselves, and there was perhaps even ritual use of the burial area via the courtyard and ceremonial room.

Several compounds or "houses" at Casas Grandes are likely elite residential areas. These include the House of the Serpents, the House of the Dead, and possibly the House of the Macaws (DiPeso 1974). In each case the structures are basically single-storied, and have interior courtyards. Some have ceremonial rooms, and access to portions of all of them was restricted. In the House of the Dead, there is a multiple burial with a considerable quantity of grave goods. This multiple burial possibly represents relatives of actual status individuals. The rest of the site's population lived in multistoried roomblocks, and were buried in flexed positions with no more grave goods than found in much of the rest of the Southwest.

The nature of the Casas Grandes interaction sphere outside the site of Casas Grandes itself is less well understood. There does seem to be a hierarchy of sites within the region around Casas Grandes. That is, there were a few, widely spaced, larger sites with a greater number of smaller sites in between them. The excavations that have been conducted in outlying communities, for example, the Ringo site (Johnson and Thompson 1963), the Curtis site (Mills and Mills n.d.), the Pendleton site (Kidder et al. 1949), the Walsh and Montoya sites (LeBlanc 1977), have not focused on the largest of these outlying communities. As a consequence, our characterization of outlying sites may exclude important aspects present on only the larger ones.

It is clear, however, that these sites represent a sharp break with the past. This is clearly seen in the Mimbres area. There, the Casas Grandes related sites have adobe wall construction without cobbles. Instead of the usual Mimbres roof support pattern, with three posts down the central axis of the roof, they have one or two central posts. Sometimes these principal postholes are lined with stones and have a flat slab base, a construction technique not seen before in Mimbres sites. Mimbres hearths are rectangular and lined with stone slabs. The hearths found in the Casas Grandes related sites are smaller, with perhaps one-third the area, and are round adobe basins, sometimes elevated slightly on platforms.

Nonarchitectural features are also distinct from earlier Mimbres sites.

Interments are divided between cremations in jars and subfloor burials that are flexed, with a "killed" bowl inverted over the head. These burials mimic the Mimbres burial mode except that the ceramics are different. In fact, the ceramic complex is almost completely different from that of the Mimbres. Painted wares include Chupadero Black-on-white, Three Rivers Red-on-terracotta, and El Paso Polychrome; other decorated wares include Ramos Black and Playas Red Incised. Even the utility wares are distinctly different from the previous Mimbres series.

Similar breaks with the past occur in other parts of the southern Mogollon area, but as the earlier materials are less well known, it is harder to characterize the differences. As distinctive as these manifestations are from the preceding southern Mogollon, there is regional variability as well. These Casas Grandes time period materials have been classified as the El Paso phase in the southern Jornada area, the Black Mountain phase in the central Mimbres area, and the Animas phase in Hidalgo County, with less specific designations in southeastern Arizona. Workers have also noted regional variability in northern Chihuahua (Sayles 1936; Brand 1943).

In each case, there are some architectural differences, such as entrance steps in the El Paso area, or stone wall footings in parts of northern Chihuahua. The major differences among the regions are in ceramics, with clinal changes occurring across the southern Mogollon area as a whole. For example, El Paso Polychrome and Chupadero Black-on-white decreases as one moves west; Ramos Polychrome decreases as one moves out from Casas Grandes in any direction; and Playas Red Incised decreases away from Hidalgo County.

In spite of the differences between areas and our paucity of knowledge about these remains, they are so radically different from what preceded them that we can only conclude they represent a sharp cultural break with the past.

There is little good evidence for the termination of the Casas Grandes interaction sphere. It was clearly in existence in the late 1200s. Evidence from the Mimbres area and Casas Grandes itself seems to support a termination date near A.D. 1300. F. Plog (personal communication) believes he has evidence for Casas Grandes outlier communities well into the 1300s; Wilcox and Shenk (1977) believe that major developments did not get started until after A.D. 1300 and that they lasted into the 1400s. While I believe the weight of evidence supports an early 1300s termination date, clearly the available evidence on this extremely important question is inadequate. If this dating is correct, then the existence of the Casas Grandes interaction sphere conforms very closely with the Reorganization period of the chronology defined in Chapter 1.

## Models of the Casas Grandes Interaction Sphere

Given the concept of a Casas Grandes interaction sphere, how can we account for its development and termination; and how does it relate to the disappearance of the Mimbres and to the other southern Mogollon entities? This is, of course, difficult to determine with the information at hand, but several partial models can be proposed. First, it needs to be noted that the Casas Grandes interaction sphere shares many characteristics with both the Chaco interaction sphere (Altshul 1978; Judge 1979) and the Classic Hohokam. As a consequence, it is reasonable to postulate that at a general level there were similar conditions leading to the development of all these systems. Models that fit the data for only one interaction sphere are less likely to be correct than those that can account for all three.

One can argue that the Casas Grandes interaction sphere does not represent the takeover of the southern Mogollon area by a new culture or people. The Casas Grandes interaction sphere must have developed and expanded within a century (probably within a generation or two). Even if we assume extremely high growth rates, any initial group in northern Chihuahua or elsewhere could not have more than doubled in size during this span, thus the expansion over an area of 100,000 sq km would have been impossible. In addition, there are cultural continuities such as distinctive burial practices in the Mimbres area, implying that at least some of the area's previous inhabitants were incorporated into the new interaction sphere.

It would appear, then, that the Casas Grandes interaction sphere was expansionistic, incorporating previously autonomous groups. Ethnographic examples of hierarchical societies, like the Polynesian chiefdoms (Sahlins 1958), are characterized by expansionist forms of warfare and incorporation of surrounding regimes. I find the most viable model for Casas Grandes to include many of the suggestions made by DiPeso (1974). The interaction sphere may have been dependent on trade and significant interaction with Mesoamerica and/or fringe groups. One can see Casas Grandes as developing out of a Mesoamerican interest in exploiting the American Southwest. Casas Grandes produced macaws, macaw feathers, and copper bells to trade with groups to the north, presumably for turquoise and other as yet unrecognized goods, to be sent farther south. This trade might have been quite organized and not "down the line." In arguments presented elsewhere (LeBlanc 1986), it is suggested that the Casas Grandes trade system replaced a similar position held by Chaco, leading to the demise of that interaction sphere. Such a model would have outlying areas incorporated into the Casas Grandes interaction sphere producing the goods needed for the elite and craft specialists, and perhaps some goods such as cotton for use in the trade network itself. When, for some reason, this trade was interrupted, the inter-action sphere rapidly collapsed.

It should be noted that such a model does not require a *pochteca* form of trade and control (McGuire 1980), per se. It could have been developed from an impetus further south, perhaps with some southern individuals marrying into communities and developing indigenous elites.

While such a model is rather speculative, it accounts for the rapid growth and subsequent decline of Casas Grandes, for the presence of elites when none existed before or after, and the presence of specialized produc-tion of goods that were probably traded.


## THE POST-CASAS GRANDES ERA

If we see the Casas Grandes interaction sphere as having incorporated most of the area and most of the southern Mogollon, then the consequences of its collapse must have had a major impact over all of this area. Unfortunately, the post-A.D. 1300 or Aggregation period events in the previous southern Mogollon area (now better conceived of as the northern portion of the old Casas Grandes interaction sphere) are poorly known. The Mimbres Founda-tion excavated at three sites of this period in the Mimbres Valley (Nelson and LeBlanc 1986), and work has been done at the Ormand site (Hammack 1966), Dinwiddie (Mills and Mills 1972), Kuykendall (Mills and Mills 1969), and Curtis (Mills and Mills n.d.) sites. However, most of these reports are very brief. Moreover, many workers have not attempted to, or not been able to, differentiate between sites that are pre- or post-A.D. 1300, for exam-ple, the Pendleton Ruin (Kidder et al. 1949), Box Canyon, and Clanton Draw (McCluney 1962). The question of how these sites were related to the "Salado" sites in Arizona remains fuzzy at best.

The best one can do is to sketch out what seems to be known, and then develop several models to account for this data. The post-1300 period in the Mimbres area has been termed the Cliff phase. These sites are similar enough to those in southeastern Arizona to consider them as a single entity. Sites consist of adobe-walled pueblos, some of which have two stories. Multiple roomblocks are common and if present, usually form a U or L. A plaza-like area is frequently enclosd by a free-standing adobe wall closing off the open end of the U. These free-standing walls have been termed compound walls, but it must be noted they are not like the walls of com-pound and platform mound complexes seen in the Classic Hohokam.

What appeared to be a free-standing kiva-like structure was found on the Ormand site, but in general, ceremonial architecture is absent or represents minimal construction effort. For example, at the Janss site, a small habitation room was apparently used as a ceremonial room by removing the domestic assemblage and introducing some probable ceremonial objects. In general, most Cliff phase rooms are quite large (more than 20 sq m) and there are few connecting doorways. No clear storerooms have been identified and the typical room has a large center post, and a large adobe or stone-lined hearth with a ladder through the roof just above it.

In many ways the architecture of the post-A.D. 1300 period is similar to that of the outlying Casas Grandes interaction sphere sites. There are differences, however, in posthole patterns, hearth shape and sizes, and in the use of enclosing walls. For the post-A.D. 1300 sites, walls are more massive and the rooms are somewhat larger. Thus, while differences exist, they are not of the magnitude seen between the pre-Casas Grandes sites and those of that period.

Artifacts and settlement patterns show greater differences between pre- and post-A.D. 1300 sites than architecture. Post-A.D. 1300, all interments seem to be cremations either in pits or in vessels. Burials are not within rooms, but are either in the plazas or in localized areas away from the roomblocks. Painted ceramics also differ from the previous period, but we do not have a complete replacement of types. Gila Polychrome is the dominant painted ware, and seems to be locally made. Small amounts of Chupadero Black-on-white, Ramos Polychrome, and El Paso Polychrome continue to be present, although Ramos Black and Playas Red Incised are no longer found. The utility wares change with the appearance of new shapes, new forms of texturing, and a high incidence of black burnished vessel interiors. The changes can best be characterized as gradual and not as an abrupt replacement of types.

Most important, the sites in southwestern New Mexico and southeastern Arizona represent one end of a continuum that extends westward to the Tonto Basin. For most of the cultural features just mentioned, there are clinal east to west trends. Within this continuum of sites, extending from the Mimbres Valley on the east to the Tonto Basin on the west, there is considerable variability but no clear dividing line within it.

There seems to have been a return to egalitarian, autonomous villages at this time. All manifestations of an elite group are gone. So is the association of a roomblock with a kiva seen in the Classic Mimbres period, which possibly represented a form of corporate organization within these Mimbres communities. In fact, impressionistically, one has a very different feeling about the Cliff phase. Each room seems much like another. They seem to serve as both habitation rooms and storage rooms (Nelson 1980), and there are few doorways linking adjacent rooms. In a way, these sites seem like modern apartment complexes, and perhaps the basic economic unit reverted to the nuclear family with a few cross-cutting sodalities. Whether the earlier kivas reflected kin-based or sodality groups, the importance of such organizations seems to have diminished.

Settlement patterns are only partially known, but they seem to mirror patterns over much of the Southwest at this time. Most villages are large, with 100 or more rooms. There are few small village sites; the 12 room Stailey site excavated by the Mimbres Foundation is at the low end of the size range of these communities. A few fieldhouses or special activity sites dating to this period have been identified in New Mexico. There is an interesting pattern in their occurrence. They are unknown in the Mimbres Valley and only a few are known from the Cliff area. However, they seem to be common along the Gila River west of Safford. This distribution probably reflects the relative population densities of these areas. Population densities seem to increase towards the west and with them there is an increased density of "fieldhouses."

There are also large areas with essentially no communities. Most sites seem to be concentrated along major water courses like the Mimbres and Gila Rivers. Gaps of 20 to 25 miles between site concentrations are apparently common. Population sizes are difficult to estimate. In the Mimbres Valley the population at this time was but a tenth the size of the Classic Mimbres maximum population. In the Gila Valley near Cliff, the population may have exceeded the Mimbres peak, and this may have been the case in southeastern Arizona and Hidalgo County.

Of additional note is that almost all the excavated rooms from these sites show evidence for rapid abandonment. Ceramic assemblages, metates, and even small items like bone awls, axes, and fetishes are left behind. Whether these abandonments occurred simultaneously is unknown, but it seems that the entire area east of the San Pedro River was virtually abandoned by A.D. 1450. The possible exception is the Joyce Wells site, which has C-14 dates reported in the 1500s (DiPeso 1974). However, these three dates were recalibrated (DeAtley 1980) and have an average date of 1440.

Several models can be proposed to account for the post-1300 developments. One viable interpretation would see the post-1300 sites representing the population previously included in the Casas Grandes interaction sphere, following the cessation of interaction with this former center. Previously distinct groups would have been amalgamated and shifted as a consequence of being a part of the Casas Grandes interaction sphere, and a series of new traits would have been adopted. Once the Casas Grandes interaction sphere ceased to exist there would not have been a reversion to the earlier ethnicities as reflected by the Mogollon branches, and one would expect intergroup relationships to have been tenuous and needing redefinition. The lack of large ceremonial structures and the clustering of sites may reflect a breakdown of certain cultural institutions and interactive traditions.

In broader terms, one can reevaluate the concept of Western Pueblo (Reed 1948) as representing populations once under the influence of the Chaco interaction sphere. In turn, one can view the post-A.D. 1300 population of southwestern New Mexico, southeastern Arizona, and northern Chihuahua as representing populations once under the influence of the Casas Grandes interaction sphere. In each case, local variability existed, but a broader concept is useful. A term like Southern Pueblo might be appropriate to subsume these post-Casas Grandes groups.

An alternative model would have the "Salado" expanding out of the Tonto Basin area and occupying most of the old southern Mogollon area. As previously argued, demographic considerations preclude this possibility. However, it is possible that there is a kernel of truth to this concept. If the Classic Hohokam interaction sphere included the Tonto Basin, then the sites in the eastern part of the southern Mogollon area would have been articulating with the Classic Hohokam interaction sphere. The east-west clinal variation in archaeologically visible features and the increased population size towards the west may reflect such a center-periphery relationship, with the true center being the Hohokam area.

## ABANDONMENT

All evidence points to the virtual abandonment of southwestern New Mexico and southeastern Arizona, and perhaps much of northern Chihuahua, in the years before the Entrada. Most sites seem to be deliberately and rapidly abandoned. Our evidence for the timing of these events is minimal. We have some idea about the abandonment of the three known post-A.D. 1300 sites in the Mimbres Valley. Based on various lines of evidence, the largest site, the 80+ room Disert site, was abandoned first, sometime near 1400. The two smaller sites, with 12 and 30+ rooms, were abandoned somewhat, but not much, later. Regardless of whether the smaller sites were founded by former residents of the Disert site, or were at one point contemporaneous with it, the population was dropping precipitously before the valley was completely abandoned.

The decline in population and the subsequent abandonments are surprising. The Mimbres Valley sites show evidence of adding on room groups, and Nelson (1980) has argued that the large rooms imply large families and consequent population growth. Furthermore, estimates of available wild foods suggest that the population could have subsisted quite comfortably on wild foods alone (Nelson and LeBlanc 1986). Given the availability of good farm land, it is hard to see how this population could have been under nutritional stress. The entire Mimbres drainage with its 1,400 foot elevational gradient was available to them. Hence, with changing environmental conditions, either moist, dry, cold, or warm, the small post-1300 population could have relocated settlements and/or fields to adjust to the changing climate. While the larger Disert site did have an enclosed compound, which could conceivably have been defensive, the two smaller sites were single-storied, single roomblocks in nondefensive locations. In sum, there is little evidence to argue that warfare or nutritional stress caused the village abandonments.

As unexpected as these abandonments are, they occurred over a large area. Essentially the entire area of southwestern New Mexico and southeastern Arizona to the San Pedro River seems to have been abandoned. The post-1300 population densities seem to have been higher in the west, especially to the west of the southern Mogollon area. These areas, such as the San Pedro, continued to have a resident population in the 1500s. Thus, the areas with lower population densities in the 1400s were totally abandoned by the end of that century, while those areas with higher densities in the 1400s continued to have some population in the 1500s.

Various explanations for these patterns, none satisfactory, can be proposed. There may not have been a complete abandonment at all, simply a switch to a nomadic strategy for which we have found no archaeological trace. This argument is based on no data, and such a scenario does not explain the decline in population that must have preceded such an adaptive shift. An alternative model would have nomadic groups entering the area, pushing the village horticulturalists to the west. This model also suffers from the lack of archaeological evidence for such nomadic groups. There is basically no evidence to support any such models.

A final, and little considered possibility, is that we have the dating wrong. Perhaps the sites thought to have been abandoned during the 1400s were occupied in the 1500s. European diseases preceding the Spanish could have decimated the population, leading to abandonment before actual contact was made. While this is possiible, the span between the Spanish arrival on the Mexican mainland and Coronado's entry into the Southwest is rather short. Moreover, we have little current reason to believe that the settlements in this entire area lasted beyond A.D. 1425, so our dating error would have to be in excess of 100 years. Finally, several lines of evidence suggest substantial population decline in the 1300s, which cannot be accounted for by European diseases.

## ENVIRONMENTAL CHANGE AND THE CULTURAL SEQUENCE IN THE SOUTHERN MOGOLLON AREA

There has been a long history of relying on environmental change as an explanation of events in the American Southwest. Many of these environmental changes are neither well documented nor have they been shown to be causally related to cultural change. Social, political, or cultural effects are frequently minimized or ignored. Nevertheless, one must be careful not to assume that all cultural change derives from cultural factors, ignoring the effects of environmental change.

Rainfall variability indices have been developed for the Mogollon area and it is possible to try to correlate these changes in precipitation with major cultural changes. However, these rainfall data are not nearly as good as those for the plateau area and consequently more caution is required in using these data. It is useful to begin by asking which cultural events might have had an environmental component and then to look for evidence of a correlation between changes in rainfall and the cultural change. There seem to be five such candidates; (1) the shift to settled villages beginning at A.D. 200; (2) the shift to above-ground rooms and movement into marginal areas in the early A.D. 1000s; (3) the collapse of local cultures and the developoment of the Casas Grandes interaction sphere at ca. A.D. 1130–1150; (4) the collapse of the Casas Grandes interaction sphere presumably ca. A.D. 1300; and (5) the region's abandonment at ca. A.D. 1425–1450.

The first of these events is beyond our present scope, but it is worth noting that this shift to settled, agriculture-based villages occurs over much of the Southwest, beginning earlier in the south and not occurring in the northern extremes of the Southwest until the A.D. 500s. It is hard to see how any single environmental shift could produce such a pattern.

The second event, the shift to above-ground rooms and increasing use of marginal areas, has been discussed. While it may be argued that favorable rainfall patterns in the A.D. 1000s allowed for the use of marginal areas, and other cultural changes helped make possible the shift in adaptive strategy, it seems more reasonable to argue a different relationship. Increased population led to food provisioning problems, and because of fairly good rainfall patterns, a strategy involving a shift into more marginal areas was possible. At best we can see the environment as allowing for the change, not causing it.

In summary, one can best see the long Mimbres-Mogollon sequence, and probably the parallel sequence in the rest of the southern Mogollon, as a gradual development. Any significant environmental shifts were adapted to without major cultural reorganization of the scale that is later seen for Casas Grandes. Thus, environmental change does not seem to play a critical role in accounting for cultural change prior to A.D. 1150.

The most obvious question is what happened at A.D. 1150, the end of the Mimbres sequence? Did an environmental shift, even a minor one, lead to the collapse of the Mimbres culture? Or, did the development of the Casas Grandes interaction sphere result in the takeover of the Mimbres and other southern Mogollon areas? Was the development of the Casas Grandes interaction sphere itself triggered by an environmental shift? There is simply too little information to answer any of these questions directly. However, some points can be made. Deleterious environmental change would not automatically cause a cultural collapse. It is possible that in the wake of decreasing precipitation, the Mimbres, and presumably other populations, could have declined in size without disappearing as cultural entities until they reached a population density level that could have been supported by the available resources. It also seems implausible that the development of the Casas Grandes interaction sphere and the collapse of the Mimbres and other entities were coincidental. A more likely scenario would involve the growth of the population in the southern Mogollon area, and as a consequence of this population expansion, they were undergoing food procurement stress in the early A.D. 1100s. As a result, they were far more susceptible to being incorporated into the Casas Grandes interaction sphere regardless of how that incorporation took place.

The remaining question is whether environmental change played a role in the development of the Casas Grandes interaction sphere. If one sees the possibility that Casas Grandes replaced Chaco as the center of a trading network, then an environmentally related collapse of Chaco could have led to the development of Casas Grandes. The development of the Casas Grandes interaction sphere could be viewed as an indirect result of environmental change at Chaco. The topic of the Chaco collapse is considered in other chapters, but as yet no strong case has been made for environmental change being the major factor. If the Chaco collapse was linked with the development of Casas Grandes, it seems more likely that the causes in both cases were sociopolitical. At best, deteriorating conditions on the plateau may have helped precipitate these changes, but we cannot expect to understand them simply by appealing to environmental change.

The collapse of Casas Grandes is the event for which one can best suggest an explanation principally involving environmental factors. If, as suggested, the collapse occurred in the late 1200s, then it coincided with the "Great Drought" on the Colorado Plateau, a time of major settlement pattern shifts and abandonments over much of the Plateau (see Chapter 10).

Assuming that Casas Grandes needed to trade with the plateau and mountain area populations for its continued existence, then the effect of the
drought may have been enough to disrupt this trade, leading to the collapse
of the interaction sphere. While this is far from demonstrated, one can see a
mechanism for how such an environmental shift might have had an effect
on Casas Grandes. Again, however, sociopolitical factors must have been
very important and cannot be ignored in either model building or future
research.

## CONCLUSION

Several conclusions can be drawn. The two most important determinants of
cultural change in the years between A.D. 750 and A.D. 1450 seem to have
been population growth during the first 400 years and the development and
decline of the Casas Grandes interaction sphere during the subsequent 300
years. Environmental factors may have been involved in some of these
changes, for example, favorable rainfall regimes may have resulted in population growth in the A.D. 1000s, or drought in the late 1200s affecting the
Casas Grandes collapse. However, understanding the sociopolitical changes
within the region is critical to an understanding of the cultural developments following the mid 1100s. Moreover, the southern Mogollon area, as
large as it was, cannot be understood in isolation. The region's population
may have been subsumed within the Casas Grandes interaction sphere, and
following A.D. 1300 it seems somehow linked with events and populations
farther to the west.

We can see three possible major changes in social organization. The
first, a postulated shift from patrilocal to matrilocal residence perhaps coincided with a shift to larger fundamental economic units. This may have
taken place in the A.D. 750–1150 interval. In a general sense the southern
Mogollon was occupied by an egalitarian tribal society, with the population
dispersed among small (under 300 individuals) villages. The second shift
was the development of some form of stratified or hierarchical society possibly approximating a chiefdom, centered at Casas Grandes. This seems to
have lasted for no more than 150 years and may have been the result of
external stimuli. After this interval the final shift was a "devolution" back to
tribal society, but with more aggregation than before.

In the Mimbres area, population grew at least tenfold between A.D. 200
and A.D. 1100. By A.D. 1400 it declined to the A.D. 200 level, and then there
was complete abandonment. The growth rate during the 900 years between
A.D. 200 and A.D. 1100 must have greatly exceeded that for the prior Archaic

period. After the A.D. 1100s or 1200s such growth stopped and the population dwindled. We cannot account for either the growth or decline by migration alone, and the causes of both changes are unclear.

Finally, while the timing of specific events differs, the changes seen in the southern Mogollon are paralleled by similar changes in the northern Mogollon and most of the Anasazi area. Models constructed to account for the situation in the southern Mogollon may, and should in a general way, be capable of dealing with many other aspects of southwestern prehistory.

## REFERENCES

Altshul, Jeffrey H.
    1978      The Development of the Chacoan Interaction Sphere. *Journal of Anthropological Research* 34(1):109–146.

Anyon, Roger
    1983      *Divergent Mogollon Evolution and the Development of Ceremonial Structures.* M.A. Thesis, Department of Anthropology, University of New Mexico.

Anyon, Roger, and Steven A. LeBlanc
    1980      The Evolution of Mogollon-Mimbres Communal Structure. *The Kiva* 45(3):253–277.
    1984      *The Galaz Ruin: A Mimbres Village in Southwestern New Mexico.* University of New Mexico Press.

Anyon, Roger, Patricia Gilman, and Steven A. LeBlanc
    1981      A Reevaluation of the Mogollon-Mimbres Archaeological Sequence. *The Kiva* 46(4):209–225.

Blake, Michael, Steven A. LeBlanc, and Paul E. Minnis
    1986      Changing Settlement and Population in the Mimbres Valley. *Journal of Field Archaeology* 13:439–464.

Blake, Michael, and Susan Narod
    1977      Archaeological Survey and Analysis in the Deming Region, Southwestern New Mexico. Paper presented at the Annual Meeting of the Society for American Archaeology, New Orleans.

Brand, Donald D.
    1943      The Chihuahua Culture Area. *New Mexico Anthropologist* 6–7(3):115–158.

Brody, J. J.
    1977      *Mimbres Painted Pottery.* University of New Mexico Press, Albuquerque.

Brook, Vernon R.
    1965      Cultural Traits of the El Paso Phase Pueblos of the West Texas and South New Mexico Areas. *Transactions of the 1st Regional Symposium for Southeastern New Mexico and Western Texas.*
    1966      The McGregor Site. *Artifact* 4(4).

Carey, Henry A.
1931    An Analysis of the Chihuahua Culture. *American Anthropologist* 33(3):325–374.

DeAtley, Suzanne P.
1980    *Regional Integration of Animas Phase Settlements on the Northern Casas Grandes Frontier.* Ph.D. dissertation, Department of Anthropology, University of California, Los Angeles.

DiPeso, Charles C.
1974    *Casas Grandes: A Fallen Trading Center of the Gran Chichimeca.* Amerind Foundation Publications 9, Northland Press, Flagstaff.

Eggan, Fred
1950    *Social Organization of the Western Pueblos.* University of Chicago Press, Chicago.

Fitting, James E.
1972    Preliminary Notes on Cliff Valley Settlement Patterns. *The Artifact* 10(4):15–30.

Graybill, Donald A.
1975    *Mimbres-Mogollon Adaptations in the Gila National Forest, Mimbres District, New Mexico.* U.S. Forest Service, Southwestern Region, Archaeological Report 9.

Hammack, Laurens C.
1966    *Diablo Highway Salvage Archaeology.* Laboratory of Anthropology Notes No. 41. Santa Fe.

Hard, Robert J.
1982    A Model of Land Use for the Jornada Area. Paper presented at the Mogollon Conference, Oct. 21., Las Cruces.

Haury, Emil W.
1936    *The Mogollon Culture of Southwestern New Mexico.* Medallion Papers 20. Globe, Arizona.
1950    A Sequence of Great Kivas in the Forestdale Valley, Arizona. In *For the Dean, Essays in Honor of Byron Cummings,* edited by Erik K. Reed and Dale S. King, pp. 29–39. University of Arizona Press, Tucson.
1976    *The Hohokam.* University of Arizona Press, Tucson.

Herrington, S. L. C.
1979    *Settlement Patterns and Water Control Systems of the Mimbres Classic Phase, Grant County, New Mexico.* Ph.D. dissertation, Department of Anthropology, University of Texas at Austin.

Johnson, A. E., and Raymond H. Thompson
1963    The Ringo Site: Southern Arizona. *American Antiquity* 28:465–481.

Judge, W. James
1979    The Development of a Complex Cultural Ecosystem in the Chaco Basin, New Mexico. In *Proceedings of the First Conference on Scientific Research in the National Parks,* volume 3, edited by R. M. Linn, pp. 901–906. National Park Service Transactions and Proceedings Series 5.

Kidder, A. V., Harriet S. Cosgrove, and C. B. Cosgrove
    1949      The Pendleton Ruin, Hidalgo County, New Mexico. *Contributions to American Anthropology and History* 50. Carnegie Institute of Washington, Publication 585.

LeBlanc, Steven A.
    1977      The 1976 Field Season of the Mimbres Foundation in Southwestern New Mexico. *Journal of New World Archaeology* 2(2).
    1980a     The Dating of Casas Grandes. *American Antiquity* 45(4):799–806.
    1980b     The Early Pithouse Period. In *An Archaeological Synthesis of South Central and Southwestern New Mexico,* edited by S. A. LeBlanc and M. E. Whalen, pp. 119–141. Office of Contract Archeology, University of New Mexico.
    1983      *The Mimbres People: Ancient Painters of the American Southwest.* Thames and Hudson, London.
    1986      Aspects of Southwestern Prehistory: A.D. 900–1400. In *Ripples in the Chichimec Sea,* edited by Randall H. McGuire and Frances J. Mathien, pp. 105–134. Southern Illinois University Press, Carbondale.

LeBlanc, Steven A., and Michael E. Whalen (editors)
    1980      *An Archaeological Synthesis of South Central and Southwestern New Mexico,* with contributions by R. Anyon, P. A. Gilman, P. E. Minnis, and M. Nelson. Office of Contract Archeology, University of New Mexico, Albuquerque.

Lehmer, Donald J.
    1948      The Jornada Branch of the Mogollon. *University of Arizona Bulletin* 19(2).

Lekson, Stephen H.
    1978      *Settlement Patterns in the Redrock Valley, Southwestern New Mexico.* M.A. Thesis, Department of Anthropology, Eastern New Mexico University.

Lightfoot, Kent G., and Gary M. Feinman
    1982      Social Differentiation and Leadership Development in Early Pithouse Villages in the Mogollon Region of the American Southwest. *American Antiquity* 47(1):64–86.

Lister, Robert H.
    1946      Survey of Archaeological Remains in Northwestern Chihuahua. *Southwestern Journal of Anthropology* 2(4):433–453.

McCluney, Eugene B.
    1962      *Clanton Draw and Box Canyon: An Interim Report on Two Prehistoric Sites in Hidalgo County, New Mexico.* School of American Research, Monograph 26.

McGuire, Randall H.
    1980      The Mesoamerican Connection in the Southwest. *The Kiva* 46:(1–2):3–38

Mills, Jack P., and Vera M. Mills
    1969      *The Kuykendall Site.* El Paso Archaeological Society, Special Report 6.
    1972.     The Dinwiddie Site: A Prehistoric Salado Ruin on Duck Creek, Western New Mexico. *The Artifact* 10(2)i–iv:1–50.
    n.d.      *The Curtis Site: A Prehistoric Village in the Safford Valley.* Privately printed.

Minnis, Paul E.
    1980      Population Size and Settlement Configuration in Southwestern New Mex-

ico. In *An Archaeological Synthesis of South Central and Southwestern New Mexico*, edited by S. A. LeBlanc and M. E. Whalen, pp. 460–503. Office of Contract Archeology, University of New Mexico.

1982    Pithouse Occupation in the Deming Region. Paper presented at the Mogollon Conference, Oct. 22. Las Cruces.

1985    *Social Adaptation to Food Stress: A Prehistoric Southwestern Example.* University of Chicago Press, Chicago.

Nelson, Ben A.
1980    *Cultural Responses to Population Change: A Comparison of Two Prehistoric Occupations in the Mimbres Valley, New Mexico.* Ph.D. dissertation, Department of Anthropology, Southern Illinois University.

Nelson, Ben A., and Steven A. LeBlanc
1986    *Short-term Sedentism in the American Southwest: The Mimbres Valley Salado.* University of New Mexico Press, Albuquerque.

Nelson, Ben A., Margaret C. Rugge, and Steven A. LeBlanc
1978    LA12109: A Small Classic Mimbres Ruin, Mimbres Valley. In *Limited Activity and Occupation Sites*, edited by Albert E. Ward, pp. 191–206. Contributions to Anthropological Studies No. 1. Center for Anthropological Studies, Albuquerque.

Pailes, R. A.
n.d.    Agricultural Development and Trade in the Rio Sonora Valley. Paper in possession of the author.

Reed, Erik K.
1948    The Western Pueblo Archaeological Complex. *El Palacio* 55:9–15.

Sahlins, Marshall D.
1958    *Social Stratification in Polynesia.* University of Washington Press, Seattle.

Sayles, E. B.
1936    *Some Southwestern Pottery Types.* Medallion Papers 21. Globe, Arizona.
1945    *The San Simon Branch Excavations at Cave Creek and in the San Simon Valley.* Medallion Papers 34. Globe, Arizona.

Service, Elman R.
1962    *Primitive Social Organization: An Evolutionary Perspective.* Random House, New York.

Wilcox, David R., and Lynette O. Shenk
1977    *The Architecture of the Casa Grande and Its Interpretation.* Arizona State Museum Archaeological Series 115.

Wilcox, David R., Thomas R. McGuire, and Charles Sternberg
1981    *Snaketown Revisited.* Arizona State Museum Archaeological Series 155.

Wobst, H. Martin
1974    Boundary Conditions for Paleolithic Cultural Systems: A Simulation Approach. *American Antiquity* 39:147–178.

W. JAMES JUDGE 7

# Chaco Canyon-San Juan Basin

## PROLOGUE

This paper was written in the summer of 1983 in preparation for the SAR conference that fall. At that time, I was director of the Chaco Project, the National Park Service's long-term research project in Chaco Canyon, which then employed eight archaeologists involved in writing the results of the research. Since that summer, a great number of changes have taken place that affect, among other things, the revision of this chapter. I resigned from the project in the spring of 1985. A year later, the National Park Service terminated both the project and its affiliation with the University of New Mexico, and the archaeologists working at the time were moved to the Park Service offices in Santa Fe. At this writing, only two archaeologists are working to finish the project's reports, and one of them only part-time.

Even under these difficult circumstances, a number of important research publications on Chacoan archaeology have been produced since 1983, among them Lekson (1984a), Judge and Schelberg (1984), McKenna (1984), Mathien (1985), Akins (1986), Windes (1987), and two "popular" summaries, Noble (1984) and Frazier (1986). In addition, at least two dissertations have been completed since then (Toll 1985, Sebastian 1988), and two others are being written. As a result of this wealth of recently published material, when I faced the task of revising this manuscript in 1987, the question arose whether to undertake major rewriting based on the recent publications, or to keep the revisions to a minimum, update the references, and offer information on new interpretations, differences of opinion, etc., in separate additions to the text. I have opted for the latter, partially because of time, and partially because major reports on the project are still in preparation. I apologize to the reader for this, because I dislike the discontinuity created by prologue, epilogue, and end notes as much as anyone.

## INTRODUCTION

This chapter deals with the prehistory of the San Juan Basin, a geological structure of some 26,000 square miles, which comprises most of northwestern New Mexico and adjacent parts of Colorado, Utah, and Arizona (Fig. 19). The focus herein will be largely on the New Mexico portion of this entity, which will frequently be referred to as "the Basin." In some instances, however, such as when data from the San Juan Basin Regional Uranium Study (SJBRUS) computer site files are used, the entire San Juan Basin will be dealt with.

Chaco Canyon and the Chacoan "system" dominate the discussion. The intent is not to slight Anasazi occupations that occurred earlier or later than the Chacoan manifestation, nor to ignore the non-Chacoan evidence that existed contemporaneously with Chaco. The problem is that attempting to synthesize the Chacoan data alone is an almost overwhelming task, and given limitations on space, Chaco is treated in most detail. Further, there is little question that the influence of the Chacoan system was pervasive throughout the Basin during its tenure there.

The term "Chacoan system" will be used to refer to that widespread manifestation of structures, sites, communities, roads, ceramics, and so forth, which are the material remains of a social-religious-economic network that functioned as a highly effective, well-integrated system in the San Juan Basin from about A.D. 900 to the mid 1100s. This adaptive system has also been referred to as the "Chaco Phenomenon," and the terms are used interchangeably here.

Due to the tremendous amount of archaeological information available from the San Juan Basin, discussion will focus primarily on the most recent evidence. A brief review of past environments is presented, followed by a more detailed discussion of settlement, demography, site structure, subsistence, and material culture, serving to combine the culture history of the area with an overview of recent research. Finally, an attempt is made to

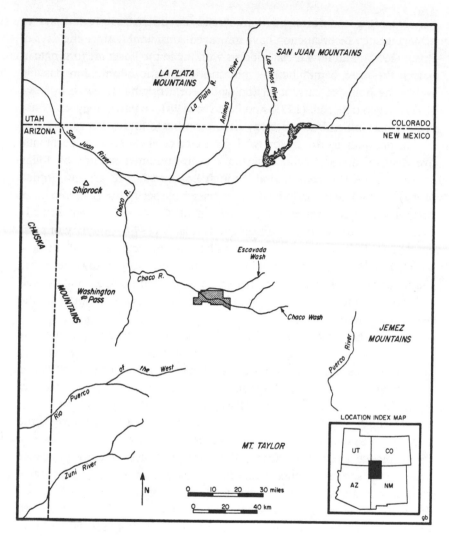

*Fig. 19. The San Juan Basin*

provide a trial reconstruction of the Chacoan system that conforms to the empirical evidence currently available and presented herein.

## PAST ENVIRONMENTS

Since the initiation of archaeological interest some 90 years ago, the San Juan Basin has also been the subject of intensive investigation and speculation regarding the reconstruction of past environments. Techniques of achieving such reconstuction have improved considerably since the days of Bryan (1954), and now archaeologists working in the Basin are fortunate in having the most comprehensive prehistoric climatic information possible within the limits of current technology. Recent original research by Love (1977) in geology, Hall (1975) and Petersen (1981) in palynology, and Rose et al. (1982) in dendroclimatology have contributed to this record.

In addition to the major work by Euler et al. (1979), paleoclimatic overviews of the San Juan Basin have been presented recently by Judge (1982) for the Holocene period through Basketmaker III and by Cordell (1982) for the Pueblo period. Other overviews of specific areas, presented as components of cultural resource management (CRM) reports, are virtually too numerous to mention. An example is Allan's (1977) summary of present and past climates in the Coal Gasification Project's report. Schelberg (1982) has summarized environmental information specifically relevant to Chaco Canyon, particularly with respect to growing season and rainfall records. Gillespie and Powers (1983) have provided such a summary for the region as a whole.

By far the most detailed work on precipitation is that produced by Rose et al. (1982) in their retrodiction of summer, winter, spring, and annual precipitation based on tree-ring indices for the period A.D. 900 to the present. The results of this study have been analyzed by Gillespie and are presented in graphic form in Powers et al. (1983:Figs. 145 and 146). Though the record speaks for itself, of primary interest to this study is the summer precipitation series, reproduced here as Figure 20. Four aspects of this sequence are noteworthy: (a) the frequent lack of correspondence between the summer sequence and the annual record; (b) the considerable variability in the record for the extended period from A.D. 900 to 1050, (c) the period of generally above-average precipitation from A.D. 1050 to 1130 (with the exception of the 1090s), and (d) the period of reduced moisture from A.D. 1130 to 1180. I will rely heavily on this sequence in examining the development and collapse of the Chaco system.

Among those who have dealt with the issue there is general agreement that much of the San Juan Basin, and Chaco Canyon in particular, is environmentally marginal to agriculturalists and presents a challenge in coping with subsistence needs. Though one can place too much emphasis on environmental determinism, it would also be naive to assume that sociocultural development in the Basin took place in the absence of environmental constraints. Here, these constraints are viewed as providing both the fundamental stimulus for the rise of sociocultural complexity in the tenth and eleventh centuries and the underlying cause of its decline.

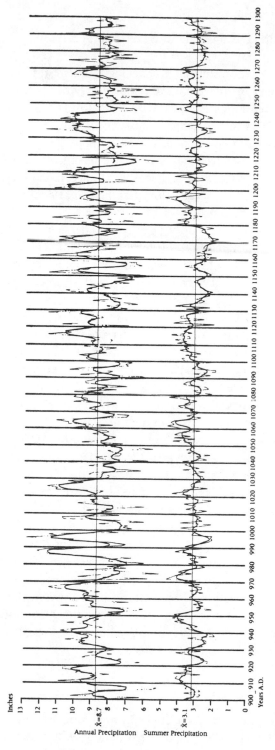

*Fig. 20. Summer and annual precipitation: northwest New Mexico*

# CULTURE HISTORY OF THE SAN JUAN BASIN

In addition to its long history of archaeological interest, the Basin has recently seen a flurry of archaeological research spawned by energy development and the need for compliance with federal historic preservation policies. So many CRM-related projects have been undertaken in the past 15 years I would guess that no one, except perhaps the office of the State Historic Preservation Officer, has a complete record of all research. In an effort to simply keep track of archaeological surveys alone, the National Park Service initiated the "SJBRUS" data base in 1979, which now has some 5,000 surveys recorded.

I will not attempt to list all the projects undertaken in the Basin; even synthesizing the most recent contributions to culture history is a major undertaking. Instead I will simply refer to some of the more recent or comprehensive overviews that have been published; among these are summaries by C. Breternitz (1982), Cordell (1982), Hayes (1981), Judge (1982), Marshall et al. (1979), Powers et al. (1983), Schelberg (1982), Sebastian (1983), Stuart and Gauthier (1981), Tainter and Gillio (1980), R. G. Vivian (1970a), Vivian and Mathews (1965), and Winter (1980). Many of these overviews incorporate the results of recent CRM research in the outline of culture history presented.

Because the Basin has witnessed so much research over so long a period of time, it is not surprising that a number of different cultural chronologies have been constructed to account for the cultural history. Of these, the Pecos Classification has probably provided the standard, but those by Gladwin (1945) and Vivian and Mathews (1965) have seen a considerable amount of use. A number of still different chronologies will be referred to in this chapter in examining the more recent data. These are presented in Figure 21. The traditional Pecos Classification was used by the SJBRUS project in coding the data base. Hayes (1981) modified this somewhat for Chaco Canyon, and Powers et al. (1983) followed Hayes's system for the analysis of the outliers. Windes (in Toll et al. 1980) developed a chronology specific to the so-called Bonito phase or dominant development in Chaco Canyon. I have combined parts of these chronological systems with the tree-ring based building phases suggested by Lekson (1984a, 1984b) to provide an analytical framework for examining the development of the Chaco system.

## *Settlement Patterns*

Certainly one of the most useful tools in analyzing settlement in the San Juan Basin is the SJBRUS computerized data base. It now contains coded

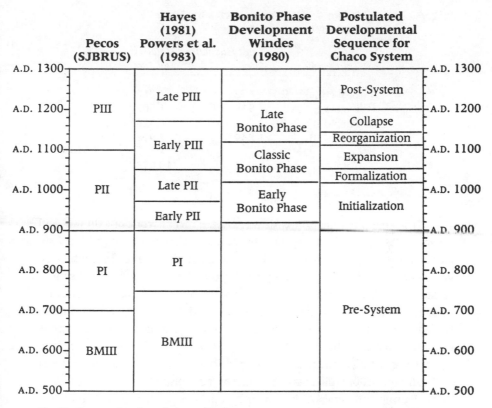

| Pecos (SJBRUS) | Hayes (1981) Powers et al. (1983) | Bonito Phase Development Windes (1980) | Postulated Developmental Sequence for Chaco System | |
|---|---|---|---|---|
| A.D. 1300 | | | | A.D. 1300 |
| PIII | Late PIII | | Post-System | A.D. 1200 |
| | Early PIII | Late Bonito Phase | Collapse | |
| A.D. 1100 | | Classic Bonito Phase | Reorganization | A.D. 1100 |
| PII | Late PII | | Expansion | |
| A.D. 1000 | | Early Bonito Phase | Formalization | A.D. 1000 |
| | Early PII | | Initialization | |
| A.D. 900 | | | | A.D. 900 |
| PI | PI | | | A.D. 800 |
| A.D. 700 | | | Pre-System | A.D. 700 |
| BMIII | BMIII | | | A.D. 600 |
| A.D. 500 | | | | A.D. 500 |

*Fig. 21. Comparative chronologies and sequences*

information on more than 27,400 archaeological sites. A basic description of the data base and its operation is provided in Wait (1982). It provides quantitative information (e.g., site frequencies broken down by time period and type) and graphic plots of both site distributions and survey loci. Its utility has been reviewed by Green (1982).

Site frequency data from the SJBRUS data base are compiled in Table 4. Habitation site frequencies are presented in addition to total frequencies by time period. Site frequency increases rapidly through the Pueblo II period, then drops during Pueblo III. These frequencies are of habitation sites only, and are based on surveys carried out in the San Juan Basin as of 1983. The surveys do not constitute an unbiased sample; thus only subjective interpretations can be made. Computer plots show that within the areas surveyed, sites increase considerably from BMIII to PI, and at the same time began a dispersion that reaches a peak during PII. Additionally, site frequency peaks. Sites then decrease in frequency and appear to cluster more during PIII.

**Table 4.  Site Frequencies by Time Period, San Juan Basin**

| Time Period | Total Habitation Sites | Total All Sites |
|---|---|---|
| Basketmaker III | 652 | 1,060 |
| Pueblo I | 939 | 1,807 |
| Pueblo II | 2,811 | 4,316 |
| Pueblo III | 1,849 | 2,915 |
| Totals | 6,251 | 10,098 |

This same phenomenon is shown by the recent work of Gillespie and Powers (1983), although they have broken down the Basin into both subregional and elevational categories. They suggest that BMIII communities are generally located in areas of optimal potential for floodwater farming (Chaco may be an exception here, because it seems to have many sites on mesa locations). Pueblo I site locations do not differ that much from BMIII. However, by Pueblo II times, site frequencies have tripled from PI. There is also an increase in the utilization of higher elevation zones. Gillespie and Powers suggest this coincides with a more optimal climatic regime between A.D. 950 and 1100, which saw both increased moisture and warmer conditions. During PIII times, site frequency declines, and they note that this correlates with the 50-year period of reduced moisture from A.D. 1130 to 1180, which would of course have the greatest effect on elevations below 6,000 ft. Although they recognize that social factors are involved in population distributions, Gillespie and Powers place a great deal of emphasis on natural environmental factors influencing site locations. Most certainly, the natural environment is something to be reckoned with in the San Juan Basin.

Based on work done by Eileen Camilli (1983) involving the division of the San Juan Basin into environmental cover-type zones from the analysis of LANDSAT imagery, a number of people have attempted to make predictions of site densities in several areas (cf. Kemrer 1982; Drager et al. 1982; McAnany and Nelson 1982; Wozniak 1982). Of these, Drager has dealt with the most extensive areal predictions. For the 21 zones where he calculated density estimations, he found an average density of 0.042 sites per hectare. Assuming the sample is representative (not a valid assumption), the projected site frequency for the total area encompassed by the 21 zones would be 51,642. This gives an idea of site densities for a major, albeit still partial, segment of the San Juan Basin. Based on these projections, the areas of highest site density occur in the Chaco Canyon area, and in the west, south-west, and southern portions of the Basin (Drager et al. 1982:Fig. 8.6).

Two separate works have been published recently that deal specifically with regional settlement of Chacoan sites (as opposed to all sites in the Basin). The first (Marshall et al. 1979) resulted from a study funded by the Public Service Company of New Mexico and the SHPO. This ambitious work provides an excellent introduction to the extent and distribution of the Chacoan system (although not all the sites dealt with in the report are Chacoan). However, it does not deal as systematically with the small site communities associated with the Chacoan structures as the other major published work on Chacoan settlement, *The Outlier Survey* (Powers et al. 1983).

The latter publication reports the results of field survey undertaken by the Chaco Project on three specific outlier communities and on a combina-tion reconnaissance-literature search carried out on 33 more. A final chapter summarizes and interprets a regional Chacoan settlement system by major time periods from BMIII to late Pueblo III (see Fig. 21 for a correlation of chronologies). Figures 22–24 show the distribution of Chacoan outliers in the San Juan Basin. Most notable is the definite focus on the southern and western portions of the Basin through the late Pueblo II period. It is not until the Classic Chacoan period (early Pueblo III in Powers et al.'s chronology) that the fuller San Juan Basin is encompassed by the Chacoan system. We will return to this point later.

Small sites, which tend to cluster around the Chacoan structures (outliers), give rise to the concept of the Chacoan "community." Though detailed survey is lacking in most cases, evidence suggests that these village sites were contemporaneous and associated with the Chacoan outliers.

In most documented cases, the communities consist of dense site clus-ters surrounding the Chacoan structure. Documented densities are as high as 27 sites per square kilometer, and estimated densities in unsurveyed areas are even higher. This contrasts with the average site density of 4.2 sites per square kilometer throughout the Basin. Further, this high site density ap-pears to drop off rapidly beyond an area of about one square kilometer (Powers et al. 1983:Table 22). Although the presence of communities has not been documented for all the Chacoan outliers currently known (as many as 70), this is felt to be more a function of lack of survey than anything else.

Clusters of high site density are, of course, not unusual in Pueblo prehis-tory. What distinguishes the Chacoan situation is that the communities (specifically the Chacoan structures within the communities) are apparently linked to Chaco Canyon and, in some cases, to each other by a system of prehistoric roadways. Though the presence of such roads has been known for some time (Judd 1964), it was primarily through the use of remote sensing techniques initiated by the National Park Service that the extensiveness of the system was realized (Obenauf 1980).

Certainly the most detailed study of the Chacoan roads is that undertaken recently by the Bureau of Land Management in conjuction with an effort to determine how best to protect and preserve known roads in the face of extensive energy development in the San Juan Basin (Kincaid 1983). In addition to providing extensive background information, the study reports the results of intensive inventory done on segments of the roads known to lie in several coal lease areas. Some inventory accomplished outside these areas is reported also.

Powers et al. (1983:272) have suggested that the roads may have divided the Chacoan outlier system into a number of segments or relatively independent subsystems, each one controlling different types of resources and/or environmental zones. Unfortunately, lack of sufficient road inventory between outliers prevents verification of this hypothesis.

Turning to the Chaco Canyon area, although a great deal of research has been undertaken there, we still lack a comprehensive analysis of settlement in the canyon. Hayes (1981) presents the results of the inventory survey of Chaco carried out under his supervision in 1972 and 1973. Although extremely useful, this cannot be considered a detailed analysis of settlement and was not intended as such. He does, however, provide some interesting data on development between BMIII and PII in Chaco Canyon. For example, there was a significant increase in site frequency following BMIII in the canyon, and an estimated 80 percent of the Pueblo I sites were built in new locations, i.e., not over existing Basketmaker sites. Site frequency then continued to increase into Pueblo II, but the majority of the sites during this period were built over earlier loci. This was accomplished by a significant shift in site locations, from the elevated mesa-top loci common to BMIII, to locations much closer to low-lying drainages. The latter loci are maintained throughout the remainder of the occupation of Chaco.

Another aspect of the Chaco Canyon settlement, which has been of interest, is that of the locations within the canyon of the major Chacoan structures or "towns." It has been suggested by some (Judge et al. 1981:86) that at least three of the sites may have been emergent central places to direct the pooling and redistribution of foodstuffs grown in drainages "controlled" by each site. The sites in question are Peñasco Blanco, Pueblo Bonito, and Una Vida, each manifesting early tenth-century construction. Though this may explain early development of large sites in Chaco, the fact remains that not all of the towns are situated at the mouths of drainages. To address this issue, Powers et al. (1983:342) have suggested that the three sites listed above, plus two others (Chetro Ketl and Pueblo Alto), served as administrative centers and canyon entry points for the major road system. Other town sites, particularly the smaller Bonito phase sites and the so-called McElmo sites, may have served specialized functions (Lekson and Judge 1978). We will reexamine the location and function of Chaco Canyon "town" sites in the final section of this chapter.

To summarize, given the amount of information available on the prehistory of the San Juan Basin, it is surprising that a detailed study of settlement has not yet been completed. Nevertheless, it has been suggested that Basketmaker populations sought optimum loci for floodwater farming in the 5,400–6,600 ft range of elevation. With the exception of Chaco Canyon itself, these loci were in the western and southern peripheries of the Basin.

Again, with the exception of Chaco Canyon, most of these optimum loci were maintained during the Pueblo I period, when site frequency increased considerably. Accompanying this increase was an expansion to higher elevations (6,600–7,000 ft range), presumably as a result of favorable moisture and temperature regimes. The Pueblo II period saw a further increase in site frequency, and the exploitation of a greater variety of environments. Again, we assume that the cause was a continuation of the favorable climatic regime. During the Pueblo III period there was a retraction of both site frequency and elevations occupied, although site frequency was not reduced to the level of the BMIII period.

Chaco Canyon mirrored these developments, with the most significant shift in site location coming between the BMIII and PI periods, when clustering along drainages became apparent. The largest expansion in Chaco took place during the Pueblo II period, and the canyon was virtually abandoned by the middle of Pueblo III.

## Demography

Certainly, another great potential of the SJBRUS data base lies in the estimation of prehistoric population levels at the regional level. Because population pressure is frequently invoked by archaeologists as a causal factor in initiating cultural change, refined estimates of population levels at different time periods would, of course, be of great value to understanding change. For the Basin, the problem lies primarily with the sample of sites within the various environmental zones established (Camilli 1983) because site frequencies were not obtained through any kind of unbiased, probabilistic sampling strategy. Instead, sites in the data base generally result from archaeological survey conducted in response to planned energy development. If more detailed research is carried out on predicting site loci within the defined zones by function and time period, the population estimates may become more reliable.

There are, of course, problems with estimating past populations from survey data in general. The inability to estimate site size, volume, room frequency, and contemporaneity accurately from the surface is something archaeologists have to live with. I do not wish to minimize these, but I doubt that they are any more severe in the San Juan Basin than elsewhere. In fact, we should probably be thankful for the tremendous amount of survey that has been carried out in the San Juan Basin and the excellent site surface visibility we have compared to other areas in this country.

Given these caveats, Table 5 presents data on site and room frequency for all habitation sites in the San Juan Basin. The large jump in site frequency from PI to PII (200 percent) is exceeded considerably by a 340 percent increase in total room frequency. This is demonstrated by the increase in the room/site ratio from 6.9 to 10.1 for the same period. Thus, not only did site numbers increase dramatically, but sites got larger.

The change from PII to PIII is equally interesting. Site frequency drops 34 percent and room counts drop 36 percent; thus, the average number of rooms per site stays virtually the same. Therefore, as represented by the SJBRUS data base, we do not see evidence of aggregation taking place from PII to PIII, merely a significant decline in site frequency and the maintenance of the prior site size.

If one equates population with room counts on a very gross basis, and I will not list all the assumptions that should accompany such an equation (see Hassan 1978 for a discussion), the population of the San Juan Basin grew gradually through Pueblo I times, then increased rapidly to Pueblo II, and decreased in Pueblo III, but not to the prior low levels. The PII population increase is probably much larger than expected for normal population growth (LeBlanc 1983) and, if at all accurate, must represent actual immigration into the San Juan Basin.

Population estimation in Chaco Canyon itself has drawn the attention of a number of archaeologists, perhaps because of the size and visibility of the large sites there and the poor quality of the environment. Estimates of total population in the canyon have been made by Fisher (1934), Pierson (1949), Vivian (1974), Drager (1976), Schelberg (1982), Lekson (1984a), and Windes (1984). These vary from 2,000 to 10,000. Hayes (1981) has provided the most detailed estimate, which deals with each major time period individually. Akins (1982:Table 3) has summarized Hayes's estimates and presented them in tabular form. When one controls for the different chronological

**Table 5.  Room Frequencies by Time Period, San Juan Basin**

| Time Period | Total Habitation Sites | Rooms | Rooms/ Site |
|---|---|---|---|
| Basketmaker III | 652 | 3,915[1] | 6.0 |
| Pueblo I | 939 | 6,461 | 6.9 |
| Pueblo II | 2,811 | 28,451 | 10.1 |
| Pueblo III | 1,849 | 18,320 | 9.9 |
| Totals | 6,251 | 57,147 | 9.1 |

[1]*Includes both "rooms" and "pithouses"*

systems used, the curves are very similar to those just noted for the San Juan Basin as a whole.

Windes (1984) has reexamined the estimates of population in the large "town" sites in Chaco by using firepit frequencies as the key criterion and suggests that there never were more than 2,000 residents at all of the large sites combined. His point is that one cannot assume that room function at the large Chaco sites was the same as that at village sites elsewhere, due to the higher frequency of nonhabitation rooms in the former.

Schelberg has reviewed all of these estimates and added his own, which combines the large site count of Windes with the village estimates of Hayes. His conclusion is that the population of Chaco Canyon, taken together with the Escavada drainage immediately adjacent to the north, never exceeded 3,669 at its peak (Schelberg 1982:121). He also evaluates the amount of arable land and suggests that this number of people could not have been supported by the local environment. We will return to this point later.

To summarize briefly, population in the San Juan Basin tracks that of the known site frequency changes through time. Population in Chaco Canyon may have behaved similarly, although recent work has suggested that the large sites were not inhabited as intensively as "normal" estimates would suggest because of noncomparability of room function.

## Site Structure

In discussing site structure for the San Juan Basin, I will again refer to data taken from the SJBRUS data base. I use the term "site structure" in a generic sense to include general concepts such as architecture, layout, and site size.

A great deal of information is available on the structural characteristics of the sites in the Chacoan outlier communities, primarily through the work of Powers et al. (1983). They provide survey data on 18 outlier communities and on the architectural characteristics of 51 Chacoan structures. Two basic site types are discussed: the Chacoan structures (which serve to define the community as a Chacoan outlying area), and the associated villages or small sites. The suggestion is made that an "elite" group resided in the structures, although mortuary evidence for this is scant (Powers et al. 1983:262).

Chacoan structures are defined by a number of criteria, including planned layout, core-veneer Chacoan masonry, large room size, ceiling height (where measurable), and Chacoan kivas. Other criteria, such as great kivas, multistory construction, and presence of a prehistoric road, are also considered, although these may not be present in each case.

As a result of their analyses, Powers et al. (1983:Table 41) divide the 51 Chacoan structures into three classes—large, medium, and small—on the basis of how they cluster in size groupings. The four large sites, Chetro Ketl, Pueblo Bonito, Aztec, and Peñasco Blanco, average 17,991 sq m in area and have an average of 474 rooms and 21 kivas each. There is no question that these are the dominant sites in the Chacoan system, at least from the standpoint of sheer size.

The medium size class contains seven sites: four located in the canyon (Pueblo del Arroyo, Una Vida, Pueblo Alto, and Hungo Pavi) and three outliers (Salmon, Kin Bineola, and Pueblo Pintado). These average 8,072 sq m in area, with an average of 181 rooms and eight kivas each. The small class comprises the remaining 40 Chacoan structures analyzed. These average 1,172 sq m in area, with an average of 41 rooms and just over two kivas each. Of these, all but four lie outside the canyon proper.

The authors also suggest functional differences in these three major site groupings, implying first, second, and third order ranking among the classes. They suggest that the third, or lowest, order, to which the majority of the sites belong, functioned as "administrative-exchange centers" for their associated communities. The second order, or medium size sites, are seen as controlling administrative functions over specific outlying road systems. Finally, the first order sites, the large sites, are seen as centrally located sites that controlled the regional system as a whole. Aztec, as one of these, is thought to be the center of the system following its shift in focus to the San Juan River area post-A.D. 1100 (see discussion below). Further, the first and second order sites were thought to have housed elites (Powers et al. 1983:344–345).

Village site structure in Chaco Canyon progresses from the rather small pithouses associated with the BMIII period to larger pit structures (but fewer per village) in Pueblo I. Pit structure size decreases again during Pueblo II, as the function changes to nonhabitation, and the structures themselves are moved close to surface rooms. Finally, the Pueblo III period sees the pit structures almost completely incorporated into the surface roomblocks, with multitiered roomblocks including both storage and habitation rooms. This, of course, is the typical Anasazi architectural progression seen elsewhere on the Colorado Plateau. McKenna (1984), who has analyzed this development in Chaco in some detail, suggests that the increase in pit structure size through the PI period indicates the need to incorporate more people as the habitation unit developed into a multifamily structure. The development of surface habitation rooms in the PII period completes this transition to multi-family units. Population increase is invoked as the primary causal factor in initiating this change.

McKenna also notes that diversity (architectural and artifactual) increases among small sites in Chaco, particularly during the early Pueblo II period, a point also stressed by Truell (1986) in her summary of village sites in Chaco. Among other things, she notes that some of the village sites contain much larger rooms than others, and are small versions of the Chacoan structures. Presumably, this diversity in structure also reflects a diversity in site function. McKenna suggests that some may have served as local centers of production and exchange for such things as turquoise, ceramics, and bone tools.

Of all the work done in Chaco Canyon, certainly the most extensive analyses of site structure have been carried out by Steve Lekson (Lekson and Judge 1978; Lekson 1982, 1983, 1984a, 1984b). Based primarily on tree-ring analyses, he has divided the construction of the Chacoan structures of the canyon into five major building periods. The first (A.D. 900–940) saw construction at three sites (Peñasco Blanco, Pueblo Bonito, and Una Vida), which consisted of large pit structures backed by a row of ramada/living rooms, a row of large, featureless rooms, and a row of storage rooms. The morphology of the sites at this time was effectively that of the basic Pueblo I structure writ large. Elsewhere we have pointed out that these sites may have been strategically located in the canyon to "control" major drainages (Judge et al. 1981).

Following the initial construction phase is an 80-year hiatus, which as Lekson (1984b) points out, may be more apparent than real (for example, one structure at Hungo Pavi may date to this period). Nevertheless, the next major building phase is that of A.D. 1020–1050, when construction took place at Pueblo Alto, Chetro Ketl, and Pueblo Bonito. The same kind of "suites" were constructed as before, but in rectangular rather than arc form. Further, the new sites of Alto and Chetro Ketl have no apparent strategic location and lack the associated small village communities.

The third period (A.D. 1050–1075) consisted primarily of additions to existing structures, except for initial construction at Pueblo del Arroyo. However, it was during the fourth period (A.D. 1075–1115) that Chaco underwent its most massive building spurt. Six major programs at four sites (Pueblo Bonito, Peñasco Blanco, Pueblo del Arroyo, and Wijiji) seemed to be scheduled in seven to ten-year units. The labor involvement was at least twice that of previous years. Further, it is apparent that "storage" rooms were the dominant type constructed and that there were many more such rooms built than normally required by contemporaneous construction of domestic space. I should add that most of the construction activity at outliers apparently took place at this time also (Powers et al. 1983:Fig. 140).

The fifth and final period (A.D. 1115–1140?) saw reduced construction activity in Chaco Canyon, limited primarily to the so-called McElmo sites plus some remodeling of existing structures. Lekson does not view this construction as "intrusive" but instead as reflecting variability in the function of public facilities at Chaco toward increased storage (cf. Lekson and Judge 1978). We should note that a considerable amount of construction took place at the northern outliers (i.e., those on the north of the San Juan River) at this time also.

Of interest in the discussion of Chacoan site structure is the procurement of trees for roofing material (i.e., primary and secondary roof beams). Lekson (1984b:64) estimates that between 200,000 and 215,000 beams were used in the total construction of Chacoan structures in the canyon as a whole. It is apparent now that the climate in the canyon during the Anasazi occupation was never such that it supported forest abundant enough to provide that much roofing material (Betancourt and Van Devender 1981), and that most of this roofing material had to be imported. That it was imported from some distance has been revealed recently in a study by Dean and Warren (in Lekson 1983) in which the existing tree-ring samples from Chetro Ketl were reanalyzed, and the remaining available wood in the site sampled. One outcome of this study is the fact that approximately 70 percent of the wood that had been identified previously as white fir is now thought to be spruce. Most certainly this indicates procurement from the periphery of the San Juan Basin.

Elsewhere, Lekson (1982) has analyzed the building construction in Chaco from the standpoint of attempting to determine the amount of labor involved. To do this, he divided the construction process into four categories: beam cutting and processing (e.g., limbing and peeling), beam transport (to Chaco), stone quarrying and other material procurement, and the actual building. He then calculated the average labor requirements (man days) for each category. To provide an example, he used the A.D. 1075–1085 construction of the east wing at Pueblo Bonito, the largest single construction unit in all of Chaco. He calculated that this event would have taken

193,000 man hours, approximately one-half of which was actual construction. Although this seems like a lot, it actually is not when spread over the ten-year period in which it presumably took place. In fact, a work crew of 30 men could have done it quite easily with an average investment of less than three months per year.

Lekson also analyzed the most intensive construction period in Chaco (A.D. 1095–1100) to determine total building requirements and found them to require no more intensive an effort than that devoted to annual ditch cleaning by San Juan Pueblo (Lekson 1982; Ford 1968), albeit of somewhat longer duration and involving more people. The point made by Lekson, and it is well taken, is that we should not use the labor organization and labor investment in Chacoan architecture as a major criterion of the level of sociocultural complexity represented there. He does not argue that Chaco was not complex, simply that we should not use Chacoan architecture as a trigger for complexity.

To summarize this discussion of site structure, it is apparent that village structure (size, layout, etc.) in the San Juan Basin is quite "normal" for that on the Colorado Plateau. As many as 70 outlier communities may have existed in the San Juan Basin during the period (A.D. 950–1200) when the Chaco phenomenon developed, flourished, and collapsed. These communities consisted of a cluster of village sites surrounding a so-called Chacoan structure, i.e., a distinct architectural unit exhibiting a number of Chacoan features. It is this configuration of small sites and Chacoan structures that distinguishes the communities of this area from elsewhere. A system of planned, prepared roadways linked the structures to Chaco Canyon and, in some instances, to each other. The structures conform to three basic size categories, with four in the large group, seven in the medium group, and the rest small. The large sites are presumed to have played the dominant role in administering the system, while the medium-size sites in Chaco Canyon may have acted as termini or control points for independent road systems. The smaller sites presumably functioned as third order centers for their respective communities.

Construction events at the outliers probably mirrored those in the canyon itself. Prior to A.D. 1050, or even until the 1080s, there were only 14 or 15 outliers. Most of the outliers were located in the southwestern quadrant of the San Juan Basin. The big push in outlier construction evidently corresponded to that in the canyon (ca. A.D. 1080–1130). At this time another 15–20 outliers were built, many in the northern segment of the Basin (Powers et al. 1983:Figure 140). In the canyon also, this was the main period of construction. Further, there is evidence that the roads may not have been constructed and used before A.D. 1050 (Kincaid 1983), thus that seems to be the date that marks the beginning of most of the activity in the Chacoan system.[1]

Regardless of the apparent intensity of construction in the canyon at the outliers, we should not overreact in attributing complexity to the system on that basis. As Lekson points out, "The scale of labor involvement was not staggering, nor stupendous, nor phenomenal . . . nor is there any . . . rational cause to consider Chacoan building a major drain on Chacoan labor" (Lekson 1982:22).

## *Subsistence*

A number of people have prepared studies recently on subsistence strategies in specific areas of the San Juan Basin, among them Reher (1977), Winter (1980), Nelson and Cordell (1982), Schelberg (1982), Powers et al. (1983), and Gillespie and Powers (1983). Most of these deal with the close association that exists between agricultural productivity and the environment of the Basin.

For example, Reher (1977), basing arguments on the work by Allan (1977) and Love (1977), who felt that agriculture was impossible in some areas of the western Basin, concluded that climatic conditions must have been better in Anasazi times, and that under such conditions catchment areas, which captured runoff, would have been productive. Winter (1980) has termed this the productivity model and has countered it with his own, which he terms the marginality model. Basically, Winter concludes that agriculture in the lower Chaco drainage would always have been marginal at best (even during the Anasazi occupation) and that permanent occupation of the area would not have been possible in the absence of some kind of energy input from outside the local environmental system. He suggests further that the source of such input was from a dendritic exchange system of trade goods under the ultimate direction of Chaco Canyon as a central control point (Winter 1980:505).

---

[1] Chacoan roads are difficult to date accurately. There seems to be general agreement that the roads date no earlier than A.D. 1050, i.e., "the late eleventh to early twelfth century" (Kincaid 1938:11–13). Yet the South Road seems to present a problem. In one place in the Bureau of Land Management study it is noted that the South Road connects early sites, but that the sites were not occupied at the time the road was built (Kincaid 1983:9–77). Yet elsewhere in the same volume it is stated that "analysis of grouped sites within the individual road corridors shows that the South Road generally dates to around the early 900s, while North and Peñasco Blanco to Ahshislepah Roads both date to the late 1000's" (Kincaid 1983:9–46). Thus it would seem we can conclude that the South Road is earlier than the North.

Regardless of the nature of the specific adaptations in various parts of the Basin, it seems that Chaco Canyon is felt to have influenced the subsistence systems in some form, at least during the Pueblo II/early Pueblo III periods. Thus, an examination of the developments in the canyon is in order.

Schelberg (1982) has emphasized the poor environmental conditions in Chaco Canyon. He notes, as Loose and Lyons (1976) did before him, the canyon's inability to support the population reconstructed on the basis of room counts for the peak period of occupation. Schelberg's study includes a detailed analysis of both historical and prehistoric climatic (rainfall) records, and an evaluation of the frost-free growing season in the canyon. His study is unique in two aspects: he takes into consideration the effect of including the Escavada drainage (to the immediate north of the canyon) as a source of arable land, and he also includes consideration of the need to have some portion of the land fallow (his figures include both 40 and 50 percent fallow). He uses Windes's revised figures for the population of the Chacoan structures in the canyon and Hayes's figures for the villages. Even including the Escavada area as a source of production, Schelberg concludes that the area still could not have supported the population indicated by the site frequency. Again, then, we see evidence of the marginality of the Basin and, in this case, of Chaco Canyon in particular.

Elsewhere, Judge et al. (1981) note the close association between productivity and climate in the Chaco area and adopt a position close to that of Reher (1977) reviewed above. In this case, it was felt that the early tenth century saw an amelioration of climate in this area, and in response to this, the early Pueblo II farmers "intensified" production by bringing more area under cultivation. Further efforts at adapting to the improved climate were seen in efforts at pooling resources, as manifest in the construction of large storage structures in the canyon, for example, the three early Bonito phase sites of Peñasco Blanco, Pueblo Bonito, and Una Vida (Judge et al. 1981).

Further responses to cope with the marginality of Chaco can be seen in the evidence of water-control systems in the canyon (Vivian 1972, 1974). It should be noted that the water-control systems in Chaco were designed to capture runoff from the lateral drainages (rincons) and not the main channel of the Chaco wash. In fact, recent research, using watershed computer modeling to analyze hydraulic and hydrologic characteristics of one of the water-control systems (at Peñasco Blanco) mapped by Vivian, has suggested that the system was unsuitable for handling runoff of the major lateral drainage. It was suited instead to a smaller watershed between two major tributary drainages (Lagasse et al. 1984). The same study also indicated that one of the major dam/reservoirs in Chaco, which evidently served the needs of Tsin Kletzin on the South Mesas, would have filled with sediment every 15–25 years and could have been overtopped by storms as often as every 2 years. This work suggests that, while effective, the water-control systems in Chaco were neither as extensive nor as productive as a cursory view would suggest, and there is no compelling reason to assume a vast amount of labor involvement in their construction and maintenance.

Analyses of material excavated by the Chaco Project has resulted in a good deal of information about subsistence in both village and town sites in the canyon. Although not yet complete, analyses of the macrobotanical and flotation samples from the villages and one town suggest more similarity between the town (Alto) and one of the small sites (629) than between the small sites themselves (627 and 629; M. Toll 1984). The key plant frequencies included are corn, beans, squash, pinyon, and prickly pear. The results of pollen analyses from the same sites tend to confirm the lack of a town-village dichotomy from the standpoint of subsistence. Further, in a study of skeletal remains from excavated town sites in Chaco, Palkovich (1984) suggests that the "elite" (as distinguished by grave goods) were not immune from subsistence stress and its consequent pathological effects.

Winter (1983) has recently investigated prehistoric corn recovered archaeologically from the San Juan Basin. On the basis of his analysis of the frequency of eight-rowed corn, he suggests the possibility of three general populations of corn: one in the Mesa Verde area, one in the western San Juan Basin-Chuska area, and possibly another one at Chaco, which might represent exchange with other areas.

Akins (1982, 1984) has also found possible evidence of exchange during the Classic Chaco period from the analysis of faunal remains from village sites and Pueblo Alto in the canyon. Although 60–65 percent of the animal diet of Chaco consisted of artiodactyls (pronghorn and deer) and two species of rabbit, it is the change in frequencies among these species that proves to be interesting. Through Red Mesa times (until ca. A.D. 1050) reliance on antelope and rabbits suggests effective communal hunting in the Chaco area. However, beginning about A.D. 1000, use of pronghorns and rabbits decreases and deer become more important. This suggests a procurement strategy from more distant areas and perhaps the transport and exchange of deer into Chaco (Akins 1982:26). (A similar increase in deer frequency was noted in the analysis of the faunal remains from the McKinley Mine area [Nelson and Cordell 1982:885].) Faunal assemblages from the trash mound at Pueblo Alto indicate much higher frequencies of bone than expected, given the size of the site and the number of rooms represented, suggesting the possibility of periodic feasting events (Akins 1982:26). Interestingly, by the peak of the Classic Chaco period, deer begin to decline in Chaco, and by the 1100s the use of turkeys for food has increased. Prior to this, turkeys were not an important food source.

One of the most comprehensive studies of subsistence recently carried out is in the Bis sa'ani area in conjunction with the mitigation project (Cully et al. 1982). In addition to studying the hydrology, physiography, soils, and vegetation of the area, modern Navajo fields were also studied to investigate suitability of field locations. The results of this multidisciplinary effort indicated that the flatlands of the community area to the south and east of the Chacoan structure (Bis sa'ani) were suitable, though marginal, for agriculture. Using the known archaeological site frequency in the community area, a population of about 100 people was estimated for the peak of occupation during the early A.D. 1100s. The study concluded that there were between 380 and 470 acres cultivable, or enough to support 123–153 people. In other words, the average yield was sufficient to supply the needs of the Bis sa'ani population in normal years, but it is doubtful that it could provide surplus to export to Chaco Canyon (Cully et al. 1982:165).

To summarize this brief examination of subsistence, as a whole, the San Juan Basin can best be characterized as generally marginal in terms of overall productivity. Obviously, some areas and some elevations were more productive than others, and it is not surprising that these would be exploited first and most continually. Less productive areas were used under more optimal moisture conditions and would thus experience fluctuations of settlement as a function of the nature of the moisture regime. Some areas, though too marginal to support a permanent population, may have done so if adequate subsistence buffers or energy subsidies could be supplied through alliance or trade networks, such as that presumably supplied by the Chacoan system during the eleventh century. However, the extensive variability of the Basin should be emphasized. The CGP-Navajo Mine area in the west-central Basin was felt to be habitable only under different climatic conditions (Reher 1977) or with subsistence trade (Winter 1980), whereas the McKinley Mine area in the southwest Basin was found to have no evidence of subsistence stress during its occupation (Nelson and Cordell 1982:888).

Bis sa'ani provides a good example of how a self-supporting outlier community may have functioned, but the question is, was Bis sa'ani a typical outlier? It was evidently settled around A.D. 1130, after the Chacoan system had peaked. Doyel et al. (1984) consider Bis sa'ani to be one of several "scion" outliers that did not contribute subsistence surplus to Chaco Canyon. They postulate that other sites (without Chacoan structures) such as those on the lower Escavada helped to meet Chaco's subsistence needs, and they define these as constituting a Chaco "halo."

In the canyon itself we have seen that there is not much difference between villages and towns with respect to the quality of subsistence, although there may be in terms of quantity. Faunal remains at village sites seem less than adequate for the size of the site represented and may indicate less than permanent (annual) occupation. On the other hand, fauna from Pueblo Alto are more abundant than expected and may indicate periodic congregation of population and/or feasting events. Subsistence patterns in Chaco seem to change during the mid 1000s, when the increases in deer frequencies and variability in corn suggest increased reliance on trade for subsistence.

## Ceramics

Cibolan wares dominate ceramic assemblages in the San Juan Basin until the A.D. 1100s, when carbon-painted wares replace them in the northern half of the Basin. Ceramic assemblages at outlier communities have been summarized by Powers et al. (1983), and initial reports on extensive analyses of Chaco Canyon assemblages have been presented by Toll et al. (1981), Toll and McKenna (1983), and Toll (1984, 1985). Of primary interest here are the results of the source-area studies of Chaco Canyon, based on temper analysis.

Prior to A.D. 920, BMIII and PI ceramic assemblages show the highest percentage of local temper throughout the Anasazi period. From A.D. 920 to 1020, when Red Mesa dominates the assemblages, chalcedonic-cemented sandstone attains its highest percentage (up to 30 percent of the gray wares), suggesting sources in the southern portion of the Basin (possibly the Red Mesa Valley). At the same time trachyte-tempered vessels, particularly gray wares, begin to appear from the Chuska area, 60 km to the west of Chaco Canyon.

During the next period (A.D. 1020–1120), Gallup, Escavada, and Puerco types dominate the assemblages, and there is a dramatic increase in the frequency of ceramics imported from the Chuskas. By the early 1100s trachyte-tempered gray wares reach 49 percent and Chuskan white wares increase sharply to 26 percent (Toll 1985:Tables 3–5). Also, some standardization of vessel form is indicated, suggesting limited areas of production of these vessels. One reason for the sharp increase in vessel imports to Chaco may well have been depletion of fuel for firing during the latter part of the eleventh century in the canyon itself (Betancourt and Van Devender 1981), though Toll (1985:437) points out that fuel shortage was not the sole reason.

During the final ceramic period at Chaco (A.D. 1120–1220), carbon-painted wares from the San Juan area became dominant. Again, imports are very high in frequency. In fact, if coarse-sand tempered gray wares were imported, as suspected, the figure reaches as high as 98.5 percent (Toll and McKenna 1983:145).

With the exception of Pueblo Alto (see below), there is little ceramic evidence to suggest any dramatic distinction between towns and villages in Chaco. In fact, both seem to be importing ceramics from the same source, and imported frequencies increase at both through time.

Certainly the most intriguing and important evidence resulting from the ceramic analyses in Chaco is that of the level of ceramic consumption at Pueblo Alto. Based on ceramic frequencies recovered from a sample of the formal trash mound, as many as 150,590 ceramic vessels may have been deposited there. It is estimated that a minimum of 49,270 trachyte-tempered pots were deposited, of which 31,360 were gray ware jars. One must wonder, then, at the staggering rate of consumption of pottery at Alto, which figures to be about 125 vessels per family per year, as opposed to an estimated 17 per family at the village sites in Chaco. Toll (1984) suggests that this may indicate periodic gatherings at Pueblo Alto of nonresidents, with possible ceramic disposal associated with such gatherings.

Ceramically, Pueblo Alto turns to a more characteristic habitation pattern after A.D. 1100. As noted, non-Chuskan carbon-painted wares increase, and Alto's ceramic assemblage becomes similar to that found from excavations at the late outliers (Salmon, Aztec, Bis sa'ani) and at other late sites in the canyon (e.g., Kin Kletso).

To summarize the ceramic evidence briefly, we see increasing importation of ceramics into Chaco through time, with possible standardization of production in the Chuska area during the A.D. 1020–1120 period, and almost certainly the formalized disposal of large quantities of imported ceramics at Pueblo Alto during the same period. Late ceramics at Chaco show a return to normal consumption but a continued increase in reliance on imported wares.

## Lithic and Exotic Materials

Cameron (1984) has analyzed the lithic material recovered from the Chaco Project excavations, undertaking both formal tool and flake analyses as well as source-area studies. As a result of her studies, she concludes that the redistribution of exotic lithic material in Chaco Canyon is not supported empirically. Jacobson (1984) has undertaken regional analyses in the San Juan Basin on survey collections. Her analyses also suggest that lithic material was not redistributed in the Basin. Here we will emphasize Cameron's source-area studies.

Cameron (1984) found that the earlier time periods in Chaco Canyon exhibited a high frequency of local materials (cherts and petrified woods). In the A.D. 1000s, these local materials decrease sharply and exotics, primarily Washington Pass chert from the Chuskas, Brushy Basin chert from the Four Corners region, and a yellow-brown spotted chert from the southern portion of the Basin, increase accordingly. Washington Pass chert dominates the exotics by far, and, in fact dominates all lithic types in the canyon from A.D. 1020–1120 (Cameron 1984:139). Obsidian, another exotic, never reached more than 2 percent of the total chipped stone analyzed. In the early time periods, the exotics consisted primarily of tools, with little debitage. By the A.D. 1000s, however, this reversed, and the exotics consist mainly of cores, debitage, and utilized flakes.

Cameron estimates that 130 kg of Washington Pass chert were imported to Pueblo Alto between A.D. 1050–1100, comprising 27 percent of the chipped stone assemblage. Further, the quantity of chipped stone discarded at Alto is five times as much as that at the village sites in Chaco (Cameron 1984:146). In contrast to that suggested by Shelley (1980) at Salmon, there is little evidence of specialization of lithic manufacture in Chaco, based on the lack of formal tools and the lack of standardized reduction techniques. Nor is there evidence of selection of exotic material for specific tools. There is only the puzzling evidence of an unusually high frequency of Washington Pass chert and a high rate of lithic material consumption at Pueblo Alto.

Exotic minerals and shell (i.e., "jewelry" items) recovered by the Chaco Project have been analyzed by Mathien (1984). Through the Pueblo I period three genera of marine shell are represented. During the Bonito phase (A.D. 1020–1120), 17 new genera of shell appear, suggesting a healthy trade with areas outside the San Juan Basin. These were distributed equally between towns and villages. Beads form the most dominant jewelry items, and of these, turquoise is the most obtrusive. The canyon, of course, is well known for the tremendous quantities of turquoise found there, and there is little doubt that it exceeds that found elsewhere in the Basin (see Mathien 1981:App. B for a summary). There is considerable evidence of turquoise bead, and to some extent pendant, manufacturing workshops at Chaco. For example, sites 629, 1360, and Alto, all excavated by the Chaco Project, have such workshops. Sites Bc51 and Bc59, Pueblo del Arroyo, Una Vida, Kin Kletso, Pueblo Bonito, and possibly Kin Nahasbas, all excavated previously, do also. At site 629 not only was a great deal of turquoise found, but 70 percent of all passive abraders (presumably used in lapidary work) recovered by the Chaco Project were found there. Although workshop evidence is abundant, Mathien sees evidence of subsidized, possibly full-time craftsmen only at 629, due to the large amount of turquoise represented there in the relatively short period of occupation. (Tom Windes [personal communication] suggests this may also be true at site 626.)

In summary, there is evidence of turquoise and other jewelry manufacture at Chaco, both in villages and in towns. There is little evidence of redistribution of lithic materials. Instead, consumption of imported lithics, particularly Washington Pass chert, seems to have taken place during the A.D. 1020–1120 period at some of the town sites in the canyon, such as Pueblo Alto.

## THE CHACO SYSTEM, A.D. 900–1200: A TRIAL RECONSTRUCTION

Through the years, a great number of people have provided models, reconstructions, or just ideas on how to explain the origin, function, and demise of the Chaco Phenomenon. Before providing yet another version, it seems appropriate to acknowledge those that have gone before, both for purposes of documentation and because of the debt owed each in arriving at a formulation of the present attempt. This list is not to be considered exhaustive— instead it includes those who have dealt with the issue in a comprehensive and/or innovative sense. I apologize to those whose labors of love have been inadvertently omitted, and for having neither space nor time here to synthesize and present the views of each.

I have grouped the references into two categories: the "Mexicanists" (those who feel the system could not have developed without extensive stimulation or direct intervention from contemporary society in Mexico) and the "Indigenists" (those who feel the Chaco Phenomenon developed independently of major influence from outside the Southwest, if not the San Juan Basin). All are listed chronologically.

Mexicanists:
Ferdon (1955), DiPeso (1974), Kelley and Kelley (1975), Lister (1978), Frisbie (1980), Reyman (1980), Washburn (1980), Hayes (1981), Schroeder (1981)

Indigenists:
Judd (1964), Vivian and Mathews (1965), Vivian (1970a, 1970b, 1983), Grebinger (1973, 1978), Judge (1977, 1979), Altschul (1978), Cordell (1979, 1982), Cordell and Plog (1979), Marshall et al. (1979), Tainter and Gillio (1980), Winter (1980), Judge et al. (1981), Mathien (1981),

Schelberg (1982), C. Breternitz (1982), Powers et al. (1983), Irwin-Williams (1983), LeBlanc (1983), Sebastian (1983)

Many of these works have been reviewed, summarized, and evaluated by Hayes (1981) in his report on the results of the Chaco survey, by C. Breternitz (1982) in his report on Bis sa'ani, and by Schelberg (1982) in his study of economic and social development in Chaco Canyon. Vivian (1970a) provides an excellent critical summary of the reconstructions developed through the late 1960s.

The following reconstruction calls on a number of different aspects of many of the models referenced here. It differs from most not in its originality, but in the fact that it is based largely on data retrieved and analyses completed in the past several years by the Chaco Project, information largely unavailable to other researchers until quite recently.

Though somewhat subjective and admittedly arbitrary, the chronological divisions used here in describing the evolution of the Chacoan systems are based primarily on the building stages suggested by Lekson (1984a) in his recent review of the architectural developments in Chaco Canyon during the Pueblo period. I have named these stages initialization, formalization, expansion, reorganization, and collapse.

## Tenth-Century Developments (Initialization)

Cultural developments in the San Juan Basin during the tenth century took place in an extremely variable (quantity and disitribution) precipitation context, and this may be the key to understanding the emerging role of Chaco Canyon in the Basin. As outlined in an earlier paper (Judge et al. 1981), three sites in the canyon seem to have dominated the settlement pattern: Peñasco Blanco, Pueblo Bonito, and Una Vida. These sites, the layouts of which were Pueblo I sites writ large, were strategically located at the confluence of major drainages and the Chaco wash. We suggested that they functioned primarily as storage sites to accompany resource pooling and redistribution within the drainage systems they "controlled" (see Vivian 1983 for a critique of this). This hypothesis would most certainly be consistent with the environmental regime that we now know dominated the tenth century (cf. Toll 1985:458–460).

Although there seems to be a lapse in construction dates from A.D. 940 to 1020, as pointed out above, this may be more apparent than real. There is no doubt, however, that the dominant ceramic type of the period was Red Mesa Black-on-white. It is interesting that this type seems focused toward the southern half of the San Juan Basin, in that it occurs in high frequency at sites in that area, and may have been produced in the southern periphery of the Basin (Toll 1984).

This focus on the southern half of the Basin is manifest in the structure of the outlier communities during the early Pueblo II period (Fig. 22). Although some Chacoan structures outside the southern half are known, those with known communities (Skunk Springs, Kin Bineola, Peach Springs, and El Rito) lie within it. Presumably these communities developed in situ from a BMIII/PI base in a manner analogous to those in the canyon for the same reasons, and to perform the same function (resource pooling and redistribution). The one exception, Guadalupe, may have developed in an eastern location for a different reason (see below). The point is that Chaco Canyon is not centrally located with respect to these sites, and I would suggest that the influence of the canyon on them was minimal during this time period. It most certainly was not serving as a central place, and in all probability there was no such thing as a Chacoan system operative then. Although undoubtedly linked through reciprocity and carrying on normal trade, the communities were probably relatively independent of each other with respect to their subsistence bases. Further, population increase at this time within the Basin could easily be explained by normal growth.

In my view, one thing did take place during this period that set the stage for the formation of the Chacoan system. This was the increasingly dominant role that Chaco Canyon played as the locus of turquoise processing and the source of finished turquoise items. It may well have not been limited to turquoise (that is, Chaco may have dominated ornament production in general), but turquoise is the single type of ornament that can be well documented as concentrated in the canyon. I suggest that this dominance is related to the fact that relative to the other communities extant at the time, Chaco was effectively poorer in resources and thus increased the turquoise processing capability in order to buffer against resource deficiencies in hard times. This, again, is consistent with the variable character of the environment at the time. At any rate, one cannot question the large quantities of turquoise associated with Red Mesa sites in the canyon, the fact that it is most frequently manifest as workshop debris, and the possibility that there was some full-time specialization of production.

By the end of the tenth century, or perhaps by A.D. 1020, I suggest that Chaco Canyon was firmly established as the dominant source of finished turquoise for the southern portion of the San Juan Basin, if not the Basin as a whole. I would argue further that by the early A.D. 1000s, turquoise had become integrated into the existing exchange network in a manner that

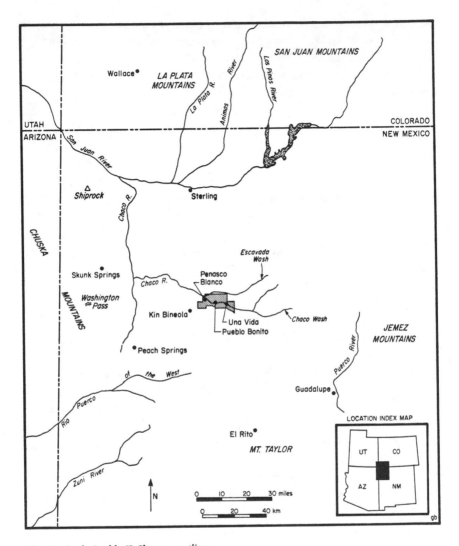

*Fig. 22. Early Pueblo II Chacoan outliers*

superceded its role as an item of primarily ritual importance. In other words, turquoise may have acquired the additional function of informally regulating exchange of other material items, both durable and perishable. If so, there would have been a brisk exchange of turquoise among the relatively independent communities of the tenth-century San Juan Basin.

Dominance by Chaco in the processing of turquoise would have been facilitated by control of the source. Thus a strong link may have existed between the canyon and the outlier at Guadalupe, the latter, serving with the canyon, to control the Cerrillos source.[2] As such, we would expect Guadalupe to manifest an early occupation as a Chacoan outlier, and that it would have little evidence of turquoise processing. In fact, both expectations are met. To be consistent with the suggestion, turquoise would pass through Guadalupe in bulk and would be carefully conserved, thus leaving little evidence. There should, however, be other evidence of strong ties between Guadalupe and the canyon, perhaps in the form of other material goods. Finally, if the hypothesis of Chaco's dominance of turquoise processing holds true, one would expect little evidence of such processing to occur at other communities in the Basin.

## A.D.1020–1050: System Formalization

About A.D. 1020 a relatively long period of above-average moisture begins in the Basin (Powers et al. 1983:Figs. 145, 146). This is especially true of summer precipitation (Fig. 20, above), and of the percentage summer moisture contributes to the annual moisture totals. A brief period of below average summer moisture occurs from A.D. 1025 to 1035, but then it remains above average until A.D. 1080. Thus, for the period in question, we see a continuation of variability from the preceding period, but by A.D. 1045, we see the beginning of what turns out to be a long trend of favorable conditions.

I would argue that during this time of continued environmental variability, Chaco's control of turquoise production increased, the role of turquoise as a ritual item became more formalized, and Chaco itself assumed an increasing role as a locus of ritual importance in the southern portion of the San Juan Basin. Many of these developments were related to precipitation variability, in that Chaco continued to rely on the needed cultural subsidies to buffer its resource deficiencies.

During this period, which can be characterized as one of transition to and formalization of the Chacoan system, Gallup Black-on-white emerges as the dominant ceramic type in the Basin. I suggest that initially Gallup was made locally in Chaco Canyon and became integrated with the emerging formalization of the turquoise exchange system. In other words, it also

---

[2] Until recently it was felt there was little evidence of Chacoan sites in the area of the Cerrillos turquoise source. However, Wiseman (1986) reports the identification of five anomalous pueblos about 1 km east of the mines. These sites are anomalous in that they are constructed of masonry instead of adobe; in the predominance of processing (mining tools, lapidary stones) rather than residential artifacts; and in the abundance of exotic sherds (Red Mesa, Gallup, Socorro Black-on-white). This is the first evidence of structural sites with Chacoan affiliation in the Cerrillos area.

became a material symbol of the emergent system, along with turquoise and a developing architectural style.

New construction in Chaco at this time is interesting because it shows the emergence of the central portion of the canyon as architecturally important. Two sites were started at this time: Chetro Ketl, in the bottom of the canyon several hundred meters east of Pueblo Bonito, and Pueblo Alto, on the mesa north of Pueblo Bonito. Prior to this we cannot say that the central portion of the canyon was dominant, but the addition of these two structures confirms the dominance of this area from then on.

These sites differ from tenth-century construction in the canyon in that neither is apparently "controlling" a particular drainage system, nor do they have clearly associated communities. This is especially true in Pueblo Alto. Although Alto may have served later as an integral component of the North Road system, there is no evidence that the road systems were built during this period. Further, Alto's elevated location, which permits visibility throughout the San Juan Basin, would have served it well were its initial function primarily related to ritual. Chetro Ketl, on the other hand, might have exercised some control over village sites on the Escavada drainage to the north; later we know it was connected to the Escavada by at least two roads, and perhaps other routes (e.g., the Jackson staircase).

During this period, developments in outlying locations continued to focus on the southern portion of the Basin. As indicated by Powers et al. (1983:Fig. 143), only one (Hogback) of the eight new outlier communities developed by this time lies outside the southern half of the Basin (Fig. 23). Again it is obvious that Chaco Canyon cannot yet be considered a central place, being located on the northeastern periphery of the established Chacoan communities. Nevertheless, the role of Chaco Canyon becomes more dominant than previously in that both architecturally and ceramically its influence is felt in the newly developed outliers. Although Red Mesa Black-on-white ceramics tend to dominate the period, Gallup Black-on-white becomes increasingly important by A.D. 1050. Architecturally, it is apparent that the Chacoan-style large structures were established in existing village communities. Of the eight new outliers, at least six had evidence of prior community development. Thus, Chaco Canyon's influence in the southern portion of the Basin seems quite prominent, yet it cannot be explained in terms of a central location with resultant economic significance.

For these reasons, it seems rational to assume that Chaco's emerging dominance was focused on a more nonmaterial realm, due to the practical economics of the Basin at the time. Again a primary ritual function, with turquoise as the durable item of symbolic value, is argued here. I would suggest that during this period the periodic visits to the canyon to obtain

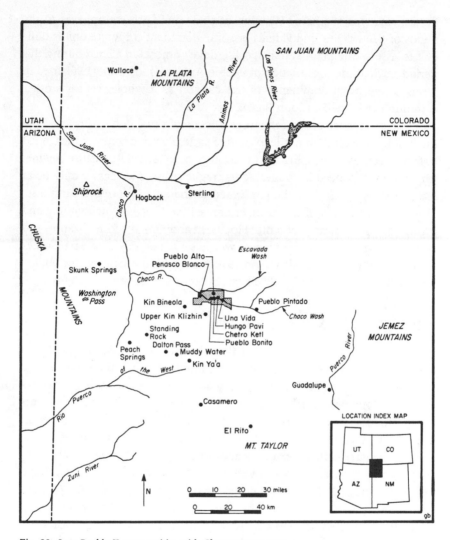

*Fig. 23. Late Pueblo II communities with Chacoan structures*

turquoise became increasingly formalized under some kind of ritual metaphor. At the same time, alliance networks between the outlying communities would become more formalized as a means of integrating those communities through exchange of nonritual material goods. As the system
formalized—that is, as it began to develop into a true system—
administration of the exchange networks would have become necessary and
could easily have fallen to those residents of Chaco Canyon, particularly if
turquoise was the primary material symbol of the ritual and was controlled

by the residents of Chaco. Whether at this point such control was in the hands of a few "elite" individuals or some dominant corporate unit is difficult to assess. The point is that specific developments in Chaco during this period, such as the construction of Pueblo Alto, are most easily explained in terms of the ritual dominance of the canyon as a whole, vis-a-vis other communities in the San Juan Basin.

The emergence of the canyon as a locus of ritual dominance, and the increasing formalization of the exchange system among communities, must both be seen as developing in the context of a variable moisture regime. Chaco Canyon's need for buffering its fragile subsistence base would be at least partially satisfied by the continued exchange of processed turquoise. This exchange would of course be enhanced for Chaco by maintaining and increasing its significance as a ritual locus. In addition, the formalization and administration of exchange alliances would serve not only to integrate other communities further but also to provide them with mechanisms for buffering against the vagaries of early eleventh-century moisture availability.

## A.D.1050–1115: System Expansion

By A.D. 1050 the basic structure of the Chacoan system was in place and operating. It is important to point out that although it had developed in a variable moisture regime (and probably largely because of such variability) the rather long period of favorable climate that followed would most certainly enhance the success of the system, particularly if it were embedded in ritual that functioned overtly to guarantee the continuation of adequate rainfall. As noted earlier, beginning about A.D. 1045 and lasting through A.D. 1080, summer precipitation was very favorable, staying well above average for most of the period and never dropping below average (Fig. 20). This 35-year "good" period was followed by a sharp, but brief, moisture reduction in the early A.D. 1080s and then a more substantial and longer reduction from A.D. 1090 to 1100. After this, another 35-year "good" period ensued until the end of the mid 1130s, when a severe and extended period of reduced moisture began.

Although the Chacoan system had developed and formalized gradually over the 100-year period from A.D. 950 to 1050 (our segmentation of the system stages is somewhat arbitrary), there is little question that a great deal of activity involving the expansion of the system took place in the latter half of the eleventh century. Gallup Black-on-white became firmly established as the dominant ceramic type, replacing Red Mesa Black-on-white. Further, the Chuskas as a source of Gallup Black-on-white and its associated gray wares became increasingly important during this period, reaching a point where the majority of the ceramics consumed in Chaco were imported from that area (Toll 1984). In addition, there is some evidence of "standardized" ceramic manufacture in the Chuska area.

During the first part of this period, from A.D. 1050 to 1075, new construction in Chaco Canyon was devoted largely to additions, although one new site (Pueblo del Arroyo) was started, and the never-completed "foundation complex" at Bonito may have been laid at this time. It was during the latter part of the period, however, that construction activity reached massive proportions in the canyon (and at the outliers also). Between A.D. 1075 and 1115, major construction programs were undertaken at Pueblo Bonito, Peñasco Blanco, Pueblo del Arroyo, and Wijiji. Interestingly, the emphasis seems to have been primarily on the construction of storage rooms (or at least nonresidential units). Accompanying this construction boom is the possibility that turquoise processing shifted from villages to the large sites, and as noted previously, there was a shift from antelope to deer as the major large animal species consumed. Presumably, deer were being imported into Chaco at this time also.

Occupancy of village sites in the canyon decreased during this period (or else the villages were simply denied access to Gallup Black-on-white ceramics), and those that were occupied seem to have been located in the central portion of the canyon (Windes and Doleman 1985). At this time in Chaco's history the population of the canyon was probably not very large: perhaps on the order of 2,000 people or less living in the canyon on a permanent, year-round basis (Windes 1984). Since it is difficult to support more than that population in the canyon (Schelberg 1982), there would be little reason for more to live there. Further, if the hypothesis of a primary ritual function is correct, only those essential to the maintenance of that function would be needed to stay.

On the other hand, it is a fact that there are "residential" facilities for a much larger population in the canyon, and estimates as high as 5,600 (Hayes 1981) have been made on that basis. Thus the reduced figure given above merits explanation. I suggest that the facilities in Chaco were constructed to accommodate periodic influxes of people in substantial numbers and that these influxes were accomplished by means of formal pilgrimages from the outlying areas to Chaco Canyon. Freidel (1981) has suggested that the concept of "pilgrimage fairs" might explain both residential dispersion and social complexity in the case of the Lowland Maya. Although his model cannot be transferred without modification to northwest New Mexico, aspects of it are attractive in explaining what appears to be the central consumption of material items from dispersed residences in the San Juan Basin during this time period. To quote Freidel, by means of these pilgrimage fairs

. . . the distribution of goods above the local level could be channeled through centers under religious sanction. Because the festivals would be scheduled and their occurrence and location well known in advance, both production and distribution of goods could be maintained in a predictable manner. Inevitably, the elite members of society responsible for the organization, size, and geographic reach of the festivals and fairs would be in a position to control and tax the distribution of goods through these centralized exchange events. If the rationale behind the fair was the festival, then the overall structure of the system would have to be a widely shared religion (Freidel 1981:378).

Again, we would not assume a one-to-one correspondence between the situation in Yucatan and that in the San Juan Basin. Freidel's model does not involve a central ritual place analogous to that which we assume for Chaco Canyon. Nor can we demonstrate at this time that festivals or fairs in the San Juan Basin involved actual economic markets, as assumed in the Mayan case. Instead, the Chacoan system seemed to involve more central consumption of goods and services rather than their redistribution at a central locus. Nevertheless, the model does provide a view of how dispersed residences may have been integrated into a single socioeconomic system through the vehicle of periodic circulation of people under a ritual principle, and how that might have served to control and regulate the distribution of both goods and services between dispersed residential communities such as the outlying components of the Chacoan system.

At least two alternative models of the operation of the Chaco system have been produced recently and should be noted here. Sebastian (1983) advocates the concept of bounded exchange groups, tied to the regional network through exchange of certain items among elites. In times of need, people (as corporate units) would be moved to areas of higher productivity, based on the established ties. Vivian (1983) minimizes the amount of interaction among outlying loci, instead emphasizing out-migration and colonization from Chaco to favorable areas as the mechanism of outlier establishment. Neither author endorses redistribution of subsistence goods between outliers, suggesting instead redistribution of people to environmentally favorable areas. Although I agree that undoubtedly people were moved frequently, I see nothing to prevent directed exchange of goods, including subsistence items, particularly between those communities relatively close to each other. This would better rationalize the structural formality of the entire system, an aspect that neither author addresses satisfactorily, in my estimation.

If the concept of pilgrimage festivals is reasonable, I would argue that the "visits" to Chaco during the prior periods developed into formal pilgrimages during this period (A.D. 1050–1115). By this I mean they became regularly scheduled ritual events where goods were transported to Chaco Canyon from outlying locations and were consumed and services performed there under a ritual metaphor. As the system expanded, these pilgrimages would be attended by increasingly larger numbers of people, involve increasingly complex ritual, and thus would require increasingly larger degrees of control and administration by those in charge, presumably those resident in Chaco Canyon. Embedded in ritual, yet tied intimately to the continuation of a favorable environment, the system would also become increasingly vulnerable to environmental fluctuation.

Although the expansion of the system can be seen in the evidence from Chaco Canyon, it is at the outlying locations that its growth becomes most apparent during this period. As noted by Powers et al. (1983:252, Fig. 1), the majority of the Chacoan outliers are dated to this period (Fig. 24). At least 19 appear to have been constructed, and with one exception (Haystack), most of the activity took place in the northern part of the Basin (i.e., north of Chaco Canyon). It is during this period, then, that Chaco Canyon finally becomes a "central place," in the geographic sense. Further, it is interesting that most of the construction activity took place toward the end of this period (after ca. A.D. 1085), when construction was at a peak in Chaco Canyon itself. Thus the system expansion, at least as manifest in architectural construction, was quite rapid indeed.

This is also the earliest period to which the construction of the roads can be attributed (Powers et al. 1983:252). Presumably, road construction began about A.D. 1050 and continued throughout the period, though roads are difficult to date. Since it is unlikely that the roads were built prior to the construction of the Chacoan structures they link, it is probable that the North Road was the last one built and, logically, that the road or roads south to Kin Ya'a were among the earliest (see note 1). In any event, by the end of this period we assume the sites of the Chacoan system were physically integrated by a road system that may have comprised five major segments, linking all but the northeast quadrant of the Basin (Powers et al. 1983:Fig. 1). With the exception of the Chimney Rock site, the latter quadrant was never a component of the Chacoan system, at least given our current knowledge of sites in the area.

These developments seem to coincide with what we have recognized previously as a substantial increase in population in the San Juan Basin during the Pueblo II period. According to the Pecos Classification, the Pueblo II period (A.D. 900–1100) includes most of the period being dealt with here (A.D. 1050–1115), thus, my guess is that much of the population increase in the San Juan Basin actually took place in the eleventh century,

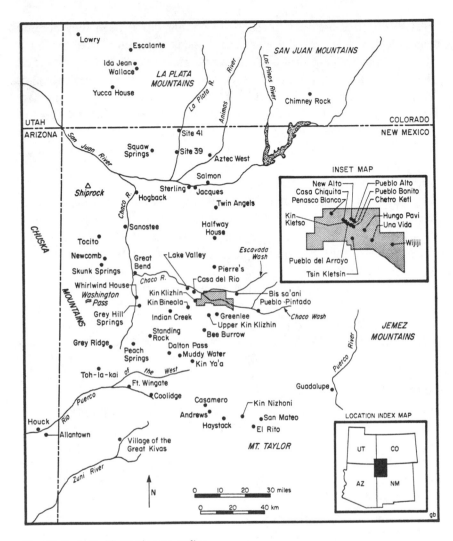

*Fig. 24. Early Pueblo III Chacoan outliers*

and probably after A.D. 1050. Given this, it most certainly would have to have taken place either through actual migration from outside the Basin or, in Stuart's (1982) terms, through the conversion of mobile, less archaeologically visible, efficiency-based groups to more visible, power-based groups. If the former was the case, and the Chaco system acted as a magnet attracting groups to it, it would be interesting to know where they came from.

In any case, it is evident that during the latter half of the eleventh century a great many more people became formally integrated into the

Chacoan network through the proliferation of communities in the Basin that elected to participate in the economic and ritual system. These communities could have arisen through the coalescence of village sites around a newly constructed Chacoan structure, through the construction of such a structure in a central location among existing village sites, or some combination of both. The benefits of such participation would lie in the ability to share in the administered exchange-redistribution network between outlying locations, as well as participating in a common religion that was seemingly successful in providing a continued favorable moisture regime. Obligations would involve participation (at some level) in periodic visitation to Chaco Canyon, and the contribution of goods and services for the common good there or elsewhere in the system.

I suggest that the Chacoan system, now fully formalized as an economic and ritual entity, functioned well and expanded rapidly due primarily to the continuation of favorable environmental (climatic) conditions in the San Juan Basin. This would be perceived indigenously as a result of adherence to an established, successful, and probably increasingly formalized ritual system controlled by Chaco Canyon. The two periods of reduced summer precipitation—one in the early A.D. 1080s and the other in the A.D. 1090s—served to challenge Chaco's ritual and administrative dominance, already made vulnerable by the formality and complexity of the system. The perception that Chaco could no longer fully control the environment might well have led to the construction of outliers in more favorable areas, such as the Salmon site on the San Juan River, where construction dates cluster at A.D. 1088 and 1094. Such challenges, I feel, set the groundwork for a major system reorganization, which was to occur during the ensuing period.

## A.D. 1115–1140: System Reorganization

The period from A.D. 1100 to 1130 was favorable climatically, particularly with respect to summer rainfall (Fig. 20). It followed two brief intervals of reduced summer moisture, one of which (A.D. 1090–1100) was more severe than any other during the eleventh century. A similar reduction took place beginning around A.D. 1130, and this initiated a very severe 50-year period of drought.

In Chaco Canyon and elsewhere in the Basin, a number of developments took place that signal major changes in the Chacoan system, changes of sufficient magnitude to suggest a significant reorganization took place. Basic to these developments was the nature and extent of new construction in the canyon. It was during this period that most of the so-called McElmo phase structures were built (e.g., Kin Kletso, Casa Chiquita, New Alto).

Additions to existing structures took the form of subdividing many of the large rooms and adding "arcs" to the sites (probably best interpreted as formally enclosing the plazas). The intensity of construction during this period returned to the "normal" level experienced before the Expansion period (A.D. 1050–1115).

Another important development at this time was the shift in location of trash deposition (Windes 1982). Extramural trash mounds were evidently seldom used. Instead, abandoned kivas and/or rooms became the locus of deposition. This shift coincides with the increase in frequency of carbon-painted wares, primarily Chaco-McElmo Black-on-white (in Chaco Canyon). Also, with respect to trash, we should recall that there is a shift in Chaco away from large mammal dominance to the increasing use of small mammals and turkeys as primary faunal subsistence items (Akins 1982). This suggests a reduction of importing large mammals (especially deer) to Chaco Canyon.

The final development in the canyon that suggests system change is an evident increase in village site frequency (Windes, personal communication) and a change in the structural character of some of the new construction at village sites. One site tested by the Chaco Project (29SJ633) may typify the late villages, which were small, single-unit versions of some of the larger McElmo phase sites, such as Kin Kletso. Truell (1986) also notes considerable diversity in village site structure during this time.

Outside the canyon proper an example of the character of this shift can be seen in the development of Bis sa'ani as an outlier, some 9.5 mi east of Pueblo Bonito. Bis sa'ani was a self-contained community of about 100 people, established sometime around A.D. 1130. The Chacoan structure has cutting dates that cluster between A.D. 1126 and 1139 (Breternitz et al. 1982:69). The community lacks a great kiva and has been classified as a "scion" community rather than an "ancestral" outlier (Doyel et al. 1984). Presumably it did not contribute subsistence goods to the canyon area.

In my view, these developments mirror a major change in function that took place in Chaco Canyon during this period. This includes change in function of sites within the canyon as well as changes in the function of the canyon vis-a-vis the San Juan Basin as a whole. Basically, Chaco appears to become more residential (domestic) and less ritual in function. Though pilgrimages may have continued, I doubt whether Chaco continued to function as the focus of such visits. Instead, I would argue that Chaco Canyon itself became the equivalent of an outlying area or, perhaps, a second order center with primarily domestic, nonritual functions.

If such a shift did indeed take place in the early twelfth century, where was the new ritual/administrative focus of the system located following reorganization? Again, one must look to the north, conceivably in the area of the San Juan River, because ceramically and architecturally, there seems to be more affinity to that area at this time. Further, sites such as Salmon and Aztec would be more centrally located with respect to the newer additions to the outlier system in southwestern Colorado. Most of the construction at outliers that can be dated to this period did take place in the northern half of the Basin, at sites such as Salmon, Aztec, Lowry, Escalante, and Ida Jean (Powers et al. 1983:252). Presumably others in the northern area would show construction activity at this time, were they tested for tree-ring dates.

Although a few sites in the southern portion of the Basin show occupation during this time period, there is little if any evidence of active construction. Actually, of the 25 Chacoan outliers in the southern half of the Basin dealt with by the Public Service Company of New Mexico's survey, only four show occupation after A.D. 1125 (i.e., middle Pueblo III) based on analysis of surface ceramics at the sites (Marshall et al. 1979). Thus, the extent to which the southern portion of the Basin was a part of the Chacoan system, or any system, during this period is simply not clear. Some archaeologists (Stein, personal communication; Lekson, personal communication) feel that this period represents a peak of activity and extensiveness of the entire system throughout the San Juan Basin and that the southern portion was very much a part of it. I feel we simply lack the chronological control at this time to be able to resolve this issue.

To summarize then, a number of changes took place in Chaco Canyon during this period that can be interpreted as suggesting a reorganization of the Chaco system. I submit that there was a shift in the administrative and ritual locus from Chaco to the San Juan area, perhaps to either Aztec or Salmon, and that this shift was the outgrowth of a brief, but relatively severe, deterioration of climatic conditions circa. A.D. 1090–1100. Gallup Black-on-white, the "symbolic" ceramic type associated with Chaco Canyon as a ritual center, became less favored than the carbon-painted wares that were dominant in the San Juan area. New sites in southwestern Colorado were incorporated into the system, but the extent to which communities south of Chaco Canyon maintained active involvement in the system is unknown. Chaco itself, I suggest, shifted its primary function to that of a residential outlying area (albeit a major one) with a supportive complement of village sites that contributed to the subsistence needs of the resident population. Chaco then participated in the redistributive exchange aspects of the system along with other outliers in its sector (e.g., Bis sa'ani, Pueblo Pintado, Kin Bineola, Casa del Rio, Upper Kin Klizhin). It is important to point out that activity in the canyon did not decline; if anything it increased when viewed from the more permanent, rather than the periodic, habitation perspective. There was, however, a fundamental change in function as Chaco lost its position of ritual dominance in the system.

## A.D. 1140–1200: System Collapse

By A.D. 1140 a period of reduced summer moisture was underway that was to last almost 50 years (Fig. 20). At virtually no time during this span did the precipitation level reach average, and for most of the time it was significantly below average. Almost certainly, the co-occurrence of this climatic deterioration with what is perceived archaeologically as the breakdown of the Chacoan system is more than coincidental. In an area like the San Juan Basin, which is environmentally marginal to begin with, moisture reduction of this extent would simply not permit the continued support of the population that the Chaco System had evidently attracted to the Basin in the previous 100 years.

In Chaco Canyon, as elsewhere in the Basin, the evidence for the "collapse" of the system is primarily negative, for example, there is a lack of evidence of construction following A.D. 1130 (A.D. 1132 at Pueblo Alto is the last known cutting date in the canyon, and may not be a construction date). This, plus stratigraphic discontinuity with the Mesa Verde reoccupation of the area in the early 1200s, suggests disuse of the area sometime in the middle of the twelfth century. At dated outliers, the situation is evidently similar. For example, construction dates at the Salmon site lapse following the end of the Chacoan construction (A.D. 1139) until the early A.D. 1260s, when the Mesa Verde construction dates cluster (Adams 1980).

If we are correct in interpreting this hiatus in construction as a "collapse" of the Chacoan system, we might speculate about the character of such a collapse. In all probability it did not involve violence, at least in Chaco Canyon, because there is little physical evidence of that. Further, the sites in the canyon seem to have been abandoned in an orderly fashion, with most of the useful material goods removed. I would guess that the collapse was probably one of the system only and that it consisted primarily of a socioeconomic reorganization and a consequent change in ritual behavior.

The mechanism of reorganization or collapse could have taken three basic forms. First, there would be a focus on the continuation of communities at the most environmentally optimal loci in the Basin. Such loci would be at a premium and perhaps even competed for. Thus certain defensive locations, such as that at Crumbled House, would not be surprising. One would expect that such locations would have been occupied throughout this period and that the occupation would continue into late Pueblo III, when Mesa Verde "influence" is manifest in the San Juan Basin.

Second, there must have been some degree of emigration from the

Basin, simply because it may well have become "supersaturated" during the eleventh century as a result of the success of the Chacoan system. The combination of an effective redistribution system and a favorable environmental regime may have attracted groups from outside the Basin as participants in the ritual metaphor. Conceivably, such groups would return to their places of origin, assuming they had maintained social ties there and were permitted to return.

For those groups that could not be accommodated in either of these two fashions, it is probable that a readaptation to a more mobile pattern with a much heavier emphasis on hunting and gathering would have been the remaining viable option, again assuming they could compete successfully in this niche with its current inhabitants. Such a lifeway is less visible archaeologically; thus it is difficult to tell the extent to which this option was invoked as a part of the "collapse."

I suggest, then, that the fundamental cause of the collapse of the Chacoan system was environmental deterioration. The system had operated very effectively in coping with variability in precipitation through a formally administered alliance network that served to redistribute goods among the outlying areas, but this coping took place in a relatively favorable climatic regime. The business of administering and scheduling the network operation was conducted in Chaco Canyon during pilgrimage festivals held as integral components of a ritual system, a system formally shared between the canyon and the outliers. As the system developed, its success attracted even more participants from outside the Basin, and this saturation of population served to make the entire network increasingly vulnerable to environmental perturbations. The role of Chaco Canyon as the ritual locus was challenged in the late eleventh century as a brief but severe reduction in summer precipitation. The system was too well integrated at that time to permit reverting to a presystem status, however, and reorganization was the most viable option. Following this reorganization, and the addition of even more groups to the north, an extended period of drought began, which was too severe for the system to handle. Perhaps another reorganization was effected as an initial response, but when this was perceived as ineffective in coping with the unfavorable climate, the three responses noted above were invoked and the Chaco system, effective for some 150 years, came to an end.

## EPILOGUE

As noted in the prologue, since this article was written three years ago, a number of reports have been published by the Chaco Project. Because the original purpose of this volume was intended to provide syntheses of the areas covered, I feel compelled to briefly review these works, which include reports by Lekson (1984a), Mathien (1985), Toll (1985), and Akins (1986). Two others, Judge and Schelberg (1984) and McKenna (1984), were essentially written at the time this article was being prepared, and many of those views are incorporated herein. I would like also to discuss a work by Sebastian (1988) which, though not published, is relevant to modeling the Chacoan system. Views are expressed in some of these works that vary with those presented herein and hopefully it will be of benefit to note them. Further, many of the Park Service publications were limited in quantity and did not receive wide distribution. The reviews that follow are presented in chronological order, with apologies to the authors that the brevity by no means does them justice.

Lekson (1984a), in a report on the great pueblo architecture in Chaco, provides a major synthesis of the construction and form of the large sites in the Canyon. In addition to describing each large site, Lekson presents construction stages, labor estimates, and interpretations of corresponding social organization. He suggests a total canyon population of 2,100–2,700 residents and notes that this is five to six times larger than the Rio Grande Pueblos as documented historically. For this and other reasons, he proposes considerable social complexity in Chaco. An early (A.D. 900–1000) settlement in Chaco of separate elite groups had, by the 1100s, attained a "level of sociopolitical complexity considerably beyond that of the ethnographic Pueblo world" (1984a:272). Lekson suggests further that Chaco reached its peak in the 1100s.

Mathien (1985) has edited a collection of major papers on the environment and subsistence of the Chaco area. Included are detailed treatments of past climates, modern vegetation and fauna of the canyon, experiments with growing corn in Chaco, and major analyses of pollen, macrobotanical, and faunal material excavated by the Chaco Project. This report is a very comprehensive summary, analysis, and interpretation of the nonartifactual data recovered by the Chaco Project.

In a very comprehensive work, Toll (1985) presents a major synthesis of recent research in Chaco Canyon, and his own interpretation of the data compiled. He builds his case cautiously and methodically on detailed analyses of Chacoan ceramics, which he carried out for the Chaco project. His insights are valuable and worth reviewing here in some detail.

Toll endorses the concept of "public architecture" as that which best describes the distinctive Chacoan structures. He notes that periods of drought occurred that created stress and resulted in intensification of energy investment in Chaco. As more favorable periods generally followed those of stress, the response to intensification was seen as successful, creating a cycle that continued throughout the Chacoan development. The nature and extent of intensification varied, and Toll makes the point that the system cannot be considered a single adaptation, rather different approaches and areas were tried through time. He notes that the early public structures of the tenth century symbolize an intensification of interactions that existed previously. Stages of intensification continued until the system achieved its peak between A.D. 1085–1110. Here he argues against Lekson's view that it peaked in the following period (A.D. 1110–1140).

Toll suggests the Chacoan sites were not intended for full-time residence, nor were they built for those of high social status. Instead they were used by the whole community, perhaps for large gatherings of people from different places participating in the Chacoan system. Though ritually sanctioned, such gatherings would have had an effect similar to that of redistribution. He deemphasizes the role turquoise might have played, as presented here, but notes that it, plus the ceramic, lithic, and constructional activities that went on in the Canyon, all represent considerable energy investments—investments which served both as "commitments to participate in the system, and . . . insurance of continued participation" (1985:507). Yet he finds little evidence that a few individuals benefitted unequally from the system and argues against the view that institutionalized elites were part of the Chacoan system. He favors instead community involvement in both production and operation of the system. In the late period (1110–1140), Toll sees a reemphasis on the domiciliary function of the public architecture, with a corresponding geographical focus to the north.

Toll notes in closing that he plans to be proved wrong in certain instances, but I imagine it will be difficult to do so. Of all Chacoan researchers, he is perhaps the most cautious in making speculations, and few of his are without substantial documentation.

Akins (1986) provides a very useful synthesis and analysis of human remains recovered from Chaco. A great deal of personal effort and expense was involved in producing this synthesis because she deals with all Chacoan burials, not just those recovered by the Chaco Project. She questions the long-held concept that Chaco lacks sufficient numbers of burials, noting in particular that the recent estimates of reduced population also require reduced expectations of burial populations. Akins is another archaeologist who endorses the concept of elites in Chaco Canyon and, in her view, the mortuary data provide the strongest evidence of social stratification.

Finally, Sebastian (1988) discusses the evolution of the Chacoan system from a broad theoretical standpoint. She challenges the view of cultural complexity rising as a buffer against the harsh environment of the San Juan

Basin. Instead, she holds that the Anasazi over-produced as a coping mechanism, then when the environment improved, complexity resulted from the strategy of successful over-production. She invokes the disparity between labor-intensive and land-intensive strategies as the specific cause of complexity, once yields increased as a result of a favorable environment. Finally, Sebastian suggests the system network functioned primarily not to move food from one location to another, but to facilitate the movement of people by providing them places to go in the event of a major subsistence failure.

Given this brief review of reports published since this article was written, it is tempting to re-think my own position and generate yet another attempt at modeling the Chacoan system. I will resist this temptation, and simply note in closing that my own views correspond most closely to those of Toll, and that I do not share the view of others that the operation of the Chaco system may have involved coercion of many by a few. In fact, I would go one step further and suggest that coercive systems require subsistence bases much more consistent (not necessarily more productive) to develop, rather than the "patchy" moisture regime of the San Juan Basin, predictable neither in quantity nor location. Having gotten myself into much trouble with that statement, I leave future modeling of the Chacoan system to others whose interest in Chaco has perhaps been kindled by the place itself and those who remain puzzled by it.

# REFERENCES

Adams, Rex K.
    1980    Salmon Ruin: Site Chronology and Formation Processes. In *Investigations at the Salmon Site: The Structure of Chacoan Society in the Northern Southwest*, vol. 1, edited by Philip Shelley and Cynthia Irwin-Williams, pp. 201–393. Eastern New Mexico University, Portales.

Akins, Nancy J.
    1982    Perspectives on Faunal Resource Utilization, Chaco Canyon, New Mexico. *Newsletter* 4(5–6):23–29. New Mexico Archaeological Council, Albuquerque.

    1984    Temporal Variation in Faunal Assemblages from Chaco Canyon. In *Recent Research on Chaco Prehistory*, edited by W. James Judge and John D. Schelberg, pp. 225–240. Reports of the Chaco Center No. 8. National Park Service, Albuquerque.

    1986    *A Biocultural Approach to Human Burials form Chaco Canyon, New Mexico*. Reports of the Chaco Center No. 9. National Park Service, Santa Fe.

Allan, William C.
    1977    Present and Past Climate. In *Settlement and Subsistence along the Lower Chaco River: The CGP Survey*, edited by C. A. Reher, pp. 127–137. University of New Mexico Press, Albuquerque.

Altschul, Jeffrey A.
1978    The Development of a Chacoan Interaction Sphere. *Journal of Anthropological Research* 34(1):109–146.

Betancourt, Julio J., and Thomas R. Van Devender
1981    Holocene Vegetation in Chaco Canyon, New Mexico. *Science* 214:656–658.

Breternitz, Cory D.
1982    *Identifying Prehistoric Activity Areas: Analysis of Temporal and Functional Variability among Dolores Area Structures, AD 575–900.* Unpublished M.A. thesis, Department of Anthropology, Washington State University, Pullman.

Breternitz, Cory D., David E. Doyel, and Michael P. Marshall (editors)
1982    *Bis sa'ani: A Late Bonito Phase Community on Escavada Wash, Northwest New Mexico.* Navajo Nation Papers in Anthropology No. 14. Window Rock, Arizona.

Bryan, Kirk
1954    *The Geology of Chaco Canyon, New Mexico in Relation to the Life and Remains of the Prehistoric Peoples of Pueblo Bonito.* Smithsonian Miscellaneous Collections 122(7). Washington, D.C.

Cameron, Catherine
1984    A Regional View of Chipped Stone Raw Material Use in Chaco Canyon, New Mexico. In *Recent Research on Chaco Prehistory*, edited by W. James Judge and John D. Schelberg, pp. 137–152. Reports of the Chaco Center No. 8. National Park Service, Albuquerque.

Camilli, Eileen L.
1983    An Ecological Cover-Type Map of the San Juan Basin, Northwestern New Mexico. In *Remote Sensing in Cultural Resource Management: The San Juan Basin Project*, edited by D. L. Drager and T. R. Lyons, pp. 39–56. Cultural Resource Management Division, National Park Service, Washington, D.C.

Cordell, Linda S.
1979    *Cultural Resources Overview: Middle Rio Grande Valley, New Mexico.* USDA Forest Service and USDI Bureau of Land Management, Albuquerque.
1982    The Pueblo Period in the San Juan Basin: An Overview and Some Research Problems. In *The San Juan Tomorrow: Planning for the Conservation of Cultural Resources in the San Juan Basin*, edited by F. Plog and W. Wait, pp. 59–83. National Park Service, Southwest Region, Santa Fe.

Cordell, Linda S., and Fred Plog
1979    Escaping the Confines of Normative Thought: A Reevaluation of Puebloan Prehistory. *American Antiquity* 44(3):405–429.

Cully, Anne C., M. L. Donaldson, M. S. Toll, and K. B. Kelley
1982    Agriculture in the Bis sa'ani Community. In *Bis sa'ani: A Late Bonito Phase Community on Escavada Wash, Northwest New Mexico*, edited by C. D. Breternitz, D. E. Doyel, and M. P. Marshall, pp. 115–166. Navajo Nation Papers in Anthropology No. 14. Window Rock, Arizona.

DiPeso, C. C., J. B. Rinaldo, and G. J. Fenner
1974    *Casas Grandes: A Fallen Trading Center of the Gran Chichimeca*, Vol. 8. The Amerind Foundation, Dragoon, Arizona.

Doyel, David E., Cory Breternitz, and Michael Marshall
    1984    Chacoan Community Structure, Bis sa'ani Pueblo and the Chaco Halo. In *Recent Research on Chaco Prehistory*, edited by W. James Judge and John D. Schelberg, pp. 37–54. Reports of the Chaco Center No. 8. National Park Service, Albuquerque.

Drager, Dwight L.
    1976    Anasazi Population Estimates with the Aid of Data Derived from Photogrammetric Maps. In *Remote Sensing Experiments in Cultural Resource Studies: Non-Destructive Methods of Archaeological Exploration, Survey and Analysis*, edited by T. R. Lyons, pp. 157–171. Reports of the Chaco Center No. 1. National Park Service, Washington, D.C.

Drager, Dwight L., James I. Ebert, and Thomas R. Lyons
    1982    Remote Sensing and Non-Destructive Archaeology: Approaches to Cultural Resources Management. In *The San Juan Tomorrow: Planning for the Conservation of Cultural Resources in San Juan Basin*, edited by F. Plog and W. Wait, pp. 219–244. National Park Service, Southwest Region, Santa Fe.

Euler, Robert C., G. J. Gumerman, T. Karlstrom, J. S. Dean, and R. H. Hevly
    1979    The Colorado Plateaus: Cultural Dynamics and Paleoenvironment. *Science* 205:1089–1101.

Ferdon, Edwin N., Jr.
    1955    *A Trial Survey of Mexican-Southwestern Architectural Parallels*. Monographs of the School of American Research 21. Santa Fe.

Fisher, Reginald B.
    1934    *Some Geographic Factors that Influenced the Ancient Population of the Chaco Canyon, New Mexico*. University of New Mexico Bulletin 244, Archaeology Series 3(1). Albuquerque.

Ford, Richard I.
    1968    *An Ecological Analysis Involving the Population of San Juan Pueblo, New Mexico*. Ph.D. dissertation, Department of Anthropology, University of Michigan. University Microfilms, Ann Arbor.

Frazier, Kendrick
    1986    *People of Chaco: A Canyon and Its Culture*. W. W. Norton and Co., New York.

Freidel, David A.
    1981    The Political Economics of Residential Dispersion Among the Lowland Maya. In *Lowland Maya Settlement Patterns*, edited by W. Ashmore, pp. 371–382. School of American Research, Santa Fe, and University of New Mexico Press, Albuquerque.

Frisbie, Theodore R.
    1980    Social Ranking in Chaco Canyon, New Mexico: A Mesoamerican Reconstruction. *Transactions of the Illinois Academy of Science* 72(4):60–69.

Gillespie, William B., and Robert P. Powers
    1983    Regional Settlement Changes and Past Environment in the San Juan Basin, Northwestern New Mexico. Paper presented at the 1983 Anasazi Symposium, Salmon Ruin, Farmington, New Mexico.

Gladwin, Harold S.
1945    *The Chaco Branch: Excavations at White Mound and in the Red Mesa Valley.*
Medallion Papers 33. Globe, Arizona.

Grebinger, Paul
1973    Prehistoric Social Organization in Chaco Canyon, New Mexico: An Alternative Reconstruction. *The Kiva* 39(1):3–23.
1978    Prehistoric Social Organization in Chaco Canyon, New Mexico: An Evolutionary Perspective. In *Discovering Past Behavior: Experiments in the Archaeology of the American Southwest*, edited by P. Grebinger, pp. 73–99. Gordon
and Breach, New York.

Green, Dee
1982    The SJBRUS Data Base: A Look at Its Utility. In *The San Juan Tomorrow:
Planning for the Conservation of Cultural Resources in the San Juan Basin*,
edited by F. Plog and W. Wait, pp. 163–170. National Park Service, Southwest Region, Santa Fe.

Hall, Steven A.
1975    *Stratigraphy and Palynology of Quaternary Alluvium at Chaco Canyon, New
Mexico.* Unpublished Ph.D. dissertation, Department of Geology, University of Michigan, Ann Arbor.

Hassan, Fekri A.
1978    Demographic Archaeology. In *Advances in Archaeological Method and
Theory*, Vol. 1, edited by Michael Schiffer, pp. 49–103. Academic Press,
New York.

Hayes, Alden C.
1981    A Survey of Chaco Canyon Archaeology. In *Archaeological Surveys of Chaco
Canyon*, by Alen C. Hayes, David M. Brugge and W. James Judge, pp. 1–
68. Publications in Archaeology 18A, Chaco Canyon Studies. National
Park Service, Washington, D.C.

Irwin-Williams, Cynthia
1983    Socio-economic Order and Authority Structure in the Chacoan Community at Salmon Ruin. Paper presented at the 1983 Anasazi Symposium,
Salmon Ruins, Farmington, New Mexico.

Jacobson, Louanne
1984    *Chipped Stone in the San Juan Basin: A Distributional Analysis.* Unpublished
M.A. thesis, Department of Anthropology, University of New Mexico,
Albuquerque.

Judd, Neil M.
1964    *The Architecture of Pueblo Bonito.* Smithsonian Miscellaneous Collections
147(1). Washington, D.C.

Judge, W. James
1977    The Emergence of Complexity in Chaco Canyon, New Mexico. Paper
presented at the 76th Annual Meeting of the American Anthropological
Association, Houston.
1979    The Development of a Complex Cultural Ecosystem in the Chaco Basin,
New Mexico. In *Proceedings of the First Conference on Scientific Research in the*

*National Parks*, edited by Robert Linn, pp. 901–905. U.S. Government Printing Office, Washington, D.C.

1982     The Paleo-Indian and Basketmaker Periods: An Overview and Some Research Problems. In *The San Juan Tomorrow: Planning for the Conservation of Cultural Resources in the San Juan Basin*, edited by F. Plog and W. Wait, pp. 5–57. National Park Service, Southwest Region, Santa Fe.

Judge, W. James, W. B. Gillespie, S. H. Lekson, and H. W. Toll

1981     Tenth Century Developments in Chaco Canyon. In *Collected Papers in Honor of Erik Reed*, edited by A. Schroeder, pp. 65–98. Papers of the Archaeological Society of New Mexico No. 6, Albuquerque.

Judge, W. James, and John D. Schelberg (editors)

1984     *Recent Research in Chaco Prehistory*. Reports of the Chaco Center No. 8, National Park Service, Albuquerque.

Kelley, J. Charles, and E. A. Kelley

1975     An Alternative Hypothesis for the Explanation of Anasazi Culture History. In *Collected Papers in Honor of Florence Hawley Ellis*, edited by T. R. Frisbie, pp. 178–223. Papers of the Archaeological Society of New Mexico No. 2. Hooper, Norman, Oklahoma.

Kemrer, Meade F.

1982     Site Predictive Models and Their Appropriate Use: An Example from the San Juan Basin. *Newsletter* 4(5–6):2–5. New Mexico Archaeological Council, Albuquerque.

Kincaid, Chris (editor)

1983     *Chaco Roads Project: Phase I*. Bureau of Land Management, Albuquerque District Office, Albuquerque.

Lagasse, Peter F., W. B. Gillespie, and K. G. Eggert

1984     Hydraulic Engineering Analysis of Prehistoric Water-Control Systems at Chaco Canyon, New Mexico. In *Recent Research on Chaco Prehistory*, edited by W. James Judge and John D. Schelberg, pp. 187–212. Reports of the Chaco Center No. 8. National Park Service, Albuquerque.

LeBlanc, Steven A.

1983     Aspects of Southwestern Prehistory: A.D. 700–1450. Paper presented at the 48th Annual Meeting, Society for American Archaeology Meeting, Pittsburgh.

Lekson, Stephen H.

1982     Labor Investment in Chacoan Building. *Newsletter* 4(5–6)21–22. New Mexico Archaeological Council, Albuquerque.

1984a    *Great Pueblo Architecture of Chaco Canyon, New Mexico*. Publications in Archaeology 18B. National Park Service, Albuquerque.

1984b    Standing Architecture at Chaco Canyon and the Interpretation of Local and Regional Organization. In *Recent Research on Chaco Prehistory*, edited by W. James Judge and John D. Schelberg, pp. 55–74. Reports of the Chaco Center No. 8. National Park Service, Albuquerque.

Lekson, Stephen H. (editor)

1983     *The Architecture and Dendrochronology of Chetro Ketl*. Reports of the Chaco

Center No. 6. Division of Cultural Research, National Park Service, Albuquerque.

Lekson, Stephen H., and W. James Judge
  1978    Architecture of the Bonito Phase of Chaco Canyon, New Mexico. Paper presented at the 77th Annual Meeting of the American Anthropological Association, Los Angeles.

Lister, Robert H.
  1978    Mesoamerican Influences at Chaco Canyon, New Mexico. In *Across the Chichimec Sea: Papers in Honor of J. Charles Kelley*, edited by Carroll L. Riley and Basil C. Hedrick, pp. 233–241. Southern Illinois University Press, Carbondale.

Loose, Richard W., and Thomas R. Lyons
  1976    The Chetro Ketl Field: A Planned Water-Control System in Chaco Canyon. In *Remote Sensing Experiments in Cultural Resource Studies: Non-Destructive Methods of Archaeological Exploration, Survey and Analysis*, edited by T. R. Lyons, pp. 133–156. Reports of the Chaco Center No. 1. National Park Service, Washington, D.C.

Love, David W.
  1977    Dynamics of Sedimentation and Geomorphic History of Chaco Canyon National Monument, New Mexico. In *New Mexico Geological Society Guidebook, 28th Field Conference, San Juan Basin*, pp. 291–300. Department of Geology, University of New Mexico, Albuquerque.

Marshall, Michael P., John Stein, Richard W. Loose, and J. Novotny
  1979    *Anasazi Communities of the San Juan Basin*. Public Service Company of New Mexico and New Mexico Historic Preservation Division, Albuquerque and Santa Fe.

Mathien, Frances Joan
  1981    Non-Utilitarian Items of the Chaco Anasazi: Social and Economic Implications. Paper presented at the 46th Annual Meeting of the Society for American Archaeology, San Diego.
  1984    Social and Economic Implications of Jewelry Items of the Chaco Anasazi. In *Recent Research on Chaco Prehistory*, edited by W. James Judge and John D. Schelberg, pp. 173–186. Reports on the Chaco Center No. 8. National Park Service, Albuquerque.

Mathien, Frances Joan (editor)
  1985    *Environment and Subsistence of Chaco Canyon, New Mexico*. Publications in Archaeology 18E. National Park Service, Albuquerque.

McAnany, Patricia, and Ben Nelson
  1982    *Cultural Resources Overview for the New Mexico Synfuels Project*. Office of Contract Archeology, University of New Mexico, Albuquerque.

McKenna, Peter J.
  1984    *The Architecture and Material Culture of 29SJ1360, Chaco Canyon, New Mexico*. Reports of the Chaco Center No. 7. National Park Service, Albuquerque.

Nelson, Ben A., and Linda S. Cordell
  1982    Dynamics of the Anasazi Adaptation. In *Anasazi and Navajo Land Use in the*

*McKinley Mine Area near Gallup, New Mexico,* Vol. 1: Archaeology, edited by Christina G. Allen and Ben A. Nelson, pp. 867–893. Office of Contract Archeology, University of New Mexico, Albuquerque.

Noble, David G. (editor)
1984    *New Light on Chaco Canyon.* School of American Research Press, Santa Fe.

Obenauf, Gretchen
1980    *The Chacoan Roadway System.* M.A. thesis, Department of Anthropology, University of New Mexico, Albuquerque.

Palkovich, Ann M.
1984    Disease and Mortality Patterns in the Burial Rooms of Pueblo Bonito: Preliminary Considerations. In *Recent Research on Chaco Prehistory,* edited by W. James Judge and John D. Schelberg, pp. 103–114. Reports of the Chaco Center No. 8. National Park Service, Albuquerque.

Petersen, Kenneth L.
1981    *10,000 Years of Climatic Change Reconstructed from Fossil Pollen, La Plata Mountains, Southwestern Colorado.* Unpublished Ph.D. dissertation, Washington State University, Pullman.

Pierson, Lloyd M.
1949    *Prehistoric Population of Chaco Canyon, New Mexico: A Study in Methods and Techniques of Prehistoric Population Estimates.* M.A. thesis, Department of Anthropology, University of New Mexico, Albuquerque.

Powers, Robert P., William B. Gillespie, and Stephen H. Lekson
1983    *The Outlier Survey: A Regional View of Settlement in the San Juan Basin.* Reports of the Chaco Center No. 3. Division of Cultural Research, National Park Service, Albuquerque.

Reher, Charles A. (editor)
1977    *Settlement and Subsistence along the Lower Chaco River: The CGP Project.* University of New Mexico Press, Albuquerque.

Reyman, Jonathan E.
1980    The Predictive Dimension of Priestly Power. *Transactions of the Illinois State Academy of Science* 72(4):40–59.

Rose, Martin R., W. J. Robinson, and J. S. Dean
1982    *Dendroclimatic Reconstruction for the Southeastern Colorado Plateau.* Final Report to the National Park Service, Division of Cultural Research, Albuquerque.

Schelberg, John D.
1982    *Economic and Social Development as an Adaptation to a Marginal Environment in Chaco Canyon, New Mexico.* Unpublished Ph.D. dissertation, Department of Anthropology, Northwestern University, Evanston, Illinois.

Schroeder, Albert H.
1981    How Far Can a Pochteca Leap Without Leaving Footprints? In *Collected Papers in Honor of Erik K. Reed,* edited by Albert H. Schroeder, pp. 43–64. Papers of the Archaeological Society of New Mexico No. 6. Albuquerque.

Sebastian, Lynne.
1983    Regional Interaction: The Puebloan Adaptation. In *Economy and Interac-*

tion along the Lower Chaco River: The Navajo Mine Archeology Program, edited by P. Hogan and J. C. Winter, pp. 445–452. Office of Contract Archeology and Maxwell Museum of Anthropology, University of New Mexico, Albuquerque.

1988     *Leadership, Power, and Productive Potential: A Political Model of the Chaco System.* Ph.D. Dissertation, Department of Anthropology, University of New Mexico, Albuquerque. University Microfilm No. 8820694.

Shelley, Philip H.
1980     Salmon Ruin Lithics Laboratory Report. In *Investigations at the Salmon Site: The Structure of Chacoan Society in the Northern Southwest,* Vol. 3, edited by Philip Shelley and Cynthia Irwin-Williams, pp. 21–159. Eastern New Mexico University, Portales.

Stuart, David E.
1982     Power and Efficiency: Demographic Behavior, Sedentism, and Energetic Trajectories in Cultural Evolution In *The San Juan Tomorrow: Planning for the Conservation of Cultural Resources in the San Juan Basin,* edited by F. Plog and W. Wait, pp. 127–162. National Park Service, Southwest Region, Santa Fe.

Stuart, David E., and Rory P. Gauthier
1981     *Prehistoric New Mexico: Background for Survey.* New Mexico Historic Preservation Bureau, Santa Fe.

Tainter, Joseph A., and David Gillio
1980     *Cultural Resources Overview: Mt. Taylor Area, New Mexico.* USDA Forest Service and USDI Bureau of Land Management, Albuquerque and Santa Fe.

Toll, H. Wolcott
1984     Trends in Ceramic Import and Distribution in Chaco Canyon. In *Recent Research on Chaco Prehistory,* edited by W. James Judge and John D. Schelberg, pp. 115–136. Reports of the Chaco Center No. 8. National Park Service, Albuquerque.
1985     *Pottery Production, Public Architecture, and the Chaco Anasazi System.* Unpublished Ph.D. dissertation, Department of Anthropology, University of Colorado, Boulder.

Toll, H. Wolcott, and Peter J. McKenna
1983     The Ceramography of Pueblo Alto. Manuscript on file at the Chaco Center, National Park Service, Albuquerque.

Toll, H. Wolcott, T. C. Windes, and P. J. McKenna
1980     Late Ceramic Patterns in Chaco Canyon: The Pragmatics of Modeling Ceramic Exchange. In *Models and Methods in Regional Exchange,* edited by Robert E. Fry, pp. 95–118. SAA Papers No. 1, Society for American Archaeology, Washington, D.C.

Toll, Mollie S.
1984     Taxonomic Diversity in Flotation and Macrobotanical Assemblages from Chaco Canyon. In *Recent Research on Chaco Prehistory,* edited by W. James Judge and John D. Schelberg, pp. 241–250. Reports of the Chaco Center No. 8. National Park Service, Albuquerque.

Truell, Marcia
1986    A Summary of Small Site Architecture of Chaco Canyon, New Mexico. In *Small Site Architecture of Chaco Canyon, New Mexico*, by Peter J. McKenna and Marcia L. Truell, pp. 115–502. Publications in Archaeology 18D. National Park Service, Santa Fe.

Vivian, Gordon, and Tom W. Mathews
1965    *Kin Kletso, a Pueblo III Community in Chaco Canyon, New Mexico*. Southwestern Monuments Association Technical Series 6. Globe, Arizona.

Vivian, R. Gwinn
1970a    *Aspects of Prehistoric Society in Chaco Canyon, New Mexico*. Ph.D. dissertation, Department of Anthropology, University of Arizona, Tucson.
1970b    An Inquiry into Prehistoric Social Organization in Chaco Canyon, New Mexico. In *Reconstructing Prehistoric Pueblo Societies*, edited by W. A. Longacre, pp. 59–83. School of American Research and University of New Mexico Press, Santa Fe and Albuquerque.
1972    *Prehistoric Water Conservation in Chaco Canyon*. Final Technical Report, NSF Grant No. GS–3100. On file, Division of Cultural Research, National Park Service, Santa Fe.
1974    Conservation and Diversion: Water-Control Systems in the Anasazi Southwest. In *Irrigation's Impact on Society*, edited by T. E. Downing and M. Gibson, pp. 95–112. Anthropological Papers No. 25. University of Arizona, Tucson.
1983    The Chacoan Phenomenon: Culture Growth in the San Juan Basin. Paper presented at the 1983 Anasazi Symposium, Salmon Ruin, Farmington, New Mexico.

Wait, Walter
1982    The Development and Application of a Computerized Data Base for the San Juan Basin, New Mexico. In *The San Juan Tomorrow: Planning for the Conservation of Cultural Resources in the San Juan Basin*, edited by F. Plog and W. Wait, pp. 171–217. National Park Service, Southwest Region, Santa Fe.

Washburn, Dorothy K.
1980    The Mexican Connection: Cylinder Jars from the Valley of Oaxaca. *Transactions of the Illinois State Academy of Science* 72(4):70–85.

Windes, Thomas C.
1982    A Second Look at Population in Chaco Canyon. Paper presented at the 47th Annual Meeting, Society for American Archaeology, Minneapolis.
1984    A New Look at Population in Chaco Canyon. In *Recent Research on Chaco Prehistory*, edited by W. James Judge and John D. Schelberg, pp. 75–88. Reports of the Chaco Center, No. 8. National Park Service, Albuquerque.
1987    *Investigations at the Pueblo Alto Complex, Chaco Canyon, New Mexico, 1975–1979, Volumes I & II*. Publications in Archaeology 18F, Chaco Canyon Studies, National Park Service, Santa Fe.

Windes, Thomas C., and William Doleman
1985    Small House Population Dynamics During the Bonito Phase in Chaco

Canyon. Paper presented at the 50th Annual Meeting, Society for American Archaeology, Denver.

Winter, Joseph C.

1980 Human Adaptation in a Marginal Environment. In *Human Adaptations in a Marginal Environment: The UII Mitigation Project,* edited by James L. Moore and Joseph C. Winter, pp. 483–520. Office of Contract Archeology, University of New Mexico, Albuquerque.

1983 A Comparative Study of Prehistoric, Historic, and Contemporary Agriculture along the Lower Chaco: I—The Anasazi. In *Economy and Interaction along the Lower Chaco River: The Navajo Mine Archeology Program,* edited by P. Hogan and J. C. Winter, pp. 421–444. Office of Contract Archeology and Maxwell Museum of Anthropology, University of New Mexico, Albuquerque.

Wiseman, Regge N.

1986 The Bronze Trail Site Group: More Evidence for a Cerrillos-Chaco Turquoise Connection. In *By Hands Unknown: Papers on Rock Art and Archaeology in Honor of James G. Bain,* edited by Anne Poore. Papers of the Archaeological Society of New Mexico No. 12, Albuquerque.

Wozniak, Frank E.

1982 *A Cultural Overview and Predictive Model in the Eastern San Juan Basin for the Contintental Divide Pipeline Company's Pipeline Route from Thoreau, New Mexico to near Ignacio, Colorado.* Office of Contract Archeology, University of New Mexico, Albuquerque.

# The Sinagua and Their Relations

## INTRODUCTION

This chapter is divided into four major sections. In the first two, I identify the spatial and temporal frameworks that I will use in interpreting the prehistory of the Sinagua area. In the third, I describe patterns of sociocultural change that occurred in the Sinagua area beginning at about A.D. 700. In the final section I discuss causes of these events, relying on a recent paper by Dean et al. (1985).

## DEFINITIONS: SPACE

Harold S. Colton (1939) provided an initial definition of the Sinagua, which he based upon a long and comprehensive list of cultural traits. While he recognized a complex overlap between these traits and ones characteristic of the Hohokam, Anasazi, Mogollon, and other groups with whom the Sinagua interacted, it was his conviction that they were sufficiently distinct to require investigation of the Sinagua as a separate "branch." In his frame of reference, a branch was the rough equivalent of a tribe. While his conclusion ultimately involved the entire constellation of traits that he utilized, he emphasized the distinctive ceramics and architecture of the area. The timber and masonry pithouses found were different from house forms typical of the Anasazi, Hohokam, and Mogollon. Crushed rock-tempered pottery, the Alameda Brown Wares, differed from the Tusayan Gray Ware of the Anasazi and the sand-tempered Mogollon Brown Ware. While the contrast with the Hohokam was not and is not as clear, this issue was not troublesome to Colton because of the many other distinctive features of Hohokam material culture.

The current status of Colton's concept is anything but clear. For example, in the recent southwestern volume of the *Handbook of North American Indians* (Ortiz 1979), Schroeder (1979) treats the Sinagua as one of the Hakataya groups while I (Plog 1979) label the area as the "Flagstaff province" of the Anasazi. Hohmann (1983) provides no definition of the term in his analysis of Sinagua social organization, but simply uses "Sinagua" in reference to the material remains in the Flagstaff area. These circumstances are not unique to the Sinagua, but reflect a general lack of attention to spatial variation at the regional level in the U.S. Southwest. It is unclear how most other branches defined by southwestern archaeologists during the period since the 1930s would fare if analyzed in relation to the massive quantities of data generated since that time.

For the purposes of identifying the spatial focus of this chapter, my intention is to rely heavily on the distribution of ceramic materials. I suggest that the architectural pattern used by Colton in defining Sinagua is far less clear than was the case forty years ago. It remains clear, however, that there is a relatively large spatial area in which Alameda Brown Wares are the predominant ceramic type. While this area extends below the Mogollon Rim, I do not intend to discuss the prehistory of this area because I am less familiar with it and because there is substantially less "southern Sinagua" literature. Furthermore, the inhabitants of sites south of the Rim do not seem to have participated to any major degree in the manufacture and/or exchange of the black-on-white types that occur on Sinagua sites north of the Rim.

The western boundary of the Sinagua region is a few miles to the west of Flagstaff where materials assignable to the Cohonina culture become abundant. The eastern boundary is near Heber, Arizona. My survey data indicate that east of this point, Alameda Brown Wares are rare to nonexistent. The northern boundary is between the line along which the foothills of the mountain belt meet the grasslands of the Little Colorado desert and the Little Colorado River. It is in this zone that the Tusayan Gray Wares gradually replace Alameda Brown Wares.

Thus, the area I will focus on includes Flagstaff and Chevelon-Chavez "provinces," as I have previously defined them (1979, 1983). I use the term province to refer to areas where material culture shows some continuity over space and time and some contrast with surrounding areas, not because of any specific organizational mechanism, but because of relatively high level, long-term interaction. In the Flagstaff province, Alameda Brown Wares constitute the overwhelming majority of the plain ware assemblages. In the Chevelon-Chavez province, these are mixed with Mogollon Brown Wares and Tusayan Gray Wares in percentages that vary from time period to time period and that generally decrease as one moves from west to east.

## DEFINITIONS: TIME

The basic cultural sequence for the Sinagua area was developed by Colton on the basis of his excavations and the derived tree-ring samples. Compared to other areas, the density of dated specimens is high. However, given the changed archaeological understanding of how such dates are interpreted, it is not surprising that there are now some problems with Colton's chronology. I intend to use Hohmann's (1983) summary of the Colton chronology and then suggest modifications that are necessary based on information that was not available to Hohmann (who actually wrote the 1983 publication in 1980 and 1981).

Colton originally defined the following phases for the Flagstaff area: Cinder Park (A.D. 500–700), Sunset (A.D. 700–900), Rio de Flag (A.D. 900–1070), Padre/Angell/Winona (A.D. 1070–1120), Elden (A.D. 1120–1200), Turkey Hill (A.D. 1200–1300), and Clear Creek (A.D. 1300–1400). Subsequently, Colton and Wilson (Wilson 1969) devised a series of ceramic groups based on the relative abundance of different types, providing somewhat finer temporal control. However, these ceramic groupings have been used primarily for assigning sites to appropriate phases.

In Hohmann's recent review of the chronology, several revisions are suggested, principally on the basis of new evidence concerning local architectural practices. Hohmann (1983) retains Colton's definitions of the first two phases. The ending date for the Rio de Flag phase is changed from A.D. 1070 to A.D. 1050. Hohmann suggests that Angell and Winona be treated as a single phase occurring between A.D. 1050 and 1100. He argues that the Padre phase dates from A.D. 1100 to 1130. The Elden phase is dated from A.D. 1130 to 1250, Turkey Hill phase from A.D. 1250 to 1300, and Clear Creek from A.D. 1300 to 1400.

In an effort to understand Hohmann's proposed revisions and to determine if an alternative and/or a more precise chronology could be prepared for the area, I reviewed all the published tree-ring dates and associated site reports for the area. I tried to work from the highest to the lowest quality of evidence available: from well-excavated sites with substantial numbers of dates to poorly excavated and/or complex sites with few dates. In other words, a noncutting date from a poorly dated context could not contradict a cutting date from a well-dated context, especially if the ring sequence was very short. In addition, I utilized radiocarbon and tree-ring dates available from the Chevelon and Chavez projects. Finally, I relied on two studies that allow improved means of interpreting the tree-ring record. S. Plog (1980) published data on the average length of ring sequences in the area. My interpretations of noncutting dates, especially if they were few in number from a particular site, were based on his approach.

Second, Hantman (1983) completed a study showing that small sites occupied for more than 30 years and large sites occupied for more than 80 years are extremely rare in the northern Southwest. Unless there were data clearly to the contrary, I used Hantman's study in estimating site occupation spans. This analysis suggested considerable need for revision in the chronologies. Finally, I reviewed the chronometric information recovered during work in the Chavez and Chevelon areas to determine if these data suggest a need for any major modifications of Colton's chronology. The massive number of tree-ring dates obtained by Colton remain the primary basis for regional chronology. The fewer numbers of tree-ring and the large numbers of radiocarbon dates from Chevelon and Chavez are neither so numerous nor so reliable as to provide an alternative basis for dating. At the same time, there is general agreement with Colton's dates. Few tree-ring specimens submitted from Chevelon sites have proved datable. Therefore, the vast majority of the dates are radiocarbon determinations. The tree-ring dates suggest an initial occupation at about A.D. 1100, with the majority of recorded sites occupied between A.D. 1160 and 1325, while the radiocarbon dates suggest a much longer and more continuous sequence. However, 14 of the 23 corrected radiocarbon dates are not separable from the tree-ring dates. The remaining radiocarbon dates (those that are significantly different) evidence an earlier occupation that could have been contemporaneous with either the Cinder Park or the Sunset phase, although the latter is more likely. The principle revisions that I believe to be necessary are as follows:

1. The utility of the concept Cinder Park phase is questionable. Only a single site, dated to A.D. 675–700, is clearly associated with this phase. It does have an early ceramic complex, but the architectural pattern is not distinguishable from later periods. At best, a very limited occupation of the area is indicated prior to A.D. 700.

2. The best dates for the Sunset phase are A.D. 800 to 950. There are no dated sites occupied between A.D. 700 and 800.

3. There is little evidence that the Rio de Flag phase as previously dated exists. There are no well-dated sites in the Flagstaff area between A.D. 950 and 1050, only sites with a few noncutting dates. In addition, a seriation of ceramic materials from apparent Rio de Flag sites, and sites occupied just before or just after the period, shows a sharp break, not the pattern of gradual change in ceramic types that one would expect during a transitional period. This phenomenon has been noted previously (Schroeder 1979, 1982). Whether the area was abandoned or simply occupied by more mobile peoples who did not build permanent structures is an important question that will be addressed later.

4. Using the ceramic seriation and the associated tree-ring dates, there are five separable clusters of sites dating between A.D. 1050 and 1200. Thus, Colton's original perception of successive changes in the artifactual and architectural record is verified. In fact, even finer distinctions than those he proposed can be defined.

5. There are no well-dated sites in the area between about A.D. 1200 and 1270, and the latter date represents the construction of the Clear Creek phase sites such as Grapevine, Kinnikinnick, and Nuvakwewtaqa (Chavez Pass) and, interestingly, other large sites in mountainous Arizona, e.g., Grasshopper and Point of Pines. This period is, in part, the Turkey Hill phase postulated by Colton on the basis of the ceramic type of that name, Turkey Hill Red. Subsequently, "pure" sites of this phase have not been located. Either the area was abandoned, as suggested by Pilles (1978), or it was occupied by more mobile peoples who did not live in permanent structures.

6. The ending date for the Clear Creek phase, on the basis of radiocarbon and tree-ring dates from Nuvakwewtaqa, is about A.D. 1425 to 1450. It is not surprising that Colton's date is somewhat early as little material from this period occurs near Flagstaff, where he did most of his work.

On the basis of these analyses, I would suggest reformulating the chronology as follows:

Cinder Park phase (?) A.D. 675–700
HIATUS A
Sunset phase A.D. 800–950
HIATUS B
Rio de Flag phase A.D. 1050–1075
Angell phase A.D. 1075–1100
Padre phase A.D. 1100–1125
Elden phase A A.D. 1125–1150
Elden phase B A.D. 1150–1200
HIATUS C
Clear Creek phase A.D. 1269–1450

Some of the reasons for defining the phases in the manner I have used will be clarified subsequently. My principle argument, however, is based on ceramic seriation and associated dates. I suspect that the two main reasons archaeologists have not previously suggested these revisions are: (1) our standards concerning the definition of "high quality context" and "well-dated site" have changed enormously in recent years, and (2) archaeologists have worked primarily with Breternitz's (1966) suggested dates, rather than attempting to determine if a more refined sequence could be derived using only the dates and materials from this (and most other) local areas. In short, I worked with the best dated contexts and asked if conclusions based on these contexts could be contradicted by more poorly dated contexts, rather than trying to make sense of all available data, whatever their quality, at once.

Because the ceramic dates that result from examining well-dated sites in the area are basic to the revisions I have suggested, these are reproduced in Table 6. I should note that Hantman's (1983) analysis of tree-ring dated ceramic types on Black Mesa and the Apache-Sitgreaves Forests are almost identical to mine.

Perhaps the most controversial aspect of the chronology that I have developed is the suggestion of three hiatuses at A.D. 700 to 800, A.D. 950 to 1050, and A.D. 1200 to 1269. I, too, was concerned about the reality of these events, however one interprets them. For this reason, I undertook an investigation of all the published tree-ring dates for the northern Southwest.

In an initial analysis, I used only well-dated sites (the Schifferian approach). At the suggestion of Steve Plog (who wondered why I had developed a sudden fondness for Schifferian as opposed to statistical procedures), I used all sites with three or more clustered tree-ring dates, even if these were "vv" dates. The analyses did not differ. Figure 25 illustrates the curve for the Southwest, except for the Mesa Verde region.[1] This curve is inconsequentially different from that discussed by Berry (1982), even though his assumptions appear very different from mine. Hiatuses, gaps in the tree-ring record, centering on about A.D. 975 and A.D. 1225, are evident throughout the northern Southwest. The gaps in the Flagstaff area are about average in length: there are longer ones in some areas and shorter ones in others. There are only a few areas where these gaps do not occur and these are themselves

---

[1] Mesa Verde presents unique problems, the discussion of which would require an additional paper. Basically, it appears that even single beams or pieces of fuelwood were preserved in the dry caves of the area, thereby biasing the record relative to the majority of areas in which preservation of even single large beams was an exception.

**Table 6. Ceramic Dates, Flagstaff Area**

*Plain Wares*

| | | |
|---|---|---|
| Lino Gray | A.D. | 675–850 |
| Deadmans Gray, Fugitive Red | | 925–1200 |
| Tusayan Gray | | 1050–1075 |
| Angell, Winona, Youngs Brown | | 1075–1200 |
| Sunset Red | | 1075–1200 (more abundant at end) |
| Elden Corrugated | | 1050–1075 |
| Little Colorado Corrugated | | 1075–1125 |
| Rio de Flag Brown | | 925–1100 (peak 900–950) |
| Tusayan Corrugated | | 1050–1200 |

*Painted Wares*

| | |
|---|---|
| Lino Black-on-gray | 675–850 |
| Kana-a | 900–950 |
| Black Mesa | 1050–1175 |
| Sosi | 1125–1175 |
| Holbrook | 1075–1200 |
| Flagstaff, Walnut, Kayenta | 1125–1200 |
| Tusayan Black-on-red | 1050–1175 |
| San Juan Orange | 1125–1200 |
| White Mountain Redwares | 1125–1200 |

interesting. For example, there is no gap at ca. A.D. 1225 in the tree-ring quadrangle containing the Chaco area because of the presence of the enigmatic "Gallina" sites, which very precisely fill in what would otherwise be a gap in that sequence. I will return to the question of how these gaps are to be interpreted later.

## PATTERNS OF CHANGE

In this section, I will attempt to summarize the current understanding of some of the major patterns of change that occurred in the Sinagua area between A.D. 700 and A.D. 1450. I will rely primarily on four data sets: Colton's original study of the Flagstaff area (1946), my own work in the Chevelon area (Plog et al. 1976), Jeff Reid's work in the Chevelon area (1982), and a large quantity of substantially unpublished material on Nuvakwewtaqa (Chavez Pass) and its environs. The discussion will focus on four topics: patterns of settlement, exchange, social stratification, and subsistence.

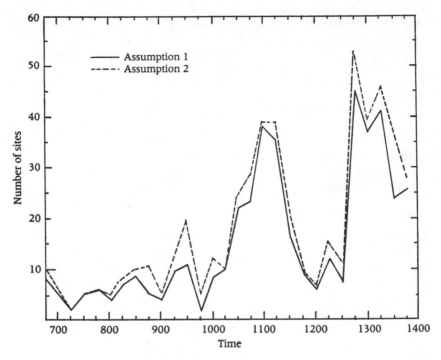

*Fig. 25. Variability in the presence of tree-ring dated sites.*

## Patterns of Settlement

In characterizing the settlement patterns of the Sinagua area, I do not intend to attempt a comprehensive regional analysis. Such analyses exist for only limited localities within the area. Instead, I intend to consider three specific issues: the permanence of settlement within the area, the existence of central places, and because interpretation of this phenomenon is based largely on settlement data, demography.

### Permanence of Settlement

Several studies have focused on the question of the permanence of settlement in the area. Interpretations have varied between claims for permanent occupation and claims for ephemeral occupation. Pilles (1978) began the dialogue over this issue by drawing a nicely documented contrast between fieldhouses and relatively more permanent settlements. He was able to show that small one- and two-room sites in the Flagstaff area had artifactual inventories that were, on the one hand, different from larger sites, and on the other hand, suggestive of temporary, special purpose occupations. Pilles notes the substantial difference in the reconstruction of regional population that results, especially during later time periods, if one treats the fieldhouses as special purpose sites and subtracts them from population reconstructions.

Partially in response to Pilles's position and a growing discussion of how small sites were to be interpreted, S. Plog (1980) undertook a study of bowl/jar ratios on sites in the Chevelon area. He reasoned that because they are larger and less portable, higher percentages of jars were likely to be found on more permanent sites. On the basis of this argument and the bowl/jar ratios, he concluded that there were permanently occupied settlements in the area, even given the small overall average size of the sites in question.

Whittlesey and Reid (1982) and Reid (1982) approached the question on the basis of the overall diversity of artifactual remains found on the sites. They argued that more permanent settlements are characterized by a higher diversity of artifactual materials. Their analyses of the Chevelon sites also suggested the presence of some permanent sites, with temporary movement to special purpose sites during a portion of the year. In fact, despite their small size, the Chevelon settlement pattern seemed to have more permanent sites than was characteristic of other areas analyzed in the Cholla Project. The only noted exception occurred during the early occupation of the area. However, I believe this apparent exception was noted only because none of the large White Mound-style villages that occur in the Chevelon area fell into the construction zone of the Cholla line.

Thus, given the relatively high number of fieldhouses in the Flagstaff and Chavez Pass areas and "limited activity sites" in the Chevelon area, there is good evidence for some degree of permanent occupation/habitation sites despite the disagreements that exist concerning the "best approaches" to establishing the degree of permanence. The two major studies undertaken to date indicate that even some small sites of the Chevelon area are likely to have been occupied for most of the year.

## Central Places[2]
The earliest candidates for central places in the Sinagua area are the White Mound-style pithouse villages characterized by Kana-a-style pottery. Unfortunately, so little excavation has occurred at sites of this time period that no detailed consideration of their function is possible. The sites in question appear to be relatively evenly distributed over the area. If, after excavation, they prove to be similar to other such sites, trade goods suggesting a central exchange and ceremonial function will be found.

---

[2] I will use the term "central places" in reference to larger than normal sites that may have served as social, political, economic, and/or ceremonial centers. Size is the only criterion clearly documented at present.

By about A.D. 1075, there is a clear candidate for a central place within the Sinagua area—Winona Village, east of Flagstaff. In addition to its considerable size, this site has a ballcourt, a fairly large burial population, and an artifactual assemblage suggesting substantial trade with other areas. There are no other sites of this time period in the area that are similar to Winona Village in size, in the presence of a ballcourt, or in artifactual remains. Thus, the site appears to have played a pivotal role. I will return to this issue in a later section.

Between A.D. 1150 and 1200 the settlement pattern in the Flagstaff area is complex. Gratz and Pilles (1979) identify what they call primary, secondary, and tertiary sites. There were three primary sites: Ridge Ruin, Juniper Terrace, and Three Courts Pueblo. These sites share common architectural features: several dozens of rooms, compounds, inner courtyards, community rooms, and ballcourts. They contain more exotic trade items than either secondary or tertiary sites. Secondary sites are smaller, about twenty rooms, and lack the formal architecture of the primary sites. They have community rooms. Tertiary sites are smaller still, about 7 to 15 rooms.

During this time period, Henderson (1979) also finds a three-tiered hierarchy in the Chavez Pass area. However, her largest sites correspond in size to secondary sites in the Flagstaff area. Interestingly, sites of similar rank in this area and around Flagstaff seem to cluster spatially, a pattern that does not suggest the existence of a settlement hierarchy. Chevelon settlement patterns appear to be more similar to those of Chavez Pass than to those of Flagstaff.

After about A.D. 1270, a relatively complex site hierarchy is evident in the area. Upham (1982) argues that Nuvakwewtaqa, with at least 1,000 rooms, was then the largest site in the area. Grapevine, Kinnikinnick, and Chevelon Ruin with several hundreds of rooms are second order sites. Survey between Chavez Pass and the Grapevine-Kinnikinnick area has now identified several sites of approximately 30 to 50 rooms (Kauffman n.d.). There is no concurrent evidence of occupation of the Flagstaff area. The Chevelon area was occupied until about A.D. 1325, but sites were generally quite small; Chevelon Ruin is the major exception. Interestingly, sites with four full masonry walls (as opposed to the more typical three-wall pattern) have large quantities of trade items, suggesting that they may have functioned as local exchange centers. In summary, the pattern of the period is a complex hierarchy, with Nuvakwewtaqa the apparent center of the settlement system.

## Demography

Virtually every effort to reconstruct demographic patterns in the area has been based on room counts. The best of these are "site based" rather than

**Table 7. Corrected Population Densities: Apache-Sitgreaves Study Areas**

| | | | Number of People per km² | | | |
|---|---|---|---|---|---|---|
| Date (A.D.) | Chevelon Juniper-Push | Purcell-Larson | Pinedale | Snowflake | Hay Hollow Valley | Alpine-Springerville |
| 650–700 | .0 | .2 | .00 | .1 | 1.1 | .0 |
| 701–750 | .0 | .2 | .05 | 1.5 | 1.2 | .0 |
| 751–800 | .0 | .2 | .05 | 1.5 | 1.2 | .0 |
| 801–850 | .0 | .2 | .05 | 1.5 | 1.2 | .0 |
| 851–900 | .5 | 2.2 | .05 | 1.5 | 1.2 | .5 |
| 901–950 | .5 | 2.2 | .60 | .4 | 4.8 | .5 |
| 951–1000 | 6.0 | 2.2 | .60 | .4 | 4.8 | .5 |
| 1001–1050 | 6.0 | 2.2 | .60 | .4 | 4.8 | .5 |
| 1051–1100 | 2.8 | 1.9 | .60 | .4 | 4.8 | 2.1 |
| 1101–1150 | 2.8 | 3.4 | 4.20 | 10.0 | 5.1 | 2.1 |
| 1151–1200 | 1.8 | 4.8 | 4.20 | 10.0 | 5.1 | 2.2 |
| 1201–1250 | .0 | 8.9 | 4.20 | 10.0 | 5.1 | 2.2 |
| 1251–1300 | .0 | 8.9 | 3.10 | 4.3 | .6 | .0 |
| 1301–1350 | .0 | .0 | 3.10 | 4.3 | .6 | .0 |
| 1351–1400 | .0 | .0 | .00 | 4.3 | .6 | .0 |

*(from Hantman 1983)*

"phase based"; dates are assigned to individual sites and the resulting data summed rather than treating sites as if they were occupied for the entire phase. Hantman (1983) has summarized existing information for the western portion of the area of concern and some nearby localities. These data are reproduced in Table 7. Two points are noteworthy. First, the area with the highest population varies over time. This variation is of sufficient magnitude to suggest regional population shifts rather than differential natural growth rates. Second, most areas experience a rapid period of population growth in the period between A.D. 1050 and 1150. This same trend occurs in the Flagstaff area and in the Chavez Pass area (Pilles 1978) even when one corrects for temporarily occupied fieldhouses.

## Exchange

Several studies have attempted to describe patterns of exchange within the area. I will summarize these by the nature of the trade item. Subsequently, I will return to the question of variation in the magnitude of exchange over time.

"Mundane" lithic raw materials, those available locally, have received very little study. Le Pere (1979, 1981) has examined such materials for the Chevelon and Chavez Pass regions. In the former, she found that the use of cherts, chalcedonies, and quartzites was primarily a function of local availability. Discrete zones where particular materials predominated could be defined over the area, but sources were always nearby. The same pattern was characteristic in the Chavez Pass area, with one exception. Throughout the occupation of Nuvakwewtaqa, raw materials were obtained from distant sources. Moreover, the abundance of these raw materials increased over time, while it declined, relative to sample size, at sites in the surrounding area.

Obsidian provides somewhat better exchange data. Green (1975) was able to show that obsidian artifacts occurred in a relatively localized area within the Chevelon drainage. The area was wedge-shaped, with the base on the western edge of the drainage. The presence of larger than normal quantities of Sunset Red on the same sites suggests that obsidian exchange with peoples of the Flagstaff area was most important during the twelfth century.

Hantman (1983) has summarized the results of sourcing studies undertaken by Findlow and his colleagues for the Chavez Pass and Chevelon areas. As one might anticipate, most of the obsidian is from the Government Mountain source. However, Red Hill obsidian does occur in the area as far west as the Chavez Pass. Findlow's studies also indicate that obsidian at Nuvakwewtaqa was obtained from a diversity of different sources. There is obsidian at the site from as far north as northern Utah and as far south as central Chihuahua. While the majority of the material is from Government Mountain, up to 30 percent of the obsidian may have come from the Polvadera Peak source in the Jemez mountains of New Mexico. Interestingly, outside of Nuvakwewtaqa, the majority of Polvadera and Red Hill obsidian was recovered from sites with ten or more four-walled masonry rooms, suggesting that these may have been local exchange centers.

Turquoise specimens from Nuvakwewtaqa have been subjected to neutron activation analysis by Phil Wiegand (personal communication) and his associates from SUNY-Stonybrook and Brookhaven Laboratory. While I sympathize with many archaeologists' current reservations concerning the reliability of the techniques used by this team, the results bear mentioning. The majority of the turquoise is from the Azure or Burro Mountain Mine near Tyrone, New Mexico. The second most important site is the Cerillos mining area near Santa Fe, New Mexico. A few specimens that may be from Colorado and Mexico were also identified.

Plain ware ceramic materials have been poorly studied using modern physical and chemical techniques. Nevertheless, important results have been obtained. First, ever since Colton's original description of Sinagua sites in the Flagstaff area, it has been clear that the distribution of these wares and types is relatively localized. The assemblages from the earliest sites in the area, for example, define two clear spatial zones. In one of these, Rio de Flag Brown predominates, while in the other, Deadman's Gray predominates. I recognize that these types are generally utilized to identify Sinagua and Cohonina, respectively. At the same time, it is worth noting that the two zones are adjacent to one another and that the pottery occurs in complexly mixed assemblages in the interface area.

It is my perception that this situation is common in the area during most time periods. Tusayan Gray Wares and Mogollon Brown Wares occur along with the typically predominant Alameda Brown Wares at most time periods. In some time periods the "imported" types are the most abundant, as, for example, during the initial occupation of Chavez Pass when Lino Gray predominates and Alameda Brown Wares are present only in limited quantities (Batcho 1982). Furthermore, different types of Alameda Brown Ware predominate in different localities. For this reason, it appears to me that plain wares were manufactured at local centers.

I do not intend to claim that there was a single center of manufacture for each type, although an analysis undertaken by Swarthout and Dulaney (n.d.) provides suggestive evidence that such may have been the case; that tin cans were, then as now, tin cans in that they were "mass produced" at a few centers, but never exchanged over great distances. However, it does seem to me highly problematical to ascribe cultural or ethnic significance to these types given their relatively localized distributions. This is not to argue that relatively long distance trade in these types did not occasionally occur. Henderson (1980), for example, argues that at about A.D. 1100 to 1150 significantly increased quantities of nonlocal Mogollon Brown Wares are found on sites in the Chavez Pass area.

Evidence for trade is reinforced when one compares the distribution of plain ware to black-on-white types. Hantman (1983) has summarized a number of studies of the distribution of these types beginning with S. Plog's (1980) efforts to characterize interaction in the area. On the basis of Garrett's (1982) petrographic study of materials from the area, he argues that one can distinguish discrete traditions of ceramic manufacture focused on the eastern and western ends of the Apache-Sitgreaves Forests. While materials appearing to have been made in both areas occur in varying quantities over the forests, there is a clear local predominance of one tradition at the eastern and western ends. Hantman further notes that, during early time periods, differences between Black Mesa ceramics and those of the forest areas were minimal. After about A.D. 1000, there was a marked contrast.

Upham and I (Plog and Upham 1982) have examined ceramic materials with results that differ from Hantman's only in the degree of complexity they suggest. Some types that have been analyzed petrographically are extremely complex in relation to, for example, feldspar types, sand grain sizes, and inclusions of rare minerals, suggesting multiple loci of production (e.g., St. John's Polychrome). Other types are so similar wherever they are found that a single source of manufacture is suggested (e.g., Homolovi Polychrome, Holbrook Black-on-white). Most other types fall somewhere in between. In some instances, there is an apparent source of manufacture. Given its similarity to other local types, Homolovi Polychrome was most certainly manufactured at Nuvakwewtaqa. In other cases, there is no such clarity. While S. Plog (1980), Douglass (1982), and Hantman (1983) believe that Holbrook Black-on-white was manufactured in the Hopi Buttes area, the petrographic evidence indicates to me that it was more likely made in the Flagstaff area.

Another important line of evidence suggesting exchange and trade derives from Colton's studies in the Flagstaff areas. By the tree-ring dates, certain types are far earlier at and in the vicinity of particular sites than in the surrounding area. For example, Holbrook Black-on-white appears to be abundant at Winona and nearby sites 25 to 50 years before it is present in appreciable quantities in sites of the surrounding area. Similarly, at about A.D. 1125 Flagstaff and Walnut Black-on-white begin to appear at sites in the Juniper Terrace area, while Sosi and Dogozhi Black-on-white begin to appear in the Wupatki area, less than a dozen miles away. Such patterns suggest the existence either of centers of production or centers of import within particular local areas. In any case, the common notion of village level production of ceramic vessels for village use is no longer viable given the petrographic and distributional data generated in recent years.

Upham (1982) has undertaken the most exhaustive analyses of patterns of ceramic exchange of fourteenth-century types in the area. He argues that the Jeddito Yellow Wares and the White Mountain Redwares show a pattern of directed exchange. Sherds and vessels of these wares occur at some sites in far greater proportions than would be expected given a pattern of down-the-line exchange. Winslow Orange Wares and Zuni Glaze Wares do show a distributional pattern indicative of down-the-line or village-to-village exchange. Thus, for at least this time period, the simultaneous presence of different mechanisms and spheres of ceramic exchange is suggested.

Except for shell, most exotic trade materials are relatively rare in the Sinagua area. For example, the work done at Nuvakwewtaqa during the last 80 years has resulted in the recovery of one copper bell and no macaws or other indications of trade with areas far to the south. (At the same time, a Quetzalcoatl glyph at the site is suggestive of southern contacts.) Shell, on the other hand, seems to have been an important trade item (Fish, Pilles, and Fish 1980) at most time periods in the post-eruptive epoch. This material occurs in both worked and unworked form and appears to be most abundant at central places such as Winona Village and Nuvakwewtaqa.

In summary, the evidence for both far-flung and, sometimes, relatively intense trade networks is substantial.

## Social Stratification

Gratz and Pilles (1979) have argued that by the Elden phase, ranked systems were present in the area. Their argument is based, in part, on the settlement data discussed earlier. However, they also incorporate data on the distribution of trade items, subsistence, and burials.

The most comprehensive study of patterns of social stratifications in the area is that underaken by Hohmann (1983). He analyzes several hundred burials, basically from the post-eruptive period, in the area immediately surrounding Flagstaff. His analysis indicates that inhumations and cremations "mirror" one another. The same apparent degrees of status differentiation are represented in each. He suggests, I believe correctly, that this pattern indicates some symbolic differentiation within local groups in the area rather than the presence of two distinct ethnic groups.

Between A.D. 1050 and 1150, his results suggest that burial goods are nonrandomly distributed among the burials; approximately 60 percent of these differences are associated with age and/or sex differences. Only about 22 percent of the differences are associated with the categories of burial furniture that are most likely to be indicative of differences in status. Much the same pattern exists during the succeeding period, A.D. 1100 to 1130.

However, at some point around A.D. 1130, the situation changes drastically. During the Elden phase (A.D. 1130 to 1200 or 1225), differences in the quantity of grave goods not associated with either age or sex account for about 47 percent of the variance. This is of course the period of burials such as that of the "magician" at Ridge Ruin. It is also interesting to note that while trade goods appear to be indicative of high status burial, these are unevenly distributed. Most burials contain trade goods of a single type; few contain goods of a mixed type. Hohmann concludes that some form of ranking/stratification existed during this period. Upham (1978, 1982) has reached similar conclusions regarding the succeeding (Clear Creek phase) period.

Reid (1985; this volume) has objected to conclusions such as those reached by Hohmann and Upham. For example, he has suggested that similar differences in Grasshopper burials are ascribable to the number of ceremonial organizations in which particular individuals participated. Apart from significant problems with the data and analyses on which he relies, I have extreme reservations concerning the extent to which archaeologists will ever be able to specify the precise ideological bases that underlay the differentiation of burial populations. Whether the high status of some individuals was vested and cognized primarily in wealth, productive expertise, power, ritual knowledge, or religiosity is a difficult issue given the data with which we deal. However, it seems clear to me that in most analyses, one finds a clear distinction between age/sex based distinctions of earlier time periods and those of later time periods when distinctions beyond age and sex occur. In my mind, this pattern is one of stratification, whatever the ideological base with which it was rationalized.

## Subsistence

Current understanding of subsistence practices in the area as related to the direct analysis of floral and faunal materials is weak. I have no direct experience in the Flagstaff area. However, in Chevelon and the Chavez Pass area, both floral and faunal preservation are extremely poor. While we have not yet begun flotation analysis of the Chavez Pass materials, that done on Chevelon materials yielded virtually no macroscopically recognized materials. Studies undertaken on the Nuvakwewtaqa faunal materials suggest patterns of species utilization similar to Grasshopper, Awatovi, and other large sites in the area. The only notable faunal evidence is the presence of substantial quantities of avifauna in one room near the great kiva at Nuvakwewtaqa, suggesting a pattern of ritual utilization.

Soil and water control systems, suggestive of intensified agricultural practices, have been found throughout the area. These may date as early as A.D. 1050. They are most abundant in the Chavez Pass area where terraces, grid systems, and irrigation ditches have been recorded. Some of the terraces in this area have artificial soils manufactured by mixing trash with the natural substrate. Unfortunately, given the presence of a very wide temporal range of trash deposits available in the area, dating is somewhere between problematical and impossible.

## STRUCTURE AND STRUCTURAL CHANGES

Earlier, I noted that a vast amount of data remain to be incorporated into a coherent picture of spatial structure in this and other areas of the Southwest. I believe that this problem exists for a number of reasons. The first is the enormous quantity of data that has been generated in recent years. Second, most of our recent effort to discuss prehistoric social structure of the Southwest has focused on sites. Yet, individual sites are only in rare instances appropriate as the exclusive foci of such analyses. While such sites may be "communities" or even the abode of multiple communities, it is also the case that communities can be dispersed over relatively broad areas. Finally, social boundaries can exist simultaneously at multiple spatial levels and we will fail to understand spatial and social structure if these various levels are not investigated together.

For these reasons, I will discuss spatial structure at several different levels, beginning with individual sites and working up to the issue of the North American Southwest in relation to Mesoamerica. Much of what I will consider is empirically founded, but much more is grasping at threads or worse. The effort must begin somewhere. Having laid out some basic ideas concerning structure, I will turn to the question of causality.

## Site Structure

During the pre-eruptive period, characterization of the spatial structure of sites is not possible. Few sites have been excavated and most of these are quite small. The existence of White Mound-style villages is an inference based on surface evidence alone.

During the post-eruptive period, the picture begins to become somewhat clearer. Hohmann (1983:66) suggests that sites such as Winona are characterized by ". . . six to eight clusters of two to four habitation units and one to two trash mounds. These village clusters usually share a communal structure, either a ball court or a community room." Hohmann argues, and I agree, that there is little evidence that the basic units at such sites represent more than a single extended family. At the same time, evidence developed earlier that Winona was a central trading center suggests to me the possibility that during the Angell phase (A.D. 1075–1100), large numbers of more ephemeral structures existed at such sites.

Known Padre phase sites are typically small, and there is again insufficient information to discuss community structure.

For the Elden phase, A.D. 1125–1200, there is only a single site (Elden Pueblo) excavated in sufficient detail to allow discussion of community patterns. To date, so little work has been done with this site that it is only possible to note that it appears to have begun with two community rooms, one of which was ultimately remodelled as a roomblock. Ridge Ruin, less well excavated, also has a ballcourt. In both cases, however, there is evidence of pithouses contemporary with the masonry architecture. These two architectural patterns suggest the possibility of a community with at least two divisions, sharing a ballcourt or community room.

The most complete data concerning community structure during the Clear Creek phase comes from Nuvakwewtaqa. Three aspects of our data are of particular interest. First, the site was composed of three separate roomblocks. Logistically, these could have been built as a single roomblock on the south mesa, but they were not. Earlier investigators, who relied heavily on surface ceramic data, interpreted these roomblocks as successive occupations. Were one to attempt to resolve this issue exclusively on the basis of surface ceramic materials today, the same conclusion would be reached. However, the chronometric data clearly indicate a period of con-temporaneity at the beginning of the occupation. Thus, the inhabitants of the site chose to construct three separate roomblocks and continued to use somewhat different cultural materials. The probable ballcourt at the site lies between the three roomblocks.

Second, there are masonry pithouses surrounding the roomblocks that are comtemporaneous with at least the early occupation of those roomblocks. Thus, a fourth "community" of some sort is suggested.

Finally, the architectural pattern of the roomblocks is unique. In each of the roomblocks, the east-west running walls are thick, roughly shaped masonry walls that run all or most of the distance through the site. The north-south running walls are of virtually every architectural style known in the Southwest. It appears that communal effort was invested in laying out the main "grid" of the site, but the definition of family or lineage space (our data are inadequate to distinguish) was left to small subsets of the community group. The style of the primary walls is sufficiently similar among the three roomblocks that it is possible that this architectural task was done for the three roomblocks simultaneously.

## Locality Structure

Very few analyses of artifactual distributions at the locality level have been undertaken. However, those that do exist suggest great potential for the definition of structure at this level. Even a careful reading of Colton's (1946) characterization of artifactual variation within the area emphasizes this potential. During the Sunset phase he notes a clear contrast between a zone in which Rio de Flag pottery predominates and one in which Deadman's predominates. While no such contrasts can be drawn during the Rio de Flag phase (A.D. 1050–1075), by the Angell phase there is evident contrast between the northern sites in the Flagstaff area, where Flagstaff and Walnut Black-on-white predominate, and the southern sites, where Holbrook predominates. Similarly, Deadman's Gray and Rio de Flag Brown predominate in the north, while Winona, Young, and Angell Brown are most characteristic in the south. At this same time, Diablo and Yaeger Brown are characteristic of the Chavez Pass area (Batcho 1982). This pattern of contrasts continues until abandonment of the area.

Several investigators have attempted to address this same issue for the area to the east of Flagstaff. Brunson (1979) studied the distribution of "styles" of corrugated pottery, McAllister (1978) and Lerner (1979), the distribution of different painted wares, and Le Pere (1979), the distribution of chipped stone raw materials. Hantman (1983) has summarized the results of these studies. They suggest what might be termed "neighborhoods," approximately 14 km in diameter (160 sq km). Hantman shows that the size of these neighborhoods fits well with the expected results using Wobst's (1974) "Maximum Equilibrium Size" simulations in relation to likely local population densities. The data in question are best for the time periods between A.D. 1100 and 1300. Hantman does note that the likely size of networks during earlier time periods, when population densities were lower, would have been much larger. This observation might explain the apparently even distribution of White Mound sites.

## Alliances

Following Upham (1982), I have used the term alliance in reference to the existence during some periods and in some places of strong normative patterning in material traits. I argue that such patterning is not likely to result from casual interaction among nearby peoples, but from strong organizational entities characterized by central places and varying degrees of trade, social stratification, and agricultural intensification. The record of the Sinagua areas suggests the existence of several such alliances.

1. *White Mound.* During the period between A.D. 800 and 950, one finds evidence in the area of widespread distribution of Kana-a and related design styles occurring in villages consisting of arcs of surface rooms with pithouses in front. Excavated examples of these sites show considerable evidence of trade goods. As noted earlier, local data are insufficient to elaborate on this pattern. For the northern Southwest, this phenomenon generally appears to date between A.D. 775 and 875. Whether the time of its manifestation at the Sinagua area is actually different is unclear at present. This alliance appears to have been characterized primarily by horizontal differentiation. Available evidence suggests more or less similar local centers without any evident hierarchy among them.

2. *Winona.* During the period between A.D. 1050 and 1100, a local

alliance centered on Winona Village seems to have existed. The alliance is characterized architecturally by masonry pithouses. The central site also had a ballcourt. Winona Village appears to have been a center for the production and/or exchange of Holbrook Black-on-white and for Angell, Youngs, and Winona Brown, and possibly, Sunset Red. Douglass (1982) has summarized evidence for directed exchange of Holbrook, although much of the trade was probably still down-the-line. Petrographic studies suggest a single local point of origin for this type. Fish, Pilles, and Fish (1980) have summarized evidence for substantial trade during this period centering on Winona Village. Settlement data are insufficient for considering the question of vertical differentiation beyond noting the existence of one large central site. There is no indication of strong organizational ties to other parts of the Southwest. Winona appears to have been a local alliance.

3. *Elden Alliance.* This alliance appears to have been centered on Gratz and Pilles's (1979) primary sites. These sites are distinctive in their architecture and in the presence of exotic goods. Ceramic exchange involved late Alameda Brown Wares and Flagstaff and Walnut Black-on-white. Sites in the Chavez Pass and Chevelon areas are secondary sites in the Gratz-Pilles classification. Thus, the alliance appears to have been centered in the Flagstaff area, but encompassed peoples living a fairly substantial distance to the east.

4. *The Jeddito Alliance.* Upham (1982) has discussed this alliance in detail. I do not intend to repeat this account. This alliance is characterized by very large central sites, vertical differentiation in the form of a complex site hierarchy, and the directed exchange of Jeddito Yellow and White Mountain Redwares. I might simply note that it is intriguing to me that so many of the large pueblos in the area appear to have initial construction dates of about A.D. 1270, and that three of them, Nuvakwewtaqa, Grapevine, and Kinnikinnick, appear to have closely aligned subsequent construction or repair sequences. These data suggest a high degree of integration of this alliance from the very beginning.

In summary, there were four time periods when there is evidence of strong material patterning in the area. I infer that these were also periods of stronger than normal interactive and organizational ties. It is noteworthy that each alliance appears to be stronger and more vertically differentiated than the preceding one.

## Hiatuses

Except for the Winona and Elden alliances (and even here the intervening Padre phase seems a less organized phenomenon), alliances are separated from one another by hiatuses in the tree-ring record. At the outset, I should acknowledge the possibility that this pattern might simply represent sampling error—that archaeologists have not excavated sites falling into these periods. Should this explanation be correct, it is, in and of itself, interesting. It is unclear at the outset why such sites should have been missed, and not just in this one area. It is also possible that the region was abandoned during these time periods.

However, I propose another explanation more in accord with the observations I have made and with the cautions mentioned above. Rather than an index of regional population per se, the tree rings reflect the construction of relatively larger and more permanent sites. If there were periods when a more mobile pattern of existence was characteristic, a "resilient" adaptation (Cordell and Plog 1979; Upham 1984), archaeologists might well fail to recognize sites left by the groups in question. There are several lines of evidence indicating that such may have been the case.

1. Especially early in the sequence, sedentism was not a well-established pattern of existence. Mobile lifestyles, as they are in many societies where both patterns are present, may have been preferred. Thus, return to a more mobile existence would not have been something that people "didn't want to do."

2. The only sites in the area which are potential candidates for filling the A.D. 1200 to 1270 hiatus are in the Chevelon drainage. In comparison with both the earlier and later alliance sites, these are small and ephemeral. Masonry typically encloses only three sides of the structures and forms what is more properly described as a foundation than a wall.

3. There are large numbers of "limited activity sites" in the area. That these are, in fact, special purpose sites associated with larger masonry settlements is a hypothesis that has not been adequately tested anywhere in the Southwest (Upham 1984). The alternative hypothesis, that the sites were left by more mobile peoples, is equally viable.

4. Dee Green and I (Plog and Green 1983) recently completed an analysis of the Southwestern Archaeological Research Group (SARG) data base in an attempt to differentiate the alliance sites from those of resilient peoples. The results largely fit our expectations about several locational and environmental considerations. For example, large masonry sites are about where one would expect them to be if they were occupied by agricultural peoples. At the other extreme, one class of sites stood out like a sore thumb: large artifact scatters. Our analysis showed that these sites tend to occur in locations that were characterized by their topographic and environmental variability, the locational strategy that one would expect a resilient group to pursue. In preparing this chapter, I checked this class of sites to see what

other characteristics they might have. I discovered, first, that they tend to have limited quantities of pottery. Secondly, even when painted pottery is abundant, these sites are difficult to date because of the diversity of different ceramic materials occurring on them (either S. Plog or I suggested no date or we disagreed). Thus, the sites lack a strong normative pattern, a characteristic postulated for resilient peoples.

5. The Rio de Flag phase, which occurs immediately after the A.D. 950–1050 hiatus, is complex in architecture and material culture. Percentages of different ceramic materials, for example, vary widely from one site to another even when these sites are in close proximity. One would anticipate this pattern if formerly resilient peoples were returning to alliance behavior—if groups that had possessed very different technological traditions were settling into a more stable pattern.

In summary, my argument, granting the lack of satisfactory evidence at present, is that these hiatuses were not periods of abandonment, but times when resilient strategies were in widespread use in the Sinagua area. Perhaps the major belief held by archaeologists that runs against such an interpretation is the widely held sense of technological continuity in the area, especially in ceramics. Despite objections to "ceramic genetics" and the derivation of styles from styles, a strong sense of technological and design continuity is implicit in virtually every interpretation of southwestern ceramic variation. There is not time in this article to present detailed arguments against such an interpretation. I will only suggest that the notion of stylistic and technological continuity is fundamentally based on perceptions of chronometric continuity, perceptions that I have shown to be incorrect.

Yes, designs can be shown to be related to one another, as can technologies. But precisely how much time elapses between epochs in the evolution of design or technology is an issue on which archaeologists should be, but are not, able to comment. If Black Mesa designs indeed evolve from Kana-a designs, this event may have taken, or could have taken, decades or a century. Thus, I submit that a highly circular patterning of reason underlies our perception of material continuity.

At the same time, I acknowledge that the survival of styles and technologies through "hiatuses" is a problematical phenomenon. One might postulate relict groups maintaining these traditions. One might consider individuals who maintain "systems of knowledge." One might postulate no more than a combination of environmental determinism and recycling/reuse. These are important empirical issues.

But our lack of knowledge of the mechanisms that may bridge the increasingly clear documented gaps in the record is not a reason for questioning the existence of those hiatuses. If they are there, they are there. If our theories are inadequate to account for the transmission of technological traditions through them, we need new theories.

## Anasazi or Hakataya?

I do not regard the question of whether the Sinagua were Hakataya or Anasazi as a trivial question of classification. It is an empirical question concerning the nature of interaction between inhabitants of the Sinagua and nearby areas. The strongest case that can be made for regarding the Sinagua as Hakataya is the allegedly paddle-and-anvil Alameda Brown Ware traditions. However, Whittlesey and Reid (1982) have recently shown that paddle-and-anvil, coil-and-scrape, and paddle-and-anvil coil-and-scrape sherds can and do occur on the same site. Similarly, as I have argued earlier, plain wares are more localized than painted wares throughout the northern Southwest. (I recently read an article reporting a few southwestern painted sherds on "Plains" sites in southeastern Colorado. The percentages of painted sherds was sometimes as high as is typical of sites in the regions where I have worked.) For these reasons, I see the pattern of plain ware ceramics in the Sinagua area as typical of most of the surrounding territory. Thus, plain wares provide no basis for separating Sinagua from Anasazi. The painted types found in the Sinagua area are typical Anasazi painted types.

Most other material traits that one might consider I also view as having highly localized distributions. One might argue that masonry pithouses are localized, but if so, they occur over much of the area on which this discussion focuses.

Thus, if one views the question of classifying Sinagua as resolvable on the basis of patterns of interaction, the Sinagua interacted with Mogollon and Hohokam to some degree, but with other Anasazi peoples to so substantial a degree that drawing a cultural boundary between Anasazi and Sinagua is questionable.

## The Mesoamerican Connection

There are very few data in the area to use in arguing for such a connection. These have all been mentioned earlier. Nevertheless, data in nearby areas do suggest some sort of low-level interaction with groups to the south. The strongest case for a Mesoamerican connection is one that can be made on the basis of the initial construction dates for large sites in this and nearby mountainous areas, about A.D. 1270. This dates the beginning of major activity at Casa Grandes. While I recognize that this date is at variance with that suggested by LeBlanc (this volume), other analyses indicate a circa A.D. 1270 date (Lekson 1983; Batcho 1983).

## Summary

What I have tried to describe is a very complex but definable spatial pattern. While there were site, local, and regional boundaries, these were at most times highly permeable because of the different exchange systems involving different materials, on which prehistoric peoples relied. These boundaries are clearest during periods when prehistoric peoples participated in alliances; they are completely unclear for resilient epochs.

# SUGGESTED EXPLANATIONS

The term explanation almost defies definition in the context of a chapter such as this one simply because of the many diverse topics that have been covered. However, it seems reasonable to suggest the directions that efforts to develop explanations might most profitably go. I intend to consider both environmental and cultural explanations for some of the patterns and changes in question.

## Environmental Causality

I have recently worked with Dean, Gumerman, and Euler (Dean et al. 1985) in attempting to construct a synthetic model of variation in the Colorado Plateaus environments and cultural responses to this variation. In this effort, we considered a variety of responses to environmental change, including range expansion, migration, storage, exchange, interaction, and territoriality. In general, the Sinagua area fits well with the predictions made on the basis of the model. In relation to this chapter, I wish to stress one important aspect of environmental causality.

I have reviewed (Dean et al. 1985) variability in tree-ring indicators of precipitation in the northern Southwest from a somewhat different perspective than has been characteristic. Most studies have focused on temporal variation in the magnitude of precipitation, wetness, and dryness. I instead focused on spatial variability: how uniform or varied conditions were over the area, irrespective of the overall wetness or dryness. There was significant variation ranging between periods with conditions far more varied than those of the present, and periods with conditions far more uniform than those of the present. The periods I have argued for the existence of alliances were characterized in this area by high spatial variability in precipitation. Interestingly, there were also periods when alliances formed elsewhere in the Southwest, but not in the Sinagua area. These were periods when high spatial variability was characteristic elsewhere but not in the Sinagua area. Furthermore, the period of the widespread White Mound alliance is characterized by the most widespread pattern of spatial variability in precipitation. Thus, I argue that enhanced exchange behavior, resulting in alliances, is an effort to overcome productive differentials created by increased locality-to-locality variation in precipitation.

A second environmental issue concerns the abandonment of the area. In this instance, I do not suggest environmental change per se as the culprit, but human induced environmental change. Using USDA Forest Service records of fuelwood availability and ethnographic data on fuelwood use, one can easily show that population densities as high as those reached at about A.D. 1150 and as high as those reached in areas of surrounding sites like Nuvakwewtaqa at about A.D. 1350, would have rapidly depleted local fuelwood supplies. Similar analyses have been undertaken in the cases of the Chaco and Dolores areas with similar results (Kohler et al. 1984; Betancourt and VanDevender 1981). In regard to this and other issues, southwestern archaeologists can no longer afford to ignore the substantial impacts that prehistoric populations could have had on their environments.

## Cultural Causality

While I believe that there is much that can be explained on the basis of environmental variables, much cannot. There are several pertinent examples.

1. The secular increase in Sinagua population and southwestern population generally transcends a variety of different environmental regimes. Whether natural growth, immigration, or a combination of the two were occurring, investigation of the details of the southwestern adaptations seems necessary to explain this pattern.

2. Alliances seem to have become stronger in the intensity of trade and more vertically differentiated over time. It appears that some "alliance" behavior was retained through the resilient epochs and is built on in the succeeding alliance. The political and economic processes underlying this pattern are probably best explored using theories such as those of Lightfoot and Feinman (1982).

3. The question of why the central places of the alliance occur in particular locations is probably best explained in relation to the nature of the political and economic patterns of those alliances, and locational and demographic theory, rather than environmental variables.

Thus, while environmental factors seem important for some aspects of the changes under consideration, there are others for which a clearer understanding of human adaptive and behavioral patterns is clearly necessary.

## REFERENCES

Batcho, D.
  1982    *Archaeological Investigations at the Chavez Pass.* Report submitted to the USDA Coconino National Forest, Flagstaff.
  1983    The Airport Site and the Dating of Casas Grandes. Manuscript on file. Department of Sociology and Anthropology. New Mexico State University, Las Cruces.

Berry, M.
  1982    *Time, Space, and Transition in Anasazi Prehistory.* University of Utah Press. Salt Lake City.

Betancourt, J., and T. VanDevender
  1981    Holocene Vegetation in Chaco Canyon, New Mexico. *Science* 214:656–658.

Breternitz, D.
  1966    *An Appraisal of Tree-ring Dated Pottery in the Southwest.* Anthropological Papers of the University of Arizona No. 10. Tucson.

Brunson, J.
  1979    *Corrugated Ceramics as Indicator of Interaction Spheres.* Manuscript on file, Department of Sociology and Anthropology, New Mexico State University, Las Cruces.

Colton, H.
  1939    *Prehistoric Cultural Units and Their Relationship in Northern Arizona.* Museum of Northern Arizona Bulletin 17. Flagstaff.
  1946    *The Sinagua: A Summary of the Archaeology of the Region of Flagstaff, Arizona.* Museum of Northern Arizona Bulletin No. 22. Flagstaff.

Cordell, L., and F. Plog
  1979    Escaping the Confines of Normative Thought. A Reevaluation of Puebloan Prehistory. *American Antiquity* 44:405–429.

Dean, J. S., Robert C. Euler, George J. Gumerman, Fred Plog, Richard H. Hevly, and Thor N. V. Karlstrom
  1985    Human Behavior, Demography, and Paleoenvironment on the Colorado Plateaus. *American Antiquity* 50:537–554.

Douglass, A.
  1982    Before the Jeddito Alliance. Manuscript on file. Department of Sociology and Anthropology, New Mexico State University, Las Cruces.

Fish, P., P. Pilles, and S. Fish
  1980    Colonies, Traders, and Traits: The Hohokam in the North. In *Current Issues in Hohokam Prehistory,* edited by D. Doyel and F. Plog, pp. 151–175. Anthropology Research Papers, Arizona State University. Tempe.

Garrett, E.
   1982      *A Petrographic Analysis of Ceramics from Apache-Sitgreaves National Forests.*
            Ph.D. dissertation in Science Education. Western Michigan University,
            Kalamazoo.

Gratz, K., and P. Pilles
   1979      Sinagua Settlement Patterns and Organizational Models: A Trial Survey.
            Paper presented at the 50th Annual Meeting, Southwestern Anthropologi-
            cal Association. Santa Barbara.

Green, M.
   1975      *Patterns of Variation in Chipped Stone Raw Material from the Chevelon
            Drainage.* Unpublished M.A. thesis, Department of Anthropology, SUNY.
            Binghamton.

Hantman, J.
   1983      *A Socioeconomic Interpretation in Ceramic Style Distribution in the Prehistoric
            Southwest.* Unpublished Ph.D. dissertation. Department of Anthropology,
            Arizona State University. Tempe.

Henderson, K.
   1979      *Archaeological Survey at Chavez Pass: The 1978 Field Season.* Report submit-
            ted to the USDA Coconino National Forest. Flagstaff.
   1980      Social Interaction and Organizational Change. Paper presented at the 45th
            Annual Meeting. Society for American Archaeology. Philadelphia.

Hohmann, J.
   1983      *Sinagua Social Differentiation: Inferences Based on Prehistoric Mortuary Prac-
            tices.* The Arizona Archaeologist No. 17, Arizona Archaeological Society.
            Phoenix.

Kauffman, B.
   n.d.      Spatial Analysis of Prehistoric Social Systems: An Example from the Pla-
            teau Southwest. Manuscript on file, Department of Sociology and Anthro-
            pology. New Mexico State University. Las Cruces.

Kohler, T., et al.
   1984      Modelling Wood Resource Depletion in the Grass Mesa Locality. In *Dolo-
            res Archaeological Program: Scientific Report 1978–1981,* pp. 99–104. US
            Department of the Interior, Bureau of Reclamation, Denver.

Lekson, S. (editor)
   1983      *The Architecture and Dendrochronology of Chetro Ketl.* Reports of the Chaco
            Center No. 6. Division of Cultural Research, National Park Service,
            Albuquerque.

LePere, L.
   1979      Factors Influencing the Distribution of Lithic Materials in Archaeological
            Sites. Apache-Sitgreaves National Forests. Unpublished Manuscript, De-
            partment of Sociology and Anthropology. New Mexico State University.
            Las Cruces.
   1981      Economic and Political Change in the Prehistoric American Southwest:
            Evidence from Lithic Remains. Manuscript on file, Department of Sociol-
            ogy and Anthropology. New Mexico State University. Las Cruces.

Lerner, S.
1979    The Effect of Natural Boundaries on Settlement Systems and Interaction. Unpublished M.A. thesis, Department of Anthropology. Arizona State University. Tempe.

Lightfoot, K., and G. Feinman
1982    Social Differentiation and Leadership Development in Pithouse Villages in Mogollon Region of the American Southwest. *American Antiquity* 47:64–86.

McAllister, J.
1978    A Symap of Ceramic Distributions on the Apache-Sitgreaves National Forests. Manuscript on file, Department of Sociology and Anthropology. New Mexico State University. Las Cruces.

Ortiz, A. (editor)
1979    *Handbook of North American Indians*, Vol. 9, Southwest. Smithsonian Institution, Washington, D.C.

Pilles, P.
1978    The Field House and Sinagua Demography. In *Limited Activity and Occupation Sites*, edited by A. Ward, pp. 119–133. Center for Anthropology Studies Contributions to Anthropology No. 1., Albuquerque.

Plog, F.
1979    Prehistory: Western Anasazi, In *Handbook of North American Indians*, vol. 9, Southwest, edited by A. Ortiz, pp. 108–130. Smithsonian Institution, Washington, D.C.
1983    Political and Economic Alliances on the Colorado Plateaus, A.D. 400 to 1450. *World Archaeology* 2:289–330.

Plog, F., and D. Green
1983    SARG: A Test of Locational Diversity. Paper presented at the 49th Annual Meeting, Society for American Archaeology, Pittsburgh.

Plog, F., J. Hill, and D. Read
1976    *Chevelon Archaeological Research Project*. UCLA Archaeological Survey Monograph.

Plog, F., and S. Upham
1982    Productive Specialization, Archeometry, and Interpretation. Paper presented at the 81st Annual Meeting, American Anthropology Association, Washington, D.C.

Plog, S.
1980    *Stylistic Variation in Prehistoric Ceramics*. Cambridge University Press, Cambridge.

Reid, J.
1982    *Cholla Project Archaeology*, vols. 1 and 2. Cultural Resource Management Division of the Arizona State Museum Archaeological Series No. 161. Tucson.
1985    Measuring Social Complexity in the American Southwest. In *Status and Structure in Stratification*, edited by M. Thompson, M. T. Garcia, and F. Kense, pp. 167–174. Archaeological Association of the University of Calgary.

Schroeder, A.
1979    Prehistory: Hakataya. In *Handbook of North American Indians*, vol. 9, Southwest, edited by A. Ortiz, pp. 379–389. Smithsonian Institution, Washington, D.C.
1982    Historical Overview of Southwestern Ceramics. In *Southwestern Ceramics: A Comparative Review*, edited by A. Schroeder, pp. 1–26. Arizona Archaeologist No. 15. Arizona Archaeological Society. Phoenix.

Swarthout, J., and A. Dulaney
n.d.    A Description of Ceramic Collections from the Coronado Railroad and Transmission Line, E. Arizona. In *The Coronado Project Archaeological Investigation*, vol. 5. Museum of Northern Arizona. Flagstaff.

Upham, S.
1978    Final Report of Archaeological Investigations at Chavez Pass Ruin, Coconino National Forest, Arizona: The 1978 season. Unpublished Manuscript, Coconino National Forest. Flagstaff.
1982    *Politics and Power: An Economic and Political History of the Western Pueblo.* Academic Press, New York.
1984    Adaptive Diversity and Southwestern Abandonment. *Journal of Anthropological Research* 40.

Whittlesey, S., and J. J. Reid
1982    Analysis of Inter-Assemblage Variability. In *Cholla Project Archaeology*, edited by J. Reid, pp. 151–179. Arizona State Museum Archaeological Series No. 161. Tucson.

Wilson, J.
1969    *The Sinagua and Their Neighbors.* Unpublished Ph.D. dissertation, Department of Anthropology, Harvard University.

Wobst, M.
1974    Boundary Conditions for Paleolithic Social Systems. *American Antiquity* 39:147–178.

# Northern and Central Rio Grande

## INTRODUCTION

The geographical area included in this paper comprises the Rio Grande Valley and surrounding mountains, from the Colorado State line in the north to Elephant Butte in the south. The lower portions of Rio Grande tributaries and portions of the Upper Cimarron and Upper Pecos River Valleys are also included within this region (Fig. 26). The archaeological information has been assembled primarily from the voluminous literature of the area (see Cordell 1979) and from site records on file in the Archaeological Records Management System (ARMS) of the Laboratory of Anthropology, Museum of New Mexico, in Santa Fe.

The data are of somewhat uneven quality, and for that reason, I emphasize the results of recent intensive research projects. These include the surveys and excavations at Arroyo Hondo (Dickson 1979; Kelley 1980; Lang and Harris 1984; Wetterstrom 1986), Steen's (1977) Pajarito Plateau survey, Woosley's (1986) surveys and excavation in the Taos area, the Cochiti Reservoir studies (Biella and Chapman 1977, 1979; Chapman and Biella 1977; Biella 1979), the Tijeras Canyon work (Blevins and Joiner 1977; Cordell 1980), Lang's (1977a, 1977b) Galisteo Basin surveys, the lower Puerco and Salado surveys (Wimberly and Eidenbach 1980), and the Rio

*Fig. 26. The northern and central Rio Grande area.*

Abajo surveys (Marshall and Walt 1984) (Fig. 27). Records on the present climate are those I compiled for the Middle Rio Grande overview (Cordell 1979). The paleoclimatic data derive primarily from Rose, Dean, and Robinson's (1981) study for Arroyo Hondo.

Before proceeding to considerations of the environment and the specifics of the culture history, some general comments are in order to characterize the nature of the archaeological data. In large part, because the Rio Grande area continues to be occupied by the Pueblo Indian descendants of the Anasazi, it attracted archaeologists in the early part of this century for whom the direct historical approach was the only available method for obtaining chronological data. Much of this early work continues to be considered classic, and very little of it has been systematically reevaluated. Despite the fact that the Rio Grande area played a key role in the development of southwestern archaeology (e.g., Kidder 1924, Nelson 1914) no single institution has maintained a sustained research commitment to the area. Compared to those portions of New Mexico where recent energy development has entailed major survey and excavation efforts, relatively little excavation has been conducted, or if undertaken, reported. Further, the dense concentration of historic and modern settlements along the Rio Grande virtually precludes the representativeness of the archaeological information. Finally, the quality of the survey data is variable because some surveys continue to rely on unsystematic samples of artifacts, particularly the ceramics used for dating.

Table 8 provides some summary information for the Rio Grande area from Albuquerque north. Of the 2,022 components recorded in the ARM System, less than 1 percent have been subject to any excavation (68 have been excavated, 55 "salvaged," and 18 tested). Comparable data for the area south of Albuquerque are not available. Of the approximately 200 sites recorded in the lower Salado and Puerco survey and the Rio Abajo from Belen to Elephant Butte, only two have been partially excavated: Pottery Mound (Hibben 1975) and LA 282 (Earls 1987). Thus, most of what we know of Rio Grande prehistory derives from survey and generalizations based on excavations of less than 1 percent of known sites; a sample that is not necessarily representative of the population of sites. Although I hope that most of the survey data are accurate, I know that at least some are very misleading. For example, in the Rio Abajo it is not always possible to duplicate surface collections made in the 1940s, because results of even well-executed surveys are distorted by years of uncontrolled collecting. In the same area, surficial structural remains are often poor indicators of the extent and configuration of subsurface features. I believe these kinds of problems are not as severe in the Northern Rio Grande area.

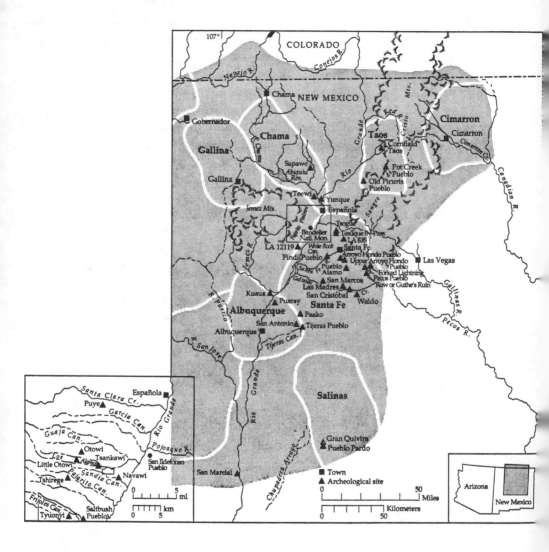

*Fig. 27. Archaeological districts and major sites in the northern and central Rio Grande (after Cordell 1979).*

**Table 8. Archaeological Status of
Northern Rio Grande Components
(ARMS File, Museum of New Mexico)**

| Status | Frequency | Percent |
|---|---|---|
| Collected | 1250 | 61.82 |
| Excavated % unknown | 50 | 2.47 |
| Mostly Excavated | 18 | 0.89 |
| Other | 2 | 0.10 |
| Salvaged | 55 | 2.72 |
| Tested | 18 | 0.89 |
| Undisturbed | 390 | 19.29 |
| Unknown | 239 | 11.82 |
| Total | 2022 | 100.00 |

## CONSIDERATIONS OF THE NATURAL ENVIRONMENT

Compared to other areas of Anasazi occupation, the Rio Grande Valley is undeniably lush, if not quite a Garden of Eden. The Rio Grande itself, and some of its tributaries, provide an abundant source of water. The mountainous regions on both sides of the river serve as large catchment areas for summer and winter precipitation. The growing season over much of the Rio Grande Valley proper is adequate for corn. Elevation differences between the valley bottoms and the bordering mountains are marked and provide situations for diversity in both floral and faunal species. Additionally, valuable raw materials (Jemez obsidian, Pedernal cherts, Cerrillos turquoise, galena, copper ores, etc.) are readily accessible and abundant.

Despite the apparent bounty, the Rio Grande Valley is not without risk for agricultural peoples (Cordell, Earls, and Binford 1984; and see Wetterstrom 1986). Before it was extensively canalized, the Rio Grande was known for devastating floods. Santo Domingo and San Marcial were virtually destroyed by flooding in 1886, and San Marcial was again destroyed in 1929. The importance of flooding in the prehistoric period is not known, although there are some hints that it might have been significant. Archaic sites along the Rio Puerco were found buried under 1 to 3 m of alluvium (Wimberly and Eidenbach 1980:7). Overgrazing has undoubtedly contributed to the severity of flooding in the historic period, however, it is worth remembering that control of major floods would have been beyond the technological abilities of the Anasazi.

Salinization and mineralization were probably also problems in local situations of poor drainage. Fosberg (1979) and Fosberg and Husler (1979) documented heavy salt concentrations in soils associated with a fieldhouse in the White Rock Canyon-Cochiti area. The full extent of salinization problems is not known, but land could have been removed from the system on a short-term basis through floods or rather longer through mineral and salt damage. Historic data discussed by Simmons (1969) and Swadesh (1974) indicate that land along the river, which could be cultivated without metal tools, was in short supply by the eighteenth century. Dense stands of hardwood along the river apparently defied the meagre tools of Hispanic colonists. There is then reason to suggest that easily cultivated, good bottomland may have been in short supply prehistorically, before Pueblo populations were decimated by European diseases.

Finally, as Ford (1972) discussed, when crops are planted along the river and irrigated, both fields and individual plants are quite close together. This situation increases the risk of crop loss due to crop disease and to insect pests. All of these factors—flooding, salinization, dense hardwood vegetation, crop disease, and insect pests—are not mitigated by labor intensification or technological solutions that were available to the Anasazi. Rather, the solutions included expanding agriculture to settings where rainfall agriculture could be practiced, buffering agricultural shortfalls through gathering and hunting, and trade or exchange with other groups. All of these were used at one time or another prehistorically.

The expansion of rainfall farming in the Rio Grande faces the same constraints as it does elsewhere in the Southwest. The data given in Table 9 were compiled from climate records of the past 50 years, except for Socorro, where only a 30-year record was available. They show the expected pattern of high rainfall and short growing seasons in the mountains and at locations north of Santa Fe. At low elevations, and south of Santa Fe, the growing season is relatively long and precipitation is scant. In the records of both rainfall and growing season, the highest and lowest precipitation figures recorded indicate considerable agricultural risk, especially in the mountainous portions of the Rio Grande area (and see Wetterstrom 1986).

Expansion of agriculture into the mountainous areas required careful selection of field locations in settings where runoff could be maximized and probably also the construction of water and soil conservation features. Table 10 provides an indication of the prehistoric investment in upland agricultural features in the Rio Grande area (and see Woosley 1986). Given the inconsistency with which agricultural features are recorded by survey archaeologists and the difficulties involved in recognizing and dating these remains, the amount of acreage devoted to them is impressive. I agree with Ford (1972) that upland agriculture was far more important prehistorically in the Rio Grande than is usually credited.

**Table 9. Precipitation and Growing Season Variability—Rio Grande Area**

| | Precipitation in cm | | | Growing Season in Days | | |
|---|---|---|---|---|---|---|
| Station | Mean | Lowest Annual Recorded | Highest Annual Recorded | Mean | Shortest Period Recorded | Longest Period Recorded |
| Santa Fe | 35.99 | 12.78 | 53.77 | 178 | 143 | 208 |
| Taos | 31.09 | 24.74 | 59.54 | 145 | 121 | 181 |
| Jemez Springs | 45.69 | 23.50 | 71.10 | 172 | 140 | 213 |
| Red River | 52.73 | 32.49 | 70.51 | 80 | 41 | 144 |
| Española | 24.89 | 9.65 | 40.13 | 163 | 120 | 193 |
| Chama | 53.59 | 26.21 | 84.07 | 109 | 83 | 134 |
| Albuquerque | 20.83 | 8.76 | 38.61 | 186 | 156 | 220 |
| Truchas | 39.62 | 18.77 | 69.09 | 138 | 111 | 166 |
| Tijeras | 34.26 | 17.12 | 80.46 | 136 | 108 | 188 |
| Socorro | 24.69 | 10.46 | 56.90 | 197 | 170 | 226 |

*(from Cordell 1979, Tuan et al. 1973, Reynolds 1956)*

With considerable risk to agriculture, gathering and hunting must have constituted important elements in the Anasazi economies. Unfortunately, detailed quantitative faunal and floral data are not consistently reported in the archaeological literature. Young (1980) analyzed quantitative faunal data from the Tijeras Canyon sites and has made a good case for the importance of hunting there. Vickery (1969) provides similarly detailed information from a small site near Taos and reached the same conclusion regarding the importance of hunting. The abundance of faunal remains in the Gallina sites has been noted for decades and is discussed in some detail by Seaman (1976). Inventories that include large and medium size game animals in numbers considered abundant by their excavators are noted for the Riana site on the Chama (Hibben 1937), Rainbow House in Frijoles Canyon (Caywood 1966), Pecos Pueblo (Kidder 1932) and Rowe Ruin (Mick-O'Hara 1987) on the Upper Pecos, and the Artificial Leg sites near Bernalillo (Frisbie 1967). Emslie (1981) discusses field hunting of avifauna at Pottery Mound. Bohrer (1986) describes the ethnobotanical data from Arroyo Hondo Pueblo, and Lang and Harris (1984) the faunal data from Arroyo Hondo Pueblo. Wetterstrom (1986) integrates these data into a model of plant and animal use at that pueblo site. Toll (1983) provides an excellent summary of the relatively little macrobotanical data that can be related to gathering for the Rio Grande area as a whole.

None of the above information is in any sense conclusive with respect to the importance of prehistoric hunting and gathering in the Rio Grande

**Table 10. Upland Agricultural Features, Northern Rio Grande Area**

| Location | Name or Site Number | Feature Type | Area |
|---|---|---|---|
| Picuris Pueblo Grant | LA 12747 | Stone grids & borders | 10,000 m² |
| | LA 12748 | Stone wall around area | 20,000 m² |
| | LA 12750 | Terraces & grids | 10,000 m² |
| | LA 12751 | Terraces & grids | 20,000 m² |
| | LA 12752 | Terraces & grids | 10,000 m² |
| | LA 926- | Terraces, waffle gardens, wing walls | ½ section |
| | Locality 1 | 14 stone alignments | |
| | Locality 2 | Grid | |
| | Locality 3 | Grid | "Extensive" |
| | Locality 4 | 40 terraces | |
| | Locality 5 | 11 terraces | |
| | Locality 6 | 14 terraces | |
| | Locality 7 | Stone alignments, grids | ½ acre |
| | OCA:PIC:1 | 5 cobble alignments | 1,200 m² |
| | OCA:PIC:5 | 2 cobble alignments | 36 m² |
| | OCA:PIC:8 | Grid system | 200 acres |
| Chama Valley | Abiquiu | Grid borders with gravel mulch bordered fields | |
| | LA 300 | Grid borders with gravel mulch | 35,916 m² |
| | Sapawe 1 | Grid borders | 7,100 ft² |
| | Sapawe 2 | 11 terraces | 1,760 ft² |
| | Tributary washes of Rio Gallina | Check dams, 21 alignments | |
| | LA 11830 | Cobble alignments, grid borders, pebble mulch | 1,755 m² |
| | LA 11831 | 7 clusters of stone alignments, gravel filled rectangles | 27,560 m² |
| | LA 11832 | Grids, some gravel filled | 1,812.5 m² |
| Rio Grande de Ranchos | | 4 sites of grid borders | |
| | | 2 contour terrace systems | |
| | | Gridded and raised fields, small borders | |
| Cochiti Reservoir | LA 13292 | | |
| | Provenience 1 | 10 terraces | 315 m² |
| | Provenience 2 | 12 terraces & grid | 600 m² |
| | LA 13293 | 2 rectangular stone alignments | 30 m² |

area. My intuitive impression is that faunal and floral species diversity and abundance in Rio Grande sites are comparable to that at very large sites in the San Juan Basin (a more impoverished natural setting), but at least faunal diversity and abundance at small Rio Grande sites are greater than at sites of similar small size in the San Juan Basin (cf. Binford 1983; Binford et al. 1982; and Judge, this volume).

Approached from a different perspective, various investigators agree that despite the fact that the Rio Grande is a relatively benign environment for horticulture compared to other parts of the Southwest, there are periods when wild resources would have been essential to prevent starvation (e.g., Anderson and Oakes 1980; Cordell 1980; Hunter-Anderson 1979; Wetterstrom 1986). Such times would have been initiated by episodes of drought or of short growing seasons when regional population densities were also high. Hunter-Anderson (1979) argues that with population increase after 1300 in the Rio Grande area, population aggregation occurred in order to vacate large "buffer" zones that could be used for hunting and gathering, and perhaps limited agriculture. Hunter-Anderson's notion is opposed by Anyon and Ferguson (1983) who maintain, on the basis of archaeological and ethnohistoric data from Zuni, that rather than requiring vacant or sparsely inhabited buffer zones, access to truly enormous amounts of territory was assured through various social ties among people living throughout the zones that were exploited. These investigators agree that access to large resource areas was important.

The question of access to specific resources, as well as resource areas, also arises within the context of prehistoric use of obsidian, chert, and especially turquoise. We know very little about the amounts of these materials that may have been traded out of the Rio Grande, or changes over time in the amounts that appear nonlocally. We are beginning to obtain good data on specific outcrops and quarries of obsidian, although our current knowledge is incomplete. Thus, Jemez obsidian is fairly easily distinguished from other obsidian sources in New Mexico and Arizona, and some specific outcrops of this source have been geochemically differentiated (i.e., Baugh and Nelson 1987; Nelson 1984). Nevertheless, outcrops of this raw material occur in many locations, not all of which have been found or examined, so that some artifacts from nearby sites cannot be matched to a specific local source. Warren (1975) has done some superficial examinations of the Pedernal chert outcrops and quarries, but we know little about the distribution of this material outside the Northern Rio Grande.

Rather more is known of the Cerrillos turquoise through Snow's (1973) careful review of historic descriptions of the mines, survey records of ceramics associated with them, and the prehistoric distribution of turquoise at various sites; Weigand's (1982) more recent discussion of ceramics from Cerrillos localities; Warren's survey of mining areas and related sites (Warren and Mathien 1985); and the work on two prehistoric lead mines in the Cerrillos area done by the Albuquerque Archaeological Society (Grigg and Sundt 1975). In addition, Snow's (1973) paper, Mathien's (1981) dissertation and subsequent papers (e.g., Mathien 1984; and see Judge, this volume), and Weigand and Harbottle's (1988) report provide information on the distribution of Cerrillos turquoise in several localities including Chaco and suggested workshops at Chacoan sites.

It is nevertheless difficult to determine how much Cerrillos turquoise was mined prehistorically or, very precisely, during which periods mining was carried out. Many of the possibly prehistoric mines are described as simple pits cut into small turquoise seams and "veinlets" through the surrounding altered monzonitic rock (Warren and Mathien 1985). Large mines, described at the turn of the century by Bandelier in 1881 (Lang and Riley 1966) and Sterrett (1911), involved the excavation of pits up to about 3 m in depth and 60 m across. Unfortunately, little datable artifactual material occurs at mining localities. Snow (1973) notes that ceramics found at Cerrillos mining areas are worn on all edges, suggesting their use as scoops. Generally, neither habitation sites nor substantial camp sites are located in the immediate vicinity of the mines. Warren's (Warren and Mathien 1985) surveys produced some ceramics suggesting that the mines may have been in use as early as A.D. 900. However, most of the ceramics collected at the Cerrillos mines date between A.D. 1150 and 1650, with a majority of these probably postdating 1350 (Snow 1973; Warren and Mathien 1985; Weigand 1982). Judge (this volume) suggests that five sites near Cerrillos, recently reported by Wiseman (1986), are of particular interest because they may relate to Chacoan use of the turquoise mines. While I agree that these sites should be examined in more detail, it is nevertheless true that there are no Chacoan outliers in the vicinity of the Cerrillos turquoise mines.

## CULTURE HISTORY

Authors use different chronological frameworks in characterizing the cultural sequences of the Rio Grande area. By far, the most common are the Pecos Classification, which is used by the ARMS file, and a scheme proposed by Wendorf and Reed (1955) specifically for the Rio Grande. These two are reproduced in Figure 28 along with the framework devised during the conference and discussed in Chapter 1. Other geographically less com-

| Dates A.D. | Pecos Classification | Wendorf and Reed 1955 | Volume Scheme |
|---|---|---|---|
| | | Historic | |
| 1600 | Pueblo V | | |
| 1500 | | | |
| 1400 | Pueblo IV | Classic | |
| 1300 | | | Aggregation |
| 1200 | Pueblo III | Coalition | Reorganization |
| 1100 | | | Transition |
| 1000 | Pueblo II | | |
| 900 | | | Expansion |
| 800 | Pueblo I | | |
| 700 | | Developmental | Initiation |
| 600 | Basketmaker | | |
| 500 | III | | |
| 400 | Basketmaker | | |
| | II | | |

*Fig. 28. Temporal frameworks used in the Rio Grande area.*

prehensive orderings used in the area include those by Wetherington (1968) and Glassow (1980). Although I attempted to use the sequence developed in Chapter I, I found that I had to group periods. Thus, I combine the Initiation and Expansion periods (from A.D. 200/500 to 1000/1050). Although the rest of the sequence seems to work quite well for the Rio Grande, I do point out time periods over which there is disagreement or problems. In the discussion that follows I begin each section with descriptive, culture historical information. The conclusion of each section consists of a more general, comparative synthesis and a somewhat, I hope, provocative, perhaps speculative, discussion.

## Initiation and Expansion (A.D. 200/500 to 1000/1050)

Evidence of Paleoindian occupation in the Rio Grande area derives from both excavation and site survey (Judge and Dawson 1972; Hibben 1955; Judge 1973; Weber and Agogino 1968; Wendorf and Miller 1959). In addition, while they are not abundant, Archaic sites are not unusually scarce (e.g., Agogino and Hester 1953; Biella and Chapman 1977; Chapman and Biella 1977; Lang 1977a, 1977b; Campbell and Ellis 1952; Schaafsma 1976, 1977; Honea 1969; Traylor et al. 1977; Steen 1955, 1977). Yet, the evidence for early Anasazi occupation is certainly scant. There are only two excavated ceramic sites that predate A.D. 600, and only a few sites have yielded archaeomagnetic or tree-ring dates older than 1050. The paucity of early sites was certainly a major factor in Wendorf and Reed's (1955) characterization of the entire period between A.D. 600 and 1200 as the Rio Grande Developmental. An examination of the data that have been obtained since Wendorf and Reed's summary suggests a sparse initial Anasazi occupation with habitation sites located in proximity to perennial water sources and arable land.

The oldest excavated and dated sites in the Rio Grande area are from the Cimarron and Upper Pecos drainages on the eastern edge of the region and from Corrales, near Albuquerque. The earliest reported date is a radiocarbon date of A.D. 510 ± 50 from MP–4, a structural site, lacking pottery, on the Middle Ponil drainage (Glassow 1980:122, 136). An archaeomagnetic date of A.D. 580 ± 40 was obtained from one pithouse at Artificial Leg site I, near Corrales. The ceramics from this structure include Lino Gray, possibly San Marcial Black-on-white, and unpolished, Mogollon trade wares (Frisbie 1967).

Slightly later dates were obtained from a component of the NP–1 site on the North Ponil drainage (Glassow 1980:136), and from two pithouses on Pecos National Monument (Nordby 1981, and personal communication 1981). NP–1 yielded two uncalibrated radiocarbon dates of A.D. 750 ± 80 and 755 ± 80. Glassow cautions, however, that both dates may be in the 800s due to secular variation of C-14 in the wood. Ceramics from this early component of NP–1 consist of unpainted oxidized ware, one sherd of Kana-a Black-on-white and one of Bluff Black-on-red (Glassow 1980:117, 137). A radiocarbon date of A.D. 850 was obtained from one of the Pecos pithouses, and two tree-ring cutting dates of 801r and 810r. The plain, oxidized ceramics from the Pecos pithouses resemble those from the Cimarron (Larry Nordby, personal communication 1981). Both Cimarron and Pecos sites consisted of shallow pithouses of irregularly oval shape. NP–1 was excavated more intensively than the Pecos site. In addition to the two shallow pithouses at NP–1, the site contained several varieties of extramural firepits, roasting ovens, bottle-shaped cists, a large exterior activity area, and abundant fire-cracked rock. Open-end trough metates, grinding slabs, corn, and beans were present.

A dozen or so sites in the vicinity of Albuquerque, which have been excavated, also seem to date to this period. These are Br–45 (Reinhart 1968), the Denison site (Vivian and Clendenen 1965), the Saint Joseph site (Schorsch 1962), the Sedillo site (Skinner 1965), one of the pithouses reported by Vytlacil and Brody (1958), Artificial Leg sites I, II, and part of III (Frisbie 1967), LA 4955 (Wiseman 1976), LA 14258 (Oakes 1979), and three pithouse sites excavated near Sandia Pueblo (Peckham 1957).

In general, these sites consist of one or or a few pithouses, which are either round or have a slight concavity on the eastern side. Where excavations have been extensive enough to reveal them, outside activity areas and associated exterior storage cists and hearths are present. Where present, floors are hard-packed clay, and there is usually a central, circular hearth. Benches, partitions, and in most cases adobe or stone deflectors, common in San Juan Anasazi pithouses, are absent. Ventilator shafts, if located, are oriented east. Roof support posts are variable in number. Some pithouses have no roof supports, some have more than four, but most have two to four. Ramp entryways, common in the Mogollon region, are unknown, except for one instance (Wiseman 1976).

All of these sites are in close proximity to intermittent tributaries of the Rio Grande. The sites are located on gravel bluffs, low terraces, sandy hills, and on hill tops. Their elevations are generally fairly low but range from 1,348 m to 1,973 m. Slab and basin metates and one-hand manos are present, and fire-cracked rock is generally abundant. Maize is present. Faunal remains include a predominance of lagomorphs, but the remains of larger animals are also noted. The faunal inventory of the Artificial Leg sites is diverse and includes beaver, antelope, deer, elk, and mountain sheep.

With the exception of LA 4955, which yielded only brown wares (Wiseman 1976), all of these sites contained Lino Gray ceramics, gray wares with fugitive red paint, Kana-a Gray, and red or brown wares, including Alma Plain and Alma Neck-banded. Obelisk Gray was identified at LA 14258. San Marcial Black-on-white is reported as present at some sites, although Marshall (1980) disagrees with some of the identifications. All of the ceramic inventories, however, are dominated by locally produced types.

A number of sites located on surveys are reported to fall within this time period, although none have been dated by chronometric techniques. Woosley (1986) reports numerous small sites consisting of pithouses, often with associated small pueblos, in the Taos area. Nonpainted utility wares and ceramics painted with mineral-based black paint, considered a variety of Kwahe'e Black-on-white, occur on these sites. Dickson (1979) reports eleven sites in the Arroyo Hondo survey area. Five of these are described as sherd and lithic scatters, pithouses were noted at three sites, and two more had incomplete records. The last site is described as a large, multicomponent site with a probable Early Developmental occupation, based on the recorded ceramics. Lino Gray and Lino Black-on-white, possibly White Mound Black-on-white, and "Early Red Mesa" are present and used as diagnostics (Dickson 1979:11). These sites appear to date after A.D. 900. According to Dickson, the sites in the Arroyo Hondo survey area are located within the Rio Grande floodplain and the Santa Fe River Canyon. These areas contain ample tillable land and perennial water from the rivers.

Wimberly and Eidenbach (1980) located one site possibly dating to this period in the Puerco drainage and four sites of this period in the lower Salado drainage. The site on the Puerco consists of a scatter of ceramics and lithics with a possible subsurface work area or pithouse. The Salado sites are all on elevated ridges. Two have pithouse depressions and two do not. Of potential interest is the observation that the site on the Puerco yielded only Lino Gray ceramics, whereas the Salado sites yielded both Lino Gray and Mogollon brown wares. There is some, though very little, evidence of occupation of the Rio Abajo, near Socorro, during this period. Sites are few, small, and apparently located in situations that are similar to those of the Archaic sites in the area.

## Discussion

As Wendorf and Reed (1955) pointed out 30 years ago, there is not a great deal of evidence of occupation in the Rio Grande area prior to A.D. 1000. The record is still scant despite recent survey efforts and evidence of Archaic occupation. The Rio Grande area thus contrasts strongly with the northern and western Colorado Plateaus (e.g., Black Mesa, Arizona and southeastern Utah), where early pithouse villages are much more common.

Two very obvious reasons may be suggested for the absence of early sites. First, sites may have been washed away or be deeply buried under alluvial deposits. Second, it is possible that the manifestations commonly associated with this time period (i.e., pithouses and ceramics) may not be characteristic in the Rio Grande area. Several investigators (e.g., Glassow 1980; Lang 1977a, 1977b) suggest that the early Anasazi occupation reflects a movement to lower elevations and to loci that are in proximity to agricultural land including the floodplains of the Rio Grande and its tributaries. If the recently constructed hydrological curves for the Colorado Plateaus (Dean et al. 1985) can be generalized to the Rio Grande area, the time period was one of relative hydrologic competence, high groundwater levels, and high effective moisture. These conditions might encourage low elevation occupation. It is likely that sites located at or near prehistoric floodplain settings are under a considerable amount of alluvium today (or have washed past El Paso). It is probably no accident that most of the excavated sites were exposed in the course of modern road-cutting activities. It seems notable that none of the really high elevation areas, in the Jemez and Sangre de Cristo Mountains, evidence any habitation sites at this time. This observation suggests that a considerable amount of territory was available for hunting and gathering and that populations may have been highly mobile. If populations were highly mobile, it is likely that an Archaic settlement pattern persisted in the higher elevation settings surrounding the Rio Grande Valley proper. If so, undifferentiated lithic scatters and isolated hearths may date to this period and be more characteristic in this area than are ceramics and pithouses.

Quite recently, as well as in the past, there have been discussions of the cultural affiliations of the early Rio Grande Anasazi, and the material assemblages have been regarded as reflecting "migrating elements" (Lang 1982) from other regions. I think there is little evidence warranting this sort of speculation. The features and artifacts seem to me to be largely local (cf. Woosley 1986). The Rio Grande pithouses lack the specific architectural features of pithouses in the San Juan area (e.g., benches and wing walls). They also lack the rampways associated with Mogollon sites (LA 4955 is a possible exception). The Lino Gray found from Santa Fe to Socorro is within the range defined by Colton (see Oakes 1979), except that it is frequently fired so that the core is reddish. Lino Gray seems to persist in the Lower Puerco, Lower Salado, and Rio Abajo areas. At least Marshall (1980) indicates that it is present on a great many later sites. Frisbie's (1967) discussion of the early Rio Grande Red Wares is still the most exhaustive, but recent reviews of these assemblages (e.g., Marshall 1980) report dissatisfaction with the applied type names. In all, specific indications of interaction with the "outside world" are rare for this period. The two exceptions are Wiseman's (1976) contention that LA 4955 represents a "pure" Mogollon pithouse, and Frisbie's (1967) observation that some of the San Marcial sherds from the Artificial Leg sites were tempered with trachyte (sanidine basalt), presumably from a source in the Chuska Mountains.

In my view, the Rio Grande area during this time period was thinly inhabited by groups pursuing highly mixed (hunting, gathering, and horticulture) subsistence strategies. There seems to have been little to constrain group mobility. I doubt if any of the excavated sites were occupied more than seasonally, because there does not appear to have been much investment in storage facilities.

## Differentiation (A.D. 1000/1050 to 1130/1150 or 1200)

In the Rio Grande area, the period between about A.D. 900 and 1300 has been divided differently by investigators causing a great deal of confusion and thwarting attempts at synthesis. For example, the ARMS files use the standard 200-year intervals, derived from the Pecos chronology, and groups sites dating from 900 to 1100 and sites dating from 1100 to 1300 into separate categories. Wendorf and Reed (1955) considered the entire period from A.D. 600 to 1200 as an entity referred to as the Rio Grande Developmental. Wetherington (1968), Lang (1977a, 1977b, 1982), Dickson (1979), and Woosley (1986) recognize smaller time segments within the Rio Grande Developmental but do not agree on the dating of these intervals. Unfortunately, it is difficult to reconcile the different subdivisions within the period by reference to synchronous changes in the archaeological record. Once again, there are only a handful of sites dated to this period by culturally independent methods. There is an archaeomagnetic date of 1100 ± 50 and two radiocarbon dates of 1190 ± 80 and 1270 ± 50 for the multicomponent Cerrita Ridge site near Taos (Woosley 1986). Archaeomagnetic dates from two pithouse sites, also near Taos, are 1120 and 1190 ± 20. Two noncutting tree-ring dates, of 1059 vv and 1106 vv, are given for two pithouse sites in the Gallina country (Seaman 1976). Four sites within the general Santa Fe, Pajarito Plateau (Alamo Canyon) area, and LA 586 in Tijeras Canyon have been tree-ring dated to this period (see Cordell 1979).

There is extreme architectural heterogeneity within the Rio Grande at this time, and most investigators rely on ceramics, rather than architecture, to assign dates to sites within this period. Unfortunately, the ceramic types that are used as temporal markers are themselves not adequately described or dated (Marshall 1980). The ceramics involved are mineral-painted black-on-white types, such as Red Mesa Black-on-white, Kwahe'e Black-on-white, Taos Black-on-white, and affiliated varieties of these, such as Kwahe'e Black-on-white-Taos variety. (Discussions of the chronological problems relating to these types are found in Cordell 1979:35–36; Marshall 1980; Stuart and Gauthier 1981:48–50.) The difficulties with the ceramic terminology transcends temporal considerations because it is important to determine how much of the ceramic inventory labeled Red Mesa actually derives from the central Chaco district. This problem is examined again below. I have used 1200 as the ending date for this period here and elsewhere (Cordell 1979), because that date seems to mark the beginning of the manufacture of carbon-painted black-on-white pottery in the Rio Grande. The carbon-based paints are recognized and noted by all investigators.

As noted, the ARMS file is organized by the standard Pecos chronology. Known sites are therefore listed as falling between A.D. 900 and 1100 or 1100 and 1300. Table 11 summarizes the sites in the ARMS file. It is noteworthy that of the 2,022 sites in the file, only 141 (0.49 percent) have been assigned to the period before 1100. Whether or not the rather dramatic increase in ARMS sites in the next period relates to sites dating before 1200 is not known. Dickson (1979) indicates a small increase in the number of sites in the Arroyo Hondo survey area before 1200. Most of these continue to be in the primary resource zones of the Rio Grande floodplain and the Santa Fe River canyon. Most of the excavated Albuquerque and Corrales

**Table 11. Archaeological Components in the Northern Rio Grande (ARMS File, Museum of New Mexico)**

| Period | Frequency |
|---|---|
| A.D. 900–1100 | 141 |
| A.D. 1100–1300 | 742 |
| A.D. 1300–1600 | 452 |
| A.D. 1100+indefinite | 691 |
| Total | 2022 |

area sites (i.e., Sedillo, the Artificial Leg sites) have components that relate to this period. Stuart and Gauthier (1981:49) make the interesting observation that in the White Rock Canyon-Cochiti and Pajarito Plateau areas, multicomponent sites and dual component sites, which have earlier component dates prior to 900, are at low elevations, whereas dual component sites that continued to be occupied after 1150 or were reoccupied after that date tend to be at higher elevations. They relate the change to climatic factors. The various Tijeras Canyon surveys, and subsequent excavations (Blevins and Joiner 1977; Oakes 1979), yielded four sites that can be assigned to this period. Within the Lower Rio Salado and Puerco areas, six sites have been assigned to this time span (Wimberly and Eidenbach 1980), and settlement is considered to be sparse and dispersed. In the Rio Abajo area, Marshall and Walt (1984) indicate an increase in the size and density of sites. They note that sites are clustered on the benchlands north of Socorro.

Despite the various problems that hinder generalization, the settlement history of the Rio Grande area suggests some interesting and complex patterning during this time period. For example, in the southern portion of the region (the Rio Abajo, Lower Salado, Lower Puerco, Tijeras Canyon, Corrales, and perhaps the Arroyo Hondo survey area), investigators indicate gradual population increase. Elsewhere, notably the Galisteo Basin and the White Rock Canyon-Cochiti areas, researchers comment on an apparent hiatus in *residential* sites. North of Santa Fe, particularly along the Chama and perhaps the Upper Pecos, there is very little indication of an in situ population. In the mountainous Gallina and Taos area, there is the first evidence of any Anasazi occupation.

As indicated above, there is considerable architectural diversity represented at the excavated sites. Given the length of the period and the limited number of excavated and dated sites, it is entirely possible that some of the variation is temporal, but this is far from adequately documented (cf. Wendorf and Reed 1955). In the Taos area, sites consist of one or a few relatively deep pithouses with associated jacal surface structures. The pithouses themselves are usually circular and, except for central hearths, lack floor features. The few Gallina sites are single pithouses. The one that has been excavated had an extensive exterior work area and surrounding stockade (Seaman 1976). The Santa Fe area sites include pithouses located under Pindi Pueblo (Stubbs and Stallings 1953), some of the apparently adobe surface structures at LA 835, tuff masonry pueblos of 23 rooms with associated circular and rectangular kivas (Traylor et. al. 1977), and basalt cobble and adobe-walled small pueblos of about 9 rooms (Honea 1971). The excavated Tijeras Canyon sites consist of a pithouse and associated extramural work area and an adobe-walled structure with a later pithouse and ramada. None of the Lower Puerco, Salado, or Rio Abajo sites has been excavated. The surface indications, however, suggest a predominance of jacal surface structures and small pueblos.

As mentioned, Red Mesa Black-on-white is the hallmark type of this period, particularly if Santa Fe Black-on-white (a carbon-painted type) is absent. Unfortunately, ceramics that are referred to as Red Mesa in the Rio Grande area represent a heterogeneous lot. All investigators seem to be talking about mineral (iron) based paint on a fairly hard white slip and either ticked or squiggle style design (Marshall 1980). For the lower Puerco, Marshall specifically states that the Red Mesa is indistinguishable from that of the central Chaco district, and Lang (1982) likewise suggests that Red Mesa in the Rio Grande is imported from the Chaco area. Yet, some of the Red Mesa from Taos or the "Red Mesa-like" ceramics reported show only resemblances to Red Mesa from the Chaco area. Ceramic associations vary depending upon location within the area, but gray wares, red wares, scored, punctate, and rubbed gray and brown wares are represented, as are San Marcial and Socorro Black-on-white. Corrugated gray utility pottery occurs at most sites, but in some localities, such as the Taos area, apparently only toward the end of the period.

## Discussion

In the Anasazi area as a whole, the period from A.D. 1000 to 1150/1175 is viewed as one of general population expansion or, in some instances, population dispersion, presumably based on appropriate and successful agricultural technology. For the eastern Anasazi, in particular, the period is dominated by events in Chaco Canyon and the San Juan Basin. If the Rio Grande Valley followed the general Anasazi pattern, greatly increased numbers of sites would be expected. If the expansion of the Chacoan system was tied to the systematic procurement, manufacture, and exchange of turquoise items, and if Chacoan turquoise were obtained from the closest turquoise source area, then there should be evidence of use of the Cerrillos mines. Finally, because the period from about 1000 to 1150 was the time when the Chacoan system seems to have been at its height, its influence on surrounding areas, including the Rio Grande, should have been at its strongest.

In fact, few of the expectations derived from the above observations are met. As noted, there is little evidence of greatly increased numbers of sites. In the Rio Abajo, Lower Salado, Lower Puerco, Tijeras Canyon, and Arroyo Hondo survey areas, investigators indicate gradual population increase during this period. In the Galisteo Basin and the White Rock Canyon-Cochiti areas, researchers comment on an apparent hiatus in residential use. Occupational evidence of any sort drops off dramatically north of Santa Fe, with the exception of the first (although minimal) indications of pithouse occupation in the Taos and Gallina areas. Although at one point I had followed Stuart and Gauthier (1981) in viewing this period as reflecting a "highland agricultural adaptation," perhaps indicative of relatively dry moisture regime (Cordell and Earls 1982), the survey data from the Salado, Puerco, and Rio Abajo, all indicating low elevation sites, suggest that this interpretation was overly simplistic. Further, the composite climatological data from the Colorado Plateaus (Dean et al. 1985) again suggest high water tables, relatively high effective moisture, and low frequency temporal variability in rainfall. Rather than a highland adaptation in the Rio Grande area, there seems to be low settlement density in general, a lot of experimentation, and probably continued local instances of residential mobility. Indeed, with a favorable climatic regime and low population density, a variety of options was probably successfully pursued.

A number of scholars who examine Rio Grande prehistory from the perspective of putative migrations from the San Juan area are troubled by the association of Red Mesa Black-on-white with pithouse complexes that lack typical San Juan features, such as "winged firepits" (McNutt 1969), or later San Juan kiva features, such as benches and pilasters. Those investigators working with models of in situ growth are troubled by the apparent occupational gaps in the Galisteo Basin and White Rock-Cochiti areas (cf. Flynn and Judge 1973; Biella and Chapman 1977). The settlement distributions and the ceramic data actually accord well with Plog's (1983) description of "weak patterns." Weak patterns are characterized by extensive (rather than intensive) agricultural production, egalitarian social organization, heterogeneity in architectural style, and little evidence of local ceramic production. The Red Mesa Black-on-white ceramics and heterogeneity in settlement form in the Rio Grande area at this time may represent this sort of pattern, although at least some of the ceramics were locally produced.

Saying that a pattern is "weak," however, does not describe the way in which it functioned or articulated with the outside world. The Rio Grande Valley is of particular interest at this time because it has been considered a possible resource area for the contemporary "strong pattern" (Plog 1983) represented by the Chacoan San Juan. Thus, Judge and others (1981; and Judge 1979, this volume) suggest that the Chacoan system functioned as a center for the redistribution of resources and that finished turquoise items may have been important to the mediation of exchange or to the ceremonial centrality of the system.

Actually, results of adequate sourcing studies of the Chacoan turquoise have not been published. Nevertheless settlement distribution in the Galisteo Basin near the Cerrillos mines, which is the closest turquoise source to the Chacoan system, merits consideration. Lang (1977a) notes an apparent hiatus in settlements in the Galisteo Basin during this time period with an absence of residential sites. There are no known Chacoan outliers in the Galisteo Basin. Guadalupe Ruin is the easternmost Chacoan outlier, but the site is about 80 km from Cerrillos. As yet, the sites recently reported by Wiseman (1986) are interesting but not conclusive evidence of a Chaco connection. The data from the mining localities themselves may not be definitive, because except for the observation that some pottery items seem to have been used as scoops (Snow 1973), there is no reason to suspect that ceramics were important to prehistoric mining activities. Nevertheless, the most recent surveys indicate that 78.7 percent of the ceramics from the Cerrillos turquoise mining areas post-date 1300 (Warren and Mathien 1983:Table 10). The ceramic evidence accords well with Snow's (1973) graphs, which demonstrate a dramatic increase in turquoise at sites in the lower Rio Grande area between 1250 and 1425. These data show that there is evidence that Chacoan people neither established a resident population in order to exploit Cerrillos turquoise nor did they apparently round up the local population to serve as resident miners.

During the conference, I suggested that it would be interesting to know if Chaco traded for turquoise that was extracted more or less casually by the local population or if people affiliated with Chaco moved with unimpeded access into the territory and extracted the mineral themselves. I proposed that the absence of substantial residential sites in the Galisteo Basin and the stockaded pithouse in the Gallina might indicate that resource areas were maintained as empty zones inhabited only at risk. Although I indicated that we need systematic examination of the ethnographic record of "long distance" resource extraction involving peoples at various levels of social integration, it appeared that the absence in the Rio Grande of anything that might in any way be construed as a port-of-trade, gateway community, or massive workshop similar to the obsidian workings of Mesoamerica, also argued against Chaco having been anything like our notions of a preindustrial state.

Having reviewed the most recent information about Chaco (Judge, this volume), the ceramic data from the Rio Grande, and Snow's (1973) original discussion of the distribution of turquoise in the prehistoric Southwest, I would pursue these issues somewhat differently. With regard to the Rio Grande ceramics, I note that in the northern part of the area, and along the Lower Puerco, Red Mesa Black-on-white and associated gray wares are common. In the Albuquerque area, Tijeras Canyon, and the Salado drainage, decorated ceramics are more generally related to San Marcial Black-on-white and utility pottery of Mogollon affiliation, if not Mogollon trade wares (Frisbie 1982). Again, this may not be terribly informative with respect to the organization of communities in the Rio Grande per se, but if we are dealing with essentially contemporary phenomena (always a problem given the lack of reliable dates), then again the pattern of influences in the Rio Grande area is of interest.

The period from 1000 to 1150/1175 was the time when the Chacoan system should have been at its height, and its influence on surrounding areas at its most obtrusive. The mixed pattern of Rio Grande assemblages may indicate affiliation with two strong traditions; the Chacoan San Juan and the Mogollon. According to Judge (1983, and this volume), the early focus of the Chacoan system was to the south. Thus, southern outliers tend to be earlier than the northern ones. In Snow's (1973) graphs, the areas showing a major increase in the frequency of turquoise in archaeological sites dating between 1050 and 1249 are the Middle Gila, Mimbres, Kayenta, Mesa Verde, Flagstaff-Verde, and Chaco areas. Turquoise mines are located in both the Mimbres and Middle Gila regions, particularly the Burro Mountains and Red Hill districts (Northrop 1975). It seems possible to me that the southern focus of the early Chacoan system, coupled with the availability of turquoise in the Middle Gila area, might indicate that the southern sources are more likely than Cerrillos to have been exploited early on by participants in the Chacoan system. Further, this suggests that the primary Chacoan trade orientation may have been to the north and south and to the northwest. If so, the sparsely inhabited Rio Grande area may have affiliated rather casually with its western, San Juan Basin neighbors.

In sum, two models have been proposed for the possible relationship between the Rio Grande area and Chaco. In the first, the Rio Grande is viewed as a resource area, but perhaps one to which participants in the

Chacoan system had unimpeded access. In the second model, the Rio Grande is viewed as peripheral to developments in the San Juan Basin. Studies evaluating both models should be pursued. With precise and accurate sourcing of the Chacoan turquoise, a test of both models would be provided.

The data from the Rio Grande area continue to reflect low population densities, heterogeneity in architecture and ceramics, and instability in settlement. In terms of the model proposed by the symposium, the Rio Grande lags behind other areas. The time period is locally characterized rather more by the terms Initiation and Expansion than Differentiation. The general problem of Rio Grande cultural lag and isolation has been addressed elsewhere (Cordell 1979) where I suggested that the abundance and diversity of plants and faunal species may have permitted the continuation of a relatively mobile settlement and subsistence strategy, with a concomitant lack of investment in structural organization, including formalized alliance networks. I continue to see this as a reasonable perspective.

## Reorganization (A.D. 1150/1175 or 1200 to 1300)

In the current volume model, this time period is one of regional heterogeneity in architectural and ceramic style and a time of pan-southwestern variation in settlement size, degree of aggregation, and system scale. For the eastern Anasazi area, the collapse of the Chacoan system is viewed as an event with widespread consequences.

Within the Rio Grande Valley area specifically, the general characteristics of this period are a great increase in the number of sites, the first evidence of quite dense occupation of the mountainous areas of the Gallina and Taos districts, a diversity in types of sites, the first good evidence of agricultural features in upland settings, the first regular appearance of surface pueblo architecture, and the local production of a distinctive ceramic type (Sante Fe Black-on-white), which has carbon-based black paint. Wendorf and Reed (1955) cite A.D. 1200 as the beginning of the Rio Grande Coalition period. They end this period at A.D. 1325 with evidence of Rio Grande Glaze A in the Santa Fe area. The choice of A.D. 1300 as the terminal date here accords with the volume scheme and reflects more recent research (e.g., Warren 1980), which has shown that Glaze A was produced in the Rio Abajo, Albuquerque, and Cochiti areas at that date. An end date of 1300 also coincides with the abandonment of large areas of the high elevation settings and the formation of large aggregated pueblos elsewhere.

As Table 11 shows, the ARMS file documents a great increase in the number of sites of this time period. Lang's (1977a, 1977b) work indicates that the Galisteo Basin was once again used for habitation. Dickson's (1979:40) data show the greatest relative increase in population within the Arroyo Hondo survey area, and a similar increase is documented for White Rock Canyon-Cochiti (Biella and Chapman 1977). There is not, however, a notable increase in number of sites at Taos, the Lower Puerco-Salado, or Rio Abajo at this time. Rather, in these areas, there is a tendency toward village aggregation (Marshall and Walt 1984; Woosley 1986).

Most investigators (i.e., Wendorf and Reed 1955; Steen 1977; Lang 1977a, 1977b; Wetherington 1968) consider middle size (i.e., 13 to 30 room) pueblo villages with one or two tiers of roomblocks facing a plaza and containing a kiva, typical of this period. Both adobe and masonry construction are used, and there is no consistent chronological transition from the former to the latter. Yet, emphasis on the typical pattern is somewhat misleading. Some sites were quite large. For example, Leaf Water in the Chama district is estimated to have consisted of more than 100 rooms, and Piedra Lumbre in the Galisteo Basin, more than 150 rooms. In the Taos area, although TA–26 (Vickery 1969) fits the typical pattern, the lack of hearths in the surface rooms at the site suggests that these did not serve a habitation function. Similarly, the excavated Tijeras Canyon site that dates to this period consisted of surface rooms and a ramada (Oakes 1979), but the surface rooms lacked interior features and were probably used for storage, whereas hearths, faunal remains, and grinding equipment were associated with the ramada. In the Gallina area, large, deep pithouses and massive "unit houses" are apparently contemporary, as are the few towers and cliff-dwellings. Gallina unit houses are surface structures built of massive, often heterogeneous, rock masonry with varying amounts of mud mortar. A north-south orientation of interior features, U-shaped deflector, slab-lined hearth, and ventilator is standard within the rectangular room. The Gallina has been viewed as aberrant with respect to architecture and ceramics. Rather than these characteristics, what is interesting about the Gallina occupation from my perspective is the fact that it is virtually restricted temporally to the period from 1200 to 1300.

The sorts of architectural variation described in the Rio Grande at this time consist of relatively minor details. The details are emphasized in the literature because they either show continuity with the previous period or continuity to the historic period. The continuity in architectural styles is generally raised as an objection to attributing the overall increase in the number of sites to an immigration of people from the San Juan Basin (an interpretation with which I disagree). Continuity of stylistic architectural elements from this time period to the present has been used to identify sites ancestral to specific modern Rio Grande Pueblos. With respect to continuity in local developments, investigators point to architecture at sites near Española, Tijeras Canyon, and the Upper Pecos that sometimes includes upright posts in the interiors of adobe or masonry walls, a feature from the previous period (and in any case local and not related to the San Juan Anasazi). Also, until the very end of this period, kivas, where present, are generally circular and incorporated into roomblocks, which is interpreted as representing a local pattern. Continuities to specific modern Pueblos include the pithouses or kivas near Taos, and rectangular rooms at Pot Creek Pueblo, that have central basins with single upright post roof supports, a pattern that is documented at historic Old Picuris. Similarly, there are a number of architectural details that relate the Gallina unit houses to the ancestral Jemez villages of Unshagi and Giusewa (Reiter 1938). Near the end of the Rio Grande Coalition period, two changes occur that are discussed in somewhat more detail below. These are the production of Galisteo Black-on-white ceramics and construction of kivas with keyhole recesses at some sites.

Except in the Gallina area, where Gallina Black-on-gray ceramics dominate the decorated ceramic assemblages, Santa Fe Black-on-white is the hallmark type of the Coalition period. This type was produced at many locations and is therefore less homogeneous than the literature indicates. Santa Fe Black-on-white is generally considered to have derived from an earlier cognate of late Chacoan ceramics based on design element and layout. In the Rio Grande area, even where Santa Fe Black-on-white makes up the majority of painted sherds from a site, it is not the exclusive painted type. Commonly occurring with Santa Fe are local variations such as Wiyo, Pindi, Poge, and "Taos/Poge" Black-on-white. Mineral-painted Chupadero Black-on-white and Taos Black-on-white may also occur as part of the local ceramic assemblage. The predominant utility types are corrugated or indented corrugated. Smeared corrugation occurs more frequently at the end of the period. A common misconception is that the various black-on-white types mentioned occur sequentially. They do not. Another misconception is that types such as Pindi and Poge characterize either a time period or make up the majority of decorated sherds at certain sites in the vicinity of Santa Fe. In fact, even at the type sites, Pindi and Poge comprise less than 1 percent of the assemblage of decorated ceramics. Furthermore, as Peckham (1981) notes, the types themselves are somewhat heterogeneous in regard to their attributes.

Largely because Santa Fe Black-on-white is consistently viewed as a local derivative of late Chacoan ceramics, and notably poorer in execution, and because Coalition period sites reflect a continuation of local stylistic treatment in architecture, most investigators view the Coalition period as an in situ development without substantial migration from the San Juan region

(Ellis 1974 is a notable exception). The slightly later, Coalition period type, Galisteo Black-on-white, which is virtually identical to Mesa Verde Black-on-white, is seen by some (e.g., Mera 1935; Wendorf and Reed 1955; Ford, Schroeder, and Peckham 1972) as indicative of a migration from the Mesa Verde area. Other manifestations that are noted in support of this view are an increase in the number of late Coalition period sites, the possibly more frequent use of masonry architecture near the end of the period, and above-ground kivas with deflectors and southern orientation of kiva floor features. In addition, two Coalition period sites in the Bandelier-Alamo Canyon area had circular kivas that were modified into kivas with southern keyhole-shaped recesses at the end of the Coalition period (Snow 1974; Traylor et al. 1977), which is again interpreted as evidence of a Mesa Verde intrusion.

In addition to the ceramics, the other artifactual materials associated with Coalition period sites include tri-notched axes in both the Taos and Gallina areas, "elbow" pipes, and a diversity of bone tools from the Gallina area, grooved axes, bone beads, awls, and slab and trough-shaped metates. As noted above, upland agricultural features are recognized for this period. These include check dams, grid alignments and fieldhouses at sites near Española and in the Taos area. The substantial reservoirs in the Gallina district may have been for domestic rather than agricultural purposes.

## Discussion

There is little question that this period sees the expansion of settlement in the Rio Grande area. It is also a time during which archaeological districts (see Fig. 27) in the area begin to show distinctive patterns. These developments suggest to me that some sort of demographic threshold was crossed. It is entirely likely that some of the population derived from the San Juan Basin, or its peripheries. It is not at all surprising that none of the known sites manifest a unit intrusion of such people, because the migration of an entire village or community into an inhabited area is an exceptionally uncommon event enthnographically (Cordell 1979:103; Upham 1984). If there were migrant families or individuals, these undoubtedly joined the local population, which accords with the degree of continuity that is emphasized in much of the literature.

Despite an apparent abundance of sites dating to this period, there is so little information about them that the Coalition must go on record as one of the more poorly understood periods in southwestern prehistory. According to both Steen (1977) and Snow (1974), sites of approximately the same size in the Pajarito Plateau area differ considerably in form. Some have one or more kivas. Others lack kivas entirely. The excavators of at least one 15-

room pueblo with two kivas and a pithouse in White Rock Canyon doubt that agriculture played a major part of the subsistence of its inhabitants because the site is in proximity to poor agricultural land, yielded no corn cobs or kernels, and lacked mealing bins (Laumbach et al. 1977). The criteria used to distinguish the various carbon paint black-on-white ceramic types differ from one investigator to another, and very little is known about the specificity of temper sources or clays among these types. Intuitively, it seems to me that this is the first period that locally made decorated ceramics occur in the Rio Grande in any abundance, and little is known of how many centers of production there were, the geographic distribution of the various types, and in some instances, their longevity.

The problem of the longevity of the Rio Grande early carbon-painted types is potentially severe, and its resolution may entail rethinking the entire period. For example, Arroyo Hondo Pueblo yielded hundreds of tree-ring dates in the 1300s, yet the ceramic assemblage is dominated by carbon paint black-on-white types (Douglas Schwartz, personal communication, 1983). Elsewhere in the Santa Fe and Albuquerque areas, sites dating in the 1300s are generally characterized by Glaze A ceramic assemblages. Similarly, the pottery from Rowe Pueblo, near Pecos, consists largely of Rowe Black-on-white, Wiyo Black-on-white, and some Santa Fe. Yet the site produced tree-ring dates in the 1290s from rooms that were not the last on the site to have been occupied. Clearly, if the situation at Arroyo Hondo and Rowe are common, then many sites that are currently attributed to the Coalition period and a pre-1300 date may, in fact, postdate 1300. This situation, in turn, would require reevaluating the increase in population attributed to the Coalition period, as well as the structural organization of the post-1300 period.

Writing a scenario of a time as poorly known as the Rio Grande Coalition period is certainly a risky undertaking. Nevertheless, some observations raise questions worth considering. First, it is of potential interest that at a time when the Chacoan system appears to have failed as a system, village occupation of the Galisteo Basin, in the vicinity of the Cerrillos mines, is in evidence. One model of Chacoan turquoise procurement, described above, proposed that Chaco maintained unimpeded access to the resource, perhaps by keeping the area vacant. Although I do not believe that Chaco attained a level of political and social complexity entirely sufficient for this task, it is suggestive that residential sites appear in the Galisteo Basin when Chaco is no longer a centralized system. On the other hand, the occupation of the Galisteo Basin may simply be the outcome of population increase and dispersion of agricultural communities throughout the area.

The Gallina occupation is one that I believe requires reevaluation and reinterpretation. Although it has long been considered unique and aberrant (Seaman 1976 provides a review), it shares some characteristics with the Taos occupation of this time period. For example, the nonpainted ceramics from the Taos and Gallina areas are much alike, as is the apparent contemporeneity of pithouse and surface structures. Some artifact forms, such as the tri-notched axes, are virtually identical in both areas. The remarkable, defensive, oft-discussed Gallina towers are in fact relatively uncommon features that were eventually used as storage structures, no matter what their original function (Dick 1976; Ellis 1974; Cordell 1979). In addition, despite the widely shared notion that Gallina sites reflect an unusual amount of burning and carnage, the number of burned Gallina pithouses is not uncommon in comparison to other southwestern pithouse villages (Cordell 1979), and some recent observations on the skeletal collections have failed to confirm great evidence of violence and burning (Maria Mercer, personal communication, 1984). The highland occupations of both the Gallina and the upland Taos areas do seem to have flourished at times when there were only relatively sparse occupations in the locations immediately surrounding them. In the Gallina case, when Chaco was at its height to the west and later, when large aggregated communities existed to the north and east in the Chama and Rio Grande Valleys, there was no obvious occupation of the Gallina proper. This seems to support Hunter-Anderson's (1979) suggestion that at times, highland areas were maintained as relatively vacant buffer zones.

In terms of the general model, particularly as reflected by data from the San Juan Basin, this period of time was one of a shift in stylistic affiliation to centers in the north, such as Mesa Verde. In the Rio Grande area, there was a parallel change in the move from Santa Fe Black-on-white to Galisteo Black-on-white, a type viewed as a Mesa Verde cognate, and construction of Mesa Verde keyhole-shaped kivas at some sites. Again, however, the stylistic heterogeneity of locally manufactured ceramics is a salient characteristic for the Rio Grande area. Finally, although there seems to have been some increase in sedentary occupation, evidenced especially by the presence of residential sites throughout most of the area, until the problem relating to the possible longevity of the carbon paint black-on-white ceramic types is resolved, the precise increase in actual numbers of sites remains unclear.

## Aggregation (A.D. 1300 to 1540)

The beginning date for this period coincides with Wendorf and Reed's (1955) beginning date for the Rio Grande Classic. They extend the period to 1600. The characteristic features of the Rio Grande at this time are the presence of very large aggregated communities and the production of Rio Grande Glaze ceramics over much of the area. Of major importance, of course, is the fact that the Rio Grande region was one of the few in the Southwest to be occupied by large villages into the historic and modern periods.

Most of the better known Rio Grande sites date to this period. Many of these sites were intensively investigated during the first half of this century, and many are inadequately dated or known by contemporary standards. Nevertheless, they include the large sites of the Chama, Pajarito Plateau, and the Taos areas, such as Te'ewi, Tsiping, Howiri, Tsama, Sapawe, Tsankawi, Tshirege, Otowi, Tyounyi, Pot Creek Pueblo, Old Picuris, and the ancestral Taos village "Cornfield Taos." Large, late sites near Santa Fe include Arroyo Hondo, Cieneguilla Pueblo, Pindi, and the Galisteo Basin pueblos—Pueblo Largo, San Cristobal, San Marcos, She, Galisteo Pueblo, Las Madres, and Pueblo Lumbre. There are a series of large sites along the Upper Pecos, including Pecos Pueblo itself, Rowe Ruin, Arrowhead, Dick's Ruin, and Loma Lothrop. Near Albuquerque, aggregated pueblos include Kuaua, Alameda Pueblo, Paa-ko, Tijeras Pueblo, and San Antonio. South of Albuquerque, Pottery Mound and the Piro Pueblos also date to this period. There were also very large pueblos in the Salinas area east of the Sandias and Manzano Mountains, such as Abo, Quarai, Tenabo, and Gran Quivira.

The sites of the Rio Grande area exhibit considerable variation in construction materials, construction technique, and site layout. Some, like Sapawe, Kuaua, Arroyo Hondo, Tijeras Pueblo, and Pottery Mound were built of adobe. The Upper Pecos sites, the sites of the Pajarito Plateau, and of the Salinas area are largely multistoried masonry pueblos. The larger sites had multiple plaza areas surrounded by roomblocks, one very large or great kiva, and frequently smaller kivas as well. The great kivas of the Rio Grande are great in terms of size. Those that have been excavated or tested lack the elaborate floor features of Chacoan great kivas (Cordell 1979, 1980).

The Rio Grande Glazes were produced between about A.D. 1300 and 1700, initially probably in imitation of the St. Johns and Heshotauthla Polychromes of the Cibola area that had been traded into the Rio Grande. Warren's (1977) temper analyses suggest that the earliest Rio Grande Glazes were made at a number of different centers in the vicinity of Cochiti and Albuquerque. Early glazes were also produced in the Rio Abajo. The early glazes were widely traded not only in the Rio Grande area itself, but also to the adjacent Plains. Clearly, not every site in the Albuquerque and Santa Fe areas either produced or traded for the early glazes. As noted above, Arroyo Hondo Pueblo is in the vicinity of one of the early glaze production areas, but retained a largely black-on-white ceramic assemblage.

By about 1450, sites in the Galisteo Basin became production centers for glazes with cream or yellow interior slips. Although glazes originating in the Galisteo Basin were traded to other localities within the Rio Grande Valley, especially to sites on the Pajarito Plateau and the Santa Fe plain, they seem not to have been distributed as widely south of Albuquerque or east of the Sandia Mountains. Finally, during the 1600s, glaze pottery was produced at only a few locations: the Rio Abajo/Salinas area, the Galisteo Basin, Pecos, and Zia Pueblos (Snow 1982). In the northern part of the Rio Grande area, especially the Chama Valley, the black-on-gray ceramic tradition persisted throughout the period in the form of Abiquiu Black-on-gray and Bandelier Black-on-gray (the "biscuit" wares). The Jemez area remained outside both glaze and biscuit traditions, producing Jemez Black-on-white until well into the historic period (Lambert 1981).

Perhaps the most striking feature of these late ceramics is the marked uniformity in design layout and style (not technological attributes) from the Rio Grande area to Hopi. A well known example is the Jeddito Sikyatki style on jars of Pottery Mound Polychrome. This symbolic interaction also extends, I believe, to the kiva mural art. The murals from Kawaika-a and Awatovi are similar in execution and pictorial treatment to those from Kuaua and Pottery Mound (Cordell 1984). It seems likely that at least some of the motifs relate to the Kachina cult. Although one view (Schaafsma and Schaafsma 1974) holds that Kachina ceremonialism entered the Western Pueblos from the Jornada and Rio Grande areas, Crotty (1987) argues persuasively that the Western Anasazi were the source of the masked representations of the kiva murals. Neither Crotty nor I, from our very different backgrounds and perspectives, see any particular similarities between the kiva art of the Southwest and Mesoamerican wall paintings (contra Brody 1979).

In terms of site layout, Hibben (1939) and Steen (1977) contrast two types of sites on the Chama and Pajarito Plateau, respectively. One type, referred to as Plaza sites, consists of masonry roomblocks around a central plaza. Entry to the plaza generally is on the east and is a small opening. The plaza contains a circular kiva. A second kiva is frequently outside the pueblo structure on the east side, south of the entry to the plaza. A second type of layout predominates among larger sites. These consist of massive roomblocks arranged around three sides of a plaza and open to the south. Both Hibben and Steen view the two types as temporally sequential, but there are insufficient dates to adequately support this interpretation. Some of the very large sites (Sapawe, Pecos, Pot Creek, Paa-ko, Kuaua, and the Galisteo Basin Pueblos) consist of multiple plazas with roomblocks massed around each plaza. At Paa-ko, the plazas are not contemporary (Lambert 1954). At Arroyo Hondo Pueblo, the construction sequence indicates different episodes of building, reuse, and abandonment. Elsewhere, there are too few dates currently on hand to make even these interpretations.

It might be reasonable to suggest organizational differences that could underlie the differences in site layout, admitting that these may well have undergone change over time. The highly organized use of space at plaza-oriented sites suggests community control lacking at sites consisting of massed roomblocks. Much of the extramural work area at Plaza sites would be in view of the entire community. Greater variation in the use work space is at least possible at sites consisting of massed roomblocks. There is an apparent difference in the kind of planning reflected in the two site layouts as well. The Plaza sites seem to have required a coordinated social effort to construct. For example, the bonding and abutting patterns of multistory room walls at Rowe clearly show that two-story rooms facing separate plazas were built at the same time (Wait and Cordell 1981). Yet, the Plaza oriented communities appear to be less flexible in response to incremental growth or minor population increases. It is difficult to add a few rooms to an enclosed rectangle. It seems to me that Plaza pueblos reflect a design for demographic (and social) stability. With regional packing, local abandonments (perhaps climatically induced), and any demographic instability, the massed roomblocks of aggregated pueblos seem more likely.

A number of investigators, from Mera (1940) on, have noted population changes and abandonments of sites within the Rio Grande area. The paleoclimatic data (Rose, Dean, and Robinson 1981) do not indicate times of regional climatic deterioration. On the other hand, given the marked population increase and regional packing of the period, even minor changes would have had great impact locally. For example, the tree-ring data indicate that Tijeras Pueblo was thriving only during a period of unusually good moisture conditions in Tijeras Canyon (Cordell 1980). With abandonments of sites, settlement instability, and concomitant population influx, one might expect the site plan of massed roomblocks to prevail.

The most common approach to the later culture history of the Rio Grande area has been to attempt correlations between ceramic types and language groups. The fact that there is little agreement among reconstructions (e.g., Ford, Schroeder, and Peckham 1972) indicates, to me, the difficulty involved in this kind of research. In fairness, however, it should be pointed out that the direct historical approach to tribal culture history is certainly thwarted by the reluctance of the modern Rio Grande Pueblos to allow archaeological investigations on their lands. Projects such as the current Santo Domingo water claim research has the potential to be highly informative in this regard (Florence Ellis, personal communication, 1982).

Finally, there seems to me to be a woefully inadequate use of historic archival and documentary materials in conjunction with the archaeology of this period. Of course, investigators working at sites where contemporary documents exist examine these for potential information (e.g., Lambert 1954, 1981; Hayes et al. 1982; Holschlag 1975). Yet, we lack the sorts of topical syntheses that would be the most valuable from an archaeological perspective. It would be useful, for example, to have a regional historical perspective on inter-Pueblo and Pueblo-Hispanic trade, on population fluctuations and village organization, and on land use patterns.

## Discussion

During the Rio Grande Classic, there was certainly a major increase in population in the area. Some of the very large sites, such as those along the Chama, probably represent amalgamations of migrants from the Northern San Juan-Mesa Verde area and indigenous Rio Grande peoples. I suspect, too, that some of the aggregated settlements were established by Rio Grande Anasazi in response to the presence of efficiently organized aggregated communities. Differentiation between these two, potentially distinctive, community types has not been attempted. The level of discrimination required may be beyond current archaeological methods, although I believe it is worth a try.

The great number of large aggregated sites in the Rio Grande area is truly impressive, as is the longevity of individual sites and the aggregated pattern in the region as a whole. This situation contrasts with that in the Grasshopper region and the Upper Little Colorado—both areas abandoned prehistorically. The Rio Grande Valley then provides a remarkable resource for understanding the organizational mechanisms of success. For example, whether or not the stability of aggregated systems in southwestern environments depends on elaborate exchange systems, as has been suggested (Upham 1982), is a question well worth investigating with Rio Grande data. As yet, this has not been done.

The similarities between the Rio Grande and Western Pueblo stylistic treatment of ceramics and kiva art indicate considerable interpueblo interaction, oriented along an east-west axis, over enormous distances—from the Hopi Mesas to the central Rio Grande and beyond. The full extent of Pueblo-Plains interaction in the prehistoric period is currently not as well known, although an excellent beginning has been made through the study of the distribution of obsidian on the southern Plains (Baugh and Nelson 1987). It is quite clear that most of the interpeublo, long distance exchange, and probably much of the Pueblo-Plains trade, was disrupted in the wake of the Spanish Conquest. It would be useful to develop methods that will enable us to precisely document both exchange paths, how they functioned, and how they were disrupted.

Two directions that might be followed, in this regard, would be to develop refined models of production and distribution of a variety of products and to fully assess and reevaluate the impact of European contact. For example, we are beginning to identify changes in the locations of glaze ware manufacture. Still, we do not know how many sites within a production center (i.e., the Galisteo Basin) were actually producing vessels nor over what precise period of time. We also require information about the distribution of well-sourced ceramics outside the Rio Grande proper. With some of these basic data, it might be productive to simulate various distribution profiles that would be useful in evaluating the distribution of the types produced. On the other hand, we should also address the organizational and settlement impacts of the demographic collapses that accompanied the introduction of Europeans, their diseases, and their domestic livestock (see Lycett 1984, 1985; Upham 1982, 1984). It is crucial to learn the timing of epidemics, including their transgenerational impacts. It is also necessary to document changes in farming strategies and hunting and gathering as Indian populations declined. It is also important to consider the loss of specialist knowledge as an effect of population loss. The Rio Grande Valley, largely because it is the home of many modern Pueblo Indians, has been interpreted primarily by extending observations about the present into the past. While it is undeniable that there are many temporal continuities in Pueblo culture, the important differences between present and past have been neglected. It is my hope that in part through isolating, describing, and attempting to explain the differences, we will gain a better understanding of the forces that operated most strongly in the formation of Pueblo cultural adaptation.

## FINAL REMARKS

At the time of the first Pecos Conference (Kidder 1927), virtually all of southwestern prehistory was described as though it represented minor variations on themes and trends observable in the Eastern Anasazi region, which includes the Rio Grande area. Subsequent research in the Lower Sonoran Desert, the Mogollon Mountains, and the western portions of the Colorado Plateaus greatly restricted the area over which an eastern Anasazi model would be applied appropriately. Yet, for those working in the Anasazi area, a model of development that was based on the San Juan Anasazi areas of Mesa Verde and Chaco Canyon continued to be viewed as the norm.

Recent research in the San Juan Basin, which has so productively begun to delimit the scale and extent of the Chacoan system, has undermined the notion that the Chaco San Juan is representative of general developments in the eastern Anasazi area. Although over the years, the Rio Grande has been viewed as more and more peripheral to developments in the eastern Anasazi area, the model developed in this volume, I believe, is a productive first step in gaining a better understanding of the similarities in overall patterning throughout the Southwest. Thus, it is quite clear that during the tenth and eleventh centuries, the Chacoan system was unique, and over much of the Southwest, settlements were more like those in the Rio Grande area.

The change in perspective generated in this volume, however, is not simply the result of an accumulation of empirical research efforts. We have moved from the comparison of isolated traits toward an emphasis on those patterns that we believe are more important to an understanding of organizational structure and behavioral strategies. I think it is an encouraging start.

# REFERENCES

Agogino, George A., and James J. Hester
    1953    The Santa Ana Pre-ceramic Sites. *El Palacio* 60(4):131–140.

Anderson, Dana, and Yvonne Oakes
    1980    A World View of Agriculture. In *Tijeras Canyon: Analyses of the Past*, edited by Linda S. Cordell, pp. 12–40. University of New Mexico Press, Albuquerque.

Anyon, Roger, and T. J. Ferguson
    1983    Settlement Patterns and Changing Adaptations in the Zuni Area after A.D. 1000. Paper presented at the Anasazi Symposium, San Juan Archaeological Research Center and Library, Bloomfield, New Mexico.

Baugh, Timothy G., and Fred W. Nelson, Jr.
    1987    New Mexico Obsidian Sources and Exchange on the Southern Plains. *Journal of Field Archaeology* 14:313–329.

Biella, Jan V.
    1979    *Archeological Investigations in Cochiti Reservoir, New Mexico, Vol. 3: 1976–1977 Field Seasons*. Office of Contract Archeology, Department of Anthropology, University of New Mexico, Albuquerque.

Biella, Jan V., and Richard C. Chapman
    1977    *Archeological Investigations in Cochiti Reservoir, New Mexico. Vol. 1: A Survey of Regional Variability*. Office of Contract Archeology, Department of Anthropology, University of New Mexico, Albuquerque.
    1979    *Archeological Investigations in Cochiti Reservoir, New Mexico, Vol. 4: Adaptive Change in the Northern Rio Grande Valley*. Office of Contract Archeology, Department of Anthropology, University of New Mexico, Albuquerque.

Binford, Martha R.
    1983     Faunal Analysis. In *Economy and Interaction Along the Lower Chaco River*, edited by Patrick Hogan and Joseph C. Winter, pp. 367–374. Office of Contract Archeology and Maxwell Museum of Anthropology, University of New Mexico, Albuquerque.

Binford, Martha R., William H. Doleman, Neale Draper, and Klara B. Kelley
    1982     Anasazi and Navajo Archeofauna. In *Anasazi and Navajo Land Use in the McKinley Mine Area Near Gallup, New Mexico. Volume 1: Archeology, Part One*, edited by Christina G. Allen and Ben Nelson, pp. 448–507. Office of Contract Archeology, University of New Mexico, Albuquerque.

Blevins, Byron B., and Carol Joiner
    1977     The Archeological Survey of Tijeras Canyon. In *The 1975 Excavation of Tijeras Pueblo, Cibola National Forest, New Mexico*, edited by Linda S. Cordell, pp. 124–196. Archeological Report 18. USDA Forest Service, Southwest Regional Office, Albuquerque.

Bohrer, Vorsila L.
    1986     Ethnobotanical Pollen. In *Food, Diet, and Population at Prehistoric Arroyo Hondo Pueblo, New Mexico* by Wilma Wetterstrom, pp. 187–250. School of American Research Press, Santa Fe.

Brody, J. J.
    1979     Pueblo Fine Arts. In *Handbook of North American Indians*, vol. 9, Southwest, edited by Alfonso A. Ortiz, pp. 603–608. Smithsonian Institution Press, Washington, D.C.

Campbell, John Martin, and Florence Hawley Ellis
    1952     The Atrisco Sites: Cochise Manifestations in the Middle Rio Grande Valley. *American Antiquity* 17(3):211–221.

Caywood, Louis R.
    1966     *Excavations at Rainbow House, Bandelier National Monument.* National Park Service, Southwest Archeological Center, Globe, Arizona.

Chapman, Richard C., and Jan V. Biella (editors)
    1977     *Archeological Investigations in Cochiti Reservoir, New Mexico, Vol. 2: Excavation and Analysis, 1975 Season.* Office of Contract Archeology, University of New Mexico.

Cordell, Linda S.
    1979     *Cultural Resources Overview of the Middle Rio Grande Valley, New Mexico.* U.S. Government Printing Office, Washington, D.C.
    1980     *Tijeras Canyon: Analyses of the Past.* University of New Mexico Press, Albuquerque.
    1984     *Prehistory of the Southwest.* Academic Press, Orlando.

Cordell, Linda S., and Amy C. Earls
    1982     Mountains and Rivers: Resource Use at Three Sites. Paper presented at the Second Mogollon Conference, Las Cruces, New Mexico.

Cordell, Linda S., Amy C. Earls, and Martha R. Binford
    1984     Subsistence Systems in the Mountainous Settings of the Rio Grande Valley. In *Prehistoric Subsistence Systems in the Southwest*, edited by Suzanne

and Paul Fish, pp. 232–242. Arizona State University Anthropological Research Paper 33, Tempe.

Crotty, Helen K.
1987      Masks Portrayed in Pueblo IV Kiva Murals. Manuscript in possession of author.

Dean, Jeffrey S., Robert C. Euler, George J. Gumerman, Fred Plog, Richard H. Hevly, and Thor N.V. Karlstrom
1985      Human Behavior, Demography, and Paleoenvironment on the Colorado Plateaus. *American Antiquity* 50(3):537–554.

Dick, Herbert W.
1976      *Archeological Excavations in the Llaves Area, Santa Fe National Forest, New Mexico, 1972–1974. Part I—Architecture.* Archeological Report 13. USDA Forest Service, Southwest Regional Office, Albuquerque.

Dickson, Bruce D.
1979      *Prehistoric Pueblo Settlement Patterns: The Arroyo Hondo, New Mexico, Site Survey.* Arroyo Hondo Archaeological Series, vol. 2. School of American Research Press, Santa Fe.

Earls, Amy C.
1987      *An Archaeological Assessment of "Las Huertas", Socorro New Mexico.* Papers of the Maxwell Museum of Anthropology, Number 3. Albuquerque.

Ellis, Florence H.
1974      Anthropological Data Pertaining to the Taos Land Claim. In *American Indian Ethnohistory, vol. 1. Indians of the Southwest,* compiled and edited by David Agee Horr, pp. 29–50. Garland Publishing Company, New York and London.

Emslie, Steven D.
1981      Prehistoric Agricultural Ecosystems: Avifauna from Pottery Mound, New Mexico. *American Antiquity* 46:853–860.

Flynn, Leo L., and W. James Judge
1973      An Archeological Assessment of the Cañada de Cochiti Grant. Manuscript on file, Department of Anthropology, University of New Mexico, Albuquerque.

Ford, Richard I.
1972      An Ecological Perspective on the Eastern Pueblos. In *New Perspectives on the Pueblos,* edited by Alfonso A. Ortiz, pp. 1–18. School of American Research and University of New Mexico Press, Albuquerque.

Ford, Richard I., Albert H. Schroeder, and Stewart L. Peckham
1972      Three Perspectives on Puebloan Prehistory. In *New Perspectives on the Pueblos,* edited by Alfonso A. Ortiz, pp. 22–40. School of American Research and University of New Mexico Press, Albuquerque.

Fosberg, S.
1979      Geologic Controls of Anasazi Settlement Patterns. In *Archeological Investigations in Cochiti Reservoir, New Mexico,* vol. 4, edited by J. V. Biella and R. C. Chapman, pp. 145–168. Office of Contract Archeology, University of New Mexico, Albuquerque.

Fosberg, S., and J. Husler
1979    Pedology in the Service of Archeology: Soil Testing at LA 13086. In *Archeological investigations in Cochiti Reservoir, New Mexico*, vol. 4, edited by J. V. Biella and R. C. Chapman, pp. 307–318. Office of Contract Archeology, University of New Mexico, Albuquerque.

Frisbie, T. R.
1967    *The Excavation and Interpretation of the Artificial Leg Basketmaker III–Pueblo I Sites Near Corrales, New Mexico*. Unpublished M.A. Thesis, Department of Anthropology, University of New Mexico, Albuquerque.
1982    The Anasazi-Mogollon Frontier? Perspectives from the Albuquerque Area, or Brown vs. Gray: A Paste Case from the Albuquerque Region. In *Mogollon Archaeology: Proceedings of the 1980 Mogollon Conference*, edited by Patrick H. Beckett and Kira Silverbird, pp. 17–25. Acoma Books, Ramona, California.

Glassow, Michael A.
1980    *Prehistoric Agricultural Development in the Northern Southwest: A Study in Changing Patterns of Land Use*. Ballena Press Anthropological Papers 16. Socorro, New Mexico.

Grigg, Paul S., William M. Sundt
1975    A Progress Report on the Archaeological Excavations of the Bethesda Mines. Manuscript on file, Albuquerque Archaeological Society, Albuquerque.

Hayes, Alden C., Jon Nathan Yound, and A. H. Warren
1982    *Excavation of Mound 7, Gran Quivira National Monument, New Mexico*. Publication in Archaeology 16. National Park Service, Washington, D.C.

Hibben, Frank C.
1937    *Excavation of the Riana Ruin and Chama Valley survey*. University of New Mexico Anthropological Series 2(1).
1955    Specimens from Sandia Cave and Their Possible Significance. *Science* 122:688–689.
1975    *Kiva Art of the Anasazi at Pottery Mound*. K. C. Publications, Las Vegas, Nevada.

Holschlag, Stephanie L.
1975    *Pot Creek Pueblo and the Question of Prehistoric Northern Tiwa Household Configuration*. Unpublished Ph.D. dissertation, Department of Anthropology, Washington State University, Pullman.

Honea, Kenneth
1969    The Rio Grande Complex and the Northern Plains. *Plains Anthropologist* 14(43):57–70.
1971    LA 272; The Dead Horse Site. In *Excavations at Cochiti Dam, New Mexico 1964–1966 Season, Volume I: LA 272, LA 9154, LA 34* edited by David H. Snow. Laboratory of Anthropology Notes No. 79, Museum of New Mexico, Santa Fe.

Hunter-Anderson, Rosalind
1979    Explaining Residential Aggregation in the Northern Rio Grande: A Competition Reduction Model. In *Archeological Investigations in Cochiti Reservoir*,

*Vol. 4. Adaptive Change in the Northern Rio Grande*, edited by Jan V. Biella and Richard C. Chapman, pp. 169–175. Office of Contract Archeology, University of New Mexico, Albuquerque.

Judge, W. James
1973    *The Paleo-Indian Occupation of the Central Rio Grande Valley, New Mexico.* University of New Mexico Press, Albuquerque.

1979    The Development of a Complex Cultural Ecosystem in the Chaco Basin, New Mexico. In *Proceedings of the First Conference on Scientific Research in the National Parks*, edited by Robert M. Linn, pp. 901–905. U.S. Government Printing Office, Washington, D.C.

1983    The Chaco System, A.D. 900–1200: A Trial Reconstruction. Paper presented at the 82nd Annual Meeting of American Anthropological Association, Chicago.

Judge, W. James, and J. Dawson
1972    PaleoIndian Settlement Technology in New Mexico. *Science* 176:1210–1216.

Judge, W. James, H. Wolcott Toll, William B. Gillespie, and Stephen H. Lekson
1981    Tenth Century Developments in Chaco Canyon. In *Collected Papers in Honor of Erik Kellerman Reed*, pp. 65–98. Papers of The Archaeological Society of New Mexico 6. Archaeological Society Press, Albuquerque.

Kelley, N. Edmund
1980    *The Contemporary Ecology of Arroyo Hondo, New Mexico.* School of American Research Press, Santa Fe.

Kidder, Alfred Vincent
1924    *An Introduction to the Study of Southwestern Archaeology, With a Preliminary Account of the Excavations at Pecos.* Papers of the Southwest Expedition I. (Reprinted in 1962 by Yale University Press, New Haven.)

1927    Southwestern Archaeological Conference. *Science* 68:489–491.

1932    *The Artifacts of Pecos.* Yale University Press. New Haven.

Lambert, Marjorie F.
1954    *Paa-ko: Archaeological Chronicle of an Indian Village in North Central New Mexico.* School of American Research Monograph 19. University of New Mexico Press, Albuquerque.

1981    Spanish Influences on the Pottery of San Jose de Los Jemez and Giusewa. In *Collected Papers in Honor of Erik Kellerman Reed*, edited by Albert H. Schroeder, pp. 215–236, Papers of the Archaeological Society of New Mexico 6. Albuquerque.

Lang, Richard W.
1977a    *An Archaeological Survey of Certain State Lands Within the Drainages of Arroyo de la Vega de los Tanos and Arroyo Tongue de los Tanos, Sandoval County, New Mexico.* School of American Research Archaeology Contract Program, Santa Fe.

1977b    *Archeological Survey of the Upper San Cristobal Arroyo Drainage, Galisteo Basin, Santa Fe County, New Mexico.* School of American Research Contract Program, Santa Fe.

1982    Transformation in White Ware Pottery of the Northern Rio Grande. In

*Southwestern Ceramics, A Comparative Review*, edited by Albert H. Schroeder, pp. 153–200. A School of American Research Advanced Seminar, Arizona Archaeologist No. 15. Arizona Archaeological Society, Phoenix.

Lang, Richard W., and Arthur H. Harris,
  1984    *The Faunal Remains from Arroyo Hondo Pueblo, New Mexico. A Study in Short-Term Subsistence Change*. School of American Research Press, Santa Fe.

Lange, Charles H., and Carroll L. Riley
  1966    *The Southwestern Journals of Adolph F. Bandelier, 1880–1882*. University of New Mexico Press, Albuquerque.

Laumbach, Karl, Toni Sudar-Murphy, Billy J. Naylor, and Shirley Rorex
  1977    Description of Five Sites in White Rock Canyon: LA 5013, LA 5014, LA 12511, LA 12512 and LA 12522. In *Archeological Investigations in Cochiti Reservoir, New Mexico, Volume 2: Excavation and Analysis 1975 Season*, edited by Richard C. Chapman and Jan V. Biella with Stanley D. Bussey, contributing editor, pp. 29–82. Office of Contract Archeology, University of New Mexico, Albuquerque.

Lycett, Mark T.
  1984    Social and Economic Consequences of Aboriginal Population Decline from Introduced Diseases. Paper presented at the 49th Annual Meeting of the Society for American Archaeology, Portland.
  1985    Archaeological Implications of European Colonial Contact: Land, Labor, and Depopulation in the Spanish Americas. Paper presented at the 83rd Annual Meeting of the American Anthropological Association, Denver.

Marshall, Michael
  1980    Preliminary Analysis of Ceramic Materials. In *Reconnaissance Study of the Archaeological and Related Resources of the Lower Puerco and Salado Drainages, Central New Mexico*, edited by Mark Wimerbly and Peter Eidenbach, pp. 165–188. Human Systems Research, Tularosa, New Mexico.

Marshall, Michael P., and Henry Walt
  1984    *Rio Abajo: The Prehistory and History of a Rio Grande Province*. New Mexico Historic Preservation Division, Santa Fe.

Mathien, Frances Joan
  1981    *Economic Exchange Systems in the San Juan Basin*. Unpublished Ph.D. dissertation, Department of Anthropology, University of New Mexico, Albuquerque.
  1984    Jewelry Items of the Chaco Anasazi. In *Recent Research on Chaco Prehistory*, edited by W. J. Judge and J. D. Schelberg, pp. 173–362. Duckworth, London.

McNutt, Charles H.
  1969    *Early Puebloan Occupation at Tesuque By-Pass and in the Upper Rio Grande Valley*. Anthropological Papers of the University of Michigan 40. University of Michigan, Ann Arbor.

Mera, H. P.
  1935    *Ceramic Clues to the Prehistory of North Central New Mexico*. Laboratory of Anthropology Technical Series. Museum of New Mexico, Santa Fe.

1940        *Population Changes in the Rio Grande Glaze Paint Area*. Laboratory of Anthropology Technical Series 9. Santa Fe.

Mick-O'Hara, Linda
1987        Identification and Analysis of the Faunal Remains From the 1984 Excavations at Rowe Pueblo. Report on file, Department of Anthropology, California Academy of Sciences, San Francisco.

Nelson, Fred W. Jr.
1984        X-ray Fluorescence Analysis of Some Western North American Obsidians. In *Obsidian Studies in the Great Basin*, edited by R. E. Hughes, pp. 27–62. Contributions of the University of California Archaeological Research Facility 45.

Nelson, Nels C.
1914        *Pueblo Ruins of the Galisteo Basin, New Mexico*. Anthropological Papers of the American Museum of Natural History 15 (Part 1).

Nordby, Larry
1981        The Prehistory of the Pecos Indians. In *Exploration*, pp. 5–11. Annual Bulletin of the School of American Research, Santa Fe, New Mexico.

Northrop, Stuart A.
1975        *Turquoise and Spanish Mines in New Mexico*. University of New Mexico Press, Albuquerque.

Oakes, Yvonne Roy
1979        *Excavations at Deadman's Curve, Tijeras Canyon, Bernalillo County, New Mexico*. Laboratory of Anthropology Notes No. 137, Santa Fe, New Mexico.

Peckham, Stewart L.
1957        *Three Pithouse Sites Near Albuquerque, New Mexico*. Highway Salvage Archaeology 3(12). Laboratory of Anthropology, Museum of New Mexico, Santa Fe.
1981        The Palisade Ruin. *Papers of the Archaeological Society of New Mexico* 6:113–148.

Plog, Fred
1983        Political and Economic Alliances on the Colorado Plateaus, A.D. 400–1450. In *Advances in World Archaeology*, vol. 2, edited by Fred Wendorf, pp. 289–330. Academic Press, New York.

Reinhart, Theodore R.
1968        *Late Archaic Culture of the Middle Rio Grande Valley, New Mexico: A Study of the Process of Culture Change*. Unpublished Ph.D. dissertation, Department of Anthropology, University of New Mexico, Albuquerque.

Reiter, Paul
1938        *The Jemez Pueblo of Unshaqi, New Mexico, with Notes on the Earlier Excavations at "Amoxiumqua" and Giusewa*. University of New Mexico Bulletin 326, Monograph Series 1(4). Albuquerque.

Reynolds, S. E.
1956        *Climatological Summary, New Mexico. Temperature 1850–1954; Frost 1850–1954; Evaporation 1912–1954*. New Mexico State Engineers Office, Technical Report No. 5. Santa Fe.

Rose, Martin R., Jeffrey S. Dean, and William J. Robinson
    1981    *The Past Climate of Arroyo Hondo, New Mexico, Reconstructed from Tree Rings.*
            Arroyo Hondo Archaeological Series 4. School of American Research,
            Santa Fe.

Schaafsma, Curtis F.
    1976    *Archaeological Survey of Maximum Pool and Navajo Excavations at Abiquiu
            Reservoir Rio Arriba County, New Mexico.* School of American Research,
            Santa Fe.
    1977    *A Road and Drill Pad Survey for the Questa Molybdenum Company, Carson
            National Forest.* In Archeological Report No. 15, pp. 1–12. Miscellaneous
            papers, USDA Forest Service Southwestern Regional Office, Albuquerque.

Schaafsma, Polly, and Curtis F. Schaafsma
    1974    Evidence for the Origins of Pueblo Katchina Cult as Suggested by South-
            western Rock Art. *American Antiquity* 39(4):535–545.

Schorsch, Russell L.
    1962    A Basket Maker III Pit House Near Albuquerque. *El Palacio* 69(2):114–
            118.

Seaman, Timothy J.
    1976    Archeological Investigations on the San Juan-to-Ojo 34KV Transmission
            Line for Public Service Company of New Mexico. Manuscript on file,
            Laboratory of Anthropology, Museum of New Mexico, Santa Fe.

Simmons, Marc
    1969    Settlement Patterns and Village Plans in Colonial New Mexico. *Journal of
            the West* 8:7–21.

Skinner, S. Alan
    1965    The Sedillo Site: A Pit House Village in Albuquerque. *El Palacio* 72(1):5–
            24.

Snow, David H.
    1973    Prehistoric Southwestern Turquoise Industry, *El Palacio* 29:33–51.
    1974    *The Excavation of Saltbush Pueblo, Bandelier National Monument, New Mex-
            ico, 1971.* Laboratory of Anthropology Notes No. 97, Santa Fe.
    1982    The Rio Grande Glaze, Matte-Paint, and Plainware Tradition. In *Southwest-
            ern Ceramics: A Comparative Review,* edited by Albert H. Schroeder, pp.
            235–278. The Arizona Archaeologist 15. Phoenix.

Steen, Charles R.
    1955    The Pigeon Cliffs Site, A Preliminary Report. *El Palacio* 62:174–180.
    1977    *Pajarito Plateau Archaeological Survey and Excavation.* Los Alamos Scientific
            Laboratories, Los Alamos, New Mexico.

Sterrett, D.B.
    1911    Mineral Resources of the United States. *U.S. Geological Survey,* Part
            2:1065–1073. Washington, D.C.

Stuart, David E., and Rory P. Gauthier
    1981    *Prehistoric New Mexico: Background for Survey.* New Mexico Historic Preser-
            vation Bureau, Santa Fe.

Stubbs, S. A., and W. S. Stallings, Jr.
1953    *The Excavation of Pindi Pueblo, New Mexico.* Monographs of the School of American Research 18. Santa Fe.

Swadesh, Frances Leon
1974    *Los Primeros Pobladores: Hispanic Americans of the Ute Frontier.* University of Notre Dame Press, South Bend.

Toll, Mollie S.
1983    Wild Plant Use in the Rio Abajo: Some Deviations from the Expected Pattern Throughout the Central and Northern Southwest. Paper presented at the Rio Abajo Area Conference Seminar on the Archaeology and History of the Socorro District, March 18–19, New Mexico Institute of Mining and Technology, Socorro.

Traylor, Diane, Nancy Wood, Lyndi Hubbell, Robert Scaife, and Sue Waber
1977    Bandelier: Excavations in the Flood Pool of Cochiti Lake, New Mexico. Manuscript on file, Southwest Cultural Resource Center, National Park Service, Santa Fe.

Tuan, Yi-Fu, Cyril E. Everard, Jerold G. Widdison, and Ivan Bennett
1973    *The Climate of New Mexico.* State Planning Office, Santa Fe.

Upham, Steadman
1982    *Polities and Power: An Economic and Political History of the Western Pueblo.* Academic Press, New York.
1984    Adaptive Diversity and Southwestern Abandonment. *Journal of Anthropological Research* 40(2):235–256.

Vickery, Lucretia D.
1969    *Excavations at Ta 26, a Small Pueblo Site Near Taos, New Mexico.* Unpublished M.A. thesis, Department of Anthropology, Wichita State University, Wichita.

Vivian R. Gwinn, and Nancy Wilkinson Clendenen
1965    The Denison Site: Four Houses Near Isleta, New Mexico. *El Palacio* 72(2):5–26.

Vytlacil, Natalie, and J. J. Brody
1958    Two Pit Houses Near Zia Pueblo. *El Palacio* 65(5):174–184.

Wait, Walter K., and Linda S. Cordell
1981    The Rowe Archeological Research Project, Final Report to the National Endowment for the Humanities for Grant RS-1144-79. Ms. on file, Southwest Regional Office, USDI National Park Service, Santa Fe.

Warren, A. Helene
1975    The Ancient Mineral Industries of Cerro Pedernal, Rio Arriba County, New Mexico. In *New Mexico Geological Society Guidebook, 25th Field Conference, Ghost Ranch,* edited by Charles T. Siemers, pp. 87–93. Albuquerque.
1977    Prehistoric and Historic Ceramic Analysis. In *Archeological Investigations in Cochiti Reservoir (vol. 2). Excavation and Analysis, 1975 Season,* edited by Richard C. Chapman and Jan V. Biella, pp. 97–101. Office of Contract Archeology, University of New Mexico, Albuquerque.

1980　Prehistoric Pottery of Tijeras Canyon. In *Tijeras Canyon: Analyses of the Past,* edited by Linda S. Cordell, pp. 149–168. University of New Mexico Press, Albuquerque.

Warren, A. Helene, and Frances J. Mathien
1985　Prehistoric and Historic Turquoise Mining in the Cerrillos District: Time and Place. In *Southwestern Culture History, Collected Papers in Honor of Albert H. Schroeder,* edited by Charles H. Lange, pp. 93–129. Papers of The Archaeological Society of New Mexico 10. Archaeological Society of New Mexico and Ancient City Press, Santa Fe.

Weber, Robert H., and George A. Agogino
1968　Mockingbird Gap Paleo-Indian Site: Excavations in 1967. Paper presented at the 33rd Annual Meeting of the Society for American Archaeology, Santa Fe.

Weigand, Phil C.
1982　Sherds Associated with Turquoise Mines in the Southwestern U.S.A. *Pottery Southwest* 9(2):4–6.

Weigand, Phil C., and Garman Harbottle
1988　The Role of Turquoises in the Ancient Mesoamerican Trade Structure. Paper presented at the 52nd Annual Meeting of the Society for American Archaeology, Toronto 1987 and revised September 1988 for *Prehistoric Exchange Systems in North America,* edited by J. E. Ericson and T. G. Baugh.

Wendorf, Fred, and Erik Reed
1955　An Alternative Reconstruction of Northern Rio Grande Prehistory. *El Palacio* 62(5–6):131–173.

Wendorf, Fred, and John P. Miller
1959　Artifacts from High Mountain Sites in the Sangre de Cristo Range, New Mexico. *El Palacio* 66(2):37–52.

Wetherington, Ronald Knox
1968　*Excavations at Pot Creek Pueblo.* Fort Burgwin Research Center Report 6. Rancho de Taos, New Mexico.

Wetterstrom, Wilma
1986　*Food, Diet, and Population at Prehistoric Arroyo Hondo Pueblo, New Mexico.* School of American Research Press, Santa Fe.

Wimberly, Mark, and Peter Eidenbach
1980　*Reconnaissance Study of the Archaeological and Related Resources of the Lower Puerco and Salado Drainages, Central New Mexico.* Human Systems Research, Inc., Tularosa, New Mexico.

Wiseman, Regge N.
1976　*An Archaeological Impact Statement and Mitigation Proposal for New Mexico State Highway Department Project F-0330-1(14) near San Ysidro, Sandoval County, New Mexico.* Museum of New Mexico, Laboratory of Anthropology Notes No. 125. Santa Fe.
1986　The Bronze Trail Site Group: More Evidence for a Cerrillos-Chaco Turquoise Connection. In *By Hands Unknown: Papers on Rock Art and Archae-*

*ology in Honor of James G. Bain,* edited by Anne Poore. Papers of the Archaeological Society of New Mexico 12. Albuquerque.

Woosley, Anne I.
1986    Puebloan Prehistory of the Northern Rio Grande: Settlement, Population, Subsistence. *The Kiva* 51(3):143–164.

Young, Gwen
1980    Analysis of Faunal Remains. In *Tijeras Canyon: Analyses of the Past,* edited by Linda S. Cordell, pp. 88–120. University of New Mexico Press, Albuquerque.

STEVEN A. LeBLANC 10

# Cibola: Shifting Cultural Boundaries

The Cibola area of east central New Mexico and west central Arizona witnessed a more complex series of events than most of the rest of the Southwest. In particular, these events included considerable changes in cultural relationships over time. These relationships changed so much that it is hard to define a Cibola area over time. Moreover, Cibola represents one of the few areas that contained a sizable population at the time of Spanish contact, thereby increasing the total span we can study. Even though the area has received considerable research activity, such efforts have rarely focused on Cibola as a region, and these efforts frequently have been on the margins of the Cibola area, or otherwise restricted to single sites or narrow slices of time. As a consequence, the history of Cibola has been the subject of confusion or misunderstanding, and is still in many ways poorly understood. The work of the Field Museum in the Vernon area is an exception, but Vernon is on the extreme western periphery of the Cibola area.

## THE AREA AND THE CULTURAL-HISTORICAL BACKGROUND

The Cibola area has historically been associated with the Zuni people, especially with the historic towns inhabited at Spanish contact. Archaeologically, it has usually been considered to encompass a much broader area (Woodbury 1956). It will be argued in this paper that the general region witnessed considerable change in cultural boundaries, so that any rigid spatial demarcation becomes impossible to utilize over time.

The Cibola area is considered here to extend as far north as the western Rio Puerco. On the east, the plateau area extending to Cebolleta Mesa seems to be a useful boundary. Less obvious boundaries exist to the south and west. In the south, a very real cultural boundary existed along an east-west line at about the latitude of Quemado. This line runs into Arizona, where it seems to fall between Showlow and the Zuni River. This boundary is distinct from before A.D. 700 until about A.D. 1000, but no longer exists after this time. After A.D. 1000, it makes sense to include the Reserve or Cibola branch of the northern Mogollon (and perhaps the Forestdale branch) in our discussion. Thus, the maximal area under consideration extends south to the Tularosa River and the area around Reserve. As such, the area would include the northern fringe of the Mogollon rim. On the west, the situation is very vague, but for this discussion it will be limited to the Holbrook-Showlow line.

A broad chronology is given in Figure 29, which extends beyond the focus of this volume. Paleoindian and Archaic remains have been recovered from much of the area (Tainter and Gillio 1980; Plog 1981; Berman 1979). The first ceramic occupations seem to date after the A.D. 300s (Wendorf 1950; Martin et al. 1962; LeBlanc 1982). The early presence of brown wares, at the Flattop site (Wendorf 1950) and along the Puerco (Wasley 1960; Ferg 1978), has long been noted. Sites as far north as the Puerco River show heavy concentrations of brown wares in an area that later was dominated by grey wares. However, architectural features, such as pithouse shape and village layouts, were always basically Anasazi.

Certainly by A.D. 800–900 the area as far south as the Quemado-St. Johns-Snowflake line is basically Anasazi; it is the nature of the earlier manifestations that is in question. The dating of sites in this earlier period is a bit fuzzy, so it is hard to characterize what happened. One model might be that much of the area was initially Mogollon-like and slow expansion by Anasazi-related peoples pushed south to the above-mentioned line. Alternatively, the area could have been inhabited basically by Anasazi peoples, initially obtaining considerable ceramics from the south that were later supplanted by local production and more tribal trade in grey wares. Yet another alternative is that the area's population during the very late Archaic was ethnically or culturally distinct from either Anasazi or Mogollon, and adopted various traits causing it to ultimately appear quite Anasazi. This last model could account for the distinctiveness of the Zuni language. Of course,

|  | Contact |
| 1540 | |
|  | Defensive Pueblos |
| 1275 | |
|  | Initial aggregation and defensive posture |
| 1260 | |
|  | Post-Chaco reorganization |
| 1130–1150 | |
|  | Chaco Sphere |
| 1000 | |
|  | Regional Diversity (various local phases) |
| 750 | |
|  | Regional Diversity (various local phases) |
| 550 | |
|  | Early pottery using pithouse villages |
| 300 | |

*Fig. 29. The Cibola sequence.*

trait chasing, in the absence of attempts at understanding the processes involved, is of limited utility. Nevertheless, the Cibola area clearly did not have a single cultural manifestation or stable boundaries during the early part of the ceramic period.

What is probably pertinent to our present concerns is that the Cibola area witnessed either shifting cultural boundaries, or was some form of frontier-type in-between zone from the earliest pottery-producing periods. Thus, the pattern of changing cultural boundaries considered in this chapter actually has a time depth greater than the time range being discussed in this volume.

## THE EXPANSION PERIOD (A.D. 800–1000)

By A.D. 800, or the middle of what is considered Pueblo I, the Cibola area was Anasazi except for the area south of Quemado. Grey wares were produced, pithouses had air shafts or vestibules, not rampways; there were no rectangular great kivas, and axes were generally full-grooved. Thus, for each of the traditionally employed diagnostic trait differences between Anasazi and Mogollon, Cibola fell within the Anasazi pattern.

### Site Plans and Layouts

Between A.D. 500 and 1000, pithouse villages with below-ground storage facilities were first supplanted by villages with stone-lined cists, which were, when covered, considerably above-ground. These, in turn, were supplanted by actual above-ground storage rooms. These were made of slab and jacal walls and contiguous or almost contiguous groups of storage rooms were built (Gladwin 1945; Roberts 1939). This produced the "unit house" or front-oriented plan, as Bullard (1962) noted. He points out that this basic unit, storage units with a habitation unit to the south or southeast, which in turn had a trash area to the south or southeast of it, is neither a dwelling nor a village. Such a unit consists of more than one structure, but the unit, what he termed habitation, can be combined in groups to produce a village.

There are several interesting aspects of the unit layout. First, such oriented units do not appear in Mogollon villages except on rare occasions, and they are not found in the Reserve branch of the Mogollon until after A.D. 1000. This, as will be discussed, had an important bearing on the nature of the cultural change at that time. Secondly, this orientation of storage, habitation, and trash evolves into an orientation of storage-habitation-kiva-trash from north or northwest to south or southeast, which occurs over much of the Anasazi area, including Cibola, until about A.D. 1275 when it is largely abandoned. Even Chaco bighouses preserve this pattern. That is, the orientation pattern is preserved through a considerable architectural sequence in both house form and time. It is surely a diagnostic or fundamental aspect of Anasazi behavior.

In the Cibola area, the White Mound Village (Roberts 1939), the Twin Buttes site (Wendorf 1951), Whitewater (Gladwin 1945), and the early village at Kiatuthlanna (Roberts 1931) are examples of this pattern. NA14,084 (Gratz n.d.) may be another example, but the report is not adequate enough to make an interpretation. Cerro Colorado at Mariana Mesa does not demonstrate this pattern. However, the excavators focused on houses and not extramural areas, and it does not appear that the excavations were carried out in places where storage or trash facilities would have been, had the pattern existed. Moreover, the village was earlier than most of the above examples and the pattern may not have been fully established that early. In this light it is interesting to note that Cerro Colorado has a number of bell-shaped storage pits, some of which are superimposed by slab-lined pits (which are partially above-ground). Perhaps there is an evolution in the nature of the storage facilities from bell-shaped pits to slab-lined pits and the orientation pattern also developed during this time span.

Most of these sites seem quite small. When considered at a single point in time, even in the few cases where there may have been 50 structures present, for example, Cerro Colorado (Whalen 1982), there is considerable evidence of superpositioning or abandonment of structures while the site as a whole was occupied. For example, at White Mound one can make a good argument that of the six pithouses excavated, no more than two were contemporary. Thus, it seems at present that the largest villages consisted of perhaps no more than 10–15 contemporary structures. If this is the case, then these Cibola sites were smaller than the largest contemporary sites from other areas, for example, Snaketown in the Hohokam area (Wilcox et al. 1981) and the Galaz in the Mimbres area (Anyon and LeBlanc 1984). That is, either the largest village sites in the Cibola area have not been excavated, or the largest population aggregates were considerably smaller than in other areas.

Perhaps one of the most interesting aspects of these sites is the absence or rarity of great kivas. At this time range, great kivas are known from the Anasazi area at Shabik'eshchee (Roberts 1929), and elsewhere (Marshall et al. 1979). They are frequently 9 m or more in diameter. The only candidate for such a feature in the Cibola area is the "dance plaza" at Whitewater (Roberts 1939), but this is clearly an unroofed feature. Even if some great kivas eventually turn out to exist for this time range, they would seem to be rarer than in either the Mogollon area or the northern Anasazi area.

The transition to above-ground habitation rooms seems to occur after A.D. 900. There is no strong evidence for the use of above-ground habitation rooms until after the initial construction of multistoried pueblos in Chaco Canyon. Thus the shift to above-ground rooms, which is usually seen as a gradual evolutionary process, may, in the Cibola Branch, be in part an imitation of the Chaco example.

## Settlement Patterns, Subsistence, and Artifacts

Suprisingly, settlement patterns are poorly known prior to A.D. 1000. It would appear that most sites are located in low elevations along major water courses, a pattern seen elsewhere at this interval. Exceptions seem to be very early sites located on mesa tops or other high places, for example, Flattop (Wendorf 1950). This seems to be a pattern similar to early Mogollon sites, which are also located on high, isolated landforms. However, before the end of the Initiation period (A.D. 650–750), this pattern no longer seems to exist and sites are closer to valley floors. It must be remembered that as elsewhere in the Anasazi area, sites in valley bottoms of this time range are often heavily alluviated. These sites are buried so deeply that they are encountered only by road or arroyo cuts. As a consequence, I suspect that the number of valley bottom sites is underrepresented.

In the Zuni area, there are relatively few sites recorded from this time range, and those that are, are usually found on or near major drainage bottoms. This overall pattern also holds for the Quemado area, but Whalen (1982) has noted that there are a few large sites, as well as smaller ones, located well away from major drainages. These sites, such as Cerro Colorado, are in elevated areas and some have defensive aspects to their locations. Whether we are seeing a holdover from the earlier high, isolated site locations, the utilization of a more marginal resource base, or else just differences in topography between Zuni and Quemado, is unclear.

Estimating population sizes or growth rates for the pre-A.D. 1000 time span would seem to be futile. The only systematic attempts that have been made are for the Hay Hollow Valley at the extreme western edge of the area. In general, there does not seem to be any dramatic growth during the early part of the period, and it is not until around A.D. 1000 that there is a marked rise in the number of sites.

Opinions differ considerably concerning the nature of the subsistence strategy during A.D. 800–1000. It is frequently argued (Whalen 1982; Cordell and Plog 1979) that hunting and gathering were of major importance with horticulture a backup. However, at sites like the Green Bear (Ferg 1978), the abundance of corn would argue for considerable reliance on it. Also, the mano-metate complex is dominated by two-handed manos and trough metates that, it can be argued (Lancaster 1983), are designed for corn processing.

The presence of sites like Cerro Colorado in suboptimal agricultural areas may be seen as supporting the argument for the minor importance of agriculture at this time. However, most of the village sites may be along major water courses. These are just the areas we would expect to find a low density population heavily dependent on agriculture, yet such areas are presently underrepresented in our samples. No project in the area has really addressed this issue, and it is likely that horticulture was as important in the Cibola area at A.D. 900 as it must have been in the Hohokam, the Mimbres, or the Chaco areas at this same time.

Artifactual assemblages are generally similar over most of the Anasazi area at this time. The painted wares share design styles and surface decoration techniques, and while local types have been defined, there are no local design styles. Grey ware utility vessels follow the plain-neck banded-corrugated pattern seen elsewhere in the Anasazi area, with perhaps more fugitive red introduced earlier. This may be a reflection of the "southern" connection to the Cibola area.

There is certainly less elaboration of artifact categories, such as jewelry and "ceremonial" goods, than is seen in the southern Mogollon or Hohokam areas. No complex trade networks seem to have been in existence.

## The Reserve Area

Because it is pertinent to the following discussion, a brief consideration of the Reserve area is included for the pre-A.D. 1000 interval. Village sites consisted of irregularly arranged pithouses and rectangular great kivas occurred on the larger sites (Berman 1979). Storage was in bell-shaped pits or intramurally. There was no above-ground construction of any type prior to A.D. 1000. In most ways, the sites were like those of the Three Circle phase in the southern Mogollon except, on average, they were smaller than their southern counterparts. Also, painted ceramics do not seem to be locally produced. The Vernon-Hay Hollow area seems to share many similarities with the Reserve area at this time.

In summary, the Cibola area (including the Reserve area) seems to have been simply organized during this interval. The largest communities, conceived of as either single communities or site clusters, probably held less than 150 people and most are much smaller. No evidence has been put forth that would argue for anything but an egalitarian, tribally based, exogamous society. No sumptuous burials, craft specialization, nor major public works are observed. Thus, at the pre-A.D. 1000 interval, the Cibola area is less complex and is in some ways peripheral to areas such as Chaco, Mimbres, or the Hohokam.

## THE DIFFERENTIATION PERIOD (A.D. 1000–1130) AND THE CHACO EXPANSION

The remaining history of the Cibola area cannot be understood without considering the development of the Chaco interaction sphere. Because our perception of the Chaco interaction sphere is very recent and, as yet, poorly developed, assessing the impact of it on the Cibola area is difficult. However, one point can surely be made. The more one looks for the impact, direct or indirect, of the Chaco interaction sphere, the more one finds. Thus, we must assume that we underperceive the importance of the Chaco development for the Cibola area.

The Chaco interaction sphere is considered elsewhere in this volume and only a few pertinent points need to be made. The first concerns the level of sociopolitical integration. It is increasingly clear that Chaco was a ranked or chiefdom level society in the sense of Service (1962). Schelberg (1982) has summarized much of the pertinent data and many of the arguments, and they are quite convincing. The development of a complex social organization was a unique event in the Anasazi area, and after the Chaco collapse, no ranked society ever reoccurred, although some of the tribal organizations, for example, Zuni, were rather complex.

A second point concerns the dating of the Chaco interaction sphere. By the late A.D. 800s or early A.D. 900s, the beginnings of what developed into the Chaco interaction sphere were taking place in Chaco Canyon proper. However, the interaction sphere expansion does not seem to have taken place before A.D. 1000, or if it did, it does not seem to have taken place in the Cibola area. In fact, while there is some evidence for the foundation of some Chacoan communities (outliers) in the early A.D. 1000s, the best documented proliferation of outliers occurs in the A.D. 1080s or later (Powers et al. 1983).

It is the nature of the Chaco outlying communities that is most pertinent to our understanding of the Cibola area. Our understanding has been greatly enhanced by the recent publication of two volumes dealing with outlying communities (Marshall et al. 1979; Powers et al. 1983). They, and observations by the writer, serve as the basic sources for the following discussion. In the San Juan Basin and southwestern Colorado, where they are best known, outliers consist of a "bighouse" or "great house," which is multistoried and almost always of core veneer, tabular sandstone. Rooms are larger than typical with higher ceilings (an archaeologically difficult trait to find). Bighouses are oriented with multistoried rooms generally on the north or northwest and single storied rooms in the "front," or the south or southeast. Bighouses usually have "in-roomblock" kivas. That is, kivas are set within the roomblocks themselves and are walled in. This is in contrast to kivas that are in front of, and separate from, roomblocks.

Great kivas are almost always present. They are usually more than 12 m in diameter. They are masonry-lined, and entered by a step entryway. There is often an appended room on the side opposite from the entryway. Other rooms may or may not be appended. The location of great kivas is varied. Some are appended to bighouses, but most lie elsewhere in the community. They can be far away; several hundred meters is not uncommon. Thus, their association with bighouses may go unnoticed and their absence at sites like Kiatuthlanna may be reality, or may simply result from the failure to look for them.

In addition to the bighouse, Chaco communities consist of a number of small roomblocks. These are single-storied, frequently have kivas in front of them, and range up to a kilometer or two from the bighouse. Few complete surveys around bighouses have been made, but 30 associated roomblocks are not uncommon (Marshall et al. 1979; Powers et al. 1983). Beyond this there is still another tier of sites. These seem to be special use or seasonally utilized sites associated with agriculture. Because of the frequency of walled structures and rooms open at one end, one would not associate these sites with year-round habitation. This class of sites extends 4–10 km from the bighouse-kiva center. Thus, if as argued below, Chaco communities are spaced at 13–16 km intervals in favorable locations, then one observes an almost continuous distribution of sites. Not all workers agree on what constitutes a Chacoan outlier, nor what is an associated community. There is every reason to believe that there are substantial differences among them, especially as one moves farther away from Chaco Canyon. I believe that the above definition, while perhaps "broad" in its conception, makes sense out of much information from Cibola in a way that a more "narrow" definition does not.

A final aspect of the Chacoan outlier communities is the roads. These recently rediscovered features connect the communities in a dendritic pattern with Chaco Canyon. They are strong evidence that we are not simply witnessing a fad or copying phenomenon in the development of the outlying communities, but instead we have a truly integrated system. The nature of the roads need not concern us here except that they are distinctively made features, and are not trails (Obenauf 1980).

## The Distribution of Chacoan Communities

Most of the recognized Chacoan communities are in the San Juan Basin. This is due, in large part, to their study (Marshall et al. 1979; Powers et al. 1983) and the legislation covering them (PL 96–550). However, in spite of opinions such as those of Tainter and Gillio (1980), it has long been noted that they occur far beyond the confines of the basin. In fact, most of the early recognized examples, such as Lowry (Martin 1936) 200 km to the north, Village of the Great Kivas (Roberts 1932) 120 km to the south, and Allentown (Roberts 1939) 150 km to the southwest, are outside the basin; the latter two are in the Cibola area. At least five other sites on the northern edge of the Cibola area are now generally considered as outliers: Sanders, Houck, Ft. Wingate (including Fenced-Up Horse Canyon), and two in Manuelito Canyon (Reed 1938; Fowler et al. 1987). These are basically along the Puerco.

The most important idea in this paper is that many other Chacoan outliers exist in the Cibola area. A recent survey (Fowler et al. 1987) provides new information about these and other sites, the results of which are not fully assimilated here, but only touched upon below. There are three candidates on the Zuni Reservation besides Village of the Great Kivas. There is also the well-known La Ventana site to the east of the Malpais, and possibly the Dittert site south of the Malpais. These additional communities demonstrate that Village of the Great Kivas is not exceptional, but is part of a dense concentration of outliers spread, with a few gaps, every 13–16 km in an *unbroken distribution* from Chaco Canyon. There is no appreciable gap and there are no significant differences between these outliers and many of those seen in the basin.

Some very tentative ideas can be suggested. Chaco outliers in the northern part of Cibola are generally smaller than outliers such as Kin Ya'a, but are not significantly smaller than other San Juan Basin outliers, such as San Mateo and Andrews. There are road segments at the Manuelito, La Ventana, and Dittert sites, among others (Fowler et al. 1987). Numerous definite road segments have been found in the Cibola area, and many other possibilities have been observed, but not confirmed.

The major point is that although these northern Cibola Chacoan communities are generally unrecognized as such by archaeologists, they are there and in considerable numbers. When they are visited by workers familiar with Chaco outliers, there is little question whether they are really outliers. The problem is our lack of perception, and a failure to publish the existing information.

As surprising as this distribution of Chaco outlier communities may seem to some, I consider it to be the tip of the iceberg. There are still more candidates for Chacoan outlying communities as far south as Forestdale and the Tularosa River at Apache Creek. As one moves south from Zuni, the density of recognized outlying communities drops off, but it is unclear whether this is reality or our perception. In particular, I am unfamiliar with the sites in Arizona and have had no opportunity to research the pertinent site files. However, Plog (1979) notes a number of round great kivas along the eastern periphery of his Chavez-Chevelon province that may be related to Chacoan communities.

Some communities, such as Cox Ranch Pueblo just south of Zuni Salt Lake, or the Jaralosa site, appear to be classic examples of what we expect to find for an outlier. The Cox Ranch site has a large group of single-storied roomblocks around it, and there is a large great kiva with attached rooms. The Zuni Salt Lake trail (a possible Chacoan road) would, if extended, pass very near Cox Ranch, but no linkage has been demonstrated. The ceramics are not late PIII, but earlier.

The likelihood that these sites are really Chacoan outliers is supported by the presence of a considerable number of outliers in the Cortez area of Colorado, which is equally distant from Chaco. Not counting outliers along the Mancos and otherwise south of Yucca House, a good case can be made for at least eight Chacoan communities in the Cortez area. For example, Lowry Ruin is 200 km from Chaco, the same distance as Cox Ranch Pueblo.

The western extent of Chaco outliers is far from clear. North of I-40 there are White House and Kin Li Chi, and along the Puerco the above-mentioned Allentown, Houck, and Sanders. The Sundown site has a Chaco-looking great kiva, but any possible bighouse would have been of adobe and may have been hidden by silt (Gumerman and Olsen 1968). To the south, the Linden site, reported by Hough (1907), is a potential candidate as are several near St. Johns mentioned by Spier (1918). The Forestdale Ruin (Haury 1950) also has the characteristics and dates one would expect of an outlier community. Several other candidates are discussed by Fowler et al. (1987). As discussed below, I think the Carter Ranch site attempts to mimic the attributes of a Chaco outlier, but, in fact, is not one. This then, may define the western limit of true Chaco sites.

In summary, most, if not all, of the Cibola area was in fact within the Chaco sphere. Clearly all of Zuni, probably all of the Cebolleta Mesa country, and the Upper Puerco were included. An excellent case can be made for the rest of the New Mexican Cibola area as far south as Quemado, and into east central Arizona. If correct, this would mean that all of the former Cibola area came under the Chaco interaction sphere.

Yet another possibility exists. It has long been noted that the northern portion of the Mogollon area, in particular the Reserve and Forestdale branches, began to look Anasazi beginning in the A.D. 1000s. I propose that this impression is real and what actually occurred is that, in at least portions of these areas, actual Chacoan outlying communities were founded. The Forestdale site has been mentioned, and LA 3270, along the Tularosa near Apache Creek, has similar characteristics but is undated.

Other possible candidates for Chaco outlier centers in this former Mogollon area include sites from the Danson (1957) survey, such as site 42 in the Center Fire Creek area, sites 84, 434, and 417 (one of which might be LA 3270) on the Tularosa, sites 398 and 421 in the Gallo Mountain area, sites 184, 194, and 202 in the Largo Canyon-Agua Fria area, and site 168 in the Coyote Creek area. This large number of candidates suggests that there is potential for a considerable number of outliers in the Reserve area.

This model would have Reserve Black-on-white as a local attempt at making pottery within the Chacoan tradition. That is, it is an effort to produce a type that fits within the tradition and includes Puerco Black-on-white, Escavada Black-on-white, Gallup Black-on-white, Chaco Black-on-white, Red Mesa Black-on-white, and should not be conceptualized as a Mogollon type at all. A similar argument would hold for Snowflake Black-on-white. The shift to above-ground rooms was abrupt and many of the known examples could well be the small roomblocks we associate with Chacoan outlying communities, but the community centers are unrecognized.

## The Identification of Chacoan Outliers

A major problem in identification exists with most Chaco outliers, not just those in the Cibola area. The Pecos Classification essentially assumes that multistoried sites are PIII. In areas away from Chaco, this is translated to mean post-A.D. 1100, which is then taken to be post-Chaco. When this criterion is applied, sites are frequently placed later in time than their ceramics indicate. Furthermore, excavated examples of good Chaco outliers almost always show evidence for reoccupation after the end of the Chaco interaction sphere. Thus, sites known only from survey are frequently considered to post-date Chaco when in fact they are contemporary with it.

In spite of these difficulties, we have several criteria for suggesting sites are Chaco related. Throughout the entire Ansazi area, multistoried sites are constructed between A.D. 1000 and 1130 and again post-A.D. 1240. Only a few examples are known from the interval A.D. 1130–1240. In the Cibola area, all of the post-A.D. 1240 multistoried sites are architecturally distinct from any form of Chacoan site (as is discussed below); thus, one can have some confidence about the date of a multistoried site without appeal to ceramics.

A candidate for a Chaco outlier community is a multistoried structure where rooms are to the north or west and a single-story section is to the south or east. That is, bighouses are not equally high on all sides, but tier down to the "front," just like Pueblo Bonito does. They have in-roomblocks, round kivas, frequently in two-storied areas of the structure. In addition, there is usually a round, masonry-lined great kiva and a nearby group of small single-storied roomblocks. These latter units may include jacal structures. Ceramics may include later types, such as Tularosa Black-on-white or St. Johns Polychrome, but they will also include Red Mesa Black-on-white, Reserve Black-on-white, and Puerco or early Wingate Black-on-red. In contrast, later post-Chaco sites will, if multistoried, be inward-facing around a cental plaza with two-storied rooms on all sides, and there will be virtually no early ceramics.

Great kivas present a terminological problem. Chacoan great kivas all seem to have been roofed, with full height masonry walls. Post-Chacoan large round structures seem to either be large but unroofed with low walls, or roofed but much smaller than Chacoan great kivas.

The above discussion does not imply that all big sites pre-A.D. 1130 are always Chacoan outliers, or that there is no variability among outliers. Sites like the pueblo at Kiatuthlanna (Roberts 1931) are enigmatic. It has Chaco-like features, namely the roomblock kivas and the building of suites of identically shaped rooms. It apparently lacks a great kiva and is adobe, not cored masonry. While there are outliers that have some adobe construction (e.g., Bis-sa-ani) and no great kivas, Kiatuthlanna is missing a number of the suite of traits that mark Chacoan outliers. Similarly, Carter Ranch (Martin et al. 1964) possibly had some two-storied rooms along the back portion; it has an in-roomblock kiva, an adjacent great kiva, and is apparently surrounded by smaller pueblos. However, in more subtle ways, it does not fit the model of an outlier. The great kiva does not have good Chaco features. The rooms are not extra large; there is no orderly, rapid building plan. Walls are not core and veneer. Thus, Carter Ranch seems to mimic an outlier. Obviously, if correct, this interpretation has sociopolitical implications that are important, but little can be said at this point.

## The Nature of the Chaco Interaction Sphere in the Cibola Area

It is one thing to claim the presence of Chaco related sites in the Cibola areas, it is quite another to characterize what their presence represented in terms of local sociopolitical integration. It is, of course, premature to address these questions. Only a handful of Chacoan related communities have been studied in Cibola, almost all excavations were 50 or more years ago, and none was studied with these questions in mind.

The theoretical and methodological implications of these questions are really beyond the scope of the current paper. In spite of these practical limitations, a few ideas can be presented. In the western Zuni Reservation area, it seems that outlying communities were dense, reminiscent of the pattern close to Chaco. I suspect that in this location almost all the population was integrated into the system and there were essentially no fully autonomous communities. Further south and west, the density of Chacoan communities may well be lower, and one can envision Chacoan communities surrounded by other autonomous communities that had only a loose connection with the interaction sphere.

Who occupied the outlying communities? Were these actual satellites, populated by people from Chaco Canyon, or were they inhabited by the local, previously existing population? This is one of the few aspects of the Chaco interaction sphere where fairly strong inferences can be made. Based on the estimates presented by Hayes (1981), population growth in Chaco Canyon itself was substantial between the interval A.D. 800 and 1130. Given realistic growth rates in the 0.3 percent range (or even up to 0.7 percent) (Hassan 1978; Cowgill 1975), an initial indigenous Canyon population could have just about grown to the degree observed for the Canyon itself, but could not produce a population surplus to found colonies. That is, one can make a better case that Chaco Canyon received immigration rather than produced emigrants.

Even if these population estimates are in error and the population increase in the Canyon was not as great as now perceived, and some net emigration did occur, it must have been insignificant. There are at least 100 outlying communities and an average population of 200 each is conservative. Thus, there were at least 20,000 people inhabiting Chacoan communities outside the Canyon and probably 40,000 is more realistic. At maximum, Chaco could have supplied two or three thousand of these people (net). The vast majority of population in any outlying community would have been local. Thus, Vivian's (1983) idea that Chaco outlier communities represent an effort to export extra people from the Canyon must be in error.

The fact that the majority of the population would have been indigenous in outliers does not mean that elite, or elite connected, individuals from the Canyon were not in residence. In fact, we can see the bighouses as elite residences as well as economic centers for the communities.

The question of how the Chaco interaction sphere worked and what produced such an expansion is far beyond the present scope and is considered elsewhere in the volume. However, the Chaco system was clearly elite-based, and resources must have been moved from outlying areas to the Canyon itself to support them. Heavy, low-value-per-pound items would have been moved the least distance. Thus, one can infer that items like corn would have been produced in nearby areas, such as the San Juan River, and carried to Chaco. Presumably more valuable items would have been produced in Cibola for transport to Chaco, but just what these might have been is unclear, although cotton goods would be an interesting possibility (Riley 1975). There does seem to be the idea that the caloric returns would prohibit long distance food transport (Lightfoot 1979). Although it may seem unlikely that food would have been transported over long distances, it is a distinct possibility. The Lightfoot model has faulty theoretical assumptions. He assumed that one must obtain many times more calories than consumed during transport. This misunderstands caloric consumption and human behavior. Based on time considerations and realistic caloric returns, food transport over 150 km was quite viable in the prehistoric Southwest.

In summary, the Cibola area contained a large number of outlying Chacoan communities. They must have played some important economic role in the interaction sphere as a whole, and presumably supplied some goods to the center. No models have been developed for the nature of this interaction, but it must have existed.

## The Chaco Collapse

Sometime between A.D. 1130 and 1150 the Chaco interaction sphere came to an abrupt end. Construction ceased in the Canyon and on outlier communities. No really large buildings were built anywhere in the former Chacoan area, with minor exceptions, for over 100 years, and round, roofed great kivas were never again built. This is, of course, a very broad and sweeping statement with considerable implications. There are large kivas after A.D. 1150. Upon scrutiny, they seem to be rectangular and not circular, but the rectangular ones do not have the floor area sizes of the Chacoan great kivas. Circular kivas are in the 9 m diameter or smaller range, and do not equate to the size of the Chacoan great kivas. The remaining kivas seem to never have been roofed, like Pecos (Kidder 1958) in the Rio Grande, and in Cibola. For whatever reasons, this long evolving tradition of circular great kivas seems to have undergone a radical transformation. Not only were the distinctive Chacoan features abandoned, but in some instances the round shape was no longer employed. Building roofed kivas, with their considerable labor requirements, which would hold most of a community, was either no longer important or was not possible given labor constraints. So the kiva tradition, which predated Chaco, was radically changed when the Chaco system collapsed.

The impact of this collapse seems to have been most severe in the areas close to the Canyon, while in more remote locales, there seems to have been a less precipitous drop in the sizes of the subsequent communities. However, even in Cibola, the immediate post-A.D. 1130 era seems to be one of little construction activity. However, a new set of developments was soon taking place that resulted in new and greater agglomeration of population and in the building of the largest pueblos ever seen in Cibola.

What seems to have happened in Cibola, and in the rest of the former Chacoan interaction sphere, is that the population began to revert to a more dispersed settlement pattern with no large pueblos. However, the population did not fully revert to the patterns seen before A.D. 1000. Masonry pueblos of approximately 20 to 40 rooms were common and there was still a tendency for loose agglomeration. While some of this clustering may have resulted from corporate labor for irrigation, in most areas there does not seem to be such a need. Because agglomeration continued over most of the Cibola area, if not the entire Anasazi area, it is reasonable to suspect that a series of social institutions and technologies developed during the time of Chaco that resulted in the real or perceived need to agglomerate. Such a need may have been ceremonial, social, or defensive. This real or perceived need was beyond what had existed pre-Chaco. That is, I argue that participation in the Chaco system resulted in the evolution of social institutions that required adequate numbers of participants, which were available with aggregation. These institutions, and consequently the need to agglomerate, did not disappear with the Chaco collapse.

Although there was not a full reversion to pre-A.D. 1000 behavior, there was surely a change back to a more egalitarian society; there is no evidence for anything like the Chacoan chiefdom level organization during the rest of Cibolan history.

## THE REORGANIZATION PERIOD (A.D. 1150–1300)

The period A.D. 1150–1300, termed *Reorganization*, witnessed a series of changes in the Cibola area that resulted in a major restructuring of the communities and the subsequent abandonment of much of the area. These events are paralleled over much of the Anasazi area, and both general patterns and apparently more unique aspects can be delineated. Almost everyone who has worked in the Cibola area has noted that there was a tendency for movement of population to higher elevations beginning in the 1100s, becoming most noticeable in the 1200s. Areas above 7,000 feet were only sparsely utilized previous to this time, but by the late 1200s vast areas below this elevation were uninhabited, and a considerable population resided at 7,000–7,400 feet.

As interesting as this pattern is, it is sometimes forgotton that the region's entire population did not participate in this move. There was a second locus of population, and this was in the lower reaches of the area, especially along the Little Colorado and its major tributaries (Spier 1918). Because the Cibola area is generally higher in the east than it is in the west, we find populations at high altitudes in New Mexico and at low altitudes in Arizona, with the mid elevations lightly utilized (Kintigh 1985). This is in contrast to the earlier pattern, when the middle level elevations were much more intensively utilized and the higher elevations lightly utilized. While it may appear that low, riverine areas were more intensively used than before, I suspect that this is a function of the high visibility of the later, larger sites, and the lower visibility and alluviation of the earlier communities. I suspect that the well-watered floodplains of the Little Colorado and lower Puerco were always intensively used.

While these two site location patterns may appear contradictory, I think they represent two different solutions to the same problem—namely, reduced rainfall and a consequent reduction in available farmland. Even under conditions of poor rainfall, there would have been enough water along the lower reaches of the exotic drainages to have supplied irrigation farming. In the Southwest in general, the higher the elevation, the greater the precipitation (Tuan et al. 1973). The movement to the 7,000–7,400 foot range would have been to areas of greater overall precipitation. However, at higher elevations there is a concomitant decrease in the growing season. For example, on average there should be about two inches more annual precipitation at El Morro than at Zuni Pueblo. Kintigh (1985) notes, however, at Zuni only 20 percent of the years have less than 130 frost-free days, while at El Morro 84 percent of the years have short, frost-free seasons.

Thus at El Morro, the growing season is too short for modern corn to mature in most years. Given the very large population resident in the area at A.D. 1300, corn farming must have been successfully practiced. One viable model is that with the drought conditions of the late 1200s, there was a concomitant increase in the number of frost-free days, thereby making the higher elevations a viable place to farm. A slightly different model would have little actual change in the length of the growing season, but the population switched to a faster-maturing corn (presumably with a somewhat lower yield) in order to take advantage of the greater precipitation and higher water table of the high elevation valleys.

Regardless of why the shift to higher elevation occurred, it definitely did. The clearest example of the shift is in the Zuni drainage, but other high elevation sites occur.

The history of the early period of the shift is poorly known. Sites that can definitely be placed in the A.D. 1150–1250 span are seemingly scarce (Kintigh 1985). In some ways, this 100-year span is the least understood of the entire prehistoric sequence. I believe that there was a trend toward movement to higher elevations, but it was minor until the mid 1200s, so that the residents of the area from A.D. 1150 to 1250 continued to occupy much of the areas used by the pre-A.D. 1150 population. This led to continued occupation, reoccupation, and nearby occupation of the previous site clusters associated with the Chaco communities, resulting in a very confused picture. This seems to be the case for the Vernon area in Arizona. There, Broken K Pueblo (Martin et al. 1967), Mineral Creek (Martin et al. 1961), the Joint site (Martin et al. 1975), and Rim Valley Pueblo (Martin et al. 1962) all fall within this time span. Broken K is larger than most sites in this interval. The others are typical examples of post-Chaco style site sizes and settings along the lower drainages, even though they lie at the west of the area under consideration.

The movement to high elevations accelerated after A.D. 1250 and patterns become increasingly clear. They are perhaps best known for the El Morro Valley (Watson et al. 1980; LeBlanc 1978; Kintigh 1985), but this valley is only an example of a more general pattern.

The El Morro Valley lies at an elevation of about 7,200 feet or higher. It is bounded on the northeast by the Zuni Mountains and is loosely defined on the south by a series of tilted mesas. Although it ultimately drains into the Zuni River, much of the area is in fact undrained and ponds occur even today. The mountains provide a potential source of faunal resources. The potential for water control or irrigation is minimal. There is no economic reason for the population to aggregate and good reasons not to. Sites dating prior to A.D. 1250 occur in the valley, but they are small and sparse and could not have represented a major population at any time.

## The Scribe S Phase

The initial major population in the valley must have been the result of migration. The population was seminucleated. Clusters of pueblos were founded in at least seven localities. This has been termed the Scribe S phase (Watson et al. 1980). Each locality or community consisted of up to 18 discrete pueblos spread over an area of about a square kilometer. Pueblos ranged in size from 1 or 2 rooms up to about 40, but most were under 20. They were single-storied, some with kivas in front.

In many ways these communities were like those of the Chaco interval. The individual pueblos retained the orientation pattern existing from the Initiation (BMIII) period. In contrast to the Chaco communities, there were far fewer fieldhouses or agriculture related limited use sites surrounding the Scribe S phase communities. It appears that fields were closer to the communities and less time was spent away from the community. Also, of course, there are no bighouses.

More unrecognized is that there are no great kivas. There are three potential types of public ceremonial facilities, but no round, roofed kivas of diameters in excess of 12 m. It is my opinion that this is true for all of Cibola, and in fact seems to be true for all of the Anasazi area. Great kivas of the Anasazi-Chaco tradition disappear after A.D. 1150.

Two further aspects of the Scribe S phase communities are different from Chacoan communities. First, the pueblos are clustered tightly. Generally, they are spaced 30–40 m apart so that the community is compact and discrete. Secondly, there is almost always one or more pueblos situated on a high point of land with a good view. In light of subsequent settlement patterns, I believe this site setting pattern is related to defense.

The Scribe S phase sites show only moderate trash deposition. Pueblos are built haphazardly without overall planning, and there is little remodeling or other evidence of time depth. Our current estimate is that most were founded after A.D. 1250 and all were abandoned by A.D. 1280. It is estimated that the valley contained some 2,000 rooms at the peak of the Scribe S phase, almost all of which were occupied contemporaneously (Watson et al. 1980).

## The Muerto Phase

At about A.D. 1275–1280, a radical transformation took place in El Morro that forever changed the organizational aspect of Cibola communities. This episode was not unique to the Valley, and examples from other areas will be considered later. The Scribe S phase communities were abandoned, and new, large, planned pueblos were built in their place. The large pueblos were built rapidly and the earlier Scribe S phase pueblos were dismantled so the wall stones could be reused to build the new large communities.

Sites such as Atsinna (Woodbury 1956), Kluckholn Ruin (Togeye), and Pueblo de Los Muertos contained 500–1,000 rooms and were remarkably similar. They consisted of four or more rows of rooms built around a central plaza. The outer two rows of rooms were two-storied, resulting in a two-storied unbroken wall around the perimeter. Evidence for Pueblo de Los Muertos, and to a lesser extent Atsinna, shows that the building of these pueblos was rapid and organized.

The Pueblo de Los Muertos construction plan was as follows. An interior wall was built parallel to the outer wall some 6 m away. Every 2.5 m, walls were abutted at right angles to the long walls, thereby creating rectangular modules, which were quite uniform in size (6 m by 2.5 m). These modules were each subdivided into two rooms by a partition wall narrower than any of the other interior walls. The end result was several hundred uniform cells, each measuring about 3 by 2.5 m. Additional rows of rooms were added to the inside of these double rows. It will be argued later that these sites are defensive.

A secure domestic water supply seems to have been a high priority for these sites. The Cienega site had a walk-in well; Atsinna had cisterns beside the ruin; and Pueblo de los Muertos had a short canal bringing water to the site edge.

There were three forms of ceremonial or public architecture. These were rectangular, in-roomblock kivas, generally about twice the size of a domestic room. The second type is larger. In the plaza of the Mirabal site and Atsinna are kivas that were 9 m in diameter. These were basically round but did not have great kiva-like features. Several hundred yards away from the Cienega site was a large 20+ m diameter stone-walled circle. The wall was only a few courses high and the feature had never been roofed. This feature was reminiscent of the unroofed, low walled, large circular feature McGimsey (1980) found at site 143 on Mariana Mesa. The large circular feature may have been a degenerate form of a true great kiva. The 9 m diameter kivas could have had some similarity to the previous Chaco-style great kivas, but they clearly served a different function vis-a-vis the community as a whole. Incidentally, the small, circular great kiva at the Mineral Creek site (Martin et al. 1961) seems equivalent to the El Morro kivas.

## General Patterns in the A.D. 1275–1300 Interval

The population movement into the El Morro Valley, and the shift from the discrete Scribe S phase pueblos to massive El Morro phase pueblos is replicated over a large area. In all cases, subtle ceramic changes show that the Scribe S phase communities are earlier than the massive pueblos. In the Cebolleta Mesa area, discrete pueblos much like the Scribe S phase sites are found all around the Calabash Ruin. This site sits on a mesa much like El Morro, only the access routes are blocked by massive walls. The Calabash Ruin contains upwards of 500 rooms. To the south, in Cebolla Canyon, is a cluster of pueblos equivalent to the Scribe S phase and an unfinished big pueblo is on a nearby hill. The outer walls were laid, but the rooms never completed.

Further to the south, the Newton site, again on a hill top, has a large rectangular room group and appended to it is a circular roomblock in a configuration very reminiscent of the Togeye Ruin in El Morro. Further to the east, the Gallinas Spring Pueblo, again of massive size, sits directly on the spring. Just upstream, on a hillside location, is a Scribe S-like community of discrete pueblos.

Site 616 is similar to the Muerto phase pueblos, including a walk-in well (McGimsey 1980). The nearby site, 187, seems to be a good example of a Scribe S phase-like pueblo, although the full settlement pattern was not delineated. Both McGimsey and Danson note other examples in the Quemado region. I know of no other examples further to the south in New Mexico.

A settlement complex on Coyote Creek upstream from St. Johns seems to be another example of the same pattern. Sites of this time range, however, are not limited to only high elevations. Slightly lower along major drainages are a few other examples, such as the Manuelito Canyon complex. This situation is particularly confusing because there is a Chaco community in the canyon, and while Reed (1938) perceived the difference, Weaver (1978) did not. There is a community of late A.D. 1200 discrete pueblos and a very large pueblo, and they probably represent the same temporal sequence as in El Morro.

Heshotauthla on the Zuni River is another lower-elevation example. Here, some of the earlier, detached pueblos have been excavated (Zier 1976) and they conform closely with the Scribe S phase El Morro pattern. Kintigh

(1985) has documented 17 big sites that may emulate the Muerto phase pattern, although this interpretation of them differs somewhat. Not all sites fit this pattern perfectly. Hooper Ranch is smaller (Martin et al. 1961) than most, but may have the same inward-facing plan. Table Rock is also smaller (about 60–100 rooms) than typical, and is not inward facing. The relation- ship of these sites to the larger, more typical sites of this time range is unclear.

Further afield, much of the "Kintiel Focus," and in particular, Wide Ruin to the northwest of Zuni, seem to represent the same pattern. The pattern in the Grasshopper area is quite similar (Graves et al. 1982), except that many of the big sites do not seem to be as rapidly constructed as the El Morro examples. In fact, I believe that this pattern of construction of very large sites occurs over much of the Anasazi area at this time in one form or another. In some places, the big sites are represented by cliff dwellings, and in others, by sites like the late component at Yellow Jacket in southwestern Colorado. In almost all areas, clusters of smaller pueblos are replaced by large defensive sites and after rather short periods, the big sites are aban- doned, a pattern that generally coincides with the Great Drought.

## Interpretation of the Late A.D. 1200s and Early 1300s Developments

A number of different models and interpretation of these events have, or can be, proposed. The rationale of the movement into high elevations has al- ready been mentioned. The shift from small sites to big ones is both intrigu- ing and ultimately of considerable importance. I feel the only viable model is a shift to a defensive posture, and Davis (1965) summarizes some of the arguments for the northern Southwest as a whole.

There are several lines of evidence for the shift to defensive sites. First, the preceding sites are already in a semidefensive state with their clustering and their line of sight in all directions. The rapid abandonment, dismantling of the small sites, and the organized building of the large ones was not the result of a gradual development. Not only would the size of the large sites have provided some protection, but their outer two-storied rooms would have produced a high defensive encircling wall. Moreover, the focus on secure domestic water, such as the walk-in wells and spring locations inside the walls, is unprecedented. We also have evidence of fierce conflagrations at some of the smaller, earlier pueblos. This occurred at the Scribe S site and at a small site near Grasshopper (Graves et al. 1982). There are also two apparent violent deaths (of six individuals) and 14 instances of disarticulated human bones, perhaps representing unburied bodies, at site 616 near Quemado (McGimsey 1980).

While superficially this may not appear to be much evidence for warfare or defense, what should we expect? First, we must reject the idea that warfare was not common in the prehistoric Southwest (Woodbury 1959). Warfare in one locale should result in neighboring groups taking precautionary measures. The big sites were designed as forts and most of the time should have been successful as forts. Thus, widespread and chronic warfare should by no means result in all pueblos being burnt, nor should all bodies show evidence of violent death. I believe the direct evidence for warfare, based on the amount of excavations undertaken to date, is as much as we might expect given the above premises.

This shift to defensive sites is not limited to the Cibola area. Numerous similar sites exist in the Mogollon rim country. Similar examples in the Chaco area include Crumbled House (Marshall et al. 1979), and perhaps Helicopter Mesa on the Puerco of the east. In the Mesa Verde area the Hovenweep towers, the cliff dwellings, and the fort-like constructions at Yellow Jacket and Mud Springs also point to this phenomenon. In Cibola, in Mesa Verde, and in the Rio Grande a similar pattern seems to occur. Small sites are situated high, where apparently the ability to see long distances and the height itself were important. Where sites are large, at least in a relative sense, location on a secure water source seems to be a major concern. Thus, most Hovenweep-like towns are not lookouts, but are defendable and have secure water supplies, as is the case for many cliff dwellings. The sequence in the Long House Valley-Tsegi Canyon area closely parallels the Cibola pattern—only the big sites are replaced by cliff dwellings. In sum, this shift to defensive sites just prior to A.D. 1300 occurs over most of the Anasazi area and explanations must be general enough to account for all these instances.

Viable explanations are not easily generated. There is some slight evidence that there is a north-south gradient to this shift. Defensive sites seem to be built circa A.D. 1250–1275 in the Mesa Verde area (Robinson and Harrill 1974), sometime around A.D. 1280 in the Cibola area (Watson et al. 1980), and at about A.D. 1300 at Grasshopper (Dean and Robinson 1982). Even if this time trend is real, it is at best only 40–50 years long. It is hard to see how any nomads could have either had such an impact over an area or filled it so quickly. This then leaves interpuebloan warfare. While there is historical evidence for intergroup warfare, the motivation for warfare over distances such as between Zuni and Hopi, is hard to fathom. Intermittent local raiding to capture more arable land is the most likely, but hardly demonstrated, explanation for the shift to defensive sites.

As I mentioned in Chapter 6 on the southern Mogollon, the possible impact of the collapse of the Casas Grandes interaction sphere on the Anasazi area during this time cannot be overlooked. At this point, no mechanism of how the collapse might have triggered warfare is offered, except that the presence of Casas Grandes may have imposed an artificial peace, a sort of pax Britannia, which disappeared with the Casas Grandes collapse.

## POST-A.D. 1300 DEVELOPMENTS IN THE CIBOLA AREA

Unlike many parts of the Southwest, the occupational sequence of the Cibola area did not come to a close in the A.D. 1300s. It appears that much of the southern Cibola area was abandoned by the early A.D. 1300s, as were many of the higher areas around Zuni. Population still existed along the Zuni and the Little Colorado rivers. Neighboring population in the Mogollon rim country lasted to nearly A.D. 1400. A similar series of abandonments and surviving sites occur in the Hopi area and to the west. By the late 1400s all the intervening area was devoid of pueblos, with clusters remaining only at Hopi, Zuni, and Acoma. There is no escaping the fact that the population declined. Interestingly, the size of the sites did not decline. We know that areas were abandoned because there are fewer and fewer sites, but in areas that were occupied, the population size of individual pueblos did not decline.

It appears that there was a need, real or perceived, for the minimum pueblo size to stay large. As the population of one pueblo declined, I believe they amalgamated with others so that the size of the pueblo stayed large or even grew, but the number of pueblo communities steadily dwindled.

This same phenomenon existed at a larger level. Initially, these large pueblos were spread rather evenly over much of Cibola, but as they declined in numbers, they began to occur in clusters. Not only do we end up with the Zuni and Hopi clusters, but somewhat earlier we have the Homolovi area cluster, another near Four Mile Ruin and another in the Chavez-Kinnikinnick area. In fact, for the A.D. 1400s one can see three foci: Hopi, Zuni, and the area south of the Little Colorado, each producing a distinctive pottery style—Sikyatki Polychrome, Matsaki Polychrome, and Four Mile Polychrome. These three types shared a general, and unique, design conception. Thus, in a sense, the old Cibola area was split into western (Four Mile) and eastern (Matsaki) traditions. One can trace this division back to the early A.D. 1300s, when Heshota Polychrome becomes distinctive from Pinedale Polychrome.

On the other hand, there is a new level of similarity in material culture and architecture, extending from Hopi down to the Mogollon rim and over to Zuni and Acoma, that first becomes apparent in the late A.D. 1200s. This is Reed's (1948) concept of Western Pueblo. These spatially diverse areas had distinctive histories up to the period of Chaco expansion. After it, they share a number of ceramic and architectural traits and settlement layout patterns. During the 1200s in particular, all of the area is quite similar ceramically, and local variability subsequently increases over time.

I believe that there were several factors that led to this similarity. The first was that all of this area (with exceptions, such as part of the Hopi area) was within the Chaco interaction sphere. This would lead to the development of common traditions. Secondly, all of the area underwent the shift to defensive sites in the late 1200s. This could have resulted in further shared responses to the problems inherent in living in such large communities. Finally, as the population dwindled and groups recombined, traditions became shared over a wide area. The Kayenta branch migration into the Point of Pines area was a classic example of this process (Haury 1958).

## Population Decline

The decline in population over great areas of the Southwest, beginning in the A.D. 1300s and becoming more apparent in the 1400s, is of considerable interest. I do not believe emigration can account for the decline. Although the Rio Grande area may have received an influx of people at this time, and possibly the Hopi area, they are the only areas that did. The entire former area of the Chaco interaction sphere saw marked decline, as did the southern Mogollon, the Mogollon rim, the Verde, and even the Hohokam areas.

Zuni has been considered to have received population from the rest of the Cibola region. This cannot be the case as is usually conceived because the population of the Zuni area also declined, and while the final population may have consisted of people from various parts of Cibola and beyond, the presence of a sizable population at Zuni cannot account for the declines seen elsewhere. Kintigh (1985) discusses a number of sites occupied between A.D. 1250 and 1550 in the Zuni drainage area. While I do not fully accept his interpretation, he has 14 pueblos containing 4,550 occupied rooms at A.D. 1300, 11 pueblos containing 3,250 rooms occupied at A.D. 1400, and 8 pueblos with 2,000 rooms at A.D. 1500. While these figures do not directly translate into population, they are a close enough approximation for our purposes. I believe Kintigh has underestimated the population at A.D. 1300, but even taking his lower figures, the decline is marked. His sample does not include any of the Quemado area sites, none from the Mogollon Rim, none from Cebolleta Mesa and south, and none from the rest of the Little Colorado. All these other areas eventually dropped to zero population, while the Zuni area saw a greater than 50 percent drop in 200 years.

While it is possible that some portion of this population became nomadic and therefore became archaeologically less visible, this cannot be an explanation for the population decline. First, if any large portion of the population at A.D. 1300 had become nonfarmers, they could not all have been supported in the area as hunters and gatherers. Secondly, while a small fraction of these numbers might go unnoticed, we would surely find evidence of many thousands of people operating with this strategy over several hundred years.

What caused such a population decline at Zuni and elsewhere? We can consider environment and social causes. The A.D. 1300s and 1400s do not appear to be particularly dry. However, it is possible that this was a period of much colder climate than average. Whether a "little ice age" had an impact on the Southwest is not clear, but such a possibility might exist and could conceivably be responsible for the decline.

An alternative social explanation is equally undemonstrated, but is worth considering. When the population aggregated into very large settlements in the late A.D. 1200s over most of the Southwest, this process may have set off a series of behavioral responses that were very detrimental to population growth. First, if warfare were the initial triggering mechanism, it could have continued on in the form of raiding. Warfare could have quickly become institutionalized. War priests could have had increasing power, scalp societies could have developed—warfare could have become self perpetuating. A Hatfield and McCoy process could have begun that did not immediately stop just because the causes that started it in the 1200s ceased to exist. We should expect that it would have stopped sometime after its causes disappeared, and perhaps the existence of smaller pueblos at Zuni in 1500, for example, Kwakina and Halona, which are not defensive, may be an indication warfare was on the wane. However, one pueblo, probably Hawikuh, was noted in the 1540s as having an encircling wall. It is quite conceivable that the decline in warfare was gradual and its existence in one form or another for 200 years took a considerable toll on the population.

Another factor debilitating population may have been at work. Aggregates of 1,000 or more people are not very adaptive in the Southwest. Although they did exist earlier, they were found in special areas or developed under special circumstances. The average distance to fields, wild foods, and fuel wood is greatly increased if a large number of people are all located in the same place. Moreover, the total resource area that can be exploited is smaller than if the population is spread over a large area. Exchange would provide less of a buffer under these circumstances because what would be a poor crop year for one would be poor for the total community. Turner (personal communication) feels that there was increased infant mortality due to iron deficiency anemia at this time, presumably as a result of decreased meat in the diet, or undernourishment in general. The combined effects of nutritional deficiencies, subsistence problems, the possible increase in disease because of living in large groups, and warfare may have been sufficient to cause the observed population declines. In general, this intriguing question has been too little considered, and we are far from a fully satisfactory answer.

## Settlement and Community Structure

By the A.D. 1500s all of Cibola was abandoned except for the few villages along the Zuni River. Here, based on the plan of Hawikuh, the inward-facing village plan seen for so long was breaking down. In a sense, the situation came full circle. The people of Zuni were farming along an optimal stretch of the river. They were living in basically autonomous communities, and had few public works, not a different adaptation from that seen at the beginning of PII some 600 years before.

At about A.D. 1400–1450 the former Western Anasazi and northern Mogollon area was greatly depopulated, but what was the nature of the interrelations of the remaining groups? While there still seems to have been some intergroup strife, there was also considerable interaction. By 1400 the Southwest had two polar centers: the Classic Hohokam and the upper-middle Rio Grande Valley. The former was in all likelihood a ranked society, in some ways similar to those of the Chaco and Casas Grandes systems. The Rio Grande was not as complexly organized.

Between these two population centers were a number of smaller population aggregates. These included the historic groups of Acoma, Hopi, and Zuni, and probably also included the Homolovi group. Zuni may well have served a middleman role in the exchange of goods between the Rio Grande and the Hohokam. Zuni seems to have been engaged in considerable trade in the historic period, yet had few local products that others would have wanted. As the number of small population aggregates continued to dwindle by the early A.D. 1500s, Zuni's role in any long-distance trade would have increased. Thus, in a sense, Zuni came to be on the extreme edge of the former Anasazi distribution (now centered on the Rio Grande) and served as a link to the Sonoran Desert.

The nature of the social organization at Zuni at this time is less clear. Wilcox (1981) makes the point that there is some evidence from the ethnohistoric literature for more than a purely egalitarian organization. The fact that the very late pueblos are usually in small clusters is also suggestive of some form of organization that transcended each village. Nevertheless, there is nothing in the archaeological record, nor in the ethnological record, that points to true chiefdom level organization. In particular, there is nothing to suggest a level of organization at all comparable to the one that must have existed at Chaco.

## PATTERNS AND CONCLUSIONS

The history of Cibola can be viewed from several perspectives. One perspective is the cultural and/or political affiliations of its inhabitants. In the early centuries A.D. the area had a Mogollon aspect, and at best was a fuzzy zone between the developing Anasazi and Mogollon traditions. However, by the A.D. 700–800s, the region was typically Anasazi in terms of pottery designs, house form, and other traits. It appeared to be developing into a distinct regional entity, just as the Kayenta or Mesa Verde areas.

During the A.D. 1000s, the entire region came within the influence of the Chaco interaction sphere. The northern portion of Cibola seems to have been fully integrated into the system. The southern area was at least partially integrated and the Chaco system dipped into the former northern Mogollon area, forever destroying the earlier boundary between the Cibola and northern Mogollon areas.

After the Chaco collapse, the former Cibola area was not distinct. It shared a broad series of cultural traits and a similar culture history with the inhabitants of the southern Anasazi region and northern Mogollon areas. The full effects of incorporation into the Chaco sphere and the consequences of the sphere's collapse are still largely unrecognized.

It was during the post-A.D. 1250 span that Cibola began to reemerge as a distinct entity, and then a series of settlement pattern shifts forever altered the basic community structure. There was a movement to higher elevations, and into large, agglomerated defensive pueblos. During the 1300s, the population relocated to lower areas, but the use of large pueblos continued until Spanish contact. By the 1300s, the Cibola ceramics were distinctive, but shared a ceramic tradition with the Little Colorado and the Hopi areas, a sharing that persisted until the 1800s. Dwindling population left the six Zuni pueblos as the heirs to the entire Cibola area; but, as for most of its history, Cibola was on a periphery. This time it was on the periphery of the population centered to the east, on the Rio Grande.

Demographic trends are hard to characterize except in impressionistic and general ways. For most of the Southwest there seems to have been a long-term increase in the population beginning at least by circa A.D. 300–500. This population growth seems to have peaked at the time of Chaco. At this time the population appears to have been quite high and perhaps stressing the resource base. If we assume each Chaco community consisted of 200–300 people and were, at the most dense spacing, some 16 km apart, we have densities of about 1–1.5 people per square kilometer. This density would, however, give a figure of 200 outliers, and a total population of 40,000–60,000 people for the maximum Cibola area considered here. These numbers appear to be too large. However, it is not unreasonable to believe that there were 50 outlying communities in the Cibola area (or equivalent populations not participating in the system). This would give a total population of 10,000–15,000. One could argue that this number is probably conservative.

Population estimates can be made for the Zuni area circa 1300. Taking Kintigh's (1985) conservative estimate, we have a population of about 9,300 people. As we know, this pattern was replicated over much of the rest of Cibola, so the total population must have been several times this amount. Thus, even by this conservative estimate, we get a population in excess of 20,000 and it could easily have been 40,000 at A.D. 1300. At this point we cannot tell whether the population peaked in the Chaco period or continued to grow until A.D. 1300. We cannot estimate the maximum population size in either interval and any estimate between 20,000 and 60,000 can be defended.

The population diminished dramatically over the next two centuries. Various estimates exist for the historic Zuni pueblos, but all realistic estimates are under 10,000. Reasonable room counts are under 3,000 for these pueblos (Kintigh estimates 2,400 rooms, 4,577 people). One must conclude that the total regional population declined to between a fifth and a tenth of its former maximum.

The nature of the causes of culture change in the Cibola area are hard to consider, in part because there is little agreement on what the changes were. No convincing simple environmental explanation has been put forth for the development of the Chaco system or for its ultimate expansion, nor for its collapse. While population shifts in the A.D. 1200s and 1300s may be accounted for by climatic regime changes, no model seems to be able to account for the subsequent population decline.

Thus, we must evoke sociopolitical explanations for many of the events that occurred in the post-A.D. 900 period. The two most important factors seem to be the development and collapse of the Chaco system and the outbreak of warfare or its threat in the late 1200s. Both occur over a much broader area than Cibola alone, and both must relate to events and circumstances that are pan-regional. The most intriguing aspects of Cibola history are not understandable by considering the region alone.

# REFERENCES

Anyon, Roger, and Steven A. LeBlanc
 1984 *The Galaz Ruin: A Mimbres Village in Southwestern New Mexico.* University of New Mexico Press, Albuquerque.

Berman, Mary Jane
 1979 *Cultural Resources Overview, Socorro Area, New Mexico.* USDA Forest Service, Southwestern Region, Albuquerque and Bureau of Land Management, New Mexico State Office, Santa Fe, New Mexico.

Bullard, W. R., Jr.
 1962 *The Cerro Colorado Site and Pithouse Architecture in Southwestern United States Prior to A.D. 900.* Papers of the Peabody Museum of American Archaeology and Ethnology 44(2). Harvard University, Cambridge.

Cordell, Linda, and Fred Plog
 1979 Escaping the Confines of Normative Thought: A Reevaluation of Puebloan Prehistory. *American Antiquity* 44:405–429.

Cowgill, George L.
 1975 On Causes and Consequences of Ancient and Modern Population Changes. *American Anthropologist* 77(3):505–525

Danson, Edward
 1957 *An Archaeological Survey of West Central New Mexico and East Central Arizona.* Papers of the Peabody Museum of Archaeology and Ethnology 44(1). Harvard University, Cambridge.

Davis, Emma Lou
 1965 Small Pressures and Cultural Drift as Explanations for Abandonment of the San Juan Area, New Mexico and Arizona. *American Antiquity* 30(3):353–355.

Dean, Jeffrey S., and William J. Robinson
 1982 Dendrochronology of Grasshopper Pueblo. In *Multidisciplinary Research at Grasshopper Pueblo, Arizona,* edited by W. A. Longacre, S. J. Holbrook, and M. W. Graves. Anthropological Papers of the University of Arizona, No. 40. Tucson

Ferg, Allan
 1978 *The Painted Cliffs Rest Area: Excavations along the Rio Puerco, Northeastern Arizona.* Arizona State Museum Contribution to Highway Salvage Archaeology in Arizona No. 50.

Fowler, Andrew P., John R. Stein, and Roger Anyon
 1987 *An Archaeological Reconnaissance of West-Central New Mexico: The Anasazi Monuments Project.* Submitted to Office of Cultural Affairs, Historic Preservation Division, State of New Mexico.

Gladwin, Harold S.
 1945 *The Chaco Branch: Excavations at White Mound and in the Red Mesa Valley.* Medallion Papers No. 33. Gila Pueblo, Globe, Arizona.

Gratz, Kathleen E.
    n.d.        *Archaeological Excavations Along Route Z4 Near Zuni, New Mexico.* Museum
                of Northern Arizona Research Paper 7. Flagstaff.

Graves, Michael W., Sally J. Holbrook, and William J. Longacre
    1982        Aggregation and Abandonment at Grasshoper Pueblo: Evolution Trends
                in the Late Prehistory of East-Central Arizona. In *Multidisciplinary Research
                at Grasshopper Pueblo, Arizona,* edited by W. A. Longacre, S. J. Holbrook,
                and M. W. Graves. Anthropological Papers of the University of Arizona,
                No. 40. Tucson

Gumerman, George J., and Allan P. Olsen
    1968        Prehistory in the Puerco Valley, Eastern Arizona. *Plateau* 40:113–127

Hassan, Fekri A.
    1978        Demographic Archaeology. In *Advances in Archaeological Method and
                Theory,* vol. 1, edited by Michael B. Schiffer, pp. 49–103. Academic Press,
                New York.

Haury, Emil W.
    1950        A Sequence of Great Kivas in the Forestdale Valley, Arizona. In *For the
                Dean, Essays in Honor of Byron Cummings,* edited by Erik K. Reed and Dale
                S. King, pp. 29–39.
    1958        Evidence at Point of Pines for a Prehistoric Migration from Northern
                Arizona. In *Migrations in New World Culture History,* edited by Raymond H.
                Thompson. *University of Arizona Bulletin* 29(2). *Social Science Bulletin*
                27:1–6

Hayes, Alden C.
    1981        A Survey of Chaco Canyon Archaeology. In *Archeological Surveys of Chaco
                Canyon, New Mexico,* by A. C. Hayes, D. M. Brugge, and W. J. Judge, pp.
                1–68. National Park Service Publications in Archeology 17A: Chaco Can-
                yon Studies. Washington, D.C.

Hough, Walter
    1907        *Antiquities of the Upper Gila and Salt River Valleys in Arizona and New Mexico.*
                Bureau of American Ethnology Bulletin 35.

Kidder, Alfred V.
    1958        *Pecos, New Mexico: Archaeological Notes.* Papers of the R. S. Peabody Founda-
                tion 5. Phillips Academy, Andover.

Kintigh, Keith W.
    1985        *Settlement, Subsistence and Society in Late Zuni Prehistory.* Anthropological
                Papers of the University of Arizona No. 44. University of Arizona Press,
                Tucson.

Lancaster, James
    1983        *An Analysis of Manos and Metates from the Mimbres Valley, New Mexico.* M.A.
                Thesis, Department of Anthropology, University of New Mexico.

LeBlanc, Steven A.
    1978        Settlement Patterns in the El Morro Valley, New Mexico. In *Investigations
                of the Southwestern Anthropological Research Group: An Experiment in Archaeo-*

*logical Cooperation*, edited by R. C. Euler and G. J. Gumerman, pp. 45–51. Museum of Northern Arizona, Flagstaff.

1982    The Advent of Pottery in the Southwest. In *The Development of Southwestern Ceramic Patterns: A Comparative Review*, edited by A. Schroeder, pp. 27–52. The Arizona Archaeologist, No. 15. The Arizona Archaeological Society, Phoenix.

Lightfoot, Kent G.
1979    Food Redistribution Among Prehistoric Pueblo Groups. *The Kiva* 44:319–339.

Marshall, Michael P., John R. Stein, Richard W. Loose, and Judith E. Novotny
1979    *Anasazi Communities in the San Juan Basin*. Public Service Company of New Mexico and the Historic Preservation Bureau, Planning Division, Department of Finance and Administration of the State of New Mexico.

Martin, Paul S.
1936    *Lowry Ruin in Southwestern Colorado*. Field Museum of Natural History, Anthropological Series 23(2).

Martin, Paul S., J. N. Hill, and William A. Longacre
1967    *Chapters in the Prehistory of Eastern Arizona, III*. Fieldiana: Anthropology 57.

Martin, Paul S., John B. Rinaldo, and William A. Longacre
1961    *Mineral Creek Site and Hooper Ranch Pueblo, Eastern Arizona*. Fieldiana: Anthropology 52.

Martin, Paul S., John B. Rinaldo, William A. Longacre, Constance Cronin, Leslie G. Freeman, Jr., and James Schoenwetter
1962    *Chapters in the Prehistory of Eastern Arizona, I*. Fieldiana: Anthropology 53.

Martin, Paul S., John B. Rinaldo, William A. Longacre, Leslie G. Freeman, Jr., James A. Brown, Richard H. Hevley, and M. E. Cooley
1964    *Chapters in the Prehistory of Eastern Arizona, II*. Fieldiana: Anthropology 56.

Martin, Paul S., Ezra B. W. Zubrow, Daniel C. Bowman, David A. Gregory, John A. Hanson, Michael B. Schiffer, and David R. Wilcox
1975    *Chapters in the Prehistory of Eastern Arizona, IV*. Fieldiana: Anthropology 65.

McGimsey, Charles R., III
1980    *Mariana Mesa: Seven Prehistoric Settlements in West-Central New Mexico*. Papers of the Peabody Museum of Archaeology and Ethnology 72. Harvard University, Cambridge.

Obenauf, Margaret S.
1980    *The Chaco Roadway System*. M.A. Thesis, University of New Mexico.

Plog, Fred
1979    Prehistory: Western Anasazi. In *Handbook of North American Indians*, vol. 9, Southwest, edited by A. Ortiz, pp. 108–130. Smithsonian Institution, Washington, D.C.
1981    *Cultural Resources Overview: Little Colorado Area, Arizona*. USDA Forest Service, Southwestern Region, Albuquerque and Bureau of Land Management, Arizona State Office, Phoenix.

Powers, Robert P., William B. Gillespie, and Stephen H. Lekson
  1983    *The Outlier Survey: A Regional View of Settlement in the San Juan Basin.*
          National Park Service: Reports of the Chaco Center 3. Albuquerque.

Reed, Eric K.
  1938    Archaeological Report for Proposed Anasazi National Monument, Man-
          uelito, New Mexico. Manuscript on file, National Park Service, Southwest-
          ern Region, Santa Fe.
  1948    The Western Pueblo Archaeological Complex. *El Palacio* 55(1):9–15.

Riley, Carroll L.
  1975    The Road to Hawikuh: Trade and Trade Routes to Cibola-Zuni During
          Late Prehistoric and Early Historic Times. *The Kiva* 41(2):137–159.

Roberts, Frank H. H., Jr.
  1929    *Shabik'eschee Village, a Late Basketmaker Site in the Chaco Canyon, New Mex-
          ico,* Bureau of American Ethnology Bulletin 92.
  1931    *The Ruins at Kiatuthlanna, Eastern Arizona.* Bureau of American Ethnology
          Bulletin 100.
  1932    *Village of the Great Kivas on the Zuni Reservation, New Mexico.* Bureau of
          American Ethnology Bulletin 111.
  1939    *Archaeological Remains in the Whitewater District, Eastern Arizona, Part I:
          House Types.* Bureau of American Ethnology Bulletin 121.

Robinson, William J., and Bruce G. Harrill
  1974    *Tree-ring Dates from Colorado V: Mesa Verde Area.* Laboratory of Tree-Ring
          Research, University of Arizona, Tucson.

Schelberg, John D.
  1982    *Economic Social Development as an Adaptation to a Marginal Environment in
          Chaco Canyon, New Mexico.* Ph.D. dissertation. Department of Anthropol-
          ogy, Northwestern University, Evanston, Illinois.

Service, Elman R.
  1962    *Primitive Social Organization: An Evolutionary Perspective.* Random House,
          New York.

Spier, Leslie
  1918    Notes on Some Little Colorado Ruins. *Anthropological Papers of the Ameri-
          can Museum of Natural History* 18:333–362.

Tainter, Joseph A., and David Gillio
  1980    *Cultural Resources Overview Mt. Taylor Area, New Mexico.* USDA Forest Ser-
          vice, Southwestern Region, Albuquerque, New Mexico and Bureau of
          Land Management, New Mexico State Office, Santa Fe, New Mexico.

Tuan, Yi-Fu, Cyril E. Everard, Jerold G. Widdison, and Iven Bennett
  1973    *The Climate of New Mexico.* New Mexico State Planning Office, Santa Fe.

Vivian, R. Gwinn
  1983    The Chacoan Phenomenon: Cultural Growth in the San Juan Basin. Paper
          presented at the Second Anasazi Symposium, Salmon Ruin, New Mexico.

Wasley, William W.
  1960    Temporal Placement of Alma Neck Banded. *American Antiquity*
          25(4):599–603.

Watson, Patty Jo, Steven A. LeBlanc, and Charles L. Redman
  1980    Aspects of Zuni Prehistory: Preliminary Report on Excavations and Survey in the El Morro Valley of New Mexico. *Journal of Field Archaeology* 7:201–218.

Weaver, Donald E., Jr.
  1978    *Prehistoric Population Dynamics and Environmental Exploitation in the Manuelito Canyon District, Northwestern New Mexico.* Ph.D. dissertation, Arizona State University, Tempe.

Wendorf, Fred
  1950    The Flattop Site in the Petrified Forest National Monument. *Plateau* 22:43–51.

  1951    Archaeological Investigations in the Petrified Forest: Twin Butte Site, A Preliminary Report. *Plateau* 24:77–83.

Whalen, Michael E.
  1982    Settlement System Evolution on the Mogollon-Anasazi Frontier. Paper presented at the Mogollon Conference, Las Cruces.

Wilcox, David R.
  1981    Changing Perspectives on the Protohistoric Pueblos, A.D. 1450–1700. In *The Protohistoric Period in the North American Southwest, A.D. 1450–1700,* edited by D. R. Wilcox and W. B. Masse. Arizona State University Anthropological Research Papers No. 24.

Wilcox, David R., Thomas R. McGuire, and Charles Sternberg
  1981    *Snaketown Revisited.* Arizona State Museum Archaeological Series 155.

Woodbury, Richard B.
  1956    The Antecedents of Zuni Culture. *Transactions of the New York Academy of Science,* series 2, 18:557–563.

  1959    A Reconstruction of Pueblo Warfare in the Southwestern United States. *Actas del XXXIII Congreso Internacional de Americanistas* 2:124–133.

Zier, Christian J.
  1976    *Excavations Near Zuni, New Mexico: 1973.* Museum of Northern Arizona Research Paper 2.

GREGORY A. JOHNSON 11

# Dynamics of Southwestern Prehistory

## *Far Outside—Looking In*

## INTRODUCTION

Imperial Sasanian resistance in Khuzistan (southwestern Iran) to the advance of Arab forces of the Caliphate of 'Umar ibn al-Khattab collapsed in A.D. 642 with the fall of Susa and Jundishapur. Five millennia of pre-Islamic political complexity had come to an end. To the contemporary Archaic populations of the American Southwest, Khuzistan might as well have been Mars. I take the title of my remarks on this volume from my own specialization in that other, very distant, Southwest.

Doug Schwartz had sought a discussant for the seminar that initiated this volume who, not being among the Southwest cognoscenti, might bring some additional measure of objectivity to the proceedings. My last formal exposure to southwestern archaeology had been in the mid-1960s, when James B. Griffin was wont to afflict undergraduates with such final examination questions as, "Discuss the Anasazi development." Given the monumental volume of work completed since then, I was able to arrive at the SAR Seminar House with my "objectivity" reasonably uncontaminated by knowledge of southwestern affairs.

It would be futile of me to attempt a concluding synthesis of the material presented in this volume. I will, rather, draw upon the foregoing chapters, my notes from formal seminar sessions and upon uneven recollection of lengthy evening discussions (one in unsuccessful quest of green chili burritos) to convey an outsider's impression of some of the major issues of southwestern prehistory. I will concentrate, as did the seminar, on Anasazi-Mogollon matters of the later periods—say, post A.D. 900.

## THE "TYPICAL" SOUTHWEST

The most salient characteristic of the American Southwest as viewed from Southwest Iran was its agricultural marginality. This was "marginality" considering both local social organization and techniques available for cultivation. Most chapters address this issue in some detail, discussing the relationship of both high and low frequency environmental variability (with their spatial components) to shifting patterns of settlement and land use.

Examination of any measure of central tendency in Southwest settlement and subsistence systems reveals a pattern of very small, short-lived communities engaged in precarious cultivation necessarily supplemented by utilization of wild resources. Mobility was the major strategy used to cope with local difficulty or take advantage of distant opportunities. Plog notes that sites of only one to five rooms, representing one or perhaps two residence units, were by far the most common type of settlement. Occupations were typically of one or two generations in duration (Plog, Chapter 8; Reid, Chapter 3).

Whenever and wherever possible, groups of families cooperated in egalitarian fashion to intensify production and/or buffer one another in various ways against the short term vagaries of sedentary life (Gumerman and Dean, Chapter 4). Judge (personal communication, 1984) notes that people normally cultivated as much land as they could, hoping to keep a stored reserve sufficient to maintain their families through often experienced periods of reduced or negligible yields. Given a strategy of residential mobility, it was very much in peoples' interest to remain as informed as possible about conditions in adjacent of even distant areas. One might expect that "How are things at home?" was the most frequent question asked of visitors and other travelers.

This is hardly the common perception of the Southwest, an area whose mention elicits a picture of massive pueblos with hundreds of rooms, of elaborate kiva ceremonialism, of brilliantly painted ceramics, of extensive trade in turquoise, obsidian, and other items both precious and mundane. We are increasingly told that if only rarely, the Southwest was home to hierarchically differentiated elites whose directive and integrative influence was felt over vast territories. The depredations of European diseases and other effects of the Entrada are felt by many to have produced a historical reality whose relative simplicity masked the presence of much more complex societies in earlier periods.

Commenting on Puebloan political organization seems to be one of life's "no win" pursuits. Opinions on the same cases expressed during the seminar ranged from Appolonian egalitarianism to centrally administered and socially stratified social formations. Whatever you say, some large number of folk will be in vigorous disagreement with you.

## SOUTHWESTERN ELITES?

The proposition that areas of the Southwest were periodically under the control of elites may be considered from a number of perspectives.

### Surplus

Ancient complex societies, like modern ones, were built upon surplus. The typical problem of emergent elites was to generate and then extract food, products, and labor beyond the subsistence requirements of the producing population. The greater the difference between subsistence needs and potential productivity, the greater the potential resources available for "public affairs," be they construction of public architecture or filling of public stomachs.

Without becoming entangled in the somewhat elastic nature of "subsistence requirements," we estimate on the basis of both archaeological and ethnographic data that they could have been fulfilled on a per capita basis in much of ancient Mesopotamia through utilization of about .5 hectares of land (Johnson 1987:112; Kramer 1980:328). Ethnographic data on traditional irrigation systems indicate, on the other hand, that villagers could cultivate a maximum of about two hectares per capita (Gremliza 1962; Oates and Oates 1976:120). Given much more stable agricultural conditions than in the American Southwest, this left an extractive potential for successful elites of about 1.5 hectares of production per capita agricultural population. Phrased differently, about 75 percent of potential agricultural production could be diverted to public use without endangering the producing population.

I estimate that by the mid fourth millennium b.c., administrative elites on the Susiana Plain of southwestern Iran were able to extract in excess of 70 percent of potential maximum per capita rural surplus, or the equivalent of more than 1 hectare of production per capita (Johnson 1987:120). This surplus extraction must be considered in addition to probable greater extraction of surplus from the food producing component of administrative center populations, and utilization of very substantial center and rural labor during the nonagricultural season.

Judge (Chapter 7; personal communication 1984) indicates that in a good year in the San Juan Basin, per capita subsistence requirements could have been met by the yield of about .5 hectares of dry farmed land. Given the prevailing uncertainty about subsequent yields, however, people cultivated as much land as they could or about 1.25 hectares per capita at maximum effort. Given (1) a long series of high yields, and (2) the ability to convince households to part with their individual food reserves, maximum potential surplus would have amounted to the equivalent of about .85 hectares of production, considerably less than the 1.5 hectares estimated for Mesopotamia. I suspect that this already large difference would be much greater if we were to consider comparative yield data.

The persistent association of habitation and specialized storage rooms in pueblo architecture suggests that significant household reserves were maintained whenever possible. This, in combination with probable frequent yield shortfalls even under locally favorable conditions, suggests that effective potential surplus extraction was very limited—even when enhanced by runoff irrigation.

I do not suggest the absence of surpluses in the Southwest. Neither do I suggest that surpluses were not used for community purposes. The point here is that even potential per capita surplus was very low in any comparative sense. With this limited ability of individual households to generate surplus production, accumulation of significant surpluses by an emergent elite or other centralizing institution would have necessarily entailed articulation of a comparatively much larger number of households into a "supplier" system. Irrespective of the nature of social relations, surplus accumulation must *a priori* have been much more difficult than in other areas where we know highly complex societies developed.

One point of allocation of surplus in societies containing elites is obviously the elites themselves. Diet is a fundamental aspect of elite support, and one expects them to be especially well provisioned in comparison to a nonelite majority. Differential access to food in general and epicurean delights in particular seems to be a very common elite status marker.

Redding (1981:253) reports, for example, differential elite access to gazelle at Tepe Farukhabad (Deh Luran Plain, southwest Iran) during the mid fifth millennium B.C. Perhaps a thousand years before the establishment of state level controls over the nearby Susiana Plain, elites at Farukhabad were enjoying succulent gazelle, while others made do with the meat of common ungulates. (My own experience in the area indicates that the hard and stringy flesh of aged sheep and goat has little to recommend it.)

At first glance, a similar pattern would appear to have been present in Classic Chacoan centers. Judge (Chapter 7) notes a much higher frequency of animal bone at Pueblo Alto than would be expected given its size. Were Chacoan elites feasting on meats at the expense of their less fortunate inferiors? It seems not. Judge also notes that individuals represented in artifactually defined "elite" burials from Chaco towns suffered subsistence stress sufficient to generate skeletal pathologies, and suggests that the high frequency of animal bone at Alto was the result of consumption by both its full-time residents and by large numbers of periodic visitors.

Either the Classic Chacoan system was in dire subsistence straits indeed, or potential Chacoan "elites" were fundamentally incompetent in ensuring their own well being. If they were, as seems a more likely alternative, subsisting on a diet common to village and town, their Old World equivalents of virtually any period would have looked with disfavor on their radical egalitarian tendencies.

## Labor

Elites tend to hunger for things other than food. Most importantly, they are also noted consumers of labor. Many of the more significant uses of labor in Archaic complex societies have low archaeological visibility. Of these, simple labor in the fields was undoubtedly the most important, but can be subsumed under surplus food extraction considered earlier. (Some fields, of course, could be controlled by elites either by direct ownership, or through administration in the name of sacred or secular institutions.)

Labor was important, especially in the New World, as a means of transport. Getting things from here to there was a major problem typically resolved on someone's back. Elites have notoriously weak backs when it comes to carrying prosaic loads.

Labor was important in the context of more or less formalized neighborly dispute. Whether for offense or defense, when you need bodies, the need is pressing.

Finally, if not inclusively, labor was required for construction and maintenance of public works. Hydraulic, transport, and occasionally, defensive facilities were probably most important. Archaeological emphasis is normally given, however, to monumental public buildings that are easy to detect and, significantly, look impressive.

In all deference to monumental public architecture that both symbolizes and helps to reproduce asymmetrical social relations, it was probably less important on a day-to-day basis than the other products of labor enumerated above. Given, however, the general enthusiasm of early complex societies for monumental construction, one wonders why this should have been so.

I suspect that the greatest virtue of early monumental architecture was that, when under construction, it absorbed a lot of labor, but was not a matter of pressing importance. Having laborers about does elites little good if they have difficulty getting them to work. Regularized labor dues, justified on ideological grounds, seems an excellent way of producing a body of workers accustomed to appear to undertake whatever task is required. The problem is that tasks of a truly pressing nature tend to be both episodic and only partially predictable.

What do you do with labor that needs to be used if it is to be reliable, but for which there is little immediate need? The monumental temple is truly an answer sent by the gods. Many early elites seem to have hit upon the same scheme to absorb labor—construct large platforms or similar structures atop which to place a sacred edifice and/or underneath which to place a tomb. Such structures were labor intensive, often involved minimal skill in construction, could be completed in stages, were easily justifiable in terms of homage to the gods, instilled pride of participation in great enterprise, and looked very impressive indeed when finished.

I have taken to referring to this sort of activity as "piling behavior," which sounds more interesting than "labor sink." What you have caused to be piled is of little consequence as long as the result is stable and large. Indigenous systems of the American Midwest piled basket loads of dirt. Mesoamericans favored rubble with an attractive facing. Mesopotamians excelled in creating massive piles of mud brick, while many Europeans had a penchant for large stones. Egyptians, of course, held the world piling record, an enterprise which they soon abandoned in favor of more utilitarian uses of labor. What most of these constructions had in common beyond their bulk was that they afforded a context for mass ritual in which hundreds or thousands of the lower orders could observe their betters engaged in sacred activity for the good of society.

Pueblo architecture can certainly be substantial, if in part because of its recent date and excellent preservation. Despite their imposing appearance, construction of residential roomblocks was not a particularly labor intensive activity given overall labor availability (Judge, Chapter 7). Considering the frequency of community abandonment and resettlement involved in a strategy of adaptive mobility, residential construction could not have been considered a matter of unusual concern.

There were a variety of nonresidential structures in different areas, but few that convey the impression of labor for labor's sake. Kivas certainly represented the vast majority of specifically sacred architecture, but differed from that most often associated with early complex societies in at least three interesting respects: (1) Kivas were not labor intensive per unit space enclosed in comparison to a "structure atop a massive pile" architectural format. (2) Proliferation of kivas in roughly direct proportion to community size implied a lesser degree of centralization of ritual affairs than is evident in the sacred architecture of most early complex societies. (3) The "inward" focus of kivas was inconsistent with the mass observation of ceremonialism apparently so common in early complex societies.

The one element of the Chacoan system that most strongly suggests efforts at labor control of a "piling behavior" varient was the now famous system of Chacoan roads. Given the absence of any obvious need for prepared transport surfaces, this system has a decidedly "useless" air about it that carries an implication of systematic concern with control of labor. This was not, however, an effort that seems to have been especially appropriate to enhance the social position of local elites.

## Mortuary Ritual

Elites in most areas of the world are, of course, most easily detected in evidence of mortuary ritual. Plog (Chapter 8) and Reid (Chapter 3) pay particular attention to burial data, although they reach very different conclusions about their implication for social organization. Plog notes that by the late twelfth century, age and sex account for less than 50 percent of the observed variance in Sinagua mortuary ritual, and attributes the substantial residual to a system of social stratification. Reid interprets similar variability in burials from Grasshopper as indicative of the differential affiliation of individuals with associational groups of some (perhaps ceremonial) kind, with little indication of ascriptive status differences beyond age and sex.

There was, at least, considerable variability in mortuary treatment. Most burials were very simple while others exhibited varying degrees of elaboration, and some were fancy indeed. It was my impression from seminar discussions that "fancy" burials were almost invariably those of adults. Ascriptive status differences based on kin group membership should, on the other hand, have resulted in the "fancy" burial of significant numbers of subadults too young to have achieved much in the way of social prestige. (Infants and very young children are often accorded "special" treatment and are much less indicative of persistent social asymmetry.)

The scarce and valuable resources marking "elite" burials may also have highly peculiar distributions. Plog (Chapter 8) indicates that most "elite" burials contain trade goods of a single type in a context of the availability of variety of trade items. This is apparently the same pattern encountered by Reid at Grasshopper and seems inconsistent to me with more frequently encountered patterns of elite acquisitiveness.

Burial evidence for ranking or stratification seems ambiguous at best. There appear to be no examples of the "elderly male with a couple of gold bowls and some young females" sort that speaks much more clearly of institutionalized social asymmetry linked to scarce and valuable resources (see, for example, Neghaban 1975).

## AN ORGANIZATIONAL ALTERNATIVE TO ELITES

The reader will have discerned that I harbor grave doubts about the ontological status of Anasazi chiefdoms. Residential mobility, potential surplus availability, diet, patterns of labor investment, and variability in mortuary ritual simply seem very different from those I would expect in a hierarchical world of high borns and common folk.

What then do we do with the abundant evidence of social variability, more stable population aggregates, labor coordination, trade and exchange that exist for the prehistoric Southwest? If evidence for the presence of ranked or stratified social groups is not very convincing, attribution of these processes to the activities of egalitarian groups as we usually perceive them does not seem to be a particularly appealing alternative.

### Modularity and Sequential Hierarchy

Beyond the impression of the prehistoric Southwest as a poor place to try to be a farmer, a second puebloan characteristic is particularly striking to the outsider. You could say that these people were almost maniacally modular. I have not counted the number of uses of the term "unit pueblo" in this volume, but suspect that it is impressive.

This modularity, in addition to other factors I will discuss below, leads me to suggest that pueblo organization was fundamentally one of a type that I have called "sequential hierarchy" (Johnson 1982, 1983). Sequential hierarchy is a structure for the organization of consensus among basically egalitarian aggregates of increasing inclusiveness.

This is not the place to repeat a somewhat lengthy argument for sequential organization that incorporates data from diverse fields including social-psychology, structural and organizational sociology, ethnology, and archaeology. It appears, however, that essentially biological constraints on human information processing capabilities operationally limit the size of consensual, "task-oriented," organizations in a context in which difficulty in achieving consensus is an exponential function of organization size.

The basic idea is that if a problem is being generated by an attempt to integrate the activities of too many organizational units, there are at least three potential methods of resolving these difficulties. Organizational units can be individuals, families, residence units, local exogamous clans, etc. Alternatives for resolution of scalar difficulties include: (a) institution of a nonconsensual political hierarchy, (b) group fission, (c) institution of a consensual sequential hierarchy. In the sequential solution, basal organizational units are aggregated into larger (and thus fewer) entities among which consensus can be obtained more easily. Lower order units are subject to minimal potential coercion by higher order organizational entities because the former retain the fission option characteristic of egalitarian systems that can be applied if higher order consensus is locally unsatisfactory.

Data on variability in group size, structure, and decision-making among the egalitarian !Kung San (Johnson 1982) and a variety of egalitarian pastoral nomads (Johnson 1983) are consistent with quantitative expectations of sequential operations, as is less complete information on larger egalitarian systems for lowland South America and highland New Guinea (Johnson 1982).

With apologies for generalization based on very limited data and theory, sequential systems appear to typically incorporate the following characteristics: (a) The size of higher order entities measured in terms of number of incorporated lower order units has a range rarely exceeding 15 or so and a mean in the immediate neighborhood of 6 or less; (b) Sequential systems are typically unstable in terms of group membership and size as individual organizational units at various levels of the sequential hierarchy find the larger consensus unsatisfactory and exercise their fission option; and (c) The use of the formalized behaviors and social relations of religious ritual as an interactional context is scale dependent in sequential systems. Ritual, which may not be evident as smaller organizational sizes, becomes increasingly important at larger sizes.

## Social Modules and Settlement Size Hierarchies

It was my impression from seminar discussions that a pattern mentioned by Dean for the Kayenta area in the early second millennium was very widespread. Namely, small habitation sites that might represent one to two residence units did not include a kiva, ceremonial room, or comparable structure. Dean noted that contemporaneous unit pueblos averaging perhaps 12 rooms incorporated at least one kiva. Rohn (Chapter 5) mentions that the large Cliff-Fewkes Canyon pueblo on Mesa Verde contained 60 kivas and 530–545 rooms for a kiva:room ratio of 1:8.8–9.1. These seem to be typical numbers for the Southwest. If, as was also my impression, a typical residence unit consisted of one habitation room and one storage/processing room (see Reid, Chapter 3), then typical kiva:residence unit ratios must have been on the order of 1:4–1:6 or so.

I find these to be very satisfactory numbers for a model in which small kivas or ceremonial rooms represent a level of sequential hierarchy above the household where such matters as interhousehold cooperation and dispute resolution were consensually resolved in a sanctified context. If this were the case, then the larger "special function" structures common on large sites (great kivas, bighouses, concentric wall structures, etc.) represented one or more levels of sequential hierarchy above a small kiva or "household cluster" level. Large sites would then have been organized in terms of smaller "social modules." The settlement size hierarchies that seem to be so clear in some periods may provide a direct reflection of the size of different suprahousehold cluster social groupings.

Admitting my limited exposure to Southwest settlement size frequency distributions, they strike me as disconcertingly discontinuous in comparison to those available from the Old World. Phrased differently, the southwestern distributions seem to contain very distinct size classes in which larger sites had sizes that were common multiples of smaller ones. The most common multiples I encountered during the seminar were approximations of two, three or four.

Rohn (Chapter 5 and discussion notes), for example, presented data on PIII settlement hierarchies and site structure from the Northern San Juan. He identified a three level hierarchy of settlement size based on survey count of kiva depressions and an assumption of a fairly constant kiva:habitation room ratio. I suspect that this may well have been a four rather than a three level system.

Briefly, small sites exhibit one to six kivas. A combination of about four of these would be equivalent to the most common site size of 20 kivas (range 17–40). An aggregation of about four, 20-kiva units would have produced a small "town" with an average of somewhere around 80 kivas. Yellowjacket, at about 165 kivas, was very close to twice (1.90) the size of an average smaller town, and contained a variety of specialized features including two plazas, one great kiva, and a concentric wall structure.

Judge (Chapter 7) notes a three level hierarchy of classic Chacoan settlements. Forty smaller sites averaged 41 rooms each. About four (4.4) of these would have been equivalent to the average size of an intermediate site (181 rooms, N=7). Finally, the four large Chacoan pueblos (average 474 rooms) in turn were two or three (2.6) times the size of these intermediate settlements.

While I am willing to admit that all of this may be a dubious exercise in numerology, I can only say that I wish that my own data were so well behaved. These possible "multiples of modules" in puebloan settlement structure and hierarchies are well within the numerical expectations for sequential organization. That kivas and other presumably religious architecture figure so prominently in these systems suggests sacred legitimation of consensus formulation. (I will resist the urge to elaborate on Reid's four "ceremonial societies" from Grasshopper. They fit the model to the point where only an aside is sufficient to support the argument.)

It seems that movement into growing aggregations may often have been by social modules, resulting in the construction of new roomblocks, wings, or entirely new settlements. Again, my impression is that major sections of contiguous architecture were effectively insulated from one another by the absence of interconnecting doors or passageways. This would have been useful in reducing casual intermodule interaction that could lead to unnecessary dispute and inhibit module level decision-making and cooperation. Large pueblos may not have been integrated structures as much as a pile of smaller units, each larger unit in the pile being in turn an aggregate of smaller social modules. Someone must be working on the ekistics (sensu Doxiadis 1968) of pueblo architecture, but I am simply ignorant of their efforts.

## Mobility and Politics

The key to this sequential structure, as well as to the absence of convincing evidence of political elites and hierarchies in the traditional sense, must certainly have been the adaptive mobility emphasized by all of the authors in this volume. Given that the vast majority of southwestern occupations were those of economically autonomous social units of one or two households, mobility decisions must have rested ultimately with individual households. Such households probably acted independently even if they were part of a larger coresident social module when a decision was necessary.

Seminar discussions focused on mobility as an economic response either to local scarcity or perceived distant abundance. Actual or potential mobility, however, must also have had an important political component. There could hardly have been anything more frustrating to an emerging elite than people who could tell them to drop dead, gather their chattels about them, and depart for a more amicable social environment. Elites, in other words, crave continuity—a commodity in very short supply in the prehistoric Southwest. Political power in such a fluid social matrix would have been elusive indeed.

Proponents of southwestern elites would have us believe that they were a very "on again, off again" proposition. All agree that there were periods when any evidence of complexity is difficult, if not impossible, to find. These were Plog's (Chapter 8) "resilient" phases of high population dispersion and often increasing reliance on wild resources. Plog's use of resiliance generally follows that of Adams (1978) who applied it to Mesopotamia. Adams was concerned with the tribally organized and seminomadic elements of Mesopotamian society that were most evident in periods of decay of central authority over the populations of urban centers and their hinterlands. Times of trouble in Mesopotamia were, however, noticeably different than in the American Southwest, involving as they did dynastic transitions with the clash of imperial armies, palace revolts, and similar pastimes of entrenched elites. Periodic turnovers in elite personnel did not involve the disappearance of elites as a social institution.

Social observers are fond of bemoaning the tenacity of institutionalized inequality once it has been established. Differential elite access to resources affords them a degree of "resilience" not available to common folk who are much more likely to starve to death under subsistence stress. While degree of political centralization and control may vary, a fundamental pattern in inequality shows little tendency to "wither away" in either the archaeological or historical record.

Given the coercion available to elites in traditional hierarchical systems, I suspect that had they been present, they would have survived environmental inconvenience in a area the size of the Southwest. As it was, complexity of some sort was periodic and I somehow doubt that after a period of egalitarian autonomy, people would have had great enthusiasm for resurgent chiefly arrogance and caprice.

A combination of low resource availability, egalitarian organization, and mobility with periodic sendentary aggregation and organizational complexity is not unknown in the ethnographic record. Perhaps the closest examples are of mixed strategy horticulturalist/hunter-gatherer groups from interior Amazonia (Gross 1979, 1983). These people (Xavante, Bororo, Timbara, Kayapo) are fragmented into small foraging units for much of the year, but aggregate into villages of up to 1,400 people for the agricultural rainy season. Social organization in villages includes an elaborate variety of age sets, formal friendship, nondescent moieties and men's societies. Ritual is both intense and especially complex in these large aggregations.

Neither village location nor composition is stable. Village locations change at 5 to 20 year intervals, but the general pattern of mobility includes moves by village segments of various sizes down to the level of the individual. This leads to a heterogeneous village composition in which some villages are known by place names, but there is no designation of the mixed aggregate that lives there. Other villages are called after a men's society or moiety, but contain numerous coresident individuals who are not members of the eponymous social unit. Behavioral expression of elaborate kinship organization and ritual disappear during seasonal dispersal and in villages that become largely depopulated.

I suspect that these Amazonians represent a diluted, but instructive, example of sequential organization that was periodically much more complex in the Southwest. Mixed Amazonian village composition is particularly interesting in light of the "ethnic" coresidence emphasized by Reid (Chapter 3) at Grasshopper. Whether or not one wants to play with "ethnic" differences of the sort that are so eminently manipulatable in mixed populations containing few physical differences, coresidence of social modules with very different backgrounds should have been typical in a "sequential" Southwest.

## "Ethnic" Coresidence

Mixed coresidence would have been the product of two factors: (a) consensual organization in which households retained the ability to make independent mobility decisions, and (b) complex patterns of both temporal and spatial variability in resource availability that would have often encouraged fairly long distance residential moves.

It is a virtual article of archaeological faith that important elements of social organization are reflected in ceramic assemblages. While I sometimes think that this is but one aspect of a larger "It was important because we can measure it" problem, the rich assemblages of the Southwest may well contain the kind of information we seek.

Southwest ceramic assemblages in comparison to others about which I actually know something, appear to contain an amazing variety of "someplace black-on-whites," "otherplace polychromes," "yet somewhere else color wares," and "they must be local plain stuff." The implied volume of "trade wares" would have been the envy of Wall Street.

If we make a "Wobstian" (1977) assumption that elaborately decorated Southwest ceramics carried information on social group affiliation, then it is evident that group composition was highly unstable. No one at the seminar betrayed the slightest doubt about Reid's assertion that he could get 25-year ceramic dates out of motifs and motif association. By comparison, Frank

Hole (1984) had to strive mightily to get patterned variability in motif association out of 400 years of comparably attractive fifth millennium ceramics from Southwestern Iran.

Frequent mobility and complex patterns of coresidence could, perhaps, account for much of the Southwest ceramic palimpsest. Ceramics in use by a given household or larger social module might well reflect past and present residential associations as well as interaction with more or less spatially distant friends and relatives whose own histories were equally complex. Add in a pinch of Schifferian (1976) mixing and a tendency to treat communities as if they were unitary entities and you get distance-similarity confusion (see S. Plog 1978).

Similarly, Cordell (Chapter 9) notes that attempts to get southwestern ceramic and linguistic distributions to fit one another in ethnic harmony have been remarkably unsuccessful. This is not a particular surprise in an area where not only mobility, but bi- or multilingualism were most likely very common. (People from "multiethnic" communities in southwest Iran whom we employed on our last excavation were able to acquit themselves quite nicely in anywhere from two to four languages. Anglo-Americans like myself, on the other hand, typically find language differences to be a significant barrier to interaction.)

## Trade

"Trade wares" raise the issue of trade in general, and its role in a sequentially ordered society. I might initially note that I see no compelling reason why copper bells, macaws (or the somewhat sad parts thereof), and the odd Quetzalcoatl glyph need be indicative of a world systemic Toltec conspiracy implemented by sly pochteca on unsuspecting northern innocents.

As another one of those things that we can measure, trade in attractive imperishables is often elevated to the status of a major source of inequality. We might call this the "B³E" theory of complexity (Baubles, Bangles, and Beads > Elites). Judge (Chapter 7) suggests, for example, that turquoise processing was intensified in Chaco as a buffer against resource shortage in hard times, a strategy that would have required it to have attained the status of a medium of exchange. This is very similar to the "social storage" argument advanced by Halstead and O'Shea (1982) to generate ranking in the ancient Aegean. Conversions between beads and beans may well have been possible in good times, but I suspect that people were probably reluctant to part with their beans in bad ones. Fungibility, in other words, is not a state but a continuous variable subject to overall economic conditions.

My guess would be that trade was more important as a context for maintaining more or less formalized contacts over wide areas—of monitoring how other folk were doing under conditions of considerable uncertainty. Given a strategy of mobility under duress, it would have been advantageous to have a ready answer to questions of "where do we go from here?" Local success stories would have become widely known and were likely to attract numbers of immigrants from less fortunate areas. Systems could be expected to expand by internal growth, peripheral accretion, and absorption of population from more distant areas. As far as I can tell from Judge's description (Chapter 7), this may have been the case in Chaco.

Everyone was likely to benefit from participation in such a system in good times. Even in the general context of low potential surplus productivity, a system that was large enough could have generated impressive reserves with small contributions from a very large number of households.

## A Sequential Chacoan Phenomenon

Chaco appears to have been particularly well endowed with storage facilities. Judge postulates only a modest full-time population in the canyon itself, based on frequency of rooms and hearths. Kiva:room ratios at Chacoan sites would support this view.

Judge (Chapter 7) provides average room and kiva numbers for three classes of Chacoan communities. The four largest pueblos averaged 474 rooms and 21 kivas each for a kiva:room ratio of 1:22.6. Seven medium sized settlements averaged 181 rooms and 8 kivas, again for a kiva:room ratio of 1:22.6. Forty small settlements averaged 41 rooms and 2+ kivas for a ratio greater than 1:20.5. That these ratios are (a) virtually identical, and (b) roughly twice those commonly encountered in other pueblo sites suggests that Judge is correct in his population estimates and emphasis on storage. That even elaborate burials in Chaco exhibit dietary stress suggests that this massed storage was not to the differential advantage of local residents.

Given a well-founded southwestern preoccupation with household reserves, comparatively massive storage at Chacoan centers must have had quite an impact on the participants of the larger Chacoan system. Participants could no doubt (says he) draw on these reserves in case of very local difficulties, giving them an excellent reason for continuing involvement in the system, with contribution of labor and goods to its continuation.

Chacoan storage, however, could not have been great at all when calculated on a per capita basis across the system as a whole. Such a system would have been both socially and economically fragile. Climatic deterioration leading to continued yield shortfalls would have drawn down reserves and made their replacement difficult indeed. Advantages of participation in the system would have eroded rapidly as labor and material inputs no longer provided a buffer against shortage. Given that operation of the system was predicated on a very large number of participants, withdrawal of only a modest proportion of them could have engendered a rapid collapse of the whole network. This it seems to have done.

It would no doubt be a simple matter to make the case that the world is not in grave need of yet another story about matters Chacoan, especially one perhaps more suited for bedtime than class time. It may be, however, that even the Chaco data can support a basically egalitarian interpretation.

## Casas Grandes: Something Else

The same seems doubtful in the case of Casas Grandes (LeBlanc, Chapter 6). Far more than any other material discussed during the seminar, Casas looks elite—even to me. The circumstances surrounding its foundation, hinterland relations, and ultimate demise are sufficiently obscure that I will not even attempt to deal with them.

One comparison with the Chacoan phenomenon did strike me as particularly revealing. The Chacoan collapse did not seem to have a major impact on subsequent affairs in its area. Life continued much as it had before. The Casas collapse, however, left a southern Mogollon area largely devoid of ceremonial architecture. Kivas were gone for all practical purposes and precious little else remained. This suggests that an area influenced by Casas had undergone a fundamental transformation of social relations that speaks of equally fundamental differences between the effects of egalitarian and elitist social systems.

## CONCLUSION

I was not particularly surprised to learn that southwestern archaeologists are nearly as friendly yet factious as their Near Eastern counterparts. I have probably said enough by now to have brought all parties to a slow boil, and would be well advised to hold my tongue.

I will conclude with the observation that if by happy accident I am even vaguely correct about Southwest political organization, the area would be even more interesting than it now appears to be. We have garden variety "chiefdoms" and "early states" stacked ten deep under the lab table, but elaborate sequential hierarchies may have been a rare phenomenon. (Çatal Húyúk in Anatolia [Mellaart 1967; Todd 1976] with its pueblo-like architecture and numerous "shrine" rooms may have been an early Old World example.) Having a large sample of sequential systems with the degree of preservation, environmental, and chronological control available in the Southwest would constitute an unparalleled comparative opportunity to investigate the factors that suppress or enhance the social inequality so many consider the bane of modern life.

## ACKNOWLEDGMENTS

I would like to thank Doug Schwartz and the other members of the SAR Seminar for a most enjoyable and instructive week in Sante Fe. The theoretical background of many of the remarks made here was initially developed with the support of the Alexander von Humboldt-Stiftung, the Institut für Archäologie-Seminar für Vorderasiatische Altertumskunde der Freien Universität Berlin, the Centre National de la Recherche Scientifique, and the CNRS project "Dévelopment des Sociétés complexes dans le S.O. de l'Iran," which I gratefully acknowledge. Daniel G. Bates, James B. Griffin, Robert Paynter, John D. Speth, and three anonymous reviewers were kind enough to comment upon earlier versions of the manuscript. Remaining sins of omission and commission are mine.

## REFERENCES

Adams, Robert McC.
  1978    Strategies of Maximization, Stability and Resilience in Mesopotamian Society, Settlement and Agriculture. *Proceedings of the American Philosophical Society* 122(5):329–335.

Doxiadis, Constantinos A.
  1968    *Ekistics: An Introduction to the Science of Human Settlement.* Oxford University Press, New York.

Gremliza, F. G. L.
  1962    *Ecology and Endemic Diseases in the Dez Pilot Area: A Report to the Khuzistan Water and Power Authority and Plan Organization of Iran.* Development and Resources Corporation, New York.

Gross, Daniel R.
  1979    A New Approach to Central Brazilian Social Organization. In *Brazil: Anthropological Essays in Honor of Charles Wagley,* edited by M. L. Margolis and W. E. Carter, pp. 321–343. Columbia University Press, New York.
  1983    Village Movement in Relation to Resources in Amazonia. In *Adaptive Responses of Native Amazonians,* edited by Raymond B. Hames and William T. Vickers, pp. 429–449. Academic Press, New York.

Halstead, Paul, and John O'Shea
  1982      A Friend In Need Is a Friend Indeed: Social Storage and the Origins of
            Social Ranking. In *Ranking, Resource and Exchange: Aspects of the Archaeol-
            ogy of Early European Society*, edited by Colin Renfrew and Stephen
            Shennan, pp. 92–99. Cambridge University Press, Cambridge.

Hole, Frank
  1984      Analysis of Structure and Design in Prehistoric Ceramics. *World Archaeol-
            ogy* 15(3):326–347.

Johnson, Gregory A.
  1982      Organizational Structure and Scalar Stress. In *Theory and Explanation in
            Archaeology: The Southampton Conference*, edited by Colin Renfrew, Michael
            J. Rowlands, and Barbara Abbott Segraves, pp. 389–421. Academic Press,
            New York.
  1983      Decision-Making Organization and Pastoral Nomad Camp Size. *Human
            Ecology* 11(2):175–199.
  1987      The Changing Organization of Uruk Administration on the Susiana Plain.
            In *The Archaeology of Western Iran*, edited by Frank Hole, pp. 107–139.
            Smithsonian Institution Press, Washington, D.C.

Kramer, Carol
  1980      Estimating Prehistoric Populations: An Ethnoarchaeological Approach. In
            *L'Archéologie de L'Iraq du Début de L'Époque Néolithique a 333 Avant Notre
            Ere: Perspectives et limites de l'intérpretation anthropologique des documents*,
            edited by Marie-Thérèse Barrelet, pp. 315–334. Colloques Internationaux
            du Centre National de la Recherche Scientifique No. 580. CNRS, Paris.

Mellaart, James
  1967      *Çatal Hüyük: A Neolithic Town in Anatolia*. McGraw-Hill, New York.

Negahban, E. O.
  1975      Brief Report on the Haft Tepe Excavations 1974. In *Proceedings of the IIIrd An-
            nual Symposium on Archaeological Research in Iran*, edited by F. Bagherzadeh,
            pp. 171–178. Iranian Center for Archaeological Research, Tehran.

Oates, David, and Joan Oates
  1976      Early Irrigation Agriculture in Mesopotamia. In *Economic and Social Archae-
            ology*, edited by G. de G. Sieveking, I. H. Longworth, and K. E. Wilson, pp.
            109–135. Duckworth, London.

Plog, Stephen
  1978      Social Interaction and Stylistic Similarity: A Reanalysis. In *Advances in
            Archaeological Method and Theory*, Vol. 1, edited by Michael B. Schiffer, pp.
            143–182. Academic Press, New York.

Redding, Richard W.
  1981      The Faunal Remains. In *An Early Town on the Deh Luran Plain: Excavations
            at Tepe Farukhabad*, edited by Henry T. Wright, pp. 233–261. Memoirs of
            the Museum of Anthropology University of Michigan No. 13, Ann Arbor.

Schiffer, Michael B.
  1976      *Behavioral Archeology*. Academic Press, New York.

Todd, Ian

1976      *Çatal Hüyük in Perspective.* Cummings Publishing Company, Menlo Park.

Wobst, H. Martin

1977      Stylistic Behavior and Information Exchange. In *For the Director: Research Essays in Honor of James B. Griffin,* edited by Charles E. Cleland, pp. 317–342. Anthropological Papers, Museum of Anthropology, University of Michigan No. 61.

# Index

*Smithsonian Series in Archaeological Inquiry*

Robert McC. Adams and Bruce D. Smith, Series Editors

The Smithsonian Series in Archaeological Inquiry presents original case studies that address important general research problems and demonstrate the values of particular theoretical and/or methodological approaches. Titles include well-focused, edited collections as well as works by individual authors. The series is open to all subject areas, geographical regions, and theoretical modes.

## *Advisory Board*

Linda Cordell (*California Academy of Sciences*), Kent V. Flannery (*University of Michigan*), George C. Frison (*University of Wyoming*), Roger C. Green (*Auckland University*), Olga F. Linares (*Smithsonian Tropical Research Institute*), David Hurst Thomas (*American Museum of Natural History*), and John E. Yellen (*National Science Foundation*).